SO-ADX-475

Financing the Small Manufacturer in Developing Countries

McGRAW-HILL SERIES IN INTERNATIONAL DEVELOPMENT

Alderfer   Local Government in Developing Countries

Benjamin   Higher Education in the American Republics

Brannen and Hodgson   Overseas Management

Bryce   Industrial Development: A Guide for Accelerating Economic Growth

Bryce   Policies and Methods for Industrial Development

Currie   Accelerating Development: The Necessity and the Means

Davenport   Financing the Small Manufacturer in Developing Countries

David   International Resources in Clinical Psychology

David   International Trends in Mental Health

Dunn   International Handbook of Advertising

Eicher and Witt   Agriculture in Economic Development

Ettinger   International Handbook of Management

Fryer   World Economic Development

Gross   Action under Planning: The Guidance of Economic Development

Harbison and Myers   Education, Manpower, and Economic Growth: Strategies of Human Resource Development

Harbison and Myers   Manpower and Education: Country Studies in Economic Development

Hunt   Social Aspects of Economic Development

Meier   Developmental Planning

Montgomery and Siffin   Approaches to Development: Politics, Administration and Change

Powelson   Latin America: Today's Economic and Social Revolution

Reidy   Strategy for the Americas

Reimann and Wigglesworth   The Challenge of International Finance

Singer   International Development: Growth and Change

Staley and Morse   Modern Small Industry for Developing Countries

Thut and Adams   Educational Patterns in Contemporary Societies

Walinsky   The Planning and Execution of Economic Development: A Nontechnical Guide for Policy Makers and Administrators

Financing the Small Manufacturer in Developing Countries

by Robert W. Davenport
Stanford Research Institute

McGraw-Hill Book Company

NEW YORK   LONDON   SYDNEY   TORONTO

FINANCING THE SMALL MANUFACTURER
IN DEVELOPING COUNTRIES

15444

1234567890-MP-72106987

Foreword

Modern manufacturing industry is one of the requisites for attainment of the economic, social, and political goals of developing countries—along with progress in other important fields like agriculture and education. A country usually needs to develop a nucleus of large factories in carefully chosen lines and also many smaller (but modern) factories, likewise in carefully chosen lines. Its industrialization program will then be more solid, better balanced, and more effective in meeting the needs of the people for manufactured goods and for employment than if promotional efforts were to be concentrated exclusively on very large industrial projects or on small industry alone.

This book is concerned wth financial tools for promoting the establishment, modernization, and sound growth of small factories. Perhaps small-to-medium factories might better convey to some readers the focus of the discussion. Small is a relative term, and a factory considered small in Detroit or even in Bombay would be considered large in Katmandu. In any case, what the book deals with is that type of industrial establishment that lies between household (cottage) industry and artisan enterprises on the one hand and large-scale factories on the other.

These establishments are factories, not craft or artisan shops; that is, they have considerable division and specialization of labor in production. Therefore, the coordinating function of management is very important; the manager, not the craftsman, is the key figure. On the other hand, they are not large enough to have such division and specialization of labor within management itself. In fact "one-man management" comes close to characterizing them, if one stretches the term to permit a few direct assistants to the manager and to allow for partnerships. The point is that there is no extensive array of vice-presidents or departmental managers with specialized staffs for production, sales, engineering, research, and finance. Hence, the methods by which development agencies can promote these small factories and work with them on productivity improvement or on financing problems or whatever have to be rather different from the methods suitable to larger establishments.

A further characteristic of small factories, particularly important for the topic of this book, is that they usually have no access to the organized capital market through public issue of shares or bonds, and in many countries their access even to bank credit or to any other kind of institutional financing is very inadequate. This is the sort of problem, of course, that Dr. Davenport considers in detail.

One of the strengths of Dr. Davenport's treatment of the financing problem is that he is always aware that finance is only one aspect—albeit a key aspect—of a whole complex of problems involved in the establishment, modernization, or growth of small factories in newly developing countries. His emphasis on the need to integrate financial measures with other measures to strengthen small factories—for example, management training, technical and managerial advisory services, economic information, and marketing help—is a very useful warning and corrective. In too many cases, development leaders desiring to encourage modernization and expansion of small factories have decided to set up some type of special lending facility, without doing anything at the same time to help overcome deficiencies in management skills, production techniques, marketing methods, and the like. The results have almost always been disappointing. The financial approach *alone* is not likely to be very effective in the development of small factories. But it is equally true that other approaches—for example, technical advice—in the absence of measures to make capital and credit more available for soundly conceived improvements are also likely to be fruitless. What is needed is a combination of measures—a "package"—each element reinforcing the others and making the success of the integrated program more likely. Provision of more adequate financing is generally an essential element in such a package, and often it can serve as the key element.

This book is, therefore, an important companion piece to the other studies on small industry's role in development which, like this one, have been prepared in the International Development Center of Stanford Research Institute with the aid of grants from the Ford Foundation. These studies include nine monographs and a general volume, *Modern Small Industry for Developing Countries,* by Eugene Staley and Richard Morse, which sums up what has been learned in the research program and applies it to practical problems of policy and of development technique.

Dr. Robert Davenport comes to his topic with a broad experience in financial studies and in the economic conditions and requirements of industrializing countries.

After receiving his bachelor's degree in Russian and Far Eastern affairs at the University of Washington and a master's degree from the Fletcher School of Law and Diplomacy, he underwent extensive training in Japanese and served in Japan at the close of the war. He subsequently took his doctorate in economics at Columbia University, preparing his dissertation on the subject of Soviet economic relations with Iran.

Between 1951 and 1953, Dr. Davenport coauthored *Investment in India* and *Investment in Pakistan,* which were pioneer publications in the series then being developed by the U.S. Department of Commerce to inform investors about the business and governmental backgrounds and conditions likely to be encountered abroad. He spent the next two years in the United Kingdom and South Asia analyzing the management and financing of British overseas enterprises.

Dr. Davenport joined Stanford Research Institute in 1957, where he has, through various assignments in Latin America, acquired a firsthand knowledge of the people and conditions of another major group of developing countries. His work for the Institute has also included an assignment as a regional economic adviser to the Government of India's small industry program, studies of investment conditions abroad, analyses of international trade and industrial development programs, and, of course, investigations in a variety of countries on financial institutions and the financing of small and medium enterprises.

Eugene Staley

Preface

This study examines experiences with financing programs in a wide variety of countries in an effort to distill from them more practical institutional arrangements than those generally employed for financing the establishment, growth, and modernization of small manufacturing enterprises. The primary concern is to arrive at institutional arrangements which are well adapted to the requirements of newly industrializing countries, since it is in these countries that development financing programs are the most needed and yet confront the greatest difficulties.

In focusing the investigation on institutional arrangements, I have followed the admonition of Wolf some years ago:

> The inadequacy of technology and capital formation may be due less to a shortage of information about [production] techniques or of potential savings, than to shortages of the "right" kinds of institutions—"right" implying those kinds of institutions which permit or stimulate, rather than impede, the adoption of new [production] techniques and the formation of productive capital. In other words, institutions—as well as capital and technology—are productive; or, more accurately, different institutions have differentially productive consequences. Growth-promoting institutions, without themselves adding resources to the economy—or at least by a process that is distinguishable from any resources which they directly add—may so restructure the environment in which factors of production meet that the rate at which combinations occur is accelerated.
>
> Hence, besides technological and investment surveys, as bases for programming technical assistance and capital projects, there is a need for institutional surveys and institutional programming.[1]

---

[1] Charles Wolf, Jr., "Institutions and Economic Development," *American Economic Review*, December, 1955, pp. 867–868. We have also generally followed Wolf's definition of institutions as *organizations* and *policies*, both private and public, or clusters of organizations and policies relating to one common purpose. Policies are widely conceived, encompassing accepted principles, legislation, administrative regulations, and established practices.

The primary method employed here for arriving at better institutional arrangements has been international comparative research. There has been extensive and diverse international experimentation with special measures for financing small enterprises. From both the successes and the failures of such efforts, much can be learned which is in some degree applicable to other countries. The main disadvantages of the international comparative approach is that analyzing the experience of many different countries is a research task of considerable magnitude. It is particularly difficult here where it is essential to examine not only the formal content of programs and the basic principles of particular financing techniques but also how individual measures and broad programs have actually operated within the context of local needs and other local conditions. Various compromises have had to be made to cope with these difficulties but without, it is hoped, sacrificing either the breadth of international coverage or the depth of program evaluation required.

The analysis is primarily concentrated on countries where the author had already or could acquire considerable firsthand experience with the country as a whole, its industry, and its financial system. Such countries include principally the newly industrializing nations of South Asia and Latin America and the more industrially advanced Japan and the United States. Basic field investigations were spread over a four-year period, 1961–1964. A brief trip to Japan, Turkey, Germany, Denmark, the Netherlands, and Canada in 1965 provided current information on some of the more successful financing programs for smaller manufacturers in industrially advanced countries. Experience has also been drawn from related work over the past decade, particularly from an investigation of the management and financing of British overseas enterprises (1953–1956), from service as an adviser to the small-industry program in India (1957–1959), and from more recent applied research on financing programs in various South and Central American countries.

Field investigations were supplemented with experience reported by other studies. There is now hardly a country for which there has not been some evaluation of financial institutions. The information is not always complete or up-to-date, evaluations may not be entirely candid, or, quite frequently, the information may not be for publication, but the review of such studies nevertheless has provided many valuable insights into the experience of countries where direct investigations were not possible. The author has been fortunate also in having been able to interchange ideas frequently during the investigation with colleagues in the International Development Center at Stanford Research Institute who have conducted industrial development studies bearing in part upon financing in a wide range of countries.

Many persons and organizations helped to make this study possible. The author gratefully acknowledges the grant from the Ford Foundation which supported this investigation. A supplementary grant from the Inter-American Development Bank enabled further field work to be conducted in seven Latin American countries. A special debt is owed to the Banco do Nordeste do Brasil, the Banco de Guatemala, the Instituto de Fomento Nacional of Nicaragua, the Banco Popular of Colombia, and the Fondo de Garantia y Fomento a la Industria Mediana y Pequeña of Mexico for collaborating in investigations in their respective countries. The author is also grateful to Tsutomu Nakamura and his associates at the Osaka Institute of Economic Research for investigations undertaken in Japan. The Central Small Industries Organisation and the Reserve Bank of India were most helpful in making available extensive information on programs in India.

Thanks are also due to the officers and staffs of numerous other banks, government agencies, research institutions, and related organizations in the countries surveyed who gave freely of their time and presented their candid views on lending programs and problems in financing small manufacturing enterprises. Equally important contributors to this study were the many industrialists who generously opened their business operations to critical examination and helped me to analyze their basic problems. It is not possible to list individually all those who have contributed to this study through sharing their experience, but the author wishes to express here his sincere thanks to them.

I should further like to acknowledge here the contributions of Dr. Eugene Staley, Director of Basic Research in the International Development Center at Stanford Research Institute. It was due to his clear vision of the need for the study and his convincing exposition of the problem that the essential financial support was obtained and the research begun. I wish also to express appreciation for the encouragement which he and the management of Stanford Research Institute gave to this research. Helpful suggestions on various chapters were also provided by Roland Pierotti, William A. Hurst, R. M. Oddie and other Bank of America staff, William Adams of First National City Bank, George Wyeth of the Agency for International Development, and Dr. Leonard Marks of Stanford University.

Finally, and most especially, I should like to thank Mrs. Jeannie Kimber, whose cheerful efficiency and initiative in providing a wide range of secretarial, editorial, and other supporting services during the course of the work have been of immense value in bringing the book to completion.

Robert W. Davenport

Contents

Foreword by Eugene Staley   v
Preface   ix

Part I: Introduction

1. The Nature and Significance of the Problem   3
2. India's Experience with Special Financing Measures   19
3. Puerto Rico's Experience with Special Financing Measures   53

Part II: General Strategy for Improving Financial Services

4. Formulating a Program   69
5. Supporting and Monitoring Services   77

Part III: Possible Channels of Developmental Finance

6. Stimulating Noninstitutional Sources of Finance   103
7. Mobilizing Commercial Banks and Savings Institutions   134
8. Encouraging Finance Companies   162
9. Utilizing Official and Quasi-official Organizations   194

Part IV: Some Operational Problems

10. Allocating Finance   227
11. Assuring Implementation   262

Part V: Additional Case Studies

12. Colombia   289
13. Japan   333

Index   373

Part One
Introduction

Chapter 1
The Nature
and Significance
of the Problem

WORLDWIDE, ONE FINDS the observation that inadequate access to finance is a major impediment to the establishment and growth of small, independent manufacturing enterprises. This complaint is common in countries with very different cultural and institutional backgrounds and various levels of industrialization. In newly industrializing countries, the need for improved means of financing small-factory development is especially great and, at the same time, especially difficult to satisfy. It is on the problem of improving the availability of financing for small-factory development in newly industrializing countries that this study focuses. Some idea of the nature and extent of the need for better financing facilities can be conveyed by examples from the findings of investigations in several countries.

The Need in India

A study of small metalworking firms in a north Indian town found the important productive potential of skilled entrepreneurs and their enterprises being frustrated by an inadequacy of finance. In the words of James T. McCrory, who made the study:

> By most standards, the small industrialists of Chopur[1] are good industrial entrepreneurs. They live frugally and save. They are highly skilled themselves or employ skilled personnel. They are quality-conscious, able to make improvements in technique on their own, quick to learn from others.
>
> As entrepreneurs they are tenacious to an extreme. When one industrial venture fails, their first act is to begin scraping together savings for another.

[1] Chopur is a fictitious name for a town not far from Delhi.

As manufactures they are versatile and resourceful with the few resources at their command. If they cannot buy a machine they will build it themselves. If they cannot reproduce a technique, they will improvise one of their own. Most are sensitive to new demands and market changes as their information and their circumstances permit.

The small industrialists of Chopur have every earmark of the successful entrepreneur, *except success.* By and large they do not prosper. When they do prosper, it is not for long. . . .

There is a pattern of growth in Chopur small industry. It is a pattern of alternate growth and decline, growth and decline always within the "small-scale" confines and never quite breaking outside. As will be seen the small industrialist plays a vital role in general industrial growth in India. But, insofar as the experience of the Chopur entrepreneur is typical, he is seldom able to participate in it himself, either for long or beyond a certain limited point of size. Why?[2]

McCrory held that the root cause of these entrepreneurs' lack of success was their perennial shortage of capital. Their willingness to start on a shoestring is admirable, he says, but this means they are financially vulnerable. "If there is any single reason why the small industries of the craftsmen-entrepreneurs do not grow, this is it." The Chopur small industrialist "has no satisfactory outside source of capital, either at all or dependable and on terms he is able to accept."

While McCrory limited his case studies to quite small factories (using power, but with less than 20 employees), a subsequent set of case studies by James J. Berna in south India focused on medium-scale factories (50 to 250 employees). Berna investigated 52 manufacturing firms in Madras state, all in the metalworking field (light engineering). These firms had succeeded in growing, some of them from very small beginnings.[3] The stories of how they built up their very small shops into small factories and eventually medium-scale factories show that it has been possible for some small entrepreneurs in India to break through the "size barrier." But the capital for doing so had to come mainly from the entrepreneur's own funds—plowing back of profits or investment of profits from another enterprise—or from family funds. Berna concluded from his study that such enterprises should be strengthened and helped to grow in every possible way. His first recommendation: "Coming down to particulars, there is an urgent need for adequate credit facilities for firms of the type under study."[4] He later stresses the need for a second kind of assistance: "Even

---

[2] James T. McCrory, *Small Industry in a North Indian Town: Case Studies in Latent Industrial Potential,* Government of India, Ministry of Commerce and Industry, New Delhi, 1956, p. 3.

[3] James J. Berna, *Industrial Entrepreneurship in Madras State,* International Development Center of Stanford Research Institute, Asia Publishing House, Bombay, London, New York, 1960.

[4] *Ibid.,* pp. 91–92, 218.

more than capital assistance, the enterprises included in the present study need help in solving their technical and labour problems."[5]

The Need in Colombia

A field study in Colombia included visits to and extended interviews in some 120 factories representative of significant industries and regions. The purpose was to assess the strengths and the growth capacity of small and medium manufacturing firms and to discover the chief limiting factors in their expansion and modernization.

Judgments were made on the motivation, vision, and management capabilities of each entrepreneur. Some 70 firms were judged to have real capacity for significant growth. Among these 70 "growth-potential" firms, the highest-priority requirement for significant expansion, in the judgment of the survey team, was additional financing. More than 60 percent of the growth-potential firms were judged to be able to expand significantly with financial assistance only. "This finding emphasizes the potentially great contribution which an effective credit program can make to the development of small and medium Colombian industry."[6]

The research team noted, however, that the appearance of such a high share of firms in which finance alone would promote significant growth is based on the prior selection of the outstanding entrepreneurs from among a wider number of firms. Among all the firms examined, only half were judged to have significant growth prospects if aided by loans alone. Furthermore, it was found that counsel on financial planning would be essential or important for two-thirds of the outstanding firms which could expand significantly with financial assistance alone. And the effectiveness of financial assistance would be multiplied substantially by simultaneous provision of other types of management counsel.[7]

The Need in Greece

A 1963 analysis of the structure, performance, and developmental possibilities of Greek industry emphasized the importance of small-scale units and found that the major difficulties standing in the way of higher productivity and growth were: low capitalization in equipment; inferior technology, including product design; difficult access to financing; and the limited market outlets for products. The financial difficulties of the small Greek manufacturing firms were found to stem from the fact that no specialized credit facilities for small business are available and from the limited internal

[5] Ibid., p. 221.
[6] Small and Medium Industry in Colombia's Development, report of an inquiry organized by the Banco Popular, aided by a team of consultants from Stanford Research Institute, Banco Popular, Bogotá, 1962 (English and Spanish editions), pp. 15–19 of the English edition.
[7] Ibid., p. 19.

financing ability of such firms. "Hence the inability of many small firms to grow into larger and more efficient firms, despite the fact that they may have capable management and favorable demand conditions for their products." The study further observed:

> With respect to external sources of financing, the existing financial agencies in Greece are not suitable for carrying out small-business loans because of the high risk involved, the inability of the small-scale operations to provide adequate loan security, and the high unit-cost involved in the handling of small loans. The development of a specialized financial organization to handle both short- and long-term credit financing for small manufacturing firms must be an essential part of any governmental program aimed at raising the productivity of a vast number of small-scale artisan firms."[8]

The Need in Japan

Japan has in many ways joined the ranks of the most industrially advanced nations. In Japan, however, as in many less developed countries, better financial facilities are viewed by authorities as a key requirement for promoting small-industry development.

> The weakness of the social and economic basis of the small enterprises is mainly due to the shortage of capital, and this weakness inevitably leads them into poor financial status, and any financial tightness becomes seriously intensified in smaller enterprises. Hence an important phase of the overall measure to assist smaller enterprises and to rouse them to a competitive level against big enterprises must necessarily involve the means by which their credit standing is improved and their source of finance is secured.[9]

The Need Elsewhere

Government authorities in other countries as diverse as Ghana, Kenya, Pakistan, Malaya, Cambodia, Korea, Puerto Rico, and Mexico and in such industrially advanced countries as the Netherlands, Denmark, and the United States have concluded that the financial needs of small enterprises are sufficiently distinct, urgent, and inadequately served to require special financial programs. It is not implied that there has been no dissenting opinion in some or all of these countries. A few studies of the needs, such as Sayre P. Schatz's study in Nigeria, have concluded that there is no capital shortage for local industries, that the problem rather is one of capital vainly seeking viable private projects.[10] For the most part, however, the

[8] George Coutsoumaris, *The Morphology of Greek Industry: A Study in Industrial Development*, Center of Economic Research, Athens, 1963, p. 321.

[9] *Administration for Development of Smaller Enterprises in Japan*, Government of Japan, Ministry of International Trade and Industry, Smaller Enterprise Agency, 1962, p. 4.

[10] A draft of a paper to be published entitled "Government Lending to Nigerian Corporate Enterprise: The Federal Loans Board." J. D. Nyhart also questions whether finance is the "critical bottleneck" to the development of local enterprise

dissension has been with the ways attempted to meet this need. Thus W. A. Lewis, in appraising the experience of the Industrial Development Corporation of the Gold Coast (now Ghana) in financing locally owned small industrial enterprises, concluded, "The writer does not therefore agree that the Industrial Development Corporation should cease to make small loans. He recommends that loans should be continued but the emphasis should be shifted to supervision and advice."[11] A 1962 appraisal of Ghana's problem similarly suggested various changes in approach but the continuation of special arrangements for financing small enterprises.[12] In brief, the general opinion on the subject of small industry is today pretty much as the United Nations found it in its 1950 study: "The problem of providing financial assistance to small undertakings was recognized as particularly urgent in underdeveloped countries, but differences of opinion prevailed regarding the form and nature such assistance should take."[13]

The Problem Stated

These cases illustrate the general nature and extent of the need felt in newly industrializing countries for better ways of making developmental finance available to small manufacturers. In response to the foregoing needs, there has been a proliferation in recent years of special financing programs for a broad sector variously defined but generally labelled as small or small and medium industry, enterprise, or business. Not only are significant sums already committed to existing programs, but new programs continue to be undertaken. Thailand, for example, established a new program in 1964 which is intended to provide "about US $1,000,000 each year to deserving small industries."[14]

Unfortunately, many of these efforts have not so far produced anything like the results originally anticipated. Often the programs have been hastily and vaguely conceived without clear decisions about what their precise objectives and methods should be. Many of them have proved more expensive and less effective than expected. The small industrialists have often found that administration of the programs is dilatory, the amount of financing available is too small, the requirements for qualifying too burdensome, or the terms ill-adapted to their needs. Yet the belief persists—and is con-

---

in Africa in his paper, *Notes on Entrepreneurship in Africa,* Harvard University Center for International Affairs, Development Seminar, Nov. 11, 1961. (Mimeographed.)

[11] *Report on Industrialization and the Gold Coast,* Government Printing Department, Accra, Gold Coast, 1963, p. 13.

[12] *The National Investment Bank of Ghana,* Porter International Company, Washington, D.C., 1962.

[13] *Domestic Financing of Economic Development,* United Nations, New York, 1950, p. 58.

[14] *Asian Productivity,* Apr. 30, 1965, p. 8.

firmed by this study—that financing can be an important and relatively economical tool for fostering development of small-scale manufacturing. A number of questions need answering in view of the sums being committed to these programs. To what extent and under what circumstances are such programs useful? Is there a common problem with which the various existing programs are seeking to cope and which requires a generally similar approach, or are there several fundamentally different problems? What types of units require these programs? What types of needs which are not now being met can special financing programs serve? And, above all, are there not approaches and methods for achieving program objectives which are more economical and effective than common present practice?

The object of the present study can be stated in brief. It is to explore what can be done to lessen the financial barriers to growth of modern small factories, especially in newly industrializing countries, and to determine how positive use can be made of financial means to promote such growth.

The Small Manufacturer—Definition of Terms

It will be useful at this point to comment on use of terms. Confusion over terminology has often hampered discussion of *small industry*, and failure to distinguish the different forms of small industry is sometimes responsible for unclear objectives and inappropriate measures in financial programs.

A companion study by Eugene Staley and Richard Morse[15] has gone into these problems of definition with care, and in this book we shall follow their usage. Small industry means all manufacturing carried on in relatively small establishments. It thus includes both nonfactory and factory forms. Household (cottage) industry and artisan industry are nonfactory forms of small industry. It is important to distinguish them from the *small factory*, which together with its owner-manager, the small manufacturer, is the focus of concern in this book.

Factory-type production differs from artisan-type production by greater division of labor. Consequently, "the factory has greater need for internal coordination, and the manager, rather than the craftsman, is the central figure. . . . If management plans and directs well, the factory is efficient. If management does a poor job, even great skill on the part of the individual workman is unlikely for long to give good results."[16]

The problems of nonfactory industry and the financial and other methods appropriate for dealing with such problems are rather different from those of factory-type industry. In a traditional preindustrial economy, manufacturing consists almost wholly of nonfactory producers—household and

---

[15] Eugene Staley and Richard Morse, *Modern Small Industry for Developing Countries*, Series in International Development, McGraw-Hill Book Company, New York, 1965.

[16] *Ibid.*, p. 7.

artisan industry. But as a country modernizes and its economy develops, the factory becomes the characteristic form of manufacturing. In industrially advanced, modern economies, small industry means mainly small factories, not household and artisan industry as in traditional economies. Since the present study is designed to aid countries in the process of modernization and industrial development, it concentrates on the financing problems of the small factory and does not attempt to deal with the problems of household or artisan industry.

What do we mean by a *small* factory and a *small* manufacturer? Staley and Morse have indicated that the small factory is distinguished by functional differences which give rise to the need for special kinds of development assistance. These special characteristics include:

1. *Relatively little specialization in management*. . . . One-man management. . . . this characteristic gives small industry certain special needs for types of advice and aid which are not so much needed by large manufacturing firms.

2. *Close personal contacts*. The manager is personally in touch with production workers, customers, suppliers, and owners (ownership is often identical with management). . . .

3. *Handicaps in obtaining capital and credit*. The small industrial firm cannot raise capital in the organized securities market, and . . . often finds difficulty in getting loans and credit from banks and other financial institutions. . . .

4. *Sheer numbers*. . . . It is often impracticable, or at any rate uneconomic, to apply to thousands of small units the same development techniques (e.g., individual feasibility studies) which can be applied to tens of large units. . . ."

It is often necessary for both operational and analytical purposes to set some boundary in quantitative terms, even though the boundary is arbitrary. This assures a uniform central focus. In this study, small factories will mean manufacturing enterprises which employ from 10 to 100 persons and have net assets of not more than the equivalent of US$100,000; and accordingly, small manufacturers will be the owners of such enterprises.

The quantitative boundaries most appropriate for operational programs will of course differ from one country to another or within the same country from one period to another, depending upon program resources and objectives, administrative considerations, and other factors. Many programs are directed toward both small and medium factories, extending the maximum size of enterprise served up to those employing 200 to 300 persons. This may be appropriate in some settings, particularly inasmuch as the medium-scale factories share with small ones many common problems and often need similar types of program assistance. It is often useful, however, to reserve some specific portion of program effort for the small units because

¹⁷ *Ibid.*, p. 3.

of the otherwise normal tendency of the larger units to monopolize most of the special assistance. In some cases, somewhat separate provisions may even be desirable for two or three size groups within the small-scale category.

In the case of special financing programs, the definition of small industry may need to be specifically restricted further to owner-managed enterprises which are owned and managed by persons who devote a major part of their time and resources to them—that is, excluding minor ventures of wealthy persons or firms. Such restrictions will tend to assure that the programs give primary attention to enterprises which are significantly retarded in their development by a shortage of finance. A great many of the existing "financing programs for small enterprises" turn out on close examination to be programs making small loans to borrowers with much larger resources than one would expect from statements of program objectives.

There are many other differences between enterprises which are as important as, or more important than, mere size. Among them are type of product (e.g., chemicals or furniture), location (e.g., in major cities or smaller towns), or age (e.g., new or long established). These differences usually need to be taken into account in financing programs, but they are for the most part obvious and present fewer definitional problems.

Development Financing

This study focuses on finding better ways to meet the financing problems of those small manufacturing units which are progressive in outlook and adaptable to changing conditions, which seek to draw upon modern science and invention in their production processes and to apply reasonably up-to-date ideas of organization and management in their business operations. Thus development financing is our topic. This means financing the establishment of new units which offer promise of constructive contribution in the environment of the developing economy and, even more important in most situations, financing modernization and growth in existing units which have already demonstrated growth potential.

Development financing also means a somewhat different approach to financing than that usually employed by traditional lenders in newly developing countries or by less imaginative bankers anywhere for whom lending is merely a business. It requires a much more active and selective approach than bankers, simply as businessmen, usually need to employ. It also requires a greater concern with how a recipient utilizes his financial resources. These distinctions and their important implications will be further considered in Chapters 10 and 11.

Finance is a powerful developmental tool and one of those which national and international development assistance programs can most easily mobilize and direct in accordance with policy requirements. It is nevertheless a much more complex, costly, and uncertain means of furthering development than is often realized, particularly so in the usual environment of newly industrializing countries. Moreover, it is only one tool.

Programs and methods of development finance must be so devised as to take full account of what Staley and Morse call "the principle of combinations and interactions." The development of modern small factories in newly industrializing countries depends not only on more adequate capital and credit, but also on managerial training, technical advice, market information, product design, raw material supply, an entrepreneurial spirit of innovation and drive for achievement, and a social and political climate encouraging to business growth. "Hence, any single factor approach to small industry development in a newly industrializing country is likely to be ineffective and wasteful. An integrated program that works on a carefully selected combination of factors simultaneously—the exact combination depending on local conditions—is much more likely to prove worthwhile."[18]

It is for this reason that at appropriate points in subsequent discussion we shall call particular attention to the need for interrelating developmental finance with other elements in a broad development program for modern small factories.

To be a significant and continuing development force in an economy, a financial program must not only be development-oriented and supported by and integrated with other development services; it must also be budgetarily sound. Although these objectives tend to pull program management in different directions, both can be achieved simultaneously, at least to a minimum degree essential to program viability and implementation. A careful balancing of effort is necessary to achieve this, so that the tension between these diverse requirements never becomes strained. Inadequate attention to budgetary soundness has caused many development financing programs to end in conspicuous failure, yet less apparent but probably even more common and more wasteful failures have resulted from too great concern for budgetary soundness and too little attention to orienting and equipping financial programs to make a contribution to economic development.

Obstacles to Financing Small-factory Development

There are many factors which stand in the way of financing the development of small factories, but two—risks and costs—are of special importance. It will be worthwhile to examine these two major obstacles briefly as preparation for considering policies, measures, and methods for overcoming them. A discussion of how these and other obstacles affect the services which particular sources of funds might provide to small manufacturers is furnished in Chapters 6 to 9.

[18] *Ibid.*, p. 353.

Risk Obstacles

No obstacle has been more stressed, particularly by lenders, than risk problems. This general view of the risks constitutes in itself a major obstacle to small-industry financing. Small-factory financing does, in fact, involve on the average somewhat greater risks than major alternative financing opportunities open to lenders. Although these risks can in large part be overcome by appropriate policies, even a moderate increase in risks can be a problem where lenders attach great importance to minimizing risk.

From the point of view of identifying ways of reducing risk problems, it is important to recognize that financing risks are influenced by many factors besides the characteristics of the recipient. They are also shaped by the circumstances of the supplier of funds and his financing methods. Risk, for example, often arises because of a lack of information. Not every supplier of funds is confronted with the same informational problems, and some are more able or willing than others to take the necessary measures to close such informational gaps.

Institutional and cost obstacles often severely limit what the financier is able and willing to do about reducing financing risks. Thus a major part of the solution to risk obstacles often lies in overcoming these interrelated problems.

The special risk problems involved in financing small-factory development are of two major types. The first are those which arise from the development orientation of such financing. For example:

1. Development financing focuses on *changing* enterprises; this tends to increase the hazards of miscalculation.
2. A development orientation implies acceptance of some degree of risk in order to serve purposes with a reasonable promise of providing exceptional development results.
3. The criteria for success of development financing are more complex than the criteria for financing intended only to earn a profit.

The second source of special risk problems is the general characteristic of factories of this scale. For example:

1. Management is exercised by one or two primary owners. Management capabilities are therefore likely to be weak in some aspects. Enlarging capabilities to meet changing problems tends to be particularly difficult in less-developed countries where entrepreneurs are less likely to have the long industrial experience, education, and access to knowledge helpful to such adaptations. There is the further problem in owner-managed enterprises that death, illness, and changes that come with age or shifting family interests of the owner-manager may drastically alter the enterprise's outlook. There is less possibility in the case of the small factory of strengthening it by adding to or completely changing management.

2. The small factory is highly vulnerable to environmental pressures, such as competition, shifts in supply positions, and changing government policies. It is rarely in a position to influence its environment significantly but must adapt to whatever changes come. Some small factories, moreover, are highly dependent on special situations—a particular market, location, or specialized product. Factories depending on special situations have less protection against unpredictable changes which can completely alter their prospects.

3. The risks in financing small factories are difficult to evaluate and control. There tend to be fewer reliable facts available concerning small factories, their management, or such environmental factors as competition than is the case for larger factories. Small factories are not always able to provide sufficient collateral to completely assure repayment. The practical means of applying other control over repayment is often lacking.

Not all the major characteristics of small factories tend to enlarge financing risks. There are other characteristics which, if taken advantage of, can help offset the special risk problems. For example:

1. The fact that small factories are more numerous means that risks can be more widely spread.

2. The owners of small factories with a large growth potential tend to be highly motivated, which helps them overcome problems.

3. Small manufacturers, because they are likely to have a continuing need for outside financing, are especially motivated to maintain a good credit record.

4. The operations of small factories tend to be simpler than those of large ones and their capabilities more apparent.

A program for financing smaller manufacturers can, but need not, be more risky than the financing which institutions are presently extending to larger enterprises. For example, institutions are in many cases financing new as well as longer-established large firms while refraining from financing time-tested smaller firms, even though financing the latter is unlikely to be as risky as financing new firms, large or small. In practice, the more serious loss problem of many development banks (e.g., the Bank of Northeast Brazil) has arisen with fairly large projects.[19]

[19] Although less common, higher loss rates on loans to small firms than on loans to large ones have also been experienced by some development banks, e.g., the Kerala State Finance Corporation discussed in Chap. 2. Accurate comparisons of loss experience between large and small enterprises are difficult to make, partly because of problems of definition and partly because of the irregular intervals at which losses tend to occur and the greater impact of one loss on the record in the case of large projects. One of the few financial institutions for which we have specific data on the ratio of realized net losses to amount disbursed of extinguished loans over an extended period (1934–1951) is the United States Reconstruction Finance Corporation. The ratio for borrowers with assets of less than $25,000 was about 7 percent; of $25,000 to $49,000, 3.5 percent; of $50,000 to $99,000, 2.1 percent; of $100,000

Cost and Profitability Obstacles

Costs also often impede the extension of the types and amounts of financing required for the healthy development of small manufacturing enterprises. Cost problems are of two general types. High lending costs may push lending rates up to such a level that enterprises cannot afford to utilize borrowed funds or will be at a serious competitive disadvantage with larger firms in the same line if they do. A second and in practice much more common type of problem is that costs, together with legislative or traditional ceilings on lending rates, may result in it being less profitable, or even quite unprofitable, to lend to small manufacturers in preference to alternative lending opportunities.

There are many reasons why loans to small manufacturers are less profitable than loans to larger enterprises or certain other types of borrowers when a uniform lending rate is charged. For example:

1. Small firms tend to borrow proportionately smaller amounts, and because the return is a fixed percent of the amount of the loan, the return falls progressively with the decline in the size of the loan. Costs, however, are not so directly related to the size of loan and do not decline proportionately or very regularly with a decline in loan size. A less than proportionate decline in costs is particularly to be expected in the common case where loan allocation and administrative procedures designed to serve the needs of large enterprises are applied with little modification to smaller enterprises.
2. Small manufacturers often cannot provide accounting records and standard types of collateral which facilitate the use of low-cost methods of loan allocation and control.
3. The rejection rate tends to be higher among smaller enterprises, adding to their general screening costs.
4. Special assistance to small manufacturers is sometimes of special importance in maintaining their capacity to use funds productively and repay loans.

Apart from the size factor, any effort to stress developmental financing may tend to raise costs. Allocation and administration of financing is more costly where an attempt is made to allocate funds to applicants in accordance with their capacity to apply them productively and to assure that they do so. Such costs are particularly high where very exacting standards

---

to $249,000, 5.7 percent; of $250,000 to $499,000, 2.4 percent; and of $500,000 and over, a little less than 1.5 percent. (R. J. Saulnier, A. G. Halcrow, and N. H. Jacoby, *Federal Lending and Loan Insurance,* Princeton University Press, Princeton, N.J., for the National Bureau of Economic Research, 1958, p. 481.) Thus, while this indicates losses to be generally higher on small loans than on larger ones, the pattern is very irregular. As the average loan period was about five years, even the highest loss rate could have been nearly offset by an additional one percentage point on the interest rate.

of development results are set or where general entrepreneurial shortcomings, inflation, and other conditions make the misallocation or misuse of funds a serious possibility.

Although the cost problem in serving small manufacturers is serious enough, particularly from the point of view of the lender who has to operate profitably on a uniform margin of, say, two percentage points or less, the extent of the problem is easily—and quite often—exaggerated. In the general lending conditions of most newly industrializing countries, a one- or two-percentage-point increase in the margin should in most cases make term loans as small as $50,000 to $100,000 almost as profitable as larger loans. A further one- or two-percentage-point increase in the margin might be required for loans ranging from $25,000 to $50,000. And if loan procedures can be suitably adapted to accommodate manufacturers requiring amounts as small as $10,000 and the margin widened by another one or two percentage points, even such small loans could frequently be served as profitably as larger loans.

In interpreting the above attempt to indicate the extent to which the profitability problem is influenced by the size of loans or of the borrowing enterprises, it should be borne in mind that the profitability of lending operations can also be greatly affected by such factors as: whether applicants are previous or existing clients, new clients with expansion plans, or clients with plans for new enterprises; the distance at which the applicants are located from the lending center and their dispersal; and the lending objectives and procedures used to achieve them, including especially the degree to which advisory assistance is used to foster a maximum or assure a minimum level of performance. A loan margin which would be inadequate to cover the costs of financing new and complex types of enterprises scattered in remote locations and requiring funds of from $50,000 to $100,000 could be quite adequate to cover the costs involved in financing the expansion of much smaller but well-established and prospering enterprises clustered in a major urban center. For instance, in countries such as Denmark and the Netherlands, where there are generally prosperous conditions and a large concentration of small firms which can be relied upon for the most part to maintain good accounting records and to have honest management and reasonably well worked out investment plans, an efficient lending program may not require more than a 1 or 2 percent margin between the cost of its funds and its lending rate to make term loans in amounts of $10,000 to $20,000.

It should also be kept in mind that lenders tend to be concerned about even very small differences in profitability when their funds can be entirely absorbed by the most profitable type of client. On the other hand, when resources are not limited, it is in the lender's economic interest to serve less profitable clients, provided there is a reasonable expectation of income at least equaling expenses. It may even be in the lender's interest—although bankers do not always realize it—to serve some clients where, according to conventional calculations, expenses are expected to exceed income. Where the demand of larger clients on funds and staff time fluctuate, little real cost will be incurred by serving additional clients which help to smooth out demand.[20] Moreover, part of the cost of serving small enterprises which may be expected to grow much larger with adequate financing may be regarded as promotional expenses to be recovered from future business.

There are a number of other advantages in lending to small firms which are not easily quantifiable but which, if taken properly into account, help offset the cost problem. As has been stressed by the management of some of the new development finance companies in Central America, serving the more promising small enterprises is a relatively inexpensive way to build a reputation as a public-spirited institution, which will help not only to attract some of the more desirable clients, but also to facilitate other relationships with the general public or government services.[21] Lending to small enterprises also enlarges the number and diversity of loans outstanding, thus strengthening an institution's ability to adjust to the effects of a default by one of its larger borrowers should this occur. In this way the institution also has access to more information on business conditions and the business community in general, which enhances its lending capabilities. Finally, financing small enterprises is a valuable means of providing experience to new staff, since this involves relatively simple projects and small sums of money.

The Special Problems of Newly Industrializing Countries

Some reference to the special problems of newly industrializing countries has already been made in discussing the obstacles to financing small-factory development. A brief listing of the major types of special problems may help bring these into perspective. The problems indicated cannot, of course, be expected to be of similar intensity or even common to every newly industrializing country nor to be exclusively confined to them. However, the greater frequency and intensity of these kinds of problems in newly industrializing countries does sharply distinguish them as a group; it also greatly alters the problem of financing small-factory development.

1. Economic Conditions

  a. Bottlenecks and general instability in the economy are more common because of deficiencies in such factors as foreign exchange, power, transport,

---

[20] This follows from the elementary rule of economics that the volume of business providing maximum profit or minimum loss is the volume at which marginal cost equals marginal revenue. If the minimum facilities essential to serve a small number of large, highly profitable customers are not always fully utilized, then additional clients may be profitably served if they provide a return at least greater than the variable costs incurred in extending service to them.

[21] Discussions in July, 1964.

and general government services. This increases the investment and financial-reserve requirements of factories and increases the risk involved in financing manufacturing concerns too small to afford their own power or similar services which cannot be hired on a dependable basis.

b. Dependence on imports for equipment and basic industrial materials weakens the base for desirable types of financial and other services from the suppliers, as is further discussed in Chapter 6. The dependence on imports also increases the risk of financing because little information is available about imported factory requirements, and there is less assurance that they will be supplied promptly.

c. The newness and limited number of small factories result in banks and other sources of finance being less familiar with the requirements for financing such enterprises. Factories tend to be too few to permit economies in financing methods that depend on serving a large number of enterprises. Factory assets have a narrower resale market and are less useful as collateral.

2. *Financial Conditions*

a. Savings tend to be inadequate in relation to investment requirements. An exceptionally high proportion of the savings available seeks nonrisk investments or investments under the saver's direct control. Those with the best capacity to develop small factories often do not have the savings required, and those who have savings that might be appropriately devoted to this purpose often do not have the capabilities required.

b. Inflation tends to diminish savings while increasing the demand for funds, enlarging especially the demand for funds to be used for nonproductive purposes. The allocation of funds in accordance with development priorities is made much more difficult. Lenders tend to have much less interest in financing small manufacturers.

3. *Industrial Capabilities*

a. Entrepreneurs and their enterprises more often lack the capabilities that come with experience.

b. Information important to guiding and evaluating industrial operations is less available and less reliable. Entrepreneurs and financiers tend to be conditioned by this and the general uncertainty of their environment to distrust and neglect such analysis as might be done in planning industrial and financial decisions.

c. The collection and dissemination of industrial information tends to require staff of exceptional training and experience because of the foregoing problems; such persons, however, are in exceptionally short supply.

4. *Social and Political Conditions*

a. Legislation governing financial relationships, property titles, banking, taxation, and other matters pertaining to financing tends to be deficient or inadequately enforced.

b. Governments' responsibilities tend to exceed their administrative capacity. Measures important for facilitating small-factory financing and dependent on government action may not be practical in these circumstances.

c. Society tends to be fragmented into small social groups having little knowledge of or confidence in one another. Finance is more easily extended when mutual confidence exists between the supplier and the recipient and between different suppliers of funds.

In the next two chapters, we shall explore the efforts to overcome the obstacles to financing small manufacturers in two countries at different levels of development and with different institutional and cultural backgrounds (India and Puerto Rico). This will introduce in concrete settings a wide range of measures and policies that will figure in the subsequent analytical discussions. Following this, Part 2 considers the problems of general strategy for improving the financial services available to small manufacturers. Part 3 deals in further detail with the principal channels through which development finance may be administered. Part 4 summarizes the main operational problems in financing the development of small factories, and Part 5 presents two additional country studies, one (Japan) setting forth a highly evolved program of a more advanced country and a second (Colombia) setting forth a program for a newly industrializing country which reflects an application of the author's basic concepts.

Chapter 2
India's Experience
with Special
Financing Measures

INDIA'S EXPERIENCE IS worth considering in some detail for the introduction it provides to the requirements of practical small-industry financing programs. India has experimented with an unusually wide variety of financing measures for small industry. Also, although India is larger and more industrially advanced than many developing countries, its efforts to improve small-industry finance have encountered most of the serious obstacles which usually arise in such countries.

As of 1960, India had some 36,000 registered small factories with fixed assets in the neighborhood of US$450 million and a gross output of over US$2.5 billion. Total employment was in excess of 1.3 million. These account for 38 percent of the employment and 25 percent of the net value added of all registered factories. India's special small-industry programs have not been confined to small factories but are intended to serve also a great many other smaller units. The focus in this analysis however will be on the special financial assistance going to small factories.[1]

[1] India's program covers all small industrial units with fixed capital of less than 500,000 rupees (Rs) (about US$105,000) except for enterprises served by the Khadi and Village Industries Commission, the Handloom Board, and certain other agencies (all rupee figures converted in this report at 4.76 rupees per dollar unless otherwise indicated). Small registered factories include only factories employing 10 or more workers if using power or 20 or more if without power and having fixed capital of less than Rs500,000. A recent official report considers only 16,500 of these employing 615,000 persons as being the "central object" of government small-industry assistance. However, it estimates that another 200,000 to 250,000 nonregistered units employing some 1 million persons fall within the scope of India's small-industries program. See *Development of Small-scale Industries in India—Prospects, Problems, and Policies,* Report of the International Perspective Planning Team,

Small-factory Needs for Development Financing

A theme which runs through most writings on small industry in India is that the small entrepreneurs lack adequate funds of their own to establish enterprises on a proper basis, to expand or modernize as this becomes appropriate, or to maintain their enterprise intact through periods of temporary adversity. The findings of McCrory and Berna have already been reported. Other brief surveys referred to below seem to confirm their general findings, although some are critical of efforts thus far and stress the need to concentrate on enterprises having "the seeds of progress in them."[2]

The available information on the extent to which small industrialists in India are able to obtain finance from the various sources is neither complete nor very accurate. There have been small surveys at different times and by different investigators, however, and from these the general pattern can be roughly pieced together.[3] Something like 10 to 20 percent of the small industrialists utilize no external sources of funds, with this proportion varying sharply with the size of enterprises even within the size ranges defined as small industry. The vast majority—perhaps 50 to 60 percent or more—obtain some finance from interbusiness creditors, money-lenders, friends, or relatives. The remaining 20 or 30 percent—and these primarily in the upper-size categories of small industry—obtain some funds from banks or government lending institutions as well as from non-institutional sources.

Although most firms obtain some external financing, the extent of dependence on external funds is small, as the estimates in Table 1 on the share of total funds from various sources suggest.

The data may not be sufficiently accurate, and the units sampled in the two years may not be sufficiently comparable to permit conclusions

---

sponsored by the Ford Foundation, Government of India, Ministry of Industry, New Delhi, 1963, pp. 15–21 and Table 1.

[2] See, for example, P. N. Dhar and H. F. Lydall, *The Role of Small Enterprises in Indian Economic Development*, Asia Publishing House, Bombay, 1961, pp. 70ff.

[3] For the most recent effort to assemble such data, see the Central Small Industries Organisation (CSIO), *Financing of Small Scale Industries in India*, Government of India, New Delhi, 1963. This assembled all the available data on the lending activities of major institutional sources of funds and gathered information from small industrialists by a survey of 250 units located in 12 cities in six states. Other surveys on the sources of small industry funds are reported in: State Bank of India, *Evaluation Report: Pilot Scheme for the Coordinated Conversion of Credit to Small Scale Industries, April 1956 to December 1957* (mimeographed); Sabita Banerji, "The Financial Structure of Small- and Medium-scale Industries," *The Indian Journal of Economics*, vol. 36, no. 145, October, 1956; C. K. Shah, "Commercial Banks and Finance for Small Industries in India," *Journal of the Indian Institute of Bankers*, October, 1957; Society for Social and Economic Studies, *Capital for Medium and Small Scale Industries*, Asia Publishing House, Bombay, 1959.

to be drawn on changes over time. They are adequate, however, to indicate that both banking and nonbanking sources play a relatively small role in financing small industry and that all external sources combined may not supply more than 15 to 20 percent of small-industry funds.

*Table 1. The Approximate Share of Various Sources in the Financing of Small Industry in India**

Source	Percent in 1957	Percent in 1961
Internal funds	88.0	81.0
Private nonbanking sources	3.6	6.6
Banking sources including the State Bank	7.3	6.5
Government sources excluding the State Bank	1.1	5.9
Total	100.0	100.0

* The 1957 data are based on a sample survey by the State Bank of India of small industrialists in six states in south India; the 1961 data are based on a sample survey by the CSIO of 250 units in 12 industrial centers. CSIO, *Financing of Small Scale Industries in India*, Government of India, New Delhi, 1963, p. 31.

Internal as well as external funds are in short supply for small firms. McCrory, speaking of a price war in an overexpanded industry, has dramatized this aspect of the small firm's plight:

> It is an unequal struggle. Everything is on the side of those with capital, the man who can operate longest at loss. In the face of this, the assets of the craftsman, his skill, his ingenuity, his ability to economize, become an arsenal of pop-guns. Those who survive are those with capital, regardless of whether they are good, bad or indifferent industrialists.[4]

A main reason for the shortage of internal funds, according to a common thesis, is that small enterprises are often so heavily dependent on a particular middleman for sales, supplies, and/or finance that the middleman is able— and tends—to drain off all profits but the minimum essential to continued operations. The middleman who takes a short-view of his interest may not leave his small-industry clients with sufficient income to develop their full potential or even to survive. The importance of such relationships as a cause of low profits however is uncertain in the absence of concrete information and is probably less significant for factory than for nonfactory types of small industry.

Another cause of inadequacy of internal funds is the instability of profits. As a result, accumulated profits may not coincide with the requirement for development expenditures (which must be met at specific times and in certain minimum amounts) or for sustaining a temporary loss so that development may later proceed from the stage already reached.

[4] James T. McCrory, *Small Industry in a North Indian Town: Case Studies in Latent Industrial Potential*, Government of India, Ministry of Commerce and Industry, New Delhi, 1956, p. 3.

An inadequacy of internal funds also arises because a great many of the persons with the knowledge of opportunities and the capabilities and drive to exploit small-industry opportunities do not come from families with sufficient inherited wealth to implement these potentialities and cannot accumulate the amount required in time from occupations requiring little initial capital. Such, for example, is the case of the "craftsmen entrepreneurs" in the Punjab metalworking industry, who, as McCrory has vividly illustrated, have entrepreneurial potentialities but, being sons of poor craftsmen and in some cases refugees, have not the funds to realize their potentialities on a practical basis. As the case histories in Berna and McCrory illustrate, growth often depends on the ability to seize opportunities for large profits, lasting for possibly brief periods.[5]

The inadequacy of finance is not entirely due to the difficulties small industrialists have in *obtaining* finance. It also arises because they are sometimes under heavy pressure to extend finance to their customers. Textile mills were reported to delay payment on machinery purchased from small industrialists for nearly six months.[6] According to one authority, payment held up by customers is the cause of a large part of small industry's financial difficulties. It is not only the heavy credit burden it places on small industrialists, but also the uncertainty it creates as to their working-capital requirements.[7] The problem of lengthy delays by customers in paying for purchases is particularly acute in the case of sales to government. Small industrialists with whom the author came in contact while guiding economic surveys in India between 1957 and 1959 typically reported a period of eight months to a year's wait for payment in the case of sales to government agencies.

The inadequacy of finance is not the only obstacle to small-industry development in India, although many of those directly concerned with the problem have tended to regard it as being at the root of the problem. In the words of P. C. Alexander who has served as India's Development Commissioner for Small-scale Industries:

> Among all the problems faced by small industries, absence of credit facilities has been the most serious. Small entrepreneurs invariably started their business with extremely limited capital scraped from their own assets and borrowed at exorbitant rates of interest. Even if they knew how to organize their production on efficient lines, they often failed because of their inability to

[5] James J. Berna, *Industrial Entrepreneurship in Madras State,* International Development Center of Stanford Research Institute, Asia Publishing House, Bombay, London, New York, 1960. Also, McCrory, *op. cit.,* p. 2.

[6] Society for Social and Economic Studies, *op. cit.,* p. 33. The example is cited from "Survey of Small and Medium-scale Engineering Factories in Bombay City," *University Journal,* vol. 26, p. 69.

[7] R. S. Bhatt, *Finance for Small Industries,* a talk given to the Small Industries Service Institute survey staff, 1956. (Mimeographed.) Berna also reports this problem in Madras but indicates one of much less magnitude. He reports delays of one month as examples of the problem. Berna, *op. cit.,* p. 14.

raise capital for acquiring good factory accommodation or new machinery and equipment, or for recurring expenses. As a result of this, production continued to be at low levels of efficiency yielding very little margin of profit for further investments. Banks and other institutional agencies of credit found these units generally ineligible for lending and they were thrown back to the mercies of money-lenders or to their own resources. Thus the economy was caught in a vicious circle of lack of capital leading to industrial backwardness and industrial backwardness leading to a lack of capital.[8]

The circularity or interrelationship of financial and other problems noted by Alexander has received increasing attention in recent years. The problem has tended to be viewed more and more as one of not merely finding ways of improving small-industry financing, but also of finding ways of meeting small industry's needs for financial and other types of assistance simultaneously.

Moneylenders and Other Conventional Sources of Small-industry Funds

The main lenders to small industry in India are a wide variety of individuals and partnerships engaged in money lending. These are broadly divided into two groups: (1) indigenous bankers who accept deposits and engage in a variety of banking activities but are not classified or registered as banks and (2) other professional moneylenders whose main financial activity is lending but who may also engage in commerce and other businesses. Friends and relatives are also an important source of funds, particularly for the smaller factories. Little can be said of this latter source in a general way, however, since in practice funds from friends and relatives in some cases cannot be distinguished from internal funds and in others are little different from loans by professional moneylenders.

Much of the concern with small-industry financing in India revolves around a conviction that small-industry development requires a reduced dependency by small industrialists on moneylenders. The main criticism of moneylenders has been their interest charges, or at least the effective cost of their services. There is nevertheless very little specific information about what their services typically cost small-industry borrowers, although much more has been reported on their services to agriculturists and artisans.[9] Indigenous bankers in western India are reported to lend at 9 to 12 percent on promissory notes, which they in turn discount with banks at a little over 6 percent.[10] Moneylenders in Surat were reported to charge 6 percent,

[8] P. C. Alexander, *Industrial Estates in India,* Asia Publishing House, Bombay, London, New York, 1963, p. 3.

[9] For a general description of money lending in India, see Bal Krishna Madan's chapter on India in B. H. Beckhart, *Banking Systems,* Columbia University Press, New York, 1954, pp. 373–420, and L. C. Jain, *Indigenous Banking in India,* The Macmillan Company, New York, 1929.

[10] George Rosen, *Some Aspects of Industrial Finance in India,* The Free Press of Glencoe, New York, 1962, p. 37.

and in Madras 6 to 24 percent.[11] A study in Bengal in 1953 reported rates to small engineering establishments as ranging from as low as 2 percent up to 16 percent. On the other hand, cases where the effective cost of financing has been over 50 percent are also reported.[12] Such data are of varying reliability and refer to different times and circumstances, but obviously the interest rate charged varies considerably from case to case. Rates of 10 to 20 percent do not seem to be unusual for the size of enterprise being considered here. The danger of harsher terms if dependency on moneylenders becomes complete also seems to be a real one.

Moneylenders are nevertheless widely used. This is in part because of the limited alternatives. However, small industrialists also prefer the lending methods of moneylenders to those of banks and government agencies. Moneylenders give prompt, flexible, and informal service. Collateral is often left in the possession of the borrowers so that its productive use is not impeded. Although rates may be high and an inability to repay on time may involve heavy penalties, the loan is otherwise tailored to meet the individual borrower's needs.

Money lending as such has been little distinguished in India from supplier credit or other interbusiness financing. The type of moneylender usually regarded as the most harmful to small-industry development is the one also engaged in commerce, because his clients tend to be dependent upon him in several ways. The criticism has apparent validity, for the merchant-moneylender is in a strong bargaining position. Nevertheless very little is known about these relationships in actual practice. One of the more thoughtful studies of a sample of small enterprises suggests that if the positive values of the merchant-lender's services are weighed alongside their deficiencies, the merchant-lender's services were, for the enterprises studied, the most useful source of small-industry assistance.[13] Progress has been made in recent years in increasing other channels of small-industry financing, but the moneylender continues to be a principal source.

Bank Financing of Small Industry

India's banking system consists primarily of 79 scheduled banks with over 4,600 offices. These account for over 98 percent of total bank credit. There are also 203 nonscheduled banks, which are small banks not accorded borrowing privileges from the central bank. The largest of India's banks is the government-owned State Bank of India, which in 1961 accounted for nearly one-fourth of all bank credit. The other scheduled banks are privately owned domestic and foreign commercial banks engaging principally in short-term financing.

[11] *Small-scale Engineering Industries in Surat, Bombay,* Government of India, Development Commissioner for Small-scale Industries, New Delhi, 1957, p. 42; and Berna, *op. cit.,* p. 140.

[12] Banerji, *op. cit.,* pp. 193–194.

[13] McCrory, *op. cit.,* pp. 24–26.

Scheduled bank financing of small industries has increased in recent years, rising from 207 million rupees (Rs) (US$43 million) outstanding in June, 1960, to Rs346 million (US$73 million) in June, 1962.[14] Non-scheduled banks had outstanding another Rs18 million (US$3.8 million) as of October, 1960.[15] The improvement reflects in good part government measures discussed later. The total nevertheless remains extremely small relative to the total bank credit outstanding, being less than 3 percent. It is also small compared with the total financial requirements of small industries. This is illustrated by the fact that bank credit outstanding to all small industry is equivalent to only about 3 percent of the value of gross output of registered small factories.[16] Banks are nevertheless the most important institutional source of small-industry financing.[17]

Indian banks normally extend credit on an overdraft basis for periods up to six months but renewable. Security is commonly required and is most frequently in the form of commodities stored under bank control. A cosigner is also required in many cases. Unsecured loans and loans against hypothecated security are also extended, but these form a relatively small part of total lending. Interest rates vary widely, being higher in smaller banks and for less attractive types of lending. Most scheduled bank loans bear 6 to 8 percent although range up to 10 to 12 percent on some loans. The general difficulty with banks as a source of small-industry financing is illustrated by the findings of a survey of Kolhapur in Bombay state:

> Only two of the seven banks lend money occasionally to small-scale industrial units on a short-term basis, at a rate of interest varying from 6 to 9 percent. These loans are made on the security of the fixed assets and finished goods of the industrial units. . . . From a general discussion held with them, it appears that they have adequate business by way of loans required by the merchants, Kolhapur being an important trading centre in this area. The commercial banks do not seem to be concerned about exploring the possibilities for new business outside trading. Further, their general reluctance to give advances to small-scale industries is based on the fact that up till now, they have had little occasion to get conversant with the marketing possibilities of the products of engineering units, nor do they have facilities for judging the quality and competitive status of finished goods of small-scale

[14] Reserve Bank of India, *Bulletin,* Bombay, February, 1963, p. 180.

[15] CSIO, *op. cit.,* p. 117 citing Reserve Bank of India, *Bulletin,* May, 1961.

[16] For a fairly detailed effort to relate credit availability to requirements for small industry during the second and third Five-Year Plans, see CSIO, *op. cit.,* pp. 141–148.

[17] If loans issued from 1955 to 1962 by the other main institutional sources (the state finance corporations, the National Small Industries Corporation, and the state governments) are assumed to approximate the volume outstanding in 1962—a probable overestimate, although most of their loans are term loans—the total would be still about 20 percent less than the volume of that of the private commercial banks. However, the total of all government small-industry financing, including State Bank loans and government investments in industrial estates is possibly as much as one-third larger than that of private commercial banks.

engineering units, which may be offered to them as security for working capital advances.[18]

Government Measures to Improve Small-industry Financing

Experimentation in India with ways of improving the financing services to industry, particularly new and locally owned enterprises and those of small and medium scale, have been going on for several decades. The Industrial Commission appointed in 1916 recommended financial assistance to all scales of industry. In the case of small industries, it suggested financing take the form of direct loans or the provision of plant on the hire-purchase system.[19] One of the primary channels for small-industry financing in India today was initiated in 1922 with the passage by the government of Madras state of a State-Aid-to-Industries Act. Similar acts were passed by a number of other states in the 1920s and by many of the remainder during the 1930s.[20]

Official measures to improve the financing available to small industry have multiplied rapidly in the past decade. Before examining each of these, a brief résumé of the amount of financing extended since the beginning of the second Five-Year Plan in 1956 through the various measures may help bring the total program into perspective.

Type of Financing Measure	*Amount of Loans or Investment (in millions of U.S. dollars)*
Low-interest term financing under State-Aid-to-Industries Act	31.0[a]
Experimental equity financing program of Orissa state	0.8[b]
Loans through industrial cooperatives	1.9[c]
Term financing through state finance corporations	10.5[d]
Hire-purchase equipment through the National Small Industries Corporation	19.5[e]
Factory sites and buildings on lease or installment terms	26.9[f]
Short-term credit and other State Bank assistance	17.4[g]
The credit guarantee program of the Reserve Bank	13.2[h]

[a] Loans issued up to March, 1962.
[b] Investment made through 1961.
[c] Loans issued in the five years ending 1961.
[d] Loans outstanding March, 1962.
[e] Value of equipment delivered up to September, 1962.

[f] Investments made up to March, 1962.
[g] Short-term credit outstanding at the end of 1962.
[h] Value of credit outstanding March, 1962, on which guarantees are given.

[18] *Principal Small-scale Industries in Kolhapur, Bombay,* Government of India, Development Commissioner for Small-scale Industries, New Delhi, 1957, p. 15.

[19] S. K. Basu, *Industrial Finance in India,* Calcutta University Press, Calcutta, India, 1953, p. 174 [citing Report of the Indian Industrial Commission (1916–1918), p. 184].

[20] The early history of the program is described in considerable detail in Basu, *op. cit.*

This program, unlike the foregoing, does not involve direct government lending or investment. The Reserve Bank also employs other measures which, like guarantees, are intended to stimulate the financing activity of other institutions.

Low-interest Term Financing under State-Aid-to-Industries Acts

This long-established channel acquired new importance in the mid-1950s as the result of an extension and liberalization in the provisions of the various state acts and increased appropriations. During the second Five Year Plan ending in March, 1961, approximately Rs26 million (US$5.5 million) in loans per year were extended by the various states and a further Rs20 million (US$4 million) were extended in the following year.[21] Under the present arrangements, two-thirds of the funds are derived from central government appropriations, one-third from state appropriations. Loans are administered by the state government's department of industries.

Loans under the provisions of certain state legislation extend to maximums varying from seven to twenty years; the usual loan period appears to be between three and seven years. The rate of interest is 3 percent on amounts up to Rs50,000 (about US$11,000) and 5 percent on amounts over that.[22]

The extent to which these go to small factories is difficult to estimate. Many types of nonfactory industries are eligible as well as factory enterprises; loans are typically very small, usually between US$500 and US$1,000, although the maximum loan size in some states is as high as US$21,000 (Rs100,000). The average loan size for five selected states was around $425, ranging from as low as $175 in one state (Madhya Pradesh) to over $6,000 in another (Gujerat).[23] These are of course averages. The average size of *loans* moreover may be a deceptive indicator of size of the *enterprise* of the loan recipients; loans are much sought after because of the attractive interest rate and lenient collateral requirements. Not only is there a high rejection rate, but also applicants are typically granted much smaller amounts than they request.

Screening has been a major difficulty of the program. The small volume of funds available relative to the demands increases the need for selectivity among applicants. There is a need both to identify fraudulent applications, which the favorable terms attract, and to judge relative priorities between eligible enterprises. The state department of industries depends for initial screening upon district officers who have a knowledge of local persons and conditions but no special knowledge of industrial or financial matters. Dis-

---

[21] Over one-third of the total was disbursed by two states (Punjab and Uttar Pradesh) and over one-fourth by three others (Bihar, Madras, and Bombay). For more detailed data, see CSIO, *op. cit.,* pp. 38–39.

[22] The Central Small Industries Organization has recently recommended that the interest rate on loans above Rs5,000 be raised to 5 or 6 percent, *Financing of Small Scale Industries in India,* p. 4.

[23] *Ibid.,* p. 43.

trict officers appear in practice to have too many other functions to handle loan applications expeditiously. Other departments are sometimes responsible for evaluating the collateral offered, such as the revenue department in the case of land and the public works department in the case of buildings. This often contributes to delay in loan processing. Delays also arise because final decisions for loans over a few hundred dollars must usually be made by the director of industries or higher authority in the state capital. Delays in arriving at loan decisions have been a common complaint since the program began, with the time required in recent years averaging around six to eight months.

The financing arrangements, like all the following ones in which government has a major role in determining allocation, are suspected by many small industrialists of being available only to those who have the right personal connections or who can establish them through bribes. To what extent this is merely uninformed cynicism, of which there is a great deal, and to what extent it is an accurate assessment is difficult for the outsider to judge. The author, however, found that it was widely believed. McCrory reports a similar finding:

> Only one small industrialist has had any direct contact with the loan program, and that has been unpleasant. He has so far been approached by two "elected representatives" and "several government officials". . . each of whom offered to help him secure loans of up to Rs. 25,000. The officials offered help on condition he make one of their respective relatives a partner in his business. The elected representatives offered help on condition he give them ten percent of the loan as commission.[24]

There is no well-defined arrangement for post-allocation supervision or assistance other than the collection of repayment in installments. A sample study in 1958 indicated, however, that a considerable number also received some technical assistance from the Small Industries Service Institutes.[25] Delinquencies or defaults have been high throughout the history of the program, amounting in recent years in the case of some states to as much as 35 to 50 percent of loans outstanding.[26]

The program as a whole does not seem to have provided a sufficiently effective means of financing small-factory development to justify the cost and effort required. It has lacked the proper organization and staffing to administer development financing; its financing responsibilities are much too broad for the resources it has; and both its average loan size and its return on loans are so small there is little motivation or possibility for operating it on an economically rational basis.

---

[24] McCrory, *op. cit.,* p. 33. Dhar and Lydall (*op. cit.,* p. 7) also refer to this problem in government.

[25] Unpublished study made by the Small Industries Service Institutes.

[26] CSIO, *op. cit.,* p. 44.

The program, though costly in relation to results produced, has made some contribution to small-industry growth. A 1958 evaluation of over 80 sample units indicated funds had usually been applied to specific purposes, such as equipment or buildings, and appeared to have contributed to the recipient's expansion. Moreover, some states, such as Punjab, had made much greater use of this program and obtained much better results than others. Two factors appear to account for this difference. One is the special effort that particular state governments and the individuals primarily responsible have made to make the program useful. The second is an exceptional supply in some states of entrepreneurs with potential, able to start on a very small scale with little more assistance than a small amount of finance.

The Experimental Equity Financing Program of Orissa State

The Orissa state government began an experiment in 1957 under the provision of its State-Aid-to-Industry Act to extend equity financing to industrial enterprises. By 1961, it had invested the equivalent of about $800,000 in 37 companies. Private shareholders were required to put up a minimum of at least 10 percent of the total investment with the state contributing the rest. The private owners were to be given the opportunity to repurchase government shareholding and were to have the managing responsibilities subject to the authority of the board of directors, on which the government was represented.

Deficiencies in the management of these enterprises soon became a major problem. A 1960 government evaluation concluded these stemmed largely from the indifference of entrepreneurs who had little at stake in the enterprise and from a lack of supervision.[27] Entrepreneurs, on the other hand, reported that effective management was blocked by the need for and inability to obtain decisions on operational matters from government directors who had little knowledge of the businesses and many other duties. Some also lacked the knowledge and experience to manage the enterprises in which they were engaged without competent advisory assistance.[28] The problems of this program led the state government to suspend its operations. Other equity financing arrangements have been under consideration since but not put into operation.

Loans through Industrial Cooperatives

Industrial cooperatives deserve mention primarily as a very old type of measure (the Cooperative Credit Societies Act dating from 1904) still

[27] *Second Report,* Government of India, Small-scale Industries Board, Subcommittee on Credit Facilities, New Delhi, 1960.

[28] Information based on the author's observations and interviews with entrepreneurs and Orissa state officials while a consultant to the Eastern Region, Small Industries Service Institutes, in 1959.

being pursued without much success. The cooperative movement in India has been largely concerned with agriculture. In recent years, under the stimulation of special government measures following the 1953 recommendations of the International Planning Team on small industries, nonagricultural credit cooperatives have grown in number. In 1959, the Japanese Delegation on Small-scale Industries again emphasized the value of cooperatives and the need for strengthening industrial cooperatives and industrial cooperative banks.[29] However, their financial importance remains small. Of nearly 12,000 such societies in 1961, over one-fifth were dormant and only 842 had capital and reserves in excess of Rs100,000 (about US$21,000).[30] Loans by industrial cooperatives and urban cooperative banks to small industries during the five years ending 1961 amounted to less than $2 million, and this largely to nonfactory types of enterprises.[31]

Term Finance through State Finance Corporations (SFCs)

Shortly after Independence and after establishing the Industrial Finance Corporation for large industry, the government of India undertook to encourage similar organizations to finance small and medium enterprises. The State Financial Corporations Act was enacted in 1951. Madras state, in advance of the act, had set up a corporation essentially of this type in 1949.[32] Within three years after the passage of the act, six more state finance corporations were established, and by 1961 there was one in each of the 15 states.[33]

The state finance corporations are largely state-owned corporations, most having a paid-up capital of around Rs10 million (about US$2 million). State government shareholding ranges from 32 percent to 64 percent and averages 46 percent. The Reserve Bank holds 17.5 percent of the equity in SFCs, and other financial institutions hold 32.5 percent. The general public, although permitted to hold up to 25 percent of their equity and offered a guaranteed dividend of usually 3 or 4 percent, has taken up an average of 4 percent of the equity in the SFCs, although holding as much as 10 percent in one corporation.[34]

Equity accounted for 31 percent of their resources in March, 1963. Bonds

[29] *Report of the Japanese Delegation on Small Scale Industries* (*1959*), Government of India Press, New Delhi, 1960, pp. 46–52, 65ff.

[30] Reserve Bank of India, *Bulletin*, May, 1963, p. 625.

[31] Report of the International Perspective Planning Team, *op. cit.*, p. 104. See G. M. Laud, *Cooperative Banking in India,* Co-operators' Book Depot, Bombay, 1956, for a detailed history of the subject.

[32] Treated here as one of the state finance corporations, even though it was incorporated under different legislation.

[33] Nagaland, a recently formed state, does not yet have a corporation.

[34] For a detailed account of the state finance corporations, see Reserve Bank of India, *Report of the Working Group on State Finance Corporations,* Bombay, 1964. (Mimeographed.)

guaranteed by state governments and purchased principally by commercial banks and to a lesser extent by the state bank, the government life insurance corporation, and other official agencies are an even more important source of funds. Their relative importance has rapidly increased in recent years. It amounted to 36 percent of all SFC resources in 1963.[35]

The corporations may also accept five-year deposits, but only two (in Kerala and Maharashtra) have done so, and the amount received has been small. The Madras Corporation, which is subject to separate regulations and accepts deposits for periods of 1 to 20 years, had nearly US$17 million in such deposits in 1963, and these constituted over half of its total resources.[36]

The corporations may also borrow from the Reserve Bank for temporary needs and are eligible to rediscount loans with the Industrial Development Bank. The corporations in eight states administer the larger loans extended from State-Aid-to-Industry funds, the total of such advances in 1962 amounting to about US$4.5 million. For this they receive 2 percent on these loans but are liable for only 25 percent of any losses which may arise.

The 15 state finance corporations had a volume of financing outstanding to small industries by March, 1962, of nearby US$11 million (Rs50 million). This accounted for approximately one-fifth of their total financing, the other four-fifths going to medium-scale enterprise.[37] Corporations in some states, such as Punjab and Gujerat, extended as much as 40 percent of their advances to small industry, while the share in some others was very small. Advances outstanding to small industry were rising rapidly, being over 50 percent higher in March, 1962, than in March, 1961. The number of small-industry units financed similarly rose from 845 in March, 1961, to 1,288 in March, 1962. Despite the rising loan volume, after more than a decade less than one-half of 1 percent of the registered small factories have received SFC loans.

The SFCs have not been restrained in their lending by a shortage of funds. They have, in fact, in a number of cases had much larger resources than they have been able to lend. Approximately one-third of the resources of the corporations as a whole were in cash, deposits, or government securities, and this average includes data for a few corporations in need of additional funds. However, they have not had any access to foreign exchange resources, which has been an obstacle to meeting one important type of financial need.

---

[35] By 1964, bond issues are reported to have risen to Rs206 million (about US $43 million) and to make up over 50 percent of SFC resources. (Letter from K. C. Mittra, Reserve Bank of India, June 4, 1964.)

[36] Reserve Bank of India, *Report of the Working Group on State Finance Corporations.*

[37] CSIO, *op. cit.,* p. 52.

Staffing has proven to be a bigger bottleneck than financing resources. A 1959 evaluation reported that two of the larger corporations had a staff of 13 persons each, but over half of these were clerical, and there was a general need among the corporations for more full-time staff.[38] A 1964 evaluation also found that most SFCs still did not have the minimum technical staffing required.[39] Only one corporation has a branch office outside the capital, although some others have agency arrangements with the State Bank of India for serving remote areas.

The new and difficult type of financing the corporations are expected to provide has resulted in cautious lending policies. The corporations have largely engaged in making term loans, usually for periods of 10 to 12 years.[40] The normal loan maximum is Rs2 million (about US$420,000). Individual corporations have established various minimums on loan size ranging from Rs10,000 (US$2,100) to Rs100,000 (US$21,000). The size of all SFC loans has averaged around US$48,000, although the average for loans to small industry has been about US$18,000.

Loans are made primarily to finance fixed assets. However, up to 25 percent of a loan may be authorized for working capital, or in exceptional cases the loan may go entirely for working capital. Loans do not usually exceed 50 percent of the value of fixed assets given in security except where loan guarantees under the program discussed below are available. The SFCs have so far made little use of the guarantee program. They normally have received a lien against liquid assets as well as a mortgage on fixed assets, which has made it difficult for loan recipients to obtain additional working capital from other lending institutions. Guarantees of directors, partners, or managing agents are also usually required. Collateral requirements have been relaxed for some units located in government industrial estates and in other special cases.

Interest rates charged have varied between 6 and 7 percent, with usually $\frac{1}{2}$ percent rebatable when the repayment schedule is adhered to. Applicants in some cases, however, must bear legal and valuation fees, stamp duties, registration, and other charges which can be significant costs in the case of smaller loans.[41]

Loan procedures have tended to follow those of the International Finance

---

[38] *Report of the Japanese Delegation on Small Scale Industries,* p. 65.

[39] Reserve Bank of India, *Report of the Working Group on State Finance Corporations,* p. IV-27. The Reserve Bank's high standard of "minimum staffing"—18 professional staff in engineering, economics, and accounting—however, may in part explain its emphasis on staff shortage.

[40] Reserve Bank of India, *Seminar on Financing of Small Scale Industries in India,* Hyberabad, 1959, vol. II, p. 40. Whether or not loans to small factories have averaged this long is not reported. Corporations are also authorized to underwrite shares and to guarantee loans, but only the Madras Corporation has engaged in these activities.

[41] *Society for Social and Economic Studies, op. cit.,* p. 75.

Corporation; applicants are normally expected to submit detailed information on the proposed use and expected results of financing, which is then analyzed. The exceptionally high rejection rate of small-enterprise applicants is in part a result of their difficulty in meeting these requirements. The evaluation of loan application is reported to require normally two to three months, although the maximum time has ranged in some states up to 9 to 15 months. Disbursement time after approval varies between one and four months.[42] A simplification in procedures has been recommended by a number of observers. The Reserve Bank has commented: "To expect the applicants to fill up complicated forms and answer an elaborate questionnaire without assistance is to scare them away."[43]

After loans are issued, there are provisions for following up on the performance of applicants through semiannual reports and annual inspections. How well the corporations have been able to supervise recipients in practice or provide or assist them in obtaining advisory assistance is not known. However, the Reserve Bank recommendation that the SFCs be staffed to provide postcredit services suggests this activity is not well developed at present.[44]

There is little detailed information on operating results of the state finance corporations. All but three still required some subsidy from the government in 1961 to pay the small dividends guaranteed to shareholders, but the amount of subsidy has been declining and in 1961 was equal to about 30 percent of the total dividends.

Financing is being extended to a fairly diversified range of small industries including many relatively new lines of production.[45] The share of financing going to small industry, though small, was increasing. However, particularly serious problems were being encountered with financing this sector. The Kerala Corporation, which in its first five years extended over one-third of its loans to small industry, reported a much higher default rate among such units, and in its 1959 report indicated doubt whether small industries could be financed with long-term credit.[46]

Major problems included the absence of reliable accounts to enable applications for, or uses of, finance to be economically and accurately evaluated, the inability of small units to provide the kind of information required

[42] Reserve Bank of India, *Report of the Working Committee on State Finance Corporations,* p. IV-10.

[43] *Ibid.,* p. IV-12. See also *Report of Japanese Delegation on Small Scale Industries,* p. 64.

[44] Reserve Bank of India, *Report of the Working Committee on State Finance Corporations,* pp. IV-66.

[45] See the Address of the Governor of the Reserve Bank of India to the Ninth Annual Conference of State Finance Corporations, reported in the *Economic Weekly,* Feb. 23, 1963, p. 352.

[46] *Sixth Annual Report,* 1959, cited by K. T. Ramakrishna, *Finances for Small-scale Industry in India,* Asia Publishing House, Bombay, London, New York, 1962, p. 31.

under present screening methods, and the unwillingness of small units to make full disclosure of pertinent information. Information on the credit reputation of applicants and on the economic outlook of particular industries was not readily available, adding to the screening difficulties. Small units sometimes owned very little fixed assets which could serve as collateral and could not always provide legal proof of ownership for such assets as they possessed. Finally, the need of many small units was for working capital, while the corporations were primarily prepared to finance the acquisition of fixed assets.[47]

Hire-Purchase Equipment through the National Small Industries Corporation (NSIC)

The NSIC was established in 1955 following the recommendations of the 1953 International Planning Team for Small Industry that there was need for a corporation with the primary function of assisting small industry to obtain a share in government purchases. The Team also suggested that the corporation include a separate body with power to make equipment loans. The purpose of the latter was to assure that units bidding on government contracts would be able to equip themselves properly for this purpose.

The provision of equipment on hire-purchase terms was begun by the NSIC in 1956, and in recent years it has become its principal activity, even though other activities have also multiplied.[48] By September, 1962, 7,303 machines valued at nearly US$20 million (Rs93 million) had been delivered, and nearly 6,000 more worth nearly US$10 million (Rs46 million) had been ordered. The equipment delivered up to September, 1962, went to an estimated 2,500 small-industry units, giving an average loan per unit of about US$8,000.[49]

The NSICs relatively brief history has been marked by changes in organization structure, policies, functions, and lending procedure, and recent recommendations suggest that more changes are in store for it. The NSIC was established as a government corporation. The original intention was that it would be autonomous so that it might operate along business lines, free of usual business limitations of government agencies. However, it has

[47] See the discussion of the state finance corporations in Reserve Bank of India, *Seminar on Financing Small Scale Industries In India,* Background Papers, especially pp. 40, 41.

[48] Other functions have included assistance with government procurement, assistance in developing ancillary relations between large and small enterprises, marketing assistance, establishment of two industrial estates, and the founding of two prototype production and training centers.

[49] This estimate assumes that each applicant received on the average somewhat over three machines, as was the case at least up to August, 1959. Scattered information on the number of machines and size of loan per applicant indicates they varied over a wide range. For more detailed data, see CSIO, *op. cit.,* p. 67.

had to depend upon government not only for all of its funds, but also for annual increases in the initially small amounts allocated it. It has thus remained in practice under direct government administrative control.

Administration continues to be its central problem. As a consultant to the NSIC noted with particular reference to its marketing program but which is equally applicable to the hire-purchase and other activities: " . . . most of the initial concepts have been sound. The failures are due to the inability of the organizational structure of the corporation to function efficiently with the personnel at its disposal. The failures are in *execution*, and hence *management*, and the ability to create in the NSIC a commercial atmosphere. It has retained all of the procedural impediments of other government bureaus in spite of its broad charter.[50]

The NSIC has offices in four cities, which for a time were organized as separate subsidiaries. It receives applications only after they have been screened by the director of industries of the appropriate state government. The latter is expected to verify that the unit qualifies as a small industry and has the capacity to use equipment finance productively. The NSIC's formal screening functions have been reduced in recent years but involve reviewing application information and particularly making certain that the enterprise does not fall within a changing list of industries excluded because of raw material shortages, overcapacity, or other reasons.[51] In practice it has generally accepted applications recommended by the state directors of industries.

Equipment payment terms have undergone a variety of changes but currently provide for a portion ranging from 5 to 20 percent paid down and the remainder plus interest in semiannual installments spread over seven years beginning one year after delivery.[52] Interest of $4\frac{1}{2}$ percent per annum is charged in the case of machines valued up to about US$3,200 (Rs15,000) and 6 percent in the case of those valued over that. There is, in addition, a service charge amounting to 5 percent of the value of the equipment. The program has attracted a large number of applicants not only because of its favorable financing terms, but also because it provides a means of obtaining imported equipment otherwise difficult to obtain because of exchange restrictions.

Evaluations of the programs have widely differed, although this has in part reflected simply different points of view. The Japanese delegation on small industry reported: "This system seems to be quite successful,

---

[50] *Internal Report to the NSIC,* May 16, 1960.

[51] Applicants are not required, however, to be actual or potential recipients of government contracts, despite the origin of the program.

[52] The 5 percent down payment applied to machines valued up to Rs2,000, 10 percent on those from Rs2,000 up to Rs50,000, and 20 percent on those over that. A special rate is given to cooperatives.

and during the period of our tour we happened to see many machines, especially imported ones, purchased under this system."[53] Dhar and Lydall also were favorably impressed, calling the hire-purchase program "one of the most successful schemes to be promoted in recent years."[54] Equally encouraging are the findings of a sample study of recipients in northern India in 1962 that recipients were heavily concentrated in machine tools, engineering, and chemicals, and about 45 percent were new enterprises; this is in general accordance with government objectives.[55]

There has been general unanimity in one criticism of the program—the delay involved in delivering equipment. Up until 1961, it normally required several months to process applications and a total of one or two years before the machinery was actually delivered. Three to six months of this may be attributed to import problems, over three-fourths of the equipment being procured from abroad. Special efforts since 1961 have succeeded in reducing delivery time in most cases to between 7 and 12 months.

Another criticism of the program, about which less has been done, is its financial record. The Estimates Committee of the Indian legislature suggested it raise its interest rates nearer to market level for loans of this type (around 12 percent), noting that the loan program, although intended to be self-supporting, was running at a loss.[56] This suggestion, however, was not implemented but was recommended again in 1962 in the International Perspective Planning Team report.[57]

The incidence of delinquency and default has also given rise to criticism. Recipients of about 15 percent of the machinery provided in the northern region were behind on their payments in November, 1962, and somewhat less than half of these were overdue for more than one installment. The total amount of arrears, however, was only about 2 percent of the value of the machinery which the NSIC had provided on hire-purchase terms in the region.[58]

A major cause of defaults—raw material shortages—is suggestive of other

[53] *Report of the Japanese Delegation on Small Scale Industries,* p. 106.

[54] Dhar and Lydall, *op. cit.,* p. 72.

[55] Report of the International Perspective Planning Team, *op. cit.,* pp. 73–74. The author himself also observed on numerous occasions between 1947 and 1949 hire-purchase equipment from the NSIC being put to productive use in new and growing enterprises.

[56] Estimates Committee, 1959–1960, *Seventy-ninth Report* (Second Lok Sabha), Ministry of Commerce and Industry, New Delhi, p. 19. Total NSR operating losses attributable to the hire-purchase program up to 1959 were equal to about 5 percent of the value of the equipment delivered or 2 percent of the value of equipment applications approved. Although this estimate does not appear to take into account the cost of the government funds tied up in NSIC operations, only a moderate increase in interest rates would seem necessary to put the operations on a financially sound basis.

[57] International Perspective Planning Team, *op. cit.,* p. 76.

[58] *Ibid.,* p. 70.

deficiencies in the program. In facilitating equipment imports and plant expansion without sufficiently accurate evaluations of the raw material position in the industry, there is a danger not only that some applicants may be unable to pay for equipment, but also that assisted enterprises may reduce production of other enterprises by their own increased use of scarce materials. Although the evaluation of applications was intended to check on material availability, neither the NSIC nor the state departments of industries were properly staffed to evaluate broad economic development considerations of this type.

Strong doubts about the program's capacity to allocate funds in accordance with national priorities are implied in the recent International Perspective Planning Team's recommendations on NSICs hire-purchase activities.[59] Moreover, the report questions whether loans against imported equipment are necessary, referring no doubt to the common observation of those acquainted with the program that at least some recipients are not in need of financing but only of the privilege of importing equipment. The report further questions whether small industry really requires the services of the corporation for financing domestic equipment, and if so, whether there are not better ways of extending it. It states that recent improvements in the program though significant are not sufficient; simpler and more efficient procedures are required. The total implications of these suggestions are highly critical—more critical, perhaps, than the team intended—of the program's value. They question the need for the program but do not specifically recommend its dissolution.[60] They do suggest that the functions of NSIC branch offices can be transferred to state corporations similar to the NSIC that are in the process of being formed and believe this further shift in organizational structure may contribute to efficiency and improved repayment records.

The suggestion of further decentralization of the NSIC was no doubt intended primarily to meet another criticism that has been made of the program—that 68 percent of the value of hire-purchase loans have been concentrated in the four states where the branch offices are located. The Central Small Industries Organisation in its recent assessment of the problem nevertheless concluded it would be premature in view of the foreign exchange and the limited supply of domestic machines for state corporations to undertake the supplying of machines on hire-purchase. It did suggest, however, that state corporations might usefully serve as agents of the NSIC in areas where it had subbranches.[61]

---

[59] *Ibid.*, p. 75.
[60] A later report by the Reserve Bank of India, however, did specifically suggest that the NSIC withdraw from hire-purchase operations and transfer these functions to the state finance corporations. *Report of the Working Committee on State Finance Corporations*, pp. 11–19.
[61] CSIO, *op. cit.*, p. 74.

Factory Sites and Buildings on Lease or Installment Terms

An industrial estates program was initiated in 1955, providing factory sites and buildings to small industrialists on a lease or installment basis. The program is administered by the state governments.[62] The central government provides funds to the states in the form of loans and extends some other assistance and guidance to their programs.

Around US$27 million (Rs128 million) had been invested in estates by March, 1962. The third Five-Year Plan, which commenced in April, 1961, provides for more than doubling allocations made in the previous five years to a total of about US$63 million (Rs302 million). As of March, 1962, 68 estates with a land area of over 2,600 acres, and building accommodations for 2,468 units were functioning. Another 37 estates were under construction or completed but not yet functioning. Preliminary preparations were in progress for a further 107 estates.[63] The recent evaluation of the estate program, however, recommended that further expansion be halted until all projects could be reviewed.

Industrial estates are capable of facilitating small-industry development in many ways: e.g., by providing timely availability of accommodations; lowering the total cost of accommodations; facilitating extension services and interbusiness exchange of information through the grouping of small factories; and coordinating the expansion of industrial facilities with the development of the rest of the community in an orderly and compatible manner. The Indian program has been initiated with a view to capturing the combined contributions which estates can make to small-industry development. In recent years, the estate program has been given the further objective of facilitating the industrialization of economically backward and rural areas.[64] The primary concern with the estate program here is its functioning as a financing mechanism, although obviously the program is not to be judged on this basis alone. Both the nature and the results of the program are heavily influenced by its combined objectives.

The usefulness of India's industrial estates program as a mechanism for financing small-industry development is best judged by evaluating results from two points of view. First, how easily implemented and economical

[62] The first two estates were established by the NSIC but were later transferred to the local government.

[63] For detailed data on the estate program up to 1962, see the appendix to Alexander, *op. cit.*

[64] For an official statement of program objectives see "Suitable Factory Accommodations," in *Small Scale Industries Programme and Progress,* Government of India, Ministry of Commerce and Industry, New Delhi, March, 1960, chap. 5. The evolution of program objectives has been described by Alexander, former Development Commissioner for Small-scale Industries, in his study, *Industrial Estates in India,* chap. 1, "Objectives of Industrial Estates Programme in India."

a method has it proven to be? Second, how much small-industry growth has been stimulated by its contribution to financing?[65]

The program has encountered many more economic and administrative problems than it was originally believed might be involved in an estates program. A major part of the economic and administrative problems has arisen from the location of estates in areas where there is little or no demand for these facilities. The objective of developing backward areas has been primarily responsible for this. Rapid program expansion and a general lack of investigation and planning were also important factors. Where estate facilities are intended to anticipate and in some degree stimulate demand, as has been the case in India, there is also inevitably a degree of speculation in choosing locations. Even where there is demand for facilities at the time they are constructed, there cannot be complete assurance that adequate demand will continue throughout an estate's long economic life. Business fluctuations and changes in locational influences, which are hard to anticipate, are hazards to maintaining full occupancy. A further occasional source of locational difficulties in government estates programs is the intentional mislocation of estates by those in charge in order to enable particular landowners to benefit from the appreciation in property values estates sometimes stimulate. Recent evaluations do not suggest that this has been a serious source of mislocation in India, but the possibility adds to the administrative problems in establishing estates and increases the need for careful investigation and planning in site selection.

High costs as well as locational errors have contributed to the economic and administrative problems of the estates. The estates were intended to provide a much better quality of housing than small industrialists typically employed on the valid grounds that poor quarters were in many cases expensive in terms of their influence on productivity. Space in estates was nevertheless expected to be competitively priced, since estates by their nature usually permit the use of cheaper land and more economical construction methods than can be employed by individual industrialists constructing their own buildings. However, the relative inefficiency of some of the government agencies responsible for construction and the construction of inadequately planned and needlessly elaborate facilities resulted in some estates being very costly.

Because of these disadvantages, a part of estate facilities have gone unused. The extent of this problem can be roughly gauged from data on

---

[65] The following evaluations are based primarily on the findings of the International Perspective Planning Team, *op. cit.,* and Alexander, *op. cit.* It is also influenced by the author's observation of estates in eastern India between 1957 and 1959 and by discussions with the Stanford Research Institute representatives on the International Perspective Planning Team and with Alexander while he was preparing his study during a visit to the Institute.

the 68 functioning estates indicating that 90 percent of their space had been allocated and 68 percent occupied by operating units.[66] The latter figure probably more nearly represents the extent of the problem, since the former includes space allotted to government agencies and to business-men more interested in the special privileges extended to renters than utiliz-ing the space for manufacturing. An *average* occupancy rate is also some-what misleading; estates in large cities have generally been fully occupied, and the vacancy problem has been concentrated in the smaller centers.

High occupancy rates even where they have been achieved have not assured a satisfactory rate of recovery on investment. Occupancy even in the large cities has been achieved in part by special inducements such as subsidized rents (usually for the first three years) and preference in access to rationed materials, low-cost finance, and other state-administered services. Such inducements have added to program costs, have reduced the effective return, and have increased administrative problems. The recent evaluation has recommended that all such privileges be discontinued.

Even more serious has been the rent collection problem. Critical rent collection problems were reported even in estates filled with highly produc-tive units. In part these reflect tenant dissatisfaction with the expiration of initial rent subsidies, the general level of rents, and unresolved policies on rental and installment purchase rights. In other cases, the cause is simply the low profitability of units or poor general creditworthiness of their man-agement. The International Perspective Planning Team concluded: "Rent administration is clearly the most serious of a number of estate management problems which were reported to the Team in interviews with estate officials, but which we did not examine in detail.[67]

The contributions of the program to small-industry development is worth examining separately from the economic and administrative problems that it has encountered in achieving these. It has made some real contributions to this end, particularly in the major cities. Most of the units in the estates are new, and some are growing; this is suggestive that small-industry devel-opment is taking place which might not otherwise have occurred. The criteria laid down for selecting tenants give preference to enterprises using modern methods and in industries of high national importance, to techni-cally trained young entrepreneurs and to cooperatives.[68] The general ten-dency of these should have been to favor enterprises and entrepreneurs with greater than average potential, provided other necessary characteristics have not been overlooked. However, there has been sufficient demand to

[66] Alexander, *op. cit.*, annexure VI.

[67] *Op. cit.*, p. 107. The Team found that three of the four industrial estates with the highest benefit-cost ratios had critical problems collecting rentals. The Team surveyed 12 estates and measured the benefit-cost ratio in terms of the relation of the estimated value added by tenants to the government investment in the estate.

[68] Alexander, *op. cit.*, pp. 26, 27.

permit selectivity only in the larger cities. Even in the latter, screening has not been entirely successful, as indicated by rent collection difficulties and the finding in a survey of 166 sample units that over half were operating at less than 60 percent of capacity.[69]

The financing aspects of estates has been one of its important attractions, though not in the case of all tenants. Screening has not apparently attempted to restrict tenants to those in need of outside financing or to vary the financing terms in accordance with capacity to repay. The limitation on the size of units which can be admitted to the estates has probably generally confined admission to those unable to finance buildings from their own or borrowed funds or to rent comparable quarters elsewhere. However, there has been some evasion of scale limitations.[70] One of the recommendations of the recent evaluations suggested financial need should be specifically taken into account.[71]

The general results of the program have been sufficiently satisfactory that recent evaluations have suggested that it be continued but with a major part of the responsibilities being transferred from government to the prospective tenants.[72] It is believed that in the larger cities the value of the type and quality of accommodations which estates can provide has been adequately demonstrated to induce small industrialists themselves to establish such facilities where there is a practical possibility of their doing so. It is expected the major obstacles which government will have to assist in overcoming are the acquisition of land, installation of public facilities, and financing.[73]

Arrangements have been approved under which an organization of small industrialists desiring to set up estate facilities may borrow through the government-owned Life Insurance Corporation of India up to 60 percent of funds required and borrow another 20 percent of the requirements from the state government. There is no experience as yet on which to judge whether these new arrangements for financing small-industry development through industrial estates will prove to be economically and administratively

[69] International Perspective Planning Team, *op. cit.,* p. 107.

[70] Alexander, *op. cit.,* p. 62.

[71] International Perspective Planning Team, *op. cit.,* Recommendation 15, p. 110.

[72] In the case of estates where the objective of developing a backward area is combined with the objective of developing small industries, no major reduction in government responsibilities is proposed by Alexander (*op. cit.,* p. 40). The International Perspective Planning Team's recommendations indicate they would favor reduced stress on estates for backward areas.

[73] Alexander stresses finance as a major obstacle to entrepreneurs setting up their own estates (see *op. cit.,* p. 55). The International Perspective Planning Team, however, suggest: "Provision of improved land and utilities should often be sufficient, especially in industrial cities, leaving the financing, design, and construction of buildings to individuals or cooperative associations, within standards set for the estate. If buildings are constructed by the state, they should be erected only as rapidly as there are specific industrial demands for them." (*Op. cit.,* p. 104.)

more practical and developmentally more effective than the initial ones. However, the long delay that has been involved in bringing it into actual operation does not augur well for it. The problems of site location and the long-term commitment of funds to a specific use (particular industrial buildings) remain. Nevertheless, the new arrangement gives potential tenants greater influence over site selection and over the cost, design, and construction of buildings. It is expected, as a result, that the investments in buildings will more closely conform to the effective demand for them.

Another problem that must be dealt with is that small industrialists also may misjudge their capacity to utilize estate facilities. Reliable procedures will still be required for (1) evaluating potential tenants as applicants for long-term development financing, (2) assisting them in overcoming temporary difficulties in making productive use of facilities, and (3) replacing tenants where insoluble difficulties arise. Just how these will be incorporated into the new arrangements is not known, but such responsibilities presumably will be exercised by some of the same central state government agencies administering the industrial estate and other small-industry assistance programs.

Evaluations of the program up to 1962 have stressed the need for applying stricter eligibility criteria and for recognizing that industrial estates are not "a magic wand," that an integrated approach to industrial development is necessary, and that an estate program to be useful and practical should be accompanied by other program elements, such as evaluation of industrial opportunities, improvement in material supplies, managerial and labor training, technological improvement, and so forth.[74] These remain difficult problems. There has been some effort from the beginning to integrate the estates program with other small-industry assistance measures, but the results have fallen short of expectations. Surveys to facilitate estate planning have in some cases been made, but have been loosely related, if at all, to decision making. Surveys were in many cases not carried out early enough, and often the estate planners had little appreciation of the importance of economic investigations to estate planning.[75] Common facility centers and extension services have not always corresponded to the estate tenants' needs and have imposed costs on the estate beyond that tenants have been willing to support. Special access by estate tenants to raw materials and financing have led in some cases to misuses of estate facilities.[76] Although the deficiencies of past arrangements have now been identified, detailed guidelines to more effective and practical means of integrating the estates program with other program elements remain to be worked out.

---

[74] International Perspective Planning Team, *op. cit.*, p. 108. A similar view is expressed in the earlier report of Alexander.

[75] The estate survey in Orissa, for example, which the author observed at several stages, suffered greatly from both these shortcomings.

[76] Alexander, *op. cit.*, p. 62.

Short-term Credit and Other State Bank Assistance

The State Bank program, begun in 1956, is the only government source primarily concerned with increasing the availability of short-term financing to small industry. The State Bank has also begun other services to small industry, but short-term financing remains the major one.

Starting on a pilot basis, the Bank has extended an increasing volume of credit to small units. In 1962, the Bank and its subsidiaries authorized Rs172 million (about US$36 million) credits to 3,828 small-industry applicants.[77] Loans outstanding at the end of 1962 amounted to Rs83 million (US$17 million). These constitute about one-fourth of the credit outstanding to small industry from government lending agencies (or one-fifth, if government investments in industrial estates are included). The State Bank's small-industry financing made up in 1961 about 16 percent of the total scheduled bank credits to small industry.[78]

The State Bank's small-industry financing activity appears much less important if compared with the other financing it extends—about 6 percent of its advances to industry, or 4 percent of its total advances, have gone to small industry. This is a much smaller share than small units might merit on the basis of their contribution to national production—registered factories alone accounting for about one-fourth of total factory net output.

The State Bank's experience in small-industry finance is best understood in the light of the evolution of the bank organization as a whole. The State Bank was formed in 1955 by the nationalization of the largest commercial bank in India, the Imperial Bank, which had once had many quasi-official functions. These functions gradually diminished in importance after the formation of the Reserve Bank in 1935. The State Bank's shares are now primarily held by the government-owned Reserve Bank.

A major initial responsibility given the State Bank was that of enlarging the national banking network, particularly in rural areas, it being specifically required to open 400 branches within five years of its formation. Offices of the State Bank and its subsidiaries rose from 477 in 1955 to 1,528 in 1962.[79] The State Bank's lending activities have also increased, although less spectacularly; its credit outstanding at the end of 1962 was over US$550 million and, together with another US$120 million of its subsidiaries, accounted for nearly one-fourth of the total for all banks in India. The

[77] The figure apparently includes renewals and so overstates the number of separate units served in 1962. State Bank of India, *Annual Report,* 1962.

[78] Scheduled bank credits outstanding to small industry at the end of 1961 were Rs321 million (US$67 million), of which Rs51 million (US$11 million) were accounted for by the State Bank. (Reserve Bank of India, *Bulletin,* November, 1962, p. 1787; State Bank of India, *Annual Report,* 1961, p. 13.)

[79] State Bank of India, *Annual Report,* 1962; *The State Bank of India: A Plan and its Fulfillment,* July, 1955/June, 1960. The State Bank and its subsidiaries account for 23 percent of the offices of all banks in India.

State Bank has channeled an increasing proportion of its advances to industry, the latter accounting for 72 percent of advances at the end of 1962.

The initial State Bank pilot program in small-industry financing had two important aspects. One was the arrangement by which the State Bank would serve as agent through which all the various financing and other assistance programs were to be coordinated and integrated. The second was the short-term financing services which the Bank was to extend.

The coordination scheme was a bold and imaginative concept. The experience in attempting to implement it is of some interest, even though the scheme has substantially failed in its objective. The pilot projects—nine initially selected—were to begin with a survey, jointly conducted by representatives of the State Bank, the Small Industries Service Institutes, and the state director of industries. The needs, problems, and prospects of all significant units in the area were to be analyzed on a case-by-case basis. This would provide information on every unit capable of using financing, not merely on those that might apply to official agencies. Those showing an interest in financing would be assisted by the Bank in applying for it and, depending on the nature of the financing need, the application would be directed to the appropriate lending agency. Units with promise but unsolved nonfinancial problems were to be considered for financing, but they would work out a program for overcoming these problems with the assistance and supervision of the Small Industries Service Institute or the staff of the director of industries. Financing applications which could not be approved were also to be referred to the Institute for its impartial review and for other assistance that might be appropriate.

The surveys in practice were not able to cover all units in the areas allotted, particularly since the program's official responsibilities extend to a broad concept of small industries, with some vagueness as to responsibilities for nonfactory units. The evaluation which examined the program in great detail found that although progress had not been "very remarkable nor uniform," the program merited continuation, improvement, and expansion.

In the lending operations which resulted, the screening of applications proved to be reasonably prompt in the case of short-term financing which the Bank itself extended—most applications were acted upon within three months. Other applications, however, were not always promptly and correctly directed to other agencies, the latter in many cases were slow to act on them, and no agency assumed sufficient responsibility for them. There was even less success in obtaining the coordinated assistance from agencies responsible for services other than finance. Other agencies tended to regard the program as a State Bank responsibility and, once the initial enthusiasm had worn off, tended to give priority to other matters. Also, some agencies, particularly the state departments of industries and the Small

Industries Service Institutes, were in many cases not sufficiently equipped or interested in extending the kinds of services the program envisaged. The financing extended was satisfactory in the sense that no losses resulted and firms were financed which, for the most part, had not previously been served by institutional sources.[80] However, there was some question as to whether some recipients did not exceed the size of units the program was intended to serve.[81] Security requirements were found to be unnecessarily conservative. There was great variation in the liberality and efficiency with which the lending was effected even among the various branches of the State Bank. This was attributed primarily to the attitude and capabilities of the particular staff involved and suggested the high importance of proper training and orienting of staff for this type of financing.

The aspect of the State Bank pilot program concerned with coordinating and integrating various sources of government assistance has tended to fade out of the program for lack of success, although efforts are being continued at 41 "intensive centres." The State Bank still refers some applications to other financing agencies. Also, it has arrangements with seven state finance corporations to serve as their agent in areas where the corporations have no offices. The services of Small Industries Service Institutes are in some degree still drawn upon in the State Bank program, but regular arrangements for doing so have largely disintegrated.

The State Bank has gradually improved and enlarged its own direct special lending activities to small industries begun on the pilot program. The special terms originally introduced in pilot centers are now available at all its branch offices. However, about two-thirds of the number and value of credits granted in 1962 were concentrated in the 37 "intensive centres." The volume of loans outstanding rose by 28 percent to Rs83 million (US$17 million) during 1962, and the 3,828 loans authorized during 1962 were 20 percent higher than in the previous year. Services have been extended to include applicants with a net worth of less than Rs15,000 (about US$3,200). However, the average size of loans authorized has remained about US$7,000 to US$8,000.

The terms have been further liberalized since the initial pilot experiments.

---

[80] Of the firms financed by the State Bank, about 30 percent reported having had no previous source of external finance, and another 45 percent has relied wholly or partly on friends and moneylenders.

[81] About one-fifth of the funds went to units with net assets of less than US$10,000, half to units with net assets of US$10,000 to US$40,000, and the remainder to larger units. Firms with small net assets, however, were not in all cases small in persons or capital employed. An extreme case cited was that of a firm with a net worth of less than $35,000 but employing over 200 workers and having a capital in excess of $200,000. Berna refers to the value this program was to the medium-scale enterprises he studied and notes that the State Bank was interpreting the maximum size of enterprises eligible liberally (*op. cit.*, p. 142).

Loans are for six months and renewable. The interest rate is usually 6 percent. The bank absorbs any costs for watchmen or inspection in the case of loans of less than Rs50,000 (about US$11,000). Recipients are not normally permitted to obtain short-term credits from other banks or moneylenders while a recipient of State Bank credit. Loans are extended up to 70 to 75 percent of the value of the basic security offered. Loans are normally secured by raw materials and/or finished goods, and all types are now reported to be acceptable. Bills are the next most important form of security accepted. In some cases, loans have been made on the security of fixed assets, company shares, or insurance policies or on an unsecured basis, but such loans make up only a few percent of the total. In most cases, the assets offered in security are stored in Bank-locked facilities at the applicant's plant or in warehouses. However, an increasing share of loans are made against assets stored in unlocked but segregated facilities at the plant under the supervision of a watchman. About two-thirds of the loans issued in areas where the guarantee system was in operation—or about one-third of all State Bank small-industry loans—have also been covered by guarantee certificates.[82] Other supporting collateral is also required in some cases.

The range of industries served has widened, although engineering and metal-fabricating industries remain important. Financing has gone primarily to well-established and growing units.

There have been two main criticisms of the program. The first is that it is much too small. A much larger program could undoubtedly be put to productive purposes if ably administered. How rapidly it is wise to expand such a program and how large a share of institutional funds should go to this purpose cannot be answered on the basis of available information.

The second defect, which is in part a cause of the first, is the nature of its screening procedures. A study of a small sample of enterprises in 1958 reports entrepreneurs' views on the State Bank's services: "Most of them refuse to consider the State Bank which, as one entrepreneur put it, is the citadel of orthodox high finance, where sound conservative banking principles in the truest British tradition are sought to be applied to these unfortunates. Red tapism, bureaucracy, and the arrogance of officialdom all serve to keep these small entrepreneurs well away from the State Bank."[83] Such criticism may well exaggerate the problem or be somewhat outdated; policies have been considerably liberalized in recent years. Nevertheless, many entrepreneurs may still be kept away from the Bank by such convictions. Recent observers suggest that Bank investigation procedures appear too extensive for their contribution to loan decisions. A Bank brochure's advice to applicants that "no detail is too unimportant for us" suggests

---

[82] State Bank of India, *Annual Report,* 1962, p. 12.

[83] Madav V. Rao, "Small Units in the Capital-goods Sector," *Economic Weekly,* Vol. 2, no. 13, pp. 441–445, Bombay, Mar. 28, 1959.

a policy which might give way to pointless investigation if administered by a relatively inexperienced staff.[84]

Inherited staff problems (a bureaucratic tradition and little use of modern banking methods and equipment) have been intensified by the rapid expansion of its branch offices and types of services. Expansion has created a general staff shortage and resulted in more rapid promotions and frequent transfers of staff than would normally occur. An Indian journal concludes: "The new managers and accountants are, to be fair, more polite and understanding than their predecessors in the days of the Imperial Bank, but many of them compare unfavourably with their opposite numbers in other banks."[85]

The Bank has introduced a variety of training programs to overcome staffing problems. Since 1961, it has had a systematic training program for all categories of staff. Its six training schools trained 426 officers and clerks in 1962 in addition to 156 new clerks trained at nine special training centers. It established a Staff Training College in 1961, which provided training to 136 officers during 1962. It also sent 31 officials to the Reserve Bank College, three to the government Administrative Staff College, and eight to programs abroad in 1962. It has included among the courses given at its Staff Training College one on financing small industries. Training programs, to judge from the general approach and some of the information imparted at the Staff Training College, should do much to create a staff of practical but developmentally oriented officers.[86]

The Bank has introduced two other financing programs for small industries of potential importance, although neither has yet achieved a significant volume of financing. In 1959, it undertook to lend up to 100 percent of the value of materials pledged by small enterprises having government contracts where the loan was also supported by a guarantee from the NSIC. Credit had been sanctioned to 35 units for Rs1.4 million (less than US$300,000) at the end of 1962, about half being issued in that year.

The Bank has also begun term lending to small industries. It has been permitted to extend term loans up to seven years since 1957. By the end of 1961 only 15 small-industry units had been financed. During 1962 special attention is reported to have been given to extending medium-term loans to small industries, although data are not available on the actual volume of financing.[87] The Bank also introduced in 1962 an installment credit arrangement for financing equipment purchases of small and medium enterprises, particularly those in defense industries. Loans were to be made up

---

[84] State Bank of India, *Small-scale Industries and the State Bank of India: Basic Information for Prospective Borrowers,* Bombay (n.d.), 1961?, p. 8.

[85] "State Bank," *Economic Weekly,* Mar. 2, 1963, p. 386.

[86] "Report on the Working of the Staff Training College, December, 1961 to April, 1963." (Unpublished.)

[87] State Bank of India, *Annual Report,* 1962, p. 12.

to Rs500,000 (about US$105,000) and to be amortized within five years.[88] Whether the State Bank will, through these two arrangements, become an important alternative or supplement to the several other official sources of term financing remains to be seen.

The Credit Guarantee Program of the Reserve Bank

A growing disenchantment with efforts to improve small-industry financing through government channels is reflected in an address of the Development Commissioner for Small-scale Industries in 1958. He stated that the real solution to the financial problem of small industries lay in obtaining the help of commercial banks; unlike government departments, they were not hampered by rules and regulations and could take reasonable risks.[89] One of the first steps in this direction was an effort—largely unsuccessful— to try to persuade commercial banks to undertake efforts like those of the State Bank.[90] A second approach to this end was the introduction of a credit guarantee system. The Hyderabad Seminar on Financing Small-scale Industries in 1959 had recommended that such a program be tried on a pilot basis, as a means of reducing the risks to banking institutions in financing small industry and of stimulating greater banking services to these enterprises. The Japanese delegation on small-scale industry later the same year similarly urged that a guarantee program be introduced.

In July, 1960, an experimental program was begun under the administration of the Reserve Bank of India. The guarantee was to be extended on loans for working capital, equipment, or fixed assets to manufacturing enterprises with total fixed assets (including the value of rental buildings) of not more than Rs500,000 (about US$105,000). The maximum period of guarantee is seven years. Initially only enterprises within 22 selected districts were to be served, but this was increased to 52 districts a year later. At the end of two years, the experiment was reviewed. On the basis of the review, in January, 1963, the program was put on a permanent basis and extended to the whole country. The volume outstanding of credits guaranteed rose to Rs63 million (US$13 million) in March, 1962, and to Rs97 million (US$20 million) in March, 1963.[91]

The program adopted was based on principles substantially different from those of the guarantee programs in the United States or Japan from which the original inspiration had been drawn. The Indian program does not make use of insurance principles or the involvement of a specially

---

[88] *Ibid.,* pp. 13–14.

[89] An address to the Delhi branch of the All India Manufacturers' Association, Oct. 27, 1958, reported in the *Bulletin of Small Industries,* December, 1958, p. 6.

[90] *Evaluation Report,* Government of India, Ministry of Commerce and Industry, Working Group on Small-scale Industries, August, 1959, p. 66.

[91] Reserve Bank of India, *Annual Report,* 1963, p. 35.

equipped local organization in determining an applicant's eligibility or in assuring his performance. The initial objective of the Indian program was simply to create an inducement sufficient to overcome banks' objections to the normal risks involved in financing promising small manufacturing enterprises. The charges for loan guarantees were therefore set quite low (one-fourth of 1 percent of the value of the loan authorized). The program was also designed to assure prompt service. The guarantee was to be extended almost automatically, and in practice applications have been acted upon within a few days.[92] Similarly, claims were required to be settled within 30 days.

At the same time, the program was not intended to stimulate indiscriminate financing of small enterprises, but rather selective financing of those with reasonable prospects.[93] To keep claims under the guarantees within acceptable limits, the program was to rely heavily upon the exercise of prudence by the lending institutions and upon the ability of the Reserve Bank's Guarantee Organization to confine the program to institutions that could be depended upon. Eligibility has been extended to 93 institutions: the State Bank of India, its seven subsidiaries, 50 other scheduled banks, 20 cooperative banks, and the 15 state finance corporations. These account for most bank lending in India, although numerous small banks are excluded.[94] The risks of the Guarantee Organization were also reduced by the limitations of its responsibilities to only a portion of the risks.[95] Another measure to keep losses reasonable was the requirement that banks submit documentation indicating that the enterprise was creditworthy.

In practice, the program has not yet proven to be a significant stimulant to increasing bank financing of small industries. Practically all the guarantees which have been issued relate to loans by the State Bank. The guaran-

---

[92] B. Venkatappiah, Deputy Governor, Reserve Bank of India, "The Credit Guarantee Scheme and Loans to Small Industries," *Industrial India,* Annual, 1961. There have been complaints about delays in issuing guarantees, although the validity of these is uncertain.

[93] Address by K. C. Mittra of the Reserve Bank to the State Bank's Staff Training College, 1963.

[94] India has 80 scheduled banks and over 200 nonscheduled banks. Some of the smaller banks extend a large share of their financing to small enterprises, but their total volume of financing is not large. They are, however, of special importance in south India. Even banks not eligible to obtain guarantees directly can obtain them where an eligible institution will participate in the loan, sharing at least 25 percent of the risk.

[95] All losses are guaranteed up to 20 percent of the amount authorized in the case of loans up to Rs10,000 (about US$2,000), up to 10 percent for those from Rs10,001 to Rs25,000 (about US$5,000), and 5 percent for large loans. In addition, half of the losses on the balances beyond these initial portions are also guaranteed. The maximum loss guaranteed per loan is limited to Rs100,000 (about US$20,000), and the foregoing provisions are subject to certain other qualifications.

tees, moreover, do not seem to have influenced State Bank lending significantly. Most institutions eligible under the program have made no use of it, although some have obtained guarantees on a few loans.

The reasons for the poor reception given the program are in part obscure, but a major one is the documentation requirement. In the case of working-capital loans of a short-term nature, the Reserve Bank has stressed the desirability of supporting guarantee applications with financial data such as balance sheets and profit-and-loss statements. For term loans, it would like additional information, such as evidence of technical feasibility of the project being financed, and estimates of future cash flows except where funds provide only a minor addition to well-established enterprises. Although Reserve Bank officials have stressed their willingness to issue guarantees on loans departing substantially from conventional banking standards of safety, they have also stressed that banks should obtain the above types of information from applicants, analyze it, and indicate in their application for a guarantee why an applicant appears creditworthy despite any shortcomings revealed.

Few banks in India are accustomed to screening applicants on this basis, although some of the staff of the State Bank are beginning to receive training in this approach. While theoretically banks might obtain some assistance in the economic and technical aspects of appraising enterprises on an outlook basis from the Small Industries Service Institutes, it is doubtful if such assistance can be obtained on a practical basis under present organizational arrangements. The difficulty of banks in meeting loan appraisal requirements is illustrated by the nature of the guarantee applications which have been submitted. A review of these is reported to have indicated that the banks submitting them (largely offices of the State Bank) had relied primarily on the extent and type of security offered rather than on the profitability or growth prospects of the enterprise.[96]

Another aspect of the guarantee arrangement that probably discourages banks from using it is the implicit need for supervising these loans. Guaranteed loans must be used for the specific purposes for which they have been approved. The extent to which lending institutions are to be held responsible for assuring the proper use of funds is not known, but Reserve Bank officials have stressed the value of supervision in preventing losses.

The lack of success of the guaranteeing arrangement does not seem to lie with the basic concept of the arrangement itself or the way it has been administered. The provisions provide substantial protection against risk at a nominal cost. The Reserve Bank officials appear to have been efficient and flexible in administering the program. They have guaranteed loans even where they have not been screened or supervised properly by the program's standards. They have paid claims on losses which in a number

[96] Mittra, *op. cit.*

of cases might have been avoided by the lender's closer adherence to screening and supervision standards.[97]

The fundamental difficulty seems to be that banks are ill-equipped to utilize this type of incentive and have basic objections to changing their ways of doing business sufficiently to avail themselves of it. Secondly, small-industry applicants also are in part unable and in part unwilling to provide the kind of information that banks would need.

Other Reserve Bank Programs

The Reserve Bank in many ways occupies a key role in the small-industry financing program. Besides operating the guarantee program, it is a shareholder in the state finance corporations and in the State Bank and has special responsibilities for cooperative banks. The Industrial Development Bank, authorized in 1964 to refinance term and export loans of lending institutions and serve as a direct lender of last resort for industry, is also to be a subsidiary of the Reserve Bank. As the central bank, moreover, it has the power to regulate the credit expansion of commercial banks and to supervise their lending policies. In 1961, it introduced a policy of giving banks which expand their volume of lending to small industries additional rights to borrow from the Reserve Bank at the basic rate.[98] These were continued in 1962 in a modified form, despite a generally tighter monetary policy.[99]

The Reserve Bank has also conducted or participated in various studies of small-industry problems. Its general measures, such as training programs for bank officers and the introduction of a credit information service for banks in 1963, also contribute to facilitating the financing of small industries. Some general measures have specifically taken the characteristics of small industries into account. Thus, its recent report outlining for the guidance of lending officers the principles of term lending includes a special section on small industries. Of particular interest is the recognition which the report gives to the need to simplify the normal informational requirements of term-loan applications in financing small industries. It indicates the need to draw upon the technical staff and the industrial and marketing information of the Small Industries Service Institutes in screening applications. It suggests the need for periodic personal contact with borrowers and of supervision and timely guidance. In these and many other suggestions, the report represents an important step ahead of conventional approaches to term financing, although it does not spell out how many practical economic and administrative problems involved in its suggestions are to be resolved.

[97] *Ibid.*
[98] Reserve Bank of India, *Bulletin,* December, p. 200.
[99] Reserve Bank of India, *Supplement,* August, 1963, p. 34.

The Search for Better Measures Continues

India, in groping for ways of reducing the financial obstacles to small-industry development, has experimented in many directions. Most of the better-known institutional devices for facilitating small-industry financing have been tried in some degree. The financing available to small industries has been somewhat improved, but results so far do not appear to be proportional to the effort being expended.

The basic defect of efforts to date appears to be one of trying to do too much with too little. Available resources in funds and staff have been too thinly spread by efforts to provide credit through a wide range of institutional channels on a very low cost and liberal terms for a large and diverse group of enterprises. Not enough attention has been given in individual measures to working out arrangements in sufficient depth and detail to assure that all the practical requirements for their operations will be met. Many of the financing programs are dependent on lending institutions and small enterprises being able to obtain types and qualities of information and supporting services which in practice are not available or not geared to servicing financing programs. Efforts to assure that programs work in the way they have been intended have relied too much on a detailed prescribing of operations and not enough on assuring that the means and incentives are sufficient to produce the results desired or that practical checks are available to reveal and control major deviations. There have been inadequate provisions for coordinating, monitoring, stimulating, and adjusting the various institutional arrangements to assure that they tend to meet the most pressing needs.

The International Perspective Planning Team, in reviewing the financial programs for small industry, concluded that the efforts to date were in the right direction. "The tools are there, but there is urgent need for using them more effectively."[100] How to make them more effective, however, was a problem for which the Team could provide no immediate answer. In part, they suggested, it was a matter of the outlook and habits of bankers, which could only be remolded with time and training. But beyond this, they recognized, there were probably important things that could be done, if only the problem were better understood. "The problems of better implementation of existing programs are very complex, and worthwhile recommendations could be made only on the basis of careful and extensive studies which the Team has not been in a position to undertake."[101] They urged, however, that such investigations be undertaken.

[100] *Op. cit.*, p. 100.
[101] *Ibid.*

Chapter 3
Puerto Rico's Experience
with Special
Financing Measures[1]

A BRIEF EXAMINATION of Puerto Rico's experience may further assist in illustrating the requirements of effective small-industry financing programs. The conditions and general situation of Puerto Rico contrast sharply with those of India in many ways. Nevertheless it has many characteristics in common with developing countries.

Puerto Rico has one of the longest and most successful experiences in the Western Hemisphere with programs for providing financial and other assistance for the development of industry. The usefulness of Puerto Rico's experience as a guide to other developing countries is, as has frequently been pointed out, limited by the fact that Puerto Rico's circumstances are at least in part unique. Puerto Rico's experience seems, nevertheless, of considerable value despite this limitation. On close analysis, each newly developing country will be found to have important peculiarities that distinguish it from most other countries. To derive guidance from the experience of other countries, it is always necessary to interpret such experience carefully in the light of its special setting, adopting or adapting for application elsewhere only what is truly relevant.

[1] Information for this chapter was gathered from published data and previous studies; discussion with several authors of earlier reports; interviews with the staff of Puerto Rican organizations during a visit to Puerto Rico in 1961; and subsequent correspondence with Puerto Rican officials. Particularly helpful have been the comments and suggestions on an early draft of this chapter by Amadeo I. D. Francis, Economic Adviser to the Administrator of the Economic Development Administration; Rafael Picó, President of the Government Development Bank for Puerto Rico; and H. C. Barton, Jr., Director of the Office of Economic Counseling, House of Representatives. The author is, of course, alone responsible for the facts and conclusions presented here.

Puerto Rico is an island economy, with a population of about 2.5 million in an area of less than 3,500 square miles. It has limited agricultural land relative to its population, no commercially proven mineral resources, no undeveloped hydroelectric potential. Two resources not to be underestimated, however, are an attractive climate and a highly motivated population.

Puerto Rico's historical relationships with the United States and present status as an associated commonwealth are other important special characteristics. Its general autonomy in tax matters has enabled it to establish tax inducements attractive to United States and foreign investors. At the same time, it has attained a degree of political stability and level of administration which many newly developing countries do not yet have. Its access to the market and to commercial and governmental services of the United States are unimpeded by tariffs or other political barriers. This has permitted a continuing interflow of population, technical know-how, and finance. Its proximity to the United States mainland brings both opportunities and competition closer to local industries.

The foregoing characteristics, combined with Puerto Rico's special development efforts, have provided the commonwealth with an advanced infrastructure and an annual per capita personal income of $700. For more than a decade, Puerto Rico has experienced continuous industrial growth and reasonable price stability. These are circumstances which greatly simplify the task of financing industrial enterprises.

Puerto Rico had a total of 2,042 industrial establishments employing over 71,000 persons in 1958. Roughly 40 percent of all manufacturing enterprises (or 810 establishments) employ between 10 and 99 workers, and these account for 39 percent of total manufacturing employment and 34 percent of value added. Small factories thus play a substantial role in Puerto Rico's economy. There are, in addition, over 1,000 enterprises employing less than 10 workers; these account for less than 6 percent of employment and 4 percent of value added. Enterprises employing 100 or more persons, although relatively few in number (192), account for well over half of employment and value added.

Most of the industrial growth has been accounted for by medium to large enterprises owned abroad, predominantly by United States investors. Enterprises owned abroad doubled in number between 1954 and 1958, and in the latter year accounted for over one-fourth of industrial enterprises and nearly half of industrial employment.[2] Locally owned enterprises, on

[2] Net output of manufacturing rose from $223 million in 1958 to $382 million in 1962, or about 70 percent. Total factory employment rose by 1962 to around 82,000, or about 15 percent over 1958. Factories promoted or assisted by the Economic Development Administration increased from 539 in 1958 to 963 in 1962. See Commonwealth of Puerto Rico, *Selected Indices of Social and Economic Progress: Fiscal Years 1929–1940, 1946–1947 to 1961–62.* Data by size breakdown

the other hand, declined in both number and employment during the same period. It was this trend, together with the unstable nature of export-oriented branch plants, that stimulated Puerto Ricans to restudy their progress in 1960, with a view to finding ways of providing increased assistance to local manufacturers, most of whom fall within our definition of small-factory owners.

Private Financial Institutions

Locally owned small factories have encountered growth financing problems despite a fairly advanced banking system. In 1959 Puerto Rico had 11 commercial banks with 121 offices, including 26 mobile units—actually a higher ratio of banks to income than in the United States.[3] Somewhat over one-half of the total loans were made by domestic banks, and the remainder by branches of United States or foreign banks. Bank lending increased faster than gross national product during the 1950s, and in 1959 Puerto Rico had a higher ratio of bank loans to gross product than the United States. The demand for bank loans has continued to press hard on available resources, the ratio of loans to private deposits being over 90 percent in November, 1962.

Although banks in Puerto Rico have not been quite so venturesome as banks in the United States, their record in this regard compares very favorably with banks in many other countries. About 17 percent of the number and about 31 percent of the amount of loans in Puerto Rico are made without collateral or guarantees; in the United States about one-third of the number and one-half of the amount of bank loans are unsecured. The ratio of amount of loan to value of collateral in Puerto Rico varies from case to case, falling for the most part between 50 and 90 percent.[4]

The policy of Puerto Rican banks toward term loans is more conservative. Term loans were estimated to account for less than 30 percent of loans to manufacturing in 1958 and were usually granted for a loan period of around one year. This contrasts with the policy of Federal Reserve member banks in the United States; 38 percent of their loans in 1957 were term loans, and half of these had maturities of more than five years. Commercial

---

are not available for the period since 1958. For a detailed analysis up to 1958, see Amadeo I. D. Francis, *Locally and Nonlocally Owned Enterprises in Puerto Rican Manufacturing Industries* (prepared by the Economic Development Administration of the Commonwealth of Puerto Rico for the Small Business Administration, Washington, D.C., 1963).

[3] For a full treatment of Puerto Rico's banking system, see John de Beers, *A Study of Puerto Rico's Banking System,* Finance Council of Puerto Rico, San Juan, 1960.

[4] Data are from de Beers, *op. cit.,* and refer to 1958 for Puerto Rico and 1957 for the United States.

banks in Puerto Rico nevertheless contribute in effect to the medium-term financing of enterprises, since demand loans are frequently renewed. More than half of all the borrowers in 1958, who accounted for 70 percent of the loans from commercial banks, were continuously in debt during the preceding year. Dependence on demand loans, which are callable at any time is, of course, much more risky for borrowers, but for those that can afford the risk demand loans provide a substantial amount of financing for medium-term needs.

Banks in Puerto Rico serve many manufacturing enterprises, including relatively new ones; over one-fourth of their business loans go to manufacturing, and about one-sixth go to enterprises less than two years old. About one-third of all manufacturing enterprises in Puerto Rico utilize bank loans. Although this is not a high proportion, some of those who do not use banks are foreign concerns that are financed from abroad. Interest rates are reasonably favorable, ranging from 5 to 7 percent for enterprises with over $250,000 capital up to a maximum of 9 percent for smaller enterprises.

Despite the generally favorable state of commercial banking, there are major gaps in the services so far as the needs of small manufacturing enterprises in Puerto Rico are concerned. Of the $45 million loaned to manufacturing in 1958, less than 15 percent was for the purpose of financing equipment and buildings. The primary purpose of loans to industry was to finance inventory or receivables; and financing to manufacturing even for this purpose was provided largely by foreign banks. It is probably reasonable to assume that these banks catered more to the larger foreign-owned enterprises than to the smaller and locally owned ones.

An even more important gap is reflected in the very small share of loans going to smaller enterprises. Total loans outstanding to factories with less than $250,000 assets was around $3 million in November, 1958. This was only 6 percent of all commercial bank loans outstanding to manufacturing enterprises. The share going to factories with less than $50,000 assets was a little over 1 percent.

Evolution of the Government Industrial Development Program

Government organizations in Puerto Rico extend financial and other services important to industrial growth. The government program reflects years of experimentation. One of its strengths is that it has remained dynamic, continuing to improve measures in response to experience and new assessments of requirements. Initially, following the establishment of the Government Development Bank and the Puerto Rico Industrial Development Company (PRIDCO) in 1942, a major emphasis was placed on the direct establishment and operation of new plants. Experience with five plants indicated that this approach required larger amounts of government financing and professional staff than could easily be mobilized. The five plants were therefore sold, and the emphasis shifted to stimulating private investors to establish plants.[5]

One element in the new approach was the provision of buildings for lease or sale to private enterprise, which was begun in 1946. Tax incentives were a second major element. These had been tried without much success as early as 1918, but now that they were enlarged and combined with other measures, they proved of great value. Added to these measures was a program of promotion and informational assistance to potential investors. The latter functions were enlarged in 1950 when the Economic Development Administration (EDA) was established. The EDA took over the increasingly important economic research and promotion functions and served as a central coordinating and policy-making agency for the overall economic development program. The Puerto Rican Industrial Development Company (PRIDCO) was reorganized as a subsidiary of EDA to administer the industrial estates program and special-risk financing. The Government Development Bank, which had been rechartered in 1948 to give better definition to its functions, remained autonomous but with close links to PRIDCO and EDA. The foregoing constituted the essential elements which proved so successful in bringing about a rapid industrial growth in Puerto Rico during the 1950s.

By the mid-1950s it became evident that, although this approach was eminently successful in inducing experienced investors from outside Puerto Rico to establish operations in the Commonwealth, it was much less effective in stimulating the establishment or expansion of locally owned enterprises. Efforts to find better ways of serving this sector were begun and culminated in a complete reexamination of programs in 1960 and the charting of possible new types of measures. One or two additional organizations have been suggested for implementing some of these, but new measures implemented up to the end of 1963 have involved only expansion and reorganization of the above-mentioned agencies.

The Functions of the Major Development Institutions

The Economic Development Administration (EDA)

The EDA has a wide range of functions. However, only those of its Office of Economic Research and its Department of Puerto Rican Industries

[5] For a description of the evolution of Puerto Rico's programs see H. C. Barton, "Puerto Rico's Industrial Development Program, 1942–1960," paper presented at the Center for International Affairs, Harvard University, and William H. Stead, *Fomento—The Economic Development of Puerto Rico*, National Planning Association, Washington, D.C., 1958. The Economic Development Administration and the Government Development Bank also have described their operations in some detail in both annual and special reports. See especially the Economic Development Administration papers: "An Appraisal of Fomento Programs" (1955) and "Social Directions in Industrial Development" (1957).

need to be outlined here. Its subsidiary, PRIDCO, is discussed later. EDA's activities in attracting enterprises from abroad remain important and are carried out by a separate department.[6]

EDA's Office of Economic Research carries out studies to identify industrial opportunities worthy of promotion. Its ability to do this has been greatly facilitated by the fairly advanced and constantly improving level of general statistical information in Puerto Rico, by its own attention to building up and utilizing data from the enterprises it has promoted, and by exceptional leadership and staffing of this program. These activities have expanded in recent years. Its total staff in January, 1964, numbered 33, of which two-thirds were research staff and the remainder secretarial, clerical, or administrative. During the fiscal year ending June, 1962, it carried out nine industries studies and seven more in the following year.

The Department of Puerto Rican Industries was reorganized and enlarged in 1961, absorbing some functions previously performed by other departments. It now employs 105 persons of which 66 are professional and the remainder secretarial or other supporting staff. These include:

1. A feasibility research staff of 18 and marketing staff of seven which were largely assembled after the 1961 reorganization. In fiscal year 1962–1963 they carried out 36 studies.
2. A local industry promotion staff of 24 which assists the establishment or expansion of local industrial enterprises; its staff has been greatly expanded since 1961 and includes engineers and business specialists. In fiscal year 1962–1963 it assisted the establishment of 25 enterprises and assisted the expansion of a great many more.
3. An industrial engineering staff of 16 which assists EDA-promoted enterprises with problems that develop after the enterprise has begun operations.
4. An engineering and scientific laboratory with a staff of 31 for testing materials and processes.
5. Staff concerned with special projects, financial counseling, and general administration.[7]

The Puerto Rican Industrial Development Company (PRIDCO)

PRIDCO, which is administered as a part of EDA, has had three principal functions since 1949: (1) to construct industrial buildings for lease or sale, (2) to administer incentive grants, and (3) to provide capital to new enterprises in the form of equity or, more frequently, in the form of loans subject to higher risks then other lenders are willing to bear. These have gone primarily to enterprises attracted from abroad, although in part also to local enterprises, with the share of the latter rising in recent years.

[6] Among its other responsibilities are the promotion of tourism and rum exports and supervision of the Port Authority.
[7] Staff data provided by the Economic Development Administration.

In the period from 1957 to 1963, 90 building sites valued at nearly $8 million were made available to local enterprises, in some cases at subsidized rates. This was about 13 percent of the building sites allocated by PRIDCO in this period; the other 87 percent went to enterprises attracted from abroad. Local enterprises received an average of about 15 sites valued at $1.3 million per year; however, allocations to local enterprises sharply increased in the year ending June, 1963, with 25 sites valued at $2.4 million going to local enterprises in that year.[8]

Incentive grants totaling $1.2 million were also made to 67 enterprises in the period 1957-1963. A sharp rise also occurred in these grants in the period 1961-1962, with 18 grants amounting to $402,000 being made.

Loans by PRIDCO to local manufacturing enterprises fluctuated in their annual amount between $290,000 and $300,000 in the late 1950s but rose to $609,000 in 1961-1962 and amounted to $510,000 in 1962-1963. Loans to local enterprises accounted for nearly three-fourths of PRIDCO's total manufacturing loans in the last two years, the other one-fourth going to enterprises attracted from abroad.[9] A special-risk financing fund of $700,000 was established for local enterprise in 1963. This had all been disbursed or earmarked by the end of the year, and an additional $750,000 was requested for the year 1964-1965. In addition, other risk financing to local projects is now being guaranteed by PRIDCO from its special-incentive funds.[10]

The Government Development Bank

The Bank has a variety of functions, including serving as the fiscal agent for the government, but its main activity has been to provide long-term finance to business enterprises where credit is not otherwise available. Over half of its business loans outstanding are to manufacturing. Loans outstanding to manufacturing enterprises have declined from a peak of $22 million reached in June, 1960, to somewhat over $18 million in June, 1963. Net loan approvals to manufacturing have averaged nearly $5 million a year over the past 10 years.

The Bank has divided its financing about equally between local manufacturers and those attracted from abroad. The share of local manufacturers has varied from year to year, being 58 percent of the net disbursements in year ending June, 1963, and 52 percent of the total period of the bank's history. The size of enterprises financed has varied over a wide range.

---

[8] The foregoing data were specially prepared for this study by the Economic Development Administration.

[9] EDA, *Private Loan Statistics of the Puerto Rico Industrial Development Company*, June 30, 1963, Table VI.

[10] Letter of January 24, 1964, from Amadeo I. D. Francis, Economic Adviser to the Administrator, Economic Development Administration.

The Bank's loans have averaged $42,000 but have varied greatly in size as the distribution below indicates:

Table 2. Government Development Bank Net Loan Disbursements to June, 1963*

Amount of loan	Percent of total number	Percent of total value
Less than $10,000	57	3
$10,000–50,000	26	17
$50,000–100,000	10	17
$100,000–1,000,000	7	49
Over $1,000,000	—†	14

* Government Development Bank, *Private Loan Statistics*, June 30, 1963. The data refer to all business loans. Many of the smaller loans may be accounted for by commercial and service enterprises.
† Less than 1 percent.

The Bank has made special arrangements for extending term loans up to $10,000 to enterprises having a capital of not over $25,000. A $500,000 fund was established in 1954 for such loans. Collateral requirements were made more flexible, although collateral is still required to the extent applicants can provide it. The Bank made an average of 10 such loans a year during the first five years, and by 1960 had committed most of the original funds, although funds from loan amortization should permit some new loans. The total lent, however, is small, and only one-sixth has gone to manufacturing enterprises.

The Bank's normal loan period has been about five years, although loans for industrial buildings may extend up to 10 years. The Bank usually required collateral, lending up to 50 percent of the value in the case of equipment and 70 percent in the case of real estate. Its lending rates are low, around 6 percent for industrial loans, but it has nevertheless operated at a small profit, even after making allowances for the interest-free capital it received from the government.

The Bank's ability to serve small enterprises has been limited by two characteristics: (1) its high standard of creditworthiness and (2) its lending procedures. It should be recognized that the Bank has undertaken riskier types of financing than local banking institutions; for one thing, it makes term loans, and, for another, it devotes a small proportion of its resources to risk programs such as the fund for small enterprises. Further, it accepts types of collateral banks often do not accept. In the case of loans of less than $50,000, in the period 1958–1962, about 12 percent were secured by equipment, 38 percent by equipment in combination with buildings or other guarantees, 38 percent by buildings, 11 percent by buildings and other guarantees, and 1 percent unclassified. In the case of larger loans, equipment is of somewhat less importance, and buildings and unclassified security are of greater importance.[11]

Its loss experience is suggestive of its willingness to incur risks; losses as a percent of disbursements averaged 3.2 percent from 1945 to 1951, 2.3 percent from 1952 to 1957, and 0.3 percent from 1958 to 1962. Losses on small loans have been much higher than the average.[12] Loans up to $15,000 showed an average loss of 3.9 percent between 1958 and 1962, all occurring where machinery formed a part of collateral. Where the latter was the sole collateral, the loss ratio was 12.6 percent in the case of loans up to $15,000 and 3.3 percent in the case of larger loans. This experience has caused the Bank, in recent years, to reverse in part an earlier relaxation of collateral requirements, which permitted in the years 1952–1957 a larger proportion of loans to be secured wholly or in part by machinery.

The Bank is generally not prepared to finance enterprises which are likely to require detailed guidance or supervision or which cannot provide good evidence of their general soundness. It is felt that such enterprises should look to PRIDCO, which has special financial resources and special staff for this purpose. While the Bank derives its own resources primarily from government appropriations and deposits and thus, from one point of view, might assume such risks and acquire necessary staff, there is a question of whether two government sources of this type of financing are needed. Moreover, because the Bank as the fiscal agent for government agencies must arrange bond flotations for them—and to some extent for itself—in the New York market, a conservative image must be maintained to obtain such funds at a low rate; the Bank's lending procedures reflect its conservative stance.

The main limitation of the Bank's lending procedures is its requirement that applicants submit well-documented projects. Small enterprises find these difficult, costly, and time-consuming to prepare. Critics charge that screening also is time-consuming, although the Bank indicates that once adequate information is provided the average time required is about six weeks.[13] The root of the difficulty, in any case, is that project lending of the type utilized by the Bank is not well adapted to the requirements of small factories.

[11] Government Development Bank, "Experiencia de Pago en los Préstamos Concedidos por el Banco a Empresas Manufactureras, Analizada a Base del Tipo de Colateral," internal memorandum made available through the courtesy of the president of the Bank, Rafael Picó.

[12] The source has excluded from the calculations the loan to the Caribe Nitrogen Company, in which a $3 million adjustment was made in fiscal year 1961–1962, on the ground that this is an exceptional case. Government Development Bank, *Private Loan Statistics,* June 30, 1963.

[13] Government Development Bank, internal memorandum on report by Robert R. Nathan, Oct. 24, 1960.

Other Sources of Financial and Technical Assistance

There are a number of other sources on which small industry in Puerto Rico can draw. A branch of the United States Small Business Administration provides all the normal services which the Small Business Administration provides elsewhere. It makes loans, either directly or in collaboration with private banks, to enterprises which are otherwise unable to obtain finance on reasonable terms. Loans of less than $12,000 can be made without collateral. Loans to manufacturing enterprises have made up a relatively small part of total loans, accounting for only 14 percent of the amount of loans approved from 1957 to 1960. In this period, 50 loans totaling $1.5 million were approved to manufacturing concerns. In the three fiscal years 1961–1963, 74 loans totaling over $10 million were made. While the number of loans per year has been rising, the average loan size has increased from about $40,000 in the period 1957–1960 to over $130,000 in three subsequent years.[14] Much of its financing in recent years thus appears to have gone to enterprises of larger scale than our definition of small factories.

The Small Business Administration also assists small enterprises in obtaining government contracts, sponsors management development seminars, provides publications of the many different aspects of small-enterprise operations, and extends advice on plant modernization and layout. Visits are made to the plants of loan applicants, and assistance is given in preparing loan applications. In 1964 it had a staff of 22, including nine specialists concerned with screening and reviewing loans or counseling applicants.[15]

Other groups whose programs are of some interest to industrial development are the three universities, the manufacturers' association, and the chamber of commerce. Puerto Rico, for its size, also has an exceptional number of private concerns providing economic and market research, management consulting, auditing, and other business services.

Progress in Adapting Assistance Programs to Local Industry Needs

Since the mid-1950s there has been an increasing trend to adapt program measures to the special needs of local industry. The question, however, has not been completely resolved concerning how much program emphasis should be given to local enterprises which are small or which require more than ordinary assistance.

From a purely economic point of view, development can be achieved much more rapidly and at a lower cost by attracting experienced industrialists. Puerto Rico has a special problem in developing sound enterprises

[14] The average size in 1959 and 1960, however, was much lower—less than $18,000.
[15] Information provided by the branch manager of the Small Business Administration.

starting from a small scale with relatively inexperienced industrialists. Such enterprises in Puerto Rico must be able to meet the competition of larger and more experienced enterprises. No tariff barriers exist against imports from the highly industrialized Eastern United States, and only a limited transportation barrier exists. Also, the promotion program has made Puerto Rico sufficiently attractive that experienced entrepreneurs from abroad are willing to take up locally even relatively modest-size ventures.

Another economic objection to stressing the development of local manufacturing is that local entrepreneurs can more easily acquire the necessary know-how for establishing enterprises in other fields such as agriculture and service industries. The more rapid industrialization which can be achieved by concentrating on attracting manufacturing enterprises from abroad will accelerate the creation of opportunities for agricultural and service enterprises in which local entrepreneurs will have greater comparative advantages.

The enlargement of the number of local industrial entrepreneurs appears important for the long-run welfare of the commonwealth, even though expeditures for this purpose may provide lower and slower economic results than if devoted to attracting firms from abroad. Local entrepreneurs have a more permanent commitment to local development and tend to develop a greater awareness of local opportunities. Industry and industrial leaders, moreover, will play a large role in Puerto Rico's future, and thus some local orientation is of special importance. What share of the development program should go to this purpose is a matter of intuitive judgment and political decision. It is being resolved in Puerto Rico simply by gradually increasing the emphasis on small and local enterprises, with the expectation that experience will indicate how far this trend should go.

The Puerto Rican program has involved both financial and other types of assistance, and the latter has proved to have an important bearing on the former. Among the first steps taken to enlarge assistance to local enterprises was the beginning of studies in 1954 to determine in what fields they were most likely to achieve viability. But as an EDA report commented in 1955:

> Such knowledge takes time and money to acquire. The facts that are needed must come from a number of technical fields, such as geology, chemistry, industrial engineering, economics, finance, marketing, and design, which are usually widely separated organizationally. The facts themselves must be analyzed, a project plan developed and checked, and then the whole put in a form suitable for promotion[16]

Despite the expense, EDA undertook a number of industry surveys as well as specific feasibility studies in subsequent years. The evaluation of

---

[16] "An Appraisal of Fomento Programs," 1955, p. 12.

these activities in 1960 found them useful but inadequate and recommended that they be expanded and improved.[17] It suggested enlarging EDA's staff and contracting with specialists from abroad to permit an initial target of 20 feasibility studies a year at an estimated annual cost of around $100,000. It also indicated a need for a continuous review of local industry assistance results so that programs could be altered as experience and changing circumstances might indicate. This would require the collection of special data on a regular basis and planned arrangements for periodic analysis. EDA is now moving in the directions indicated by the 1960 evaluation, although its expenditure on feasibility studies by 1963 had reached only about half of the suggested level.

Another step taken to foster local industry involved measures directed at improving the management know-how of local industrialists. One approach was the promotion of joint ventures between local entrepreneurs and more experienced industrialists abroad. Working relationships with those having advanced know-how is undoubtedly the most complete, practical, and rapid way to impart management techniques. This was expected to be of particular value for export enterprise, where knowledge of markets abroad and established connections are important to success. It would also provide a source of equity finance for enterprises requiring more funds than local industrialists could raise. Between June, 1959, and March, 1961, EDA promoted 12 joint ventures, and experience suggested that increased emphasis should be given to this program.[18] In the fiscal year 1962–1963, 19 joint ventures were promoted, ranging from knitwear and leather goods to paints and adhesives. They ranged in size of expected employment from 10 to 60 persons.[19]

Industry studies were begun by EDA in the mid-1950s to identify the technical assistance and other development needs of particular lines of production. EDA also gradually expanded the engineering and marketing assistance facilities. The 1960 evaluation of these activities indicated that marketing particularly merited expansion, in view of the need to seek export opportunities, and that special training programs were needed to increase the competence of technical-assistance officers. In the evaluation it was also recommended that more counseling assistance be given to promising enterprises and less to badly conceived or unpromising ones. It was suggested that more assistance should be given before investments were undertaken

[17] David L. Chewning, *Stimulating Greater Local Investment in Manufacturing Enterprises in Puerto Rico,* Puerto Rico Economic Development Administration for the Small Business Administration, Washington, D.C., 1960. See also the working papers for the Chewning report: Robert R. Nathan Associates, Inc., *Local Participation in Manufacturing Industries in Puerto Rico;* and Harbridge House, Inc. *Identifying and Screening Manufacturing Opportunities in Puerto Rico and Institutional Resources for the Small Manufacturer in Puerto Rico.*

[18] *Business Week,* Sept. 23, 1961, p. 138.

[19] Data provided by the Economic Development Administration.

to help entrepreneurs draw up programs required to obtain financing and also to improve the quality of planning in enterprises receiving financial or other assistance. The evaluation indicated further that the recent reorganization separating assistance to local industries from the efforts to attract enterprises from abroad was an important step to facilitating increased emphasis to local assistance activities.[20] In response to the evaluation, EDA increased its engineering advisory staff from 10 to 18, its marketing staff from five to seven, and, in general, reorganized these functions.

The EDA, together with the Small Business Administration, the Universities, and other organizations, has sponsored brief courses on various aspects of management which were favorably received by the business community. The 1960 evaluation, however, found that there was a need for more detailed management courses covering a wider range of subjects. It suggested the creation of a "management research and development center" which would not only provide comprehensive management training, but would also engage in research on local manufacturing problems and provide some consulting services to local business. This was expected to provide the nucleus for the eventual establishment of a graduate school of business administration.[21] No measures have been taken to implement the concept of an independent center with broad research, training, and counseling functions, although, as previously indicated, EDA's research and counseling functions have been strengthened in recent years.

The above-cited alterations and enlargements of nonfinancial services helped to make the special financial programs more useful to local industries. Financial programs also gave increased attention to the needs of small enterprise. The Government Development Bank established its special fund for small enterprises in 1954 and began experimenting with less-stringent collateral requirements. These programs were soon limited however by the Bank's need to maintain a reputation of general financial orthodoxy with the private financial community.

The Small Business Administration was persuaded to establish operations in Puerto Rico in 1956. Its operations have gradually increased but remain small in proportion to the financial requirements of local enterprises.

PRIDCO's program of leasing industrial sites has been of some importance to local industry and in 1962–1963 the volume of such leasing increased greatly. PRIDCO's loan program has also recently been augmented, and its current rate of lending (over $700,000 a year) is even larger than that suggested by the 1960 program review, which laid particular stress on the need for a risk financing program.[22]

PRIDCO now has adequate and appropriate staff to assist applicants in preparing sound development plans and to help them overcome many

[20] For details of these recommendations, see Robert R. Nathan Associates, *op. cit.*
[21] Chewning, *op. cit.*, pp. 113–114.
[22] Nathan, *op. cit.*, pp. 38–65, 68–72.

types of operating problems. Its encouragement of joint ventures has helped reduce the need for advisory assistance. What number of enterprises PRIDCO will be able to serve and what the economic costs and benefits of these services will prove to be is as yet unknown. It is evident that only a small part of the costs of the Department of Puerto Rican Industries can be supported by the earnings of a financing program of the present size. The extent to which the financing program will be able to generate a return will depend on whether or not it has devised adequate ways of sharing in profits where financing proves of great value, since all risk financing is committed in some degree to sharing losses where the recipient fails. This has been a major unsolved problem for many programs seeking to finance small factories; thus the Puerto Rico experiment with a risk financing program of substantial proportions is one that promises to be of great interest.

Part Two
General Strategy for Improving Financial Services

Chapter 4
Formulating a Program

THE SUCCESS OF programs for improving the financing available to small industrialists depends heavily on whether or not institutions and techniques appropriate to local requirements are adopted initially. Frequently they are not. To arrive at correct decisions on what the program elements should be, an evaluation must be made of the specific nature and extent of actual needs, the priority of each, and the practical possibilities of meeting them. This will involve essentially five types of evaluation:

1. The particular objectives to be served and their relative priority
2. The financial and human resources likely to be available to the program
3. The extent and characteristics of the institutional base on which programs can be built, including the political and economic framework in which the program must operate.
4. The extent, characteristics, and requirements of the small industry to be served
5. The merits and limitations of alternative approaches and techniques that might prove practical

Resolving Objectives and Priorities

The establishment of clear specific objectives which are reasonably attainable within the means provided is essential. It is also important to provide clear guidelines concerning how priorities between conflicting objectives are to be resolved. A common defect of programs centered around development banks is that the bank is given such excessive responsibilities that priorities are blurred and the capacity and will to perform well on any of them is diminished. Commercial banks, finance companies, and other private channels of financing also tend to have problems in resolving priorities and objectives when they are called upon to administer development financing, unless they are given clear guidelines on how to balance their own priorities and objectives as profit-maximizing business entities with those of development authorities.

The most effective development financing techniques are those specifically adapted to particular types of enterprises and needs. Programs with broad or vague objectives are likely to employ methods that are not efficient ways of serving some important groups of intended clients. The large degree to which the Indian program has been handicapped by responsibilities which are too broad and too diverse for its resources has been indicated in Chapter 2. The need for a better definition of small-factory development objectives and their priority in Brazil and Colombia has been indicated in studies of these countries.[1] The Industrial Bank of Argentina is said to have a similar problem:

> The extremely wide range of activities of the Banco Industrial, as well as its policy of handling huge quantities of extremely small transactions, does much to account for the size of the organization as well as its failure to emphasize sufficiently its primary function—the medium- and long-term financing of industrial development.[2]

The dangers of setting unattainable objectives have been well stated in a study evaluating the difficulties of the Ghana Development Corporation and a proposed scheme for a successor organization:

> Under almost any condition, the Bank will initially be overworked and under-staffed. If, in addition, the feeling sets in that the Bank has little opportunity for demonstrable success, the management may find itself in a position akin to its predecessor organizations [which failed].[3]

As will be elaborated in Chapter 5, the determination of development objectives and priorities is a task which requires a breadth and depth of knowledge on industry and the economy generally, which is likely to be possessed only by an organization having a staff with extensive professional training, regular contact with practical development problems of factories, and a developmental point of view. It is also a task which must be performed, if not on a continuous basis, at least periodically, so that services will be adapted to changing needs. This is particularly important when sufficient financing is available through the program to meet only the most critical needs not being served by other sources of financing.

[1] On Colombia, see Chap. 12. On Brazil, see R. W. Davenport, *Financing Small and Medium Manufacturing Enterprises in Latin America,* Inter-American Development Bank, Washington, 1962, mimeographed (English and Spanish editions).

[2] Arthur D. Little, Inc., *Industrial Development in Argentina,* Cambridge, Mass., 1961, p. 119.

[3] *The National Investment Bank of Ghana,* Porter International Company, Washington, D.C., 1962. The problems of the Ghana Development Corporation are further discussed in Chap. 12.

Assessment of Financial and Human Resources

Because resources are limited and priorities essential, a combined evaluation of objectives, techniques, and resources is a valuable first screening process in program formulation. Failure to choose objectives, priorities, and techniques which are compatible with *available* resources is a major reason why a number of programs have achieved little or nothing. The available resources are, of course, not fixed but tend to respond to demonstrable needs. But some estimate of probable resource availability boundaries must be made at the outset. The initial overall evaluation can be reconsidered and readjusted after other factors bearing on the program have been examined in detail.

The types of resources, both financial and human, required for different approaches and particular techniques vary greatly. The resources required for an industrial estates program, for example, have little in common with a program of credit guarantee or supervised credit. Similarly, both staff and financial resources required for a program extending short-term financing have little in common with one involving loans for periods of several years. The limits on the availability of some types of resources are often narrower than limits on the availability of others. An ideal program thus should reflect not only regard for the priority of needs, but also regard for the feasibility of meeting needs within the limits of a pool of varied resources.

Evaluation of the Foundations and Framework for Program Operations

Programs should utilize existing institutions as far as possible. This greatly economizes time as well as resources and in some cases is essential if programs are to be in the main streams of action and not running counter to them.

The creation of one or more new financial institutions may also be desirable. However, considerable time and effort is necessary to make new organizations operationally effective. For this reason, and because there is usually scope for major improvements in the financial services of existing institutions, alternatives should be carefully weighed. The danger of overemphasizing the creation of new channels of finance is particularly great where the enterprises to be assisted are relatively few in number and scattered.

Programs should be designed to operate within the existing political and economic framework, as they will normally be much too small to have a major effect on restructuring it. Nor is it of much value to draw up programs which will become effective only when ideal conditions are attained. A thorough and realistic appraisal of the foundations and framework for program operations is therefore essential before the elements of a program are decided upon.

It is sometimes assumed that a large part of the above investigations can be dispensed with when an entire program successfully operating in some other country is adopted and when the needs to be served are essentially the same. This assumption is rarely correct. For one thing, organizations going by the same name in different countries, such as development banks, commercial banks, or central banks may be quite differently constituted and have radically different capacities and limitations. Often the exceptional capacity, or lack thereof, of a few top officials may greatly alter an organization and may be an important determinant of what organization should have particular responsibilities, especially in less developed countries. Moreover, most programs are highly dependent at various critical points on certain characteristics of the general economic and political structure in which they operate. Part of the success of credit associations in Japan, for example, seems to derive from Japan's cultural traditions. Or, to take another example, in the United States the capacity and incentive of commercial banks to enter into term lending is greatly improved by factors that may not be common in other countries, such as: (1) a substantial proportion of deposits which are stable and a substantial proportion of assets in easily liquidated but low-yielding government bonds, (2) a fairly widespread use of reliable accounting practices and production planning by industrialists, and (3) the availability of extensive statistics and other information simplifying outlook evaluations and interfirm comparisons. To cite a third illustration, the differences in the institutional structures recommended in recent studies for administering financing to small enterprises in Colombia from those recommended in Pakistan reflect as much a difference in the two countries' inherited institutional structure as a difference in the local needs and program objectives.[4]

The fact that measures may have operated successfully in one country provides little assurance of success elsewhere. Great political, economic, and institutional differences exist even between countries of comparable size and development within such regional aggregations as Latin America, Asia, and Africa. Even greater differences must be expected between countries in these regions and the highly industrialized nations of Europe and North America from which policies, measures, and specific financing methods are frequently borrowed.

Determination of Small Industry's Specific Needs

An appraisal of small industry is also essential: (1) to determine what segments of it can or should be served, (2) to determine what the important

---

[4] *Small and Medium Industry in Colombia's Development: A Survey and a Recommended Program,* report of an inquiry organized by the Banco Popular aided by a team of consultants from Stanford Research Institute, Banco Popular, Bogotá, 1962 (English and Spanish editions), and *Encouraging The Growth of Small Industry in Pakistan,* a study prepared for the Ministry of Industries, Government of Pakistan, by a team of consultants from Stanford Research Institute, 1963.

needs are that should be served in view of program objectives, and (3) to evaluate what kinds of programs can fill these needs with the desired results. Actual needs are frequently quite different from commonly voiced needs. Some knowledge of how enterprises operate is often essential in order to determine the relative national consequence of serving various needs and even more importantly to determine what types of arrangements are most likely to be practical from the point of view of both the enterprise and the source of finance.

Programs for small industry sometimes serve types of enterprises of little consequence to primary program objectives and employ financing techniques unlikely to contribute to the intended objectives. Under the general mantle of *small industry* fall many types of enterprises with very different program needs. The methods used for stimulating the establishment of new enterprises are very different from those for stimulating the expansion of enterprises with several years of experience. It is not always essential to serve both; in some cases it may be premature in terms of resources and staff experience to serve new enterprises; in other cases existing enterprises may be adequately financed under existing arrangements, so that only new enterprises have a real need. Equipment financing may be the primary need to lower production costs where equipment is outmoded, as was the case of Iran according to Stepanek's evaluation in 1961; but special equipment financing may only increase the general problem if high costs stem from a shortage of working capital and consequent idle capacity, as was the case in Israel according to Tenenbaum's evaluation in 1960.[5] Because there are many different types of financing needs, when a program is to be initiated with limited resources it is important to determine which segments of small industry deserve priority. The measures adopted can then be tailored to the major specific needs of that segment.

Review of the Experience with Alternative Approaches and Techniques

There is a considerable body of experience on the way different small-industry financing programs have operated. Both favorable and unfavorable experiences can be instructive, since they reveal the major limitations as well as the merits of particular measures and reduce the need to invent and experiment. The experience of other countries may, of course, be highly misleading unless interpreted in the context of the differences in the overall circumstances in the area in which the experience was gained and in the area in which the experience is to be applied. Program ideas can often be adapted from abroad but can rarely be adopted in toto without some adjustment to local conditions. Although the dangers in borrowing from abroad in a purely casual way are real—as program results in many develop-

[5] J. E. Stepanek, "A Note on the Development of Small Industry in Iran," 1961(mimeographed), and E. A. Tenenbaum, *Israel's Industrial Finances: A Second Look,* Continental-Allied Company, Inc., Washington, D.C., 1960, p. 6.

ing countries clearly demonstrate—the experience of other countries remains the best and, indeed, practically the only source of program ideas and means of at least partially testing and evaluating possible program ingredients quickly and at a reasonable cost.

The Brief Survey—A Basis for Designing Appropriate Programs

A factual foundation for the previously suggested evaluations is not easily acquired in many countries. Most such data must be collected in the field by persons skilled in techniques of field investigation and with sufficient background in industrial and financial matters to evaluate information readily. The need to conduct these investigations with the proper care and skills is illustrated by McCrory's comments on his survey in India: "In every case the owners were reluctant, at first, to bring out their real difficulties; had we stopped, say, after the first interview meetings, we would have been forced to conclude that the chief cause of business failure in Chopur was that the proprietors fell ill with pleurisy."[6]

Domestic Information

Most of the information required for the basic evaluations involved in program formulation is normally available within the country. Experience in carrying out the case studies for this investigation suggests there are reasonably quick and economical procedures by which these essentials can be collected and analyzed. The total data collection and analysis required in formulating a program for a moderate-sized and fairly advanced country such as Colombia might require 9 to 10 man-months of qualified professional staff time. This assumes staff experienced in this type of survey work and familiarity with the local language and area. Where staff with requisite qualifications must be obtained abroad, it is important that they be supported by local staff and that a somewhat longer period be allowed for the survey. It is essential, in any case, that one (or more) of the persons who will have the responsibility of converting the conclusions of the investigations into an operating program participate throughout the survey as a regular team member. This is necessary to assure that those implementing the program have a full grasp of the survey findings and that no momentum is lost between the survey and implementation.

The survey will collect and analyze three main types of information:

1. Information largely of a background or statistical nature describing industry and the institutions serving it. This is obtained from published reports and from banking and official records.
2. Information on the experience, outlook, and problems of institutions which

---

[6] James T. McCrory, *Small Industry in a North Indian Town: Case Studies in Latent Industrial Potential,* Government of India, Ministry of Commerce and Industry, New Delhi, 1956, p. 3.

extend financial or other assistance to small industry.[7] This information
is largely obtained from interviews with the chief operational officers of
the institutions concerned. The most important institutions which must
normally be covered are government banks, monetary and financial authorities, development agencies, industrial departments, and statistical
agencies; private investment and commercial banks; applied research organizations; productivity centers; and business, industrial, and banking associations. Valuable information can also often be obtained from large suppliers of materials and equipment, large distributors of locally manufactured goods, private financiers, credit cooperatives, and public accounting
firms.

3. Information on the detailed characteristics of small manufacturing enterprises, their evolution and prospects, their problems and needs, and their
present sources of outside informational or financial assistance. Brief in-
plant analyses of selected enterprises provide useful information on plant
and management capabilities, their future potential, present sources of
finance and related services, past experience in utilizing such services,
and major problems and unfilled needs.[8] This will provide a basis for
determining the type of financial or related services which have the highest
priority, the forms in which they can be most economically and effectively
extended, and the types of enterprises which merit priority consideration
for assistance.

Information on Programs Abroad

Ideally, information on the experience of programs abroad should be
collected by surveys in countries having advanced programs in progress.
Using the same staff as carries out the domestic surveys would assure a
complete evaluation of the merits, limitations, and environmental requirements of such financing programs by persons with a full understanding
of the needs and conditions in the borrowing country. However, few developing countries can afford to evaluate programs abroad in full detail on
a firsthand basis, particularly since the program experience of several foreign
countries often needs to be evaluated.

Among the more economical alternatives, it is possible to review the
existing literature on other small-industry development programs, supplementing this data by mail inquiries on specific points. To be truly economical and productive, this will normally need to be carried out by a person
with some experience with the literature and programs abroad, since although there are an enormous number of programs and studies to choose

[7] The type of specific information required is shown in the "Basic Questionnaire
for Financial Institutions," R. W. Davenport, *Financing the Development of Small
and Medium Manufacturing Enterprises in Latin America, op. cit.,* appendix B.

[8] For an example of the specific types of information required from enterprises
see the "Basic Questionnaire for Small and Medium Manufacturing Concerns,"
Ibid., appendix A.

from, generally only a very few will be of great relevance. Later sections of the present study, particularly Parts 3 and 4, are intended to simplify the process of learning from the programs of various countries.

A review of what is written about programs is not likely to be adequate by itself. A brief visit is probably essential to a few of the countries where the review of programs has suggested methods of high relevance are being employed. The visit should be made by one or more of the persons who have the operational responsibility for implementing the program. Including a professional adviser with wide international program experience would be of special value in assuring that all important aspects are fully investigated. One further step to assure that borrowing policies and methods from other countries proves really useful is to provide thorough and specific training to the implementing staff in the new techniques. This might be accomplished by hiring someone with experience in the programs from which new techniques have been adapted to provide on-the-job training to local staff, by sending local staff to intern in the program abroad, or, preferably, both.

Satisfactory investigation of programs abroad will cost at least as much in most cases as the survey of domestic requirements. The extent to which financing programs have been handicapped by borrowed techniques which are inherently impractical or unsuited to local requirements suggests that the expense of these investigations will usually be well worthwhile.

Chapter 5
Supporting and
Monitoring Services

FINANCE IS USUALLY only one of several elements essential to a program for accelerating small-industry development. The strengthening interaction of finance, various informational services, and other possible program elements makes it desirable—and in many cases essential—for the integrated extension of a proper combination of services. The treatment here of services other than finance is intended to be narrow and selective, concentrating on services of particular importance to financing programs.[1] They are thus discussed using the kind of selective detail of interest to the development banker or individuals confronted with the immediate practical problem of designing or operating a financing program.

The relative importance of supporting and monitoring services will obviously vary with local circumstances. Improvement in access to capital and credit may, by itself, enable substantial numbers of small industrialists to forge ahead in locales where entrepreneurial capabilities and the environment are sufficiently advanced. Studies of small manufacturing concerns have indicated this to be the case in countries such as India, Colombia, and Brazil.[2] The possibilities of this approach, however, diminish—and indeed may vanish altogether—in less-favorable circumstances, such as those in Nigeria and Ghana. Although improved financial services alone may stimulate development under favorable circumstances, our case studies indicate that even in countries such as Colombia, this is probably not the most fruitful approach. Furthermore, the course of simply improving finan-

[1] For a broader analysis, including other services, see Eugene Staley and Richard Morse, *Modern Small Industry for Developing Countries,* Series in International Development, McGraw-Hill Book Company, New York, 1965.

[2] See Chaps. 2 and 13 on India and Colombia; on Brazil, see R. W. Davenport, *Financing the Development of Small and Medium Manufacturing Enterprises in Latin America,* Inter-American Development Bank, Washington, D.C., 1962, chap. 4.

cial services assumes transitional problems can be overcome without other services, which is not often the case.

The first step in improving financial services in any country should normally include an analysis of total problems of small-factory operations; this requires skills not normally maintained by financial institutions. The need for such skills persists throughout the program. Program formulation cannot be a one-shot process and still achieve substantial and sustained success. Designing, testing, and operating thus are interrelated phases of the work rather than well-defined sequential steps. New programs, particularly in less-industrialized countries, must normally be launched as pilot projects. There are no "patent formulas" for successful financing programs which are applicable to all countries. Indeed, there are as yet few programs which are entirely satisfactory in their own setting. Regular arrangements are needed for evaluating how well programs are working, how they might be improved, and what priorities are essential. Even when initial programs are relatively well designed, program monitoring remains important because both program capabilities and the priority of needs can be expected to change.

New needs for supporting services to facilitate the administration of financing arise once a program is begun. The extent to which various particular services are useful and can be afforded will vary greatly depending upon the nature and extent of the financing contemplated. These services tend to be relatively high cost in terms of the usual volume of small-industry financing. They are also large users of scarce skills. It is therefore especially important to minimize the requirements for such services through a discriminating use of them and through organizing them on an efficient basis. Some of the major considerations involved in doing so are discussed below.

Types of Services and Their Priority

There are basically four types of activities which can be important to small-industry development financing and which financial intermediaries are often not equipped to perform without special assistance: (1) training; (2) technoeconomic surveys; (3) technical, economic, and developmental appraisals of financing proposals and of financed enterprises; and (4) counseling and related services. Many of the activities of the first and second types are important even before programs are started. Those of the third type are required to implement some of the more significant types of financing. The last category is usually the most difficult to provide, but it is of increasing importance as more complex types of financing and larger, more comprehensive programs are undertaken.

Training

The two essential ingredients of a development financing program are funds and competent, resourceful, and properly motivated people. By and large, it is the latter that are in shortest supply. A fairly high minimum level of skills, ability, and character is required. A well-conceived training program can do much to enable properly selected candidates to measure up to the requirements of a development financing program. Thoroughly trained persons, however, soon find numerous other opportunities open to them, so that loss of staff to other employers must be expected. Training should therefore be a major and continuous adjunct to a development financing program.

Development banks and other term-lending institutions in industrially advanced countries have acquired the special competence needed for their operations partly by borrowing staff from older and more experienced institutions and partly by making it possible for new staff to gain experience gradually by handling increasingly complex tasks under supervision.[3] Lending institutions in the newly industrializing countries are not able to rely so heavily on such methods.

The industrially advanced countries have been building up their skills in medium- and long-term industrial lending for several decades. World War II accelerated the process. The long, fairly uninterrupted industrial boom and the advantages of highly developed economies have provided still more time for experimentation, staff training, and, in general, acquiring experience under favorable conditions. However, the need has grown so rapidly that experienced staff is still in short supply even in industrially advanced countries.

Even if experienced institutions in industrially advanced countries had the surplus staff available to provide institutions in less developed countries with the kind of nucleus staff with which the Small Business Finance Corporation in Japan, the Industriekreditbank in Germany, or the Small Business Administration in the United States started, this would still not quite solve their staffing problems. Term lending is a much more difficult and complex art in newly industrializing countries than in industrially advanced ones. In addition, language and cultural barriers must be overcome before experienced lenders from abroad can practice or teach their skills. Sending trainees to intern in experienced institutions abroad is unsatisfactory for the same reasons and for the additional one that a foreign institution concerned with its own operations often does not provide trainees with an organized program or access to information which will make the experience very meaningful.

Institutions in newly industrializing countries need to develop more rapid and efficient methods of generating staff than the traditional one of allowing staff to absorb skills through a loosely planned program of supervised work. Courses on banking or industrial operations and related academic training

[3] These and subsequent comments on the staff of term-lending institutions in advanced countries are based on discussions in 1965 with some of the more experienced institutions in the United States, Canada, Japan, Turkey, Germany, Denmark, and the Netherlands.

are useful background, but such training alone will not produce experience-hardened staff capable of assuming lending responsibilities. An organized program is required, designed to serve groups of trainees and directed by persons thoroughly experienced in industrial term lending and conversant with modern educational techniques. In most cases it will be advisable to provide at the outset an introduction to the practical operations of various types of manufacturing enterprises through brief, comparative in-plant operational studies. This should be followed by intensive transmission of principles and case experience in conducting loan operations, combined and integrated with guided on-the-job experience in loan analysis and supervision. In this way, several years of work under conventional training programs may be condensed into a year or less.

Training is usually needed not only for bank staff but for staff handling various related functions, such as industrial survey and counseling. It may also be useful or even essential to the objectives of development financing to provide some kinds of training for the industrialists receiving loans, their employees, or service enterprises such as accounting firms on which loan recipients may depend.

Surveys

The importance of coupling survey activities with financing programs tends to be overlooked, possibly because it is not a major element in the special assistance programs to industry in industrially advanced countries. There are several reasons why the latter need not stress this function in the same degree as newly industrializing countries. In the first place, where a well-diversified industrial structure exists, a large number of opportunities are easily identifiable and exploitable through the branching-off of entrepreneurs from closely related types of production. Experience provides much of the information needed. Secondly, developed countries have long-established official arrangements for regularly collecting, organizing, and disseminating a wide variety of statistical data of generally dependable reliability. Thirdly, because of the broad importance of information relating to industry in industrially advanced economies, private business services have arisen to meet these needs. Finally, their lending institutions have had years to build up important sources of information on industrial operations and trends through files on past loans, the large number of current loans outstanding, and the knowledge of experienced staff. Industrially advanced countries thus have much less need for special survey services than less developed countries. At the same time, it should be noted that even the United States and Japanese small-business programs have involved some survey activities, and both probably would greatly benefit by enlarging this function and integrating it better with financing activities.[4]

[4] The United States Small Business Administration has sponsored studies by research institutions and universities of the financial needs of small business, of the

The emphasis given to technoeconomic investigations in Puerto Rico has already been referred to. A few developing countries also have sought to establish regular survey activities. India has made the greatest progress in this respect with its Small Industries Service Institutes which regularly carry out surveys on (1) markets and marketing arrangements in particular industries; (2) technical and economic conditions, prospects, and requirements in particular industries; (3) industrial opportunities in particular areas; and (4) the evaluation of services and program measures.[5] Even India's investigation services, however, need to be broadened to provide satisfactory support for its small-industry development financing efforts. They also require much closer coordination with financing and other services.

Much less attention has been given to surveys in other countries. The Bank of Northeast Brazil has conducted several industrial surveys as a part of its development financing program but has not given great emphasis to this activity. It does, however, have a regular survey staff. The Industrial Development Bank of Turkey attempts through questionnaires and field visits to gather fairly extensive information on markets, competition, and economic trends for an industry the first time it receives an application from a firm in that industry and to build on this information as subsequent applications are received.[6] The Institute for Technological Research in Colombia has recently begun surveys as a preliminary step in its small-industry counseling program. These have been primarily concerned with technology and technical-assistance needs and have not been coordinated with financing programs, although ways of broadening and coordinating these investigations to better complement financing are being explored. A few other countries have survey activities as a part of their small-industry development effort, but none of these activities is very extensive.

A major value of regular coordinated survey programs has already been

---

functioning of particular services such as the small business finance companies, and of the opportunities for small business in particular lines of industry. The program, however, lacks continuity and planning. The Japanese have given greater stress to surveys but not to the point of having a regular program closely integrated with development financing activities. European small-industry programs give less attention to surveys, particularly on economic matters, although the Netherlands has a network of regional economic institutes which carry out market surveys and other studies and, when required, give direct assistance to special financing programs.

[5] For a full description of India's program see S. Nanjundan, H. E. Robison, and E. Staley, *Economic Research for Small Industry Development: Illustrated by India's Experience,* the International Development Center of Stanford Research Institute, Asia Publishing House, Bombay, London, New York, 1962.

[6] Discussions with the economic staff of the IDBT, October, 1965. In the opinion of the author and another observer, more emphasis on such investigations would be desirable. See *Public International Development Financing in Turkey,* Report no. 3, Columbia University School of Law, New York, 1962, p. 173. (Mimeographed.)

discussed—that of keeping financing programs properly focused and therefore effective. A review of even the best programs indicates that this function cannot be too heavily stressed if either a development or small-enterprise orientation of financing is to be maintained. Whatever the ownership or organizational structure of lending institutions, and whether in an advanced or newly industrializing country, the pressures to make operations a little safer, a little more profitable, and a little simpler and easier quickly tend to sap devotion to small-enterprise or development objectives unless there is an outside agency continually documenting unfilled needs of high priority and means for improving financial services.

Secondly, surveys can be of great assistance to financing institutions in evaluating the developmental importance of alternative allocations of financing and may be vital, particularly in the case of term loans, to appraising even the banking soundness of allocations. They provide information on markets, competitors, and other aspects of the industry in which applicants plan to operate, without which the outlook for individual loan applicants cannot be accurately appraised. Failure to obtain such information in evaluating loan applications has been a defect of many development banks.

The entire responsibility for gathering such information cannot be placed upon applicants. The industrialist usually lacks both access to important sources of information (such as competitors) and the training required to gather and evaluate the kind of information required. Much of this information can be obtained on a sufficiently economical and reliable basis in less developed countries only through the employment of industrial-survey specialists who are equipped by training and experience to ferret out and evaluate data. It is also important, as will be later elaborated, that the specialists employed be organized in a manner which facilitates easy access to basic sources of information and impartial reporting.

A further value of surveys is that they provide information on industrial opportunities and thus alert entrepreneurs to the relative attractiveness of different types of enterprises. This not only encourages a much better use of the entrepreneurs' funds, but also tends to improve the average quality of loan applications. It further enables lenders to take a more active approach to financing by making them aware of promising sectors.

Surveys are also useful in revealing whether the addition of counseling and other services might improve the results of financing or reduce the need for it. They indicate what the priorities of other services are and whether there are practical ways of combining them with financing. A broad technoeconomic analysis of whole industries is usually needed to indicate deficiencies critical enough to merit corrective measures. The operations of individual applicants are usually deficient in many respects, but it may not be feasible or necessary to remedy every deficiency.

Survey work is an excellent means of training staff required to operate a development financing program. Survey experience helps to acquaint counselors and industrial loan officers with the total operations of enterprises and provides them with a comparative view of the ways in which different enterprises function. The survey activity opens the way for contacts between the counselors and industrialists. Before counseling is begun, social and cultural barriers between the industrialists and counselors usually need to be broken down and personal relationships built up. The survey experience gives the counselor the opportunity to learn the business ways and special jargon of industrialists and the peculiarities of individual enterprises. Competence in these details is often important for its psychological as well as its operational value.

The importance of such preparatory work is confirmed by experience with counseling in many countries. In Taiwan, industrialists are said to regard the staff of the China Productivity and Trade Center as "bookworms" and "impractical."[7] Similar expressions of distrust or low regard for counselors have been voiced to the author by industrialists in India and various Latin American countries, and, though to a lesser degree, even in more advanced countries such as Japan and the United States. Although a part of the difficulty may be the initiation of counseling before staff have sufficient training and experience for this function, a great deal of it appears also to be a result of failure to build up proper relationships between industrialists and counselors.

Enterprise Appraisal

The development value of financing tends to be greatly increased where it is allocated on the basis of an overall appraisal of enterprises. This is helpful in reducing the leakage of financing to nonproductive purposes, in selecting enterprises which can make the most productive use of financing, in extending financing in the proper form and amount and with whatever supplementary services may be most appropriate, and in supervising and reviewing operations of enterprises being financed.

The thoroughness of methods of appraisal may vary, depending on the particular purpose, but there are three basic staff requirements for this function. The staff must be well trained in the basic sciences important to understanding modern industrial operations. It must have a practical knowledge of the technology and operational methods employed by typical or average firms, as well as those employed by exceptionally advanced enterprises. Finally, it must have close relationships with the business community and frequent contact with business enterprises, enabling it to carry out fruitful field investigations of enterprises being appraised.

Many financial intermediaries require assistance in appraising the prospects of manufacturing enterprises. They normally cannot afford to main-

[7] Edward A. Tenenbaum, *Taiwan's Turning Point,* Continental-Allied Company, Washington, D.C., 1961?, p. 40.

tain the regional network of specialists required to serve small manufacturers. Because of their institutional situation, such industrial specialists as they do have tend to be cut off from the kind of close regular contact with industrialists and industrial enterprises that is essential to making accurate and rapid appraisals.

Development banks and finance corporations do usually maintain small technical staffs which can appraise enterprises that provide thorough and easily verifiable records and plans. Few small enterprises, however, can provide information of this sort. Even where they can, this type of appraisal tends to be too costly and time-consuming in relation to the sums they usually require.

Appraisals of small enterprises to determine eligibility for financing or the performance of an enterprise in utilizing the financing and related services extended must be brief and simple to be practical. To make such appraisals tends to require a good knowledge of (1) a large number of other enterprises in the same industry, (2) the pattern of business relationships in the industry, and (3) the outlook for the industry as a whole. For this reason, staff well experienced or presently engaged in industry survey work have an advantage in making appraisals of small manufacturing firms. They are equipped by their broad knowledge of the industry and easy access to sources of information to make sufficiently thorough appraisals of the technical, economic, developmental, and, to some extent, management aspects of enterprises on the basis of brief interviews and observations of operations.[8]

Counseling

Counseling is to a degree involved in the services already described. Surveys bring together information useful to both industrialists and those counseling them. Appraisals create an awareness of problems and of their relative importance. Training when extended to recipients of finance is a form of counseling.

Counseling in its simplest form is primarily a liaison, coordinating, and expediting service for industrialists. Counseling at this level relies for its value primarily on its ability to make other organizations more useful to small industrialists rather than on a capacity to service directly his informational needs. This form of counseling is, as a result, relatively easy to provide, particularly where survey or other staff regularly in contact with industrialists is already available.

As simple as this level of counseling is, it can be of great value in improving industrialists' access to financing and their productive use of it.[9] The

---

[8] See Chap. 10 for a full discussion of loan applicant appraisals.

[9] This constitutes, for example, the main nonfinancial service of the United States Small Business Administration. The limited value of services of this type in some countries stems from their not being performed by an organization which has func-

need for a liaison function which will help the small industrialist in his relationships with others arises because the latter often is unaware of existing services or does not know how to go about gaining access to them. Often service organizations may not have sufficient interest in, or knowledge of, small industrialists to serve them effectively, or services may not be coordinated sufficiently to take advantage of complementarities. As such deficiencies are revealed by surveys, liaison staff are often important in facilitating the implementation of remedial measures through their awareness of the total problem and their exclusive devotion to this task. Their functions may include advising industrialists on: appropriate sources of finance and how to apply for it; the services available from research institutes, consultants, and trade associations, and the best way of utilizing them; and the services of other business enterprises.

In countries where there are extensive governmental activities or controls affecting industry—such as India—or simply where government administrative machinery is inadequate to its responsibilities—as in most developing countries—the assistance which a liaison service can provide industrialists in obtaining licenses, government contracts, or complying with government regulations may be important to the prosperity of small enterprises and thus to the sound and productive financing of them.

Counseling in the fullest sense, however, implies direct advisory assistance to industrialists and the maintenance of staff with the high level of professional training and lengthy practical experience required to understand and contribute to the solution of the operational problems of industrialists. The specialties in which industrialists may be able to benefit from counseling are numerous, ranging from accounting and financial policy to the broad fields of business management and production technology. Some types of counseling services may require extensive laboratory facilities or information-gathering services. Thus a complete counseling service is unlikely to be within the limits of the funds and specialized staff available to support the implementation of a financing program. However, some direct services may be possible and essential. Those of especial importance to financing programs merit brief consideration.[10]

Financial advisory services deserve priority as an accompaniment to financing programs. Some services of this type may even partially substitute for creating special sources of funds. Advising concerns on how to manage their finances and how to obtain finances from existing sources may in

---

tions and stature required to achieve the network of relationships needed for acting as a liaison, coordinating, or expediting agency.

[10] For a broader discussion of counseling, see Staley and Morse, *op. cit.*, and Joseph E. Stepanek, *Small Industry Advisory Services—An International Study*, the International Development Center of Stanford Research Institute, the Free Press of Glencoe, New York, 1960.

itself improve the availability or reduce the need for financing. Advice may be needed on:

1. The budgeting of internal finances
2. The relationship between other business decisions and financial needs
3. The possibilities and consequences of using and extending interbusiness finance
4. Ways of presenting one's case for financing to banks and other institutional sources
5. The obtaining and successful utilization of partnership funds or other private sources of finance

This type of assistance has been found to be an important need even in a country with as advanced financial services as the United States. Moreover, the need in the United States extends up to fairly large companies and is sufficiently great that private businesses are based on assisting companies in simply arranging term financing.[11]

The need for advisory services is much greater in less-developed countries, where, typically, financial facilities as well as the financial skills of entrepreneurs are limited. Interviews with industrialists in a wide variety of developing countries suggest that many entrepreneurs are so skeptical of obtaining bank finance and so awed by bank procedures that they do not apply for finance, or apply only when all else has failed—by which time they are usually in a very poor position to obtain the credit they need. Many entrepreneurs, moreover, are by training and temperament ill-equipped to keep the detailed accounts without which external financing may not be possible. Because finance is often the least-understood aspect of their business and because they feel there is little they can do about it, financial

[11] One private financial advisory service, for example, assists companies which need term financing. The value of these services has been described as the "ability to act as a catalyst between basically well-run small business and big lenders—and to refine the agreement so that the lender gets safety without putting the borrower in a strait jacket." Small business here means companies with assets of a few million dollars (*Business Week,* June 16, 1962, p. 47ff.) A study of the financial problems of a group of companies in the United States needing finance amounting to a few hundred thousand dollars also indicates the value of financial advisory services: "The lack or inadequacy of financial know-how on the part of the owners accounts in large measure for many, if not most, of the financial problems of the small firm which experiences a rapid rate of growth." (Flink, *Equity Financing of Small Manufacturing Companies in New Jersey,* School of Business, Rutgers—The State University, for the New Jersey Department of Conservation and Economic Development, Trenton, N.J., 1962, p. 13.) An even better indication of the need for financial advisory services in the United States is the recent uncovering of a racket in which some 5,000 businessmen were defrauded of around $2 million by a company which persuaded business to pay advance fees ranging from $200 to $3,000 on the false expectation of getting assistance in arranging loans (see *Business Week,* Aug. 19, 1961, p. 38).

management tends to be one of the most neglected aspects of industrial operations.

Accounting assistance is one form of counseling that a development financing program often cannot afford to neglect. The development value of such programs may be severely reduced if accounts are not available which show recipients' uses of finance, their economic condition, and their needs for other types of assistance. The diversion of development finance to improper uses has in itself been a major deficiency in countries where good accounts and reliable auditing have been lacking.[12]

Good accounting among industrial loan applicants is, moreover, the key to economical methods of evaluating applications, supervising borrowers, and identifying means of improving the efficiency of their operations. This is the principal reason why the administrative cost of extending loans to small manufacturers in advanced countries is often between one-half and one-third of that incurred by institutions in less developed countries. It may thus be worthwhile to incur considerable expenditures over an extended period of time to achieve economies of this magnitude.

Achieving good accounting standards by providing counseling assistance to recipients of finance does involve substantial costs and problems. The magnitude of the latter is suggested by the fact that inadequate accounting remains an obstacle of some importance to financing small firms even in industrialized countries. It is not merely that good accounting is fairly costly. Perhaps more important is the fact that small firms often do not fully appreciate what good accounting can do for them. It has become widespread in the United States, Japan, and some European countries primarily as the result of the requirements of well-enforced income tax laws. In less developed countries, on the other hand, failure to enforce the income tax laws is often a deterrent to the adoption of good accounting practices. Government-supported programs of free accounting assistance have also contributed greatly to the spread of accounting in some countries, such as Japan, Denmark, and the Netherlands.

Among newly industrializing countries, Turkey has had some success in encouraging the use of good accounting as the result of free accounting assistance by the Industrial Development Bank of Turkey. Strong resistance by industrialists to adopting modern accounting practices has gradually been weakened by the need of industrialists for term loans which the IDB will only grant where acceptable accounting standards are maintained. The spread of good accounting in Turkey, however, is not proceeding very rapidly. An effort is being made to accelerate it by getting all banks to require balance sheets, even for short-term financing. The problem, how-

[12] See, for example, M. S. Wattles' discussion of the Korean program, "The Market for Funds in Korea," *Proceedings of the 36th Annual Congress of the Western Economic Association,* Seattle, 1961, pp. 50ff., and Tenenbaum on the Taiwan program, *op. cit.,* pp. 94–95.

ever, remains that the IDB is not equipped to give extensive assistance to a large number of firms, and the accounting services available from private firms are at best limited.[13]

The Industrial Development Center in the Philippines has also emphasized accounting assistance. It has prepared accounting guides for a variety of types of industries and makes available accounting specialists for brief advisory visits at the cost of only the travel expenses involved. Whether this approach is achieving results is not known, but generally more detailed assistance is likely to be required to improve accounts to the level required for efficiently administering development financing.[14]

The problems in extending accounting assistance are several. First, most small enterprises, not merely a few, lack proper accounting. The situation in most developing countries is probably no better than that found by one study in Argentina:

> The weakness of management in medium and small firms is particularly obvious in the field of financial management and control. In most firms, sources of losses are not known daily, nor is responsibility for high costs placed on the workers or the supervisors. There is much guesswork in pricing products, and little is known about where costs can be cut to improve efficiency. In accord with the widespread custom among the smaller firms to conceal their financial situation from the tax collector, it appears that they have avoided accounting to such a degree that management is as ill-informed about the true state of operations as are the tax officials. The accounting systems of most of the smaller companies are rudimentary and do not serve the needs of management for a control tool and a guide to policy-making. Cost accounting to provide unit cost data and comparative costs on various products does not exist in most small firms. As a result, management usually does not know its costs and is not able to price sharply. Budgeting and financial planning is another area of weakness in financial management. Control over costs by modern accounting methods rarely exists.[15]

One of the reasons for the inadequacy of accounting in small firms is that the types of accounting services available are not sufficiently valuable to small firms to justify their costs. A large part of the accounting services available, even in developed countries, is useful for providing little more than accounts meeting reporting requirements of income tax authorities or requirements of sources of external finance. What is needed is accounts which will help to improve and control the efficiency of the firm without entailing excessive paper work. They need to be easily administered, low

---

[13] Discussions with IDBT staff in October, 1965.

[14] Japan also places great emphasis on accounting assistance, but such assistance does not seem to be directly linked with financing programs (see *Cost Accounting for Small Business,* Japan Productivity Center, [n.d.], ca. 1962).

[15] *Industrial Development in Argentina,* Arthur D. Little, Inc., Cambridge, Mass., 1961.

in cost, and readily intelligible to persons without special accounting train-ing. This type of accounting is more useful in relation to its costs and has more appeal to entrepreneurs.

A further problem which must be overcome is the fear that information from accounts will be utilized to the detriment of the concern. This applies particularly in countries where tax evasion is common. There is also a fear that financiers will use the information to appropriate business secrets or to gain control over the financed concern. Creating assurance that ac-counting information will be treated with the proper confidence is essential if the interest of entrepreneurs in good accounting systems is to become a reality.

The accounting assistance problem, in brief, is apt to be a large and, in many respects, complex one, as well as being very important. Thus it may be desirable to concentrate the major part of any effort to improve accounting on encouraging the establishment and expansion of accounting firms and assisting them to achieve the standards and capabilities commonly found in certified (or chartered) accountants of industrially advanced countries.

Extending counseling to the broader and more complex fields of manage-ment and production technology is more difficult. There may nevertheless be a need for selective assistance in these fields. Financing generally becomes much more productive where it can be combined with counseling to improve the quality of management and technology, and the latter may be an essen-tial requirement. An observation made in Nigeria holds true in some degree for many newly industrializing countries:

> Far and away the greatest internal impediment to the expansion of indigenous industry is a deficiency of managerial and technical skills. It is the weakness of these foundation members which is responsible for the meager results of FLB [Federal Loan Boards] and WRFC [Western Regional Finance Cor-poration] loans. Until these deficiencies are amended, further loaning activities will bear little fruit.[16]

This condition has caused another observer of Nigeria's financing programs to suggest the establishment of a "management corporation" which would "recruit overseas specialists for advisory, training, and temporary manage-ment positions in both private and public corporations." While acknowledg-ing that such heavy use of imported specialists is expensive, the source concludes, "initial costs are justifiable when measured against the costs of omitting the special skills which industry requires for growth."[17]

[16] Peter Kilby, *Measures to Promote the Development of Indigenous Industry,* report to the Federal Ministry of Commerce and Industry and the Western Nigeria Ministry of Trade and Industry, Lagos, 1962, p. 11.

[17] *Agricultural and Industrial Credit for Expanded Production in the Western Region of Nigeria,* International Development Services, Inc., New York, 1960, p. 42.

While the need for improving management and technology is common to many countries, the specific counseling needs vary greatly. The counseling priorities of Nigeria are unlikely to be the same as those of India or Colombia; similarly, the needs of various types and sizes of industry within any particular country may have little in common. There are, moreover, many types and methods of counseling which differ greatly in their cost and complexity. This also must be considered in determining what counseling should be done.

Even direct counseling services on management matters need not be elaborate to be useful. A part of the private management counseling in the United States, for example, which appears to be useful is not much more than a reminder service. It reminds entrepreneurs to carry out important tasks or make decisions which are likely to be postponed because they lack the daily urgency of other matters or because they involve matters which are unfamiliar or distasteful to the entrepreneur. It compensates for a normal human weakness that in one-man–controlled concerns can result in haphazard management.

A second level of counseling is simply adding the common sense and interchange of opinion of an outside person well trained in industrial operations and familiar with a wide variety of firms. It may assist only with the spot problems which the entrepreneur brings to the counselor, or it may consist of periodically reviewing the total operation to identify problems, their interrelationships, and their relative importance. The detail in which operations may be analyzed and in which guidance is given in remedying deficiencies uncovered may vary greatly, depending on the counseling resources that can be devoted to this purpose. For reasons of economy, most counseling programs so far have confined free assistance to spot advice and brief diagnosis of individual firms and, wherever practical, have extended counseling on a group basis. However, since recipients of finance must in any case be individually visited as part of normal loan supervision, some degree of individual counseling can be extended in the course of supervision. Combining the two functions will, moreover, tend to improve the quality of both.[18]

Organization of Supporting Services

Organizational arrangements are critical to the usefulness of supporting services. As Wolf has rightly stressed, "Overcoming imperfections of knowledge in underdeveloped countries is, however, a considerably more subtle process than simply a diffusion of information." Success depends, as he goes on to illustrate, on the particular way information is extended.[19] In

---

[18] The role of counseling and supervision in implementing the loan objectives of financial institutions is further elaborated in Chap. 11.

[19] One of the examples which Wolf cites—and which has a lesson applicable to industrial counseling—is the experience with agricultural extension services in

the case of supporting services for small-industry development financing, a fine balance of authority and responsibility among a variety of organizations and between them and entrepreneurs is essential. The balance required is often a delicate one easily upset by small defects and thus is not easily achieved.

There is not a single standard administrative set-up suitable for all programs. What administrative set-up is most appropriate will depend on the scale of the financing program and supporting services contemplated and on the types of financing and other services that will be most important. It will also depend on historical circumstances: what institutions and activities exist, how they are presently organized, and what parts government and private organizations play in the economy.

Our study of programs suggests to us five principles which might generally be useful guides in organizing supporting services where a specialized staff of a dozen or more persons are contemplated for these functions. In view of the variables cited above, these are obviously not intended as rigid principles, but rather as a convenient framework for bringing out the elements which require careful consideration in organizing supporting services:

1. The major part of supporting services should be combined in one agency, which should also be responsible for coordinating the other essential services.

2. Most supporting services should be organizationally independent of financial agencies and, preferably, independent of direct agencies of the government or organizations controlled by potential loan recipients; at the same time, the agency coordinating supporting services must be able to establish close working relationships with financial, government, and business organizations.

3. The cost of supporting services must be partly subsidized, since benefits arise in a way making it difficult to regain full costs directly from recipients; at the same time, part of the cost must be recouped on the basis of assessment for services performed so as to stimulate a high standard of service.

4. Supporting services and agencies should assist decision-making entities by gathering, analyzing, and disseminating information and suggestions but

India: "Though using the same tools of technical assistance (e.g., demonstrations, free or subsidized distribution of seed and fertilizer, etc.) as the earlier and unsuccessful 'grow-more-food' program, Community Development altered the institutional setting by organizing and training extension workers to function as residents in the rural villages. As accepted members of the community, they are able to communicate improved techniques in terms meaningful to the cultivators, . . . thereby removing some of the perceptual barriers that have diminished the effectiveness of earlier technical assistance efforts at the village level." Charles Wolf, Jr., "Institution and Economic Development," *American Economic Review,* December, 1955, pp. 877–879.

should remain one step removed from operational and policy responsibilities. They should advise, assist, and stimulate but not operate or control.

5. Services must be organized and staffed in such a way that the very high minimum requirements in competence and motivation of staff are not breached or strained.

Integrated Supporting Services

Supporting services should be integrated so that the same persons, or persons working closely together, can perform many of the required services. This tends to provide economies in operation and to enlarge the abilities of staff. The relatively high cost of supporting services and the limited availability of the persons with the capabilities required make economy essential.[20]

The various supporting services will each require some of the same specialized capabilities: business economists, financial analysts, and engineers—with some of each category having special knowledge of particular lines of industry—and special branches of these sciences. If staff required by separate supporting services are pooled, permitting individuals to be shifted between functions, specialized staff can be made available for all functions.

The pooling of specialists is particularly important, since some regional dispersion of staff is also essential, particularly in counseling and liaison work, but also in surveys and individual enterprise appraisals. Rapid collection, accurate evaluation and analysis, and effective dissemination of most of the types of information involved in these services depend on close relationships with the sources and with the recipients of information. At least one staff member must have the opportunity to make fairly regular and informal contacts with each major source or recipient of information; only in this way can close relationships be developed.

The industrialists and other businessmen who are the sources as well as the recipients of a large part of the information are located in a variety of centers. The same is true in some degree of banks and other lenders, government agencies, libraries, laboratories, research institutes, business associations, and other organizations who are also sources or recipients of information. The requirement that some staff be geographically dispersed reduces the flexibility with which they can be used and thus the portion of the total which may consist of highly specialized persons. Where one agency serves a variety of functions with the same regionally dispersed staff, duplication is reduced. This makes it economical to maintain centrally based but mobile specialists. Local staff can provide such specialists with a bridge to easy relationships with local contracts.[21]

---

[20] This is well illustrated by experience cited in Chap. 11 of lending institutions in Ghana and various other countries in trying to provide advisory services to their borrowers.

[21] The Netherlands Consulting Service regards it as essential that at least one

A close integration of functions permits each to benefit from the complementarities between them. Surveys, for example, are required to evaluate financial and other program services and to stimulate the improvement of those services. With moderate broadening of the scope of surveys it is possible to (1) obtain comparative information on enterprises for use in screening loan applicants; (2) identify industrial financing opportunities and in this way help upgrade the quality of applicants and induce a more active approach to financing; (3) provide training for staff of financial and other services—such training is valuable for the knowledge it imparts on data collection, analysis, and reporting, and also in providing a practical insight into industrial operations in general; (4) build up information and contacts helpful to other functions such as counseling and enterprise appraisal; and (5) help create an awareness among industrialists of the value of the various services and provide opportunities to extend counseling and supervision to present or potential recipients of financing.

To illustrate the complementarities further, persons engaged in appraising, counseling, or supervising individual enterprises need a knowledge of the whole industry of which the enterprise is a part; this is provided by survey experience or close contact with those having it. Such persons also need easy access to staff engaged in laboratory testing, applied research, finance, training, and other specialized functions. Research is less likely to be diverted from practical lines when it is closely associated with surveys and counseling. Integrating the various functions under one organization facilitates utilizing these complementarities in a way which improves the quality of performance of each and possibly also reduces total staff needs.

Although there are advantages in centralizing many supporting services, some functions may be more appropriately carried out by separate agencies. There would be little point, for example, in incorporating in a centralized agency services which, with a little encouragement, might be obtainable at a reasonable cost from specialized private firms. Similarly, it may be more practical to induce existing organizations to add some of these services to their present functions. Lending agencies, for example, can often extend on accounting and cost control without detriment, and indeed often with

---

person live close enough to each concentration of industrialists to build up bonds of confidence with a large part of them. Somewhat over 40 percent of its staff functions are concentrated in three major centers. The importance of personal relationships is also recognized in their training program, in which a new staff member spends six months working in the organizationally separate research institutes "in order to obtain a basic knowledge of the possibilities of these institutes and to establish personal relations with the research workers for a living contact in their future work." (F. J. N. Stades, *Report on Small Industry in India,* Government of India, Ministry of Commerce and Industry, New Delhi, 1960, p. 38. See also pp. 33ff.). The need for such arrangements will be much greater in the many countries which are not as close-knit by geography, communications, and culture as the Netherlands.

advantage, to their principal activities. Advice on financial matters is another field in which lending institutions can without difficulty provide a much-needed service.

Similarly, cooperative arrangements with technological institutes and laboratories operated by government agencies, universities, and private enterprises are usually the most practical means of obtaining assistance in physical testing, process experimentation, and similar undertakings. Collaborative arrangements with universities, technical institutes, and other institutions may provide the most efficient means of assuring training for industrialists in production technology and business management. Depending on the circumstances, a wide array of other established or potential services might be advantageously obtained through contractual or other cooperative arrangements with private firms, banking, industry and other business associations, regional or community corporations, and government agencies.

How supporting services should be spliced into the existing organizational structure of the economy, whether it should be a new organization or a part of an existing one, will depend on the nature of the existing structure. It is usually advantageous to build on or link to existing organizations where reasonably suitable ones exist. The agency with the primary responsibility for providing and coordinating supporting services will normally have to devote a large part of its resources to filling critical gaps in services and to stimulating, assisting, and coordinating the services of others. Clear-cut responsibilities should be established so that the agency will not duplicate services of other organizations. It must have the capabilities and incentives for giving the maximum support to enlarging and improving the services of other organizations where the latter are in the best position to provide them.

The development of several sources from which supporting services might be drawn could provide an alternative to the primary source and hence some competition, thereby encouraging a high standard of performance. However, because newly developing countries will be able to afford only a limited amount of such staff, aggregation rather than fragmentation will more generally be the most practical solution.

Autonomous but Coordinated Supporting Services

The first of several important elements in this principle is providing basic independence in the administration of most supporting services from that of financial institutions. There are many reasons for this.

Perhaps the most important reason for separating supporting services from the direct responsibilities of lending institutions is that one of the primary supporting functions is always program monitoring. Monitoring services are likely to be more objective in evaluation and more effective in stimulating improvements in financial services if they are substantially independent of lending institutions.

A second and even more fundamental reason for separating supporting from financial services is that the functions involved in supporting services require a close relationship with industrialists and a generally sympathetic orientation to their problems and needs. Financial institutions, on the other hand, in granting or refusing loans and insuring loan repayment must keep their relationship with industrialists on a more formal basis. Decisions on issuing or refusing loans involve many subjective judgments which can be more accurately made when the lender has no personal relationships with the applicant. Sound lending policies also sometimes require decisions which are painful to applicants. For example, it is sometimes necessary for a lending institution to refuse assistance to very good management or to liquidate a well-managed enterprise because of shifts in economic conditions or other factors beyond entrepreneurial control. Such decisions are not easily made but are facilitated by keeping relationships with clients on a business basis.

Incorporating supporting functions within banks involves hazards where a large amount of investment planning and operational advice is extended. There is a danger that counselors under direct pressure to prevent losses will get more deeply involved in management details than an outsider can have the competence to advise upon. Counseling may tend to be concentrated on firms which were financed by mistake and which should be liquidated, while neglecting those which can best make use of assistance, since the latter tend to be capable of meeting minimum performance standards without assistance. A counselor from a lending authority may also tend to usurp authority properly lying with management, thus defeating the whole purpose of counseling by killing the initiative of the entrepreneur. When counseling comes from a lender, there is a danger that borrowers will tend to shift their own responsibilities to counselors. When failure or serious difficulty occurs—as it sometimes must despite the best management—the bank may not be in a position to enforce its proper claims or to stimulate a greater effort. The client may be inclined to attribute the difficulties to bad advice, whether this has been a major contributory factor or not. His resulting aggrieved or uncooperative attitude will greatly complicate already difficult problems.

A further reason for not incorporating supporting services in a lending agency is the need to draw on a variety of sources of finance.[22] Where fairly broad integrated supporting services are required, it is particularly uneconomic to duplicate these services within several financing institutions. It would be possible to centralize the administration of services under one lending institution such as a development bank which would extend services to other financial intermediates, but possible conflicts of interest between financial intermediaries make this alternative unattractive.

[22] The reasons for this are indicated in Part 3 and are also well illustrated by Japan's experience reported in Chap. 13.

A final consideration is that the type of staff required for supporting services is not always easily accommodated in the administrative structure of financial institutions. Industrial specialists, for example, tend to be higher salaried than regular bank staff, which may cause internal friction. Furthermore, because of their specialized background, it is sometimes difficult to promote them to administrative positions. This may also contribute to unsatisfactory staff relations. Nevertheless, some lending institutions, such as the Industrial Bank of Canada, have shown that, by appropriate selection, utilization, and advancement of staff, a bank can integrate persons with engineering, economic, financial, or other diverse backgrounds harmoniously and in the process gradually round out the capabilities of at least the more able. Institutions in less developed countries, however, have generally encountered grave problems in attempting to do this.

The foregoing considerations make a strong case against incorporating broad supporting services within lending institutions. There are, however, some exceptions worth noting.

It will be desirable for banks lending to small manufacturers to have loan officers with some specialized training and practical experience in industrial operations, whether or not supporting services are available, to assist in loan appraisal. There are also some advisory services, such as on accounting and financial management, which banks may easily add to their functions. Other advisory services of a very general or liaison nature and survey activities may be a useful part of a bank's functions when the need for these is large enough to warrant some duplication of services.

There is sometimes a case also for integrating financial and nonfinancial services into the responsibilities of one institution where the dominant function undertaken is technical assistance and other nonfinancial services and the amount of financing to be extended is very small. Special problems in coordinating financial and nonfinancial services may be a further reason for giving a technical-assistance agency some lending powers.

If interdependent financial and nonfinancial services are to be extended by independent agencies, an adequate means of closely coordinating them will be essential. Poorly linked services which are interdependent tend to entail delays and may cause a complete breakdown in service. India's State-Aid-to-Industry program, for example, is a case where dependence by the financing agency on poorly linked outside services has resulted in serious delays.[23] In Pakistan, inadequate staffing and coordination of technical appraisal services with lending agencies dependent upon such services resulted in a situation which virtually halted the lending program.[24]

---

[23] See Chap. 2.

[24] *Encouraging the Growth of Small Industry in Pakistan,* a report prepared by a Stanford Research Institute team for the Ministry of Industries, Government of Pakistan, 1963. See also the similar problem of the Nigerian Western Region Finance Corporation in International Development Services, Inc., *Agricultural and*

The agency administering technical and other services supporting a financing program will need to be linked not only with lending institutions, but also with government agencies, research institutions, business associations, and other organizations on which it must depend for information, assistance, or cooperation. Ideally, the agency extending technical and other nonfinancial services should have close relationships with all these organizations without being heavily dependent upon any one of them.

The working out of properly balanced relationships of the agency administering supporting services with the various organizations and most particularly with financial institutions is more of an art than a science and depends a great deal on the personal characteristics of the top leadership involved. There are several administrative arrangements, however, which are often helpful in the establishment of liaison and coordination. Perhaps the most useful are contractual arrangements which define relationships and responsibilities and establish financial incentives and pressures for maintaining them. Financial institutions, for example, can obtain control over the timing and quality of enterprise appraisal performed by a separate technical-service agency through a contractual arrangement on this specific task. The technical-service agency's general autonomy or relationships with other organizations need not be impaired by contractual obligations on specific tasks, and, at the same time, adequate control over the specific service can be given to the financial organization for which it is performed. Similarly, the technical-service agency might perform counseling services for enterprises on a contractual basis, giving the recipient some means of controlling the quality of the services performed.

Another arrangement which is helpful in creating appropriate linkages is the organization of the technical-service agency under a board of directors on which there are representatives of financial institutions, government departments, industrial organizations, research institutes, or other groups with whom coordination is important. It may also be helpful to obtain a part of the staff of the technical-service agency, particularly in the initial period, from officers on loan from organizations with whom it must maintain close ties. This could foster a network of personal relationships out of which close official relationships will tend to grow. The training function of the technical-service agency serves the same purpose when it provides training not only to its own officers, but also to the staff of such other organizations as lending institutions, government agencies, and industrial associations.

Performance-motivating Funding

The extension agency often needs long-term funding to permit its staff to undertake training and investigations with fairly broad and long-term

---

Industrial Credit for Expanded Production in the Western Region of Nigeria, New York, 1960.

implications and to give it freedom to operate with professional objectivity. In order to encourage the use of these services by financial institutions, industrialists, and others, the ultimate cost of most of these services must ordinarily be borne largely by government. It may be advantageous, however, to pass a part of government's support through the hands of the important users of the services. If clients have some awareness of what the service costs, they may be more inclined to value the service and to insist upon a standard of service commensurate with costs.

A Service Orientation

Defining the agency's function as one of *advising* operating bodies is important to prevent it from assuming functions it usually cannot be equipped to carry out. With an advisory type of function, it will be better able to state its findings objectively and without circumlocution and to reach conclusions quickly. Maintaining good relationships with the various different groups it serves and/or is assisted by is also easier when it remains one step removed from operational responsibilities. As a purely advisory body, it is less likely to be subject to social and political pressures and to have greater opportunity to make use of foreign consultants.

Exceptional Staffing

The professional and personal abilities required for supporting and monitoring services are of a very high order. Their function is one of educational leadership. It requires the knowledge, sagacity, and personality to ascertain and communicate information and to motivate its application by others in controlling or operating positions. Many developing countries must utilize most of their best local talent in high administrative positions in government and business. Thus staff of the quality required is likely to be extremely scarce.

A partial solution to the staffing problem is to use specialists from abroad in key positions. It is much easier to utilize a substantial number of outsiders in key positions in training and information-gathering services than in regular government or business operations, because such services are politically less sensitive.

Not only are specialists from abroad easily fitted into informational services of this kind, but there are also special advantages in grouping and utilizing some specialists from abroad in these functions in newly industrializing countries. Often prejudice against local talent in these functions requires initial use of foreigners until joint work enhances the prestige and proves the equal capabilities of local staff. Also, the foreign specialists in the central service agency will provide a reservoir of special skills that are easily available to the administrators of more politically sensitive agencies, enabling local administrators to draw on the specialists' services on an occasional and informal basis. This enhances the effective resources of local administrators without detracting from their authority or affecting regular administrative procedures. Finally, even where the best expertise from abroad can be drawn upon, the problem of adapting expertise to an unfamiliar setting is too great for many individuals working alone but is much more readily achieved when several persons with complementary backgrounds are working closely together.

There are important limits on the extent to which specialists from abroad may be used. For one thing, they are expensive. Although various aid programs are favorably inclined to this type of assistance, foreign specialists are obviously a temporary solution. Moreover, obtaining qualified specialists who will stay for long periods is difficult. The specialist from abroad is less useful in directly carrying out supporting services than he is training and guiding local staff for this function because, at least initially, he may lack much knowledge of the local language and customs. Limited knowledge of local language and customs may not seriously impair the specialists' ability to train and guide local staff and generally plan and administer the program, since in this they are usually dealing with persons with sufficient education, experience, and cultural flexibility to adapt to these limitations. The main body of the staff nevertheless must consist of local persons. Thus the organization must be able to attract and train exceptional local staff. It is essential to establish firmly in the early years of the organization selection and personnel policies which will attract and hold local staff of unusual abilities. One means of assuring this is to place the authority and responsibility for this in the initial years in the hands of persons with exceptional capacity, international experience, and a general ability to resist pressures that in many countries tend to impede the adoption of such policies.

Part Three
Possible Channels of Developmental Finance

Chapter 6
Stimulating Noninstitutional
Sources of Finance

THE VIEWS WERE expressed in Chapter 4 that there are many channels through which small-factory development might be financed; that what could be accomplished through any one of these was usually subject to fairly narrow limitations, some of which are easily overcome and others with more difficulty or not at all; and, finally, that it is often the most practical approach—and also a necessary one if broad and sustained results are to be achieved—to direct efforts toward making several channels of value to the financing of small-factory development.

In order to illustrate these conclusions in concrete detail, we will examine the typical merits and limitations of the major channels, commencing in this chapter with noninstitutional channels and continuing in succeeding chapters to banks, finance companies, development organizations, and other institutional channels. At the conclusion of our examination of each channel of finance we will consider what can be done to increase its usefulness under the general conditions common in newly developing countries. Other institutional channels with distinctive characteristics of some importance which have been used to finance small-factory development, but which could not be covered in this review, such as regional, state, and community development corporations, credit cooperatives, government hire-purchase corporations, and industrial estates, are treated in the case studies.[1]

The discussion of the merits and limitations of the channels draws on the experience of developed countries as well as that of the less developed. The experience of even the most advanced economy is much more relevant

[1] For an elaboration of the author's views on the usefulness of parks as a channel of development financing, see K. Duke, P. Adams, and R. W. Davenport, *An Industrial Park Development Program for Central America,* Central American Bank for Economic Integration, Tegucigalpa, Honduras, 1964, chap. 7.

than it may appear from the contrasting environments of the most and least advanced. The problems experienced by advanced countries in financing small-factory development through particular channels are likely to be among the major problems that will confront such efforts in less-developed countries, although they may not be the only ones. The merits which there may be in utilizing particular channels in advanced countries may or may not be merits realizable through similar efforts in less-developed countries, but the experience of advanced countries at least suggests important potentialities which deserve exploration. Thus the experience of developed countries has the value of alerting us to the likelihood of particular problems and potentialities in utilizing the same channels in less developed countries. What advanced countries have done to overcome these problems or exploit these potentialities is also suggestive of promising measures worth experimenting with in less developed countries. The more abundant and better-documented experience of advanced countries has an important contribution to make, if it is kept in mind that it may tend to neglect aspects peculiar to less developed countries.

The noninstitutional sources of finance are by far the most important sources of small-factory finance in most countries, regardless of the level of industrialization. There are three main noninstitutional sources: (1) financing derived from the earnings of enterprises and other income or savings of the primary owner (internal financing), (2) equity or loan funds from friends and relatives of the primary owners or from moneylenders and other individual financiers, and (3) interbusiness creditors. Some effort expended on improving one or more of these sources is usually worthwhile. Even modest improvements can contribute significantly to small-factory development in view of the relative importance of these as a source of small-factory financing. Although noninstitutional sources of funds are rarely, if ever, a completely satisfactory substitute for institutional channels, they can be an important complement to them.

Internal Finance

By internal funds, we mean all funds that accrue or have accrued to small-factory owners; these include past or current profits of the factory in question and also the income and savings arising out of other activities. Only the financing of controlling owners will be treated as "internal"; the financing provided by minor shareholders or inactive partners will be dealt with in the following section on private lenders and investors.

Internal financing is normally the major source of small-factory financing. Many small factories rely exclusively on this source. The average share of capital derived from internal funds of small factories in a country such as India appears to be around 90 percent. In countries where institutional finance is more readily available, such as Greece, Sweden, or the United

States, the proportion of internal finance tends to fall to between two-thirds and one-half of total funds but remains the major source.[2]

Internal funds are of special importance. Because the entrepreneur is both the source and user of the funds, there is no problem of informational gaps or possible conflicts of interests which must be bridged by screening procedures, controls, or other terms which may restrict the use of the funds. Internal funds, in brief, provide equity capital (in effect if not always nominally in this form); this type of finance is the most difficult to obtain from other sources as well as being the most versatile.

The main objection to stimulating small-factory development through measures increasing the availability and use of internal funds arises from the difficulties involved in assuring internal funds are actually reinvested or in directing them into particular types or lines of investment. Some measures useful in increasing the availability of internal funds also are expensive or difficult to implement.

Most measures for increasing the internal financing of small-factory development revolve around increasing the profitability or the relative profitability of small factories. The factories' profits are themselves a major source of internal funds. The comparative profitability of the factory relative to the owner's alternative investment opportunities is, moreover, a major determinant of whether profits and other internal funds are invested in the enterprise.

Assistance in increasing the profits of small factories may be rendered in four basic ways: (1) by increasing productivity in the factory (improving management, technology, skills, plant); (2) by lowering production costs

[2] For data on India, see Chap. 2. In Greece, corporations with assets of less than $100,000 obtain about two-thirds of their funds internally, but the proportion falls progressively for larger enterprises, being only 23 percent for corporations with over $2.5 million assets. Diomedes Psilos, *Capital Markets in Greece,* p. 95, cited in Howard S. Ellis *Industrial Capital in Greek Development,* Center of Economic Research, Athens, 1964, p. 123. On Sweden, see Erik Dahmén, "Summary of the National Report for Sweden," in OEEC, *The Supply of Capital Funds for Industrial Development in Europe and the United States,* 1957, supplement III, p. 46, and Arne Ogren, "Equity Capital and Financing of Business," *Skandinaviska Banken Quarterly Review,* no. 3, 1962. Other European countries are discussed by Bruce R. Williams, *International Report on Factors in Investment Behavior,* OECD, Paris, 1962. On United States see Federal Reserve System, *Financing Small Business,* report to the Committees on Banking and Currency and the Select Committees on Small Business, 85th Cong., 2d Sess., 1958, p. 24, and Federal Trade Commission–Securities and Exchange Commission, *Quarterly Financial Report for Manufacturing Corporations,* Fourth Quarter, 1958. In Japan, statistics on companies employing between 10 and 100 workers suggest they obtain on the average as little as one-third of their funds from internal sources. See Chap. 13. A detailed study of the few enterprises and discussions with Japanese bankers, however, indicate that the data grossly understate owners' effective contribution to equity. The owners often have assets outside the firm which they lend to their firm or use as collateral for loans to the firm. See Chap. 13.

through increased productivity in related enterprises (cheaper materials, transport, marketing—or simply improved availability); (3) by reducing taxes or granting exemptions or subsidies or improving government services; and (4) by increasing the factory's bargaining power with customers or suppliers (tariffs, industrial associations, preference in government purchases).

A detailed examination of these methods of stimulating the internal financing of small-factory development is beyond the scope of this study, but the nature of the problems involved in utilizing them may be briefly noted. All these methods tend to involve some redistribution of income within the economy to the units assisted and at the expense of other units. There are limits to which this will contribute to overall long-run development. Moreover, immediate economic and political constraints may further narrow the extent to which these methods are applied. It is often possible, however, to reduce the usual extent of the several constraints. These can be facilitated by an organization well versed in small-factory development requirements and with the staff, funds, and motivation to assure such measures are designed and applied in a way to provide the greatest small-factory development at the least cost.

Several specific steps that often need to be taken in conjunction with measures of the four above types to increase their contribution to small-factory development might be cited. Most such measures, including tax exemptions, tariffs, the improvement of infrastructure, and often the extension of technical assistance, must, for economic or political reasons, be undertaken with a view to benefiting both large and small factories and possibly other types of enterprises. As a result, they tend to be designed and administered in a way that makes them of little assistance to small factories.

For example, tax exemptions may be granted under such elaborate procedures—as is the case in Brazil—that owners of small factories may not be able to comply with procedures. The reduction of transaction taxes—which bear more heavily on small factories than larger and more integrated plants—may be of more practical value in countries such as Chile and Brazil where transaction taxes are higher than the more commonly granted depreciation allowances and other income tax exemptions.[3]

Free or subsidized sources of technical assistance are made available to industries in many countries, but this assistance often concentrates on types of information and advice which is only applicable to large-scale production. Even where such assistance is equally valuable to small and large factories, if the amount available is very limited and allocation left to the discretion of program administrators, the latter often tend to give their whole attention to large-scale enterprises.

[3] See R. W. Davenport, *Financing Small and Medium Manufacturing Enterprises in Latin America,* Inter-American Development Bank, Washington, D.C., 1962 (English and Spanish editions), chap. 4.

Deficiencies such as these might be reduced by better knowledge of the special requirements of small factories and more concern with taking these into account in the design and administration of such measures. An organization primarily concerned with small-industry development can be useful in providing the information and stimulation helpful for this purpose.

Technical assistance, preferential treatment in government purchases, and other measures intended to improve the profits of small factories by lowering the costs or increasing the price of their output, need to be periodically reviewed to ascertain if they are in fact producing the intended result. They may indeed be helping to lower the cost or to increase prices of small-factory output, but without significantly enlarging profits. The interbusiness relationships of small units may result in any price or cost benefits being quickly drained away by large distributors or others doing business with small units on the basis of a strong bargaining position. If so, these also need to be corrected.

Measures tending to improve the profits of small factories contribute to the financing of small-factory development only if such funds are reinvested, and reinvested wisely. If all small-factory owners were like those in India described by McCrory, increasing small-factory profits would almost automatically increase productive investments in small factories:

> The craftsmen [owners of metal working factories employing up to 20 workers] have been willing to restrict their consumption severely over long periods in order to save; they start from such a low base that it is only forced, long-term saving that will do them any good. Perhaps it is easier for them to live frugally because their backgrounds start them out with modest standards. But easier or not, they do it. All but one live in rented quarters. Not all own even bicycles, and those are for business purposes. . . . Their dress makes it difficult to distinguish owner from employee or, for that matter, from the ordinary Chopur laborer.[4]

According to McCrory, the Indian craftsman-entrepreneur is not only highly motivated to reinvest, but also has the ability to use further funds productively. "He has the enterprise, the energy, the industrial outlook and the skill *now* to make things efficiently and well. He would like more education, more technical know-how, and a better acquaintance with business and marketing practices of course. But right now, he cannot even use what he has."[5]

The present author has come in contact with a great many small-factory owners of the type McCrory describes, not only in India but in a wide variety of other countries. In Colombia, for example, about a third of

[4] James T. McCrory, *Small Industry in a North Indian Town,* Government of India, Ministry of Commerce and Industry, New Delhi, 1956, p. 12.

[5] *Ibid.,* p. 41. Italics are McCrory's.

the small factories studied appeared to have a substantial growth potential that might be realized through increasing their access to funds.[6]

However, very little is known about the typical pattern of small enterprises in reinvesting profits in less-developed countries. In field work all types of cases can be observed, but it is difficult to quantify these impressions. One would suspect from field impressions that a greater proportion of small enterprises have a high reinvestment policy than is true of larger enterprises, but that even in the case of small enterprises the share of the total which reinvest a major part of earnings is probably small. The comments of one observer on Peru probably apply to many less-developed countries: "Unfortunately, in Peru the tradition of reinvesting profits is not well established and most industrialists apparently withdraw a large portion of the profits each year. Not only is there failure to use profits adequately for expansion and diversification, but there is frequently not even adequate use of cash flow for the purpose of maintaining the efficiency of existing plants."[7]

Where there is a probability that a large part of the profits generated by special measures will not be reinvested, it is advisable to couple assistance measures with reinvestment incentives and requirements. Thus, exempting only reinvested profits from taxes may be more useful than simply exempting industrial profits generally, provided, of course, that the former type of exemption is administratively practical in local circumstances. Where assistance such as technical services is extended directly to selected enterprises, it may be possible to establish reinvestment requirements as a condition of assistance or to select enterprises for assistance from those having the greatest proneness to reinvest earnings.

Measures enlarging the internal financial resources of firms contribute primarily to financing expansion and modernization in present lines of production, since most entrepreneurs are confined to their present lines by limited capabilities, little knowledge of opportunities, and inertia. In newly industrializing countries where there is a greater need for financing new enterprises and new lines of enterprise, enlarging the internal resources of existing enterprises is of more limited value as an industrial development financing measure than in countries with a large and diversified industrial base.[8] Better information or opportunities and assistance in entering new lines may help overcome some of these limitations by encouraging existing enterprises to diversify into more productive lines.

---

[6] See Chap. 12.

[7] *A Program for the Industrial and Regional Development of Peru,* Arthur D. Little, Inc., Cambridge, Mass., 1960, p. 26.

[8] The stress in highly industrialized countries on improving internal resources also derives in part from the fact that in these countries, where taxes on enterprises are already high, cutting taxes is an administratively simple measure to increase internal resources of enterprises.

Measures to improve internal financing need to be based on a realistic evaluation of the costs and results which they involve. Free or low-cost technical advice, tax exemptions, tariffs, subsidized transportation or power, and other such efforts to make small factories more profitable involve substantial costs to the economy directly or indirectly. Measures to improve internal financing are likely to be a useful ingredient in most small-industry financing programs, but to economize on their costs, enlarge their degree of effectiveness, and meet needs for which they are less suited, it is usually advantageous to give attention to improving other sources of financing as well.

Private Financiers or "Moneylenders"

Individuals other than principal owners are commonly the second or third most important source of finance for small industry in less developed countries. However, because these relations are usually informal and unrecorded, and because often neither the financier nor the recipient of funds is anxious to publicize their relationship, information on the operations of private financiers is extremely sketchy.[9]

There are several different types of relationships that fall within the category of financing by individuals other than the principal owners. We wish to exclude here a common type of moneylender—persons who mix financing with supplying, purchasing, or other business relations with those financed. Although many discussions would consider this type to be a "typical" moneylender, it may more appropriately be considered in this discussion under interbusiness finance.

The other main types which need to be separately distinguished here are: (1) relatives and close friends and (2) others who are "silent" partners

[9] Most of the data that have been gathered on this subject are limited by being derived from interviews with a small number of firms and by the difficulty of separating financing by private individuals outside the firms from financing by individuals within the firm and also from interbusiness financing. There are marked differences in the importance of private financiers for different scales of enterprise, even within small industry, and differences also arise between countries because of such factors as banking traditions and the extent of inflation. The following data are illustrative of the general importance of moneylenders in some countries. In India, various surveys indicate that between 30 and 50 percent of external credit comes from noninstitutional sources. (See Chap. 2.) A survey by the Bank of Korea in 1960 showed that 80 percent of the enterprises covered used private loans. (See "South Korea Monetary Measures for Economic Growth," *Far Eastern Economic Review*, Dec., 1960, p. 563.) An investigation in Taiwan estimated that private loans made up one-fourth to one-half of the volume of regular bank loans. (See Edward A. Tenebaum, *Taiwan's Turning Point,* Continental-Allied Company, Washington, D.C., 1961, p. 59.) A 1957 survey in Japan, which has a very advanced banking structure, shows the proportion of external credit from moneylenders, relatives, and acquaintances was about 20 percent for firms with 10 to 29 workers, and 12 percent for firms with 30 to 99 workers. (See Chap. 13.)

or private lenders. These distinctions are somewhat arbitrary, since they shade into one another. Financing may be derived from close or distant relatives, from friends or friends of friends, from local but socially separate acquaintances, from complete outsiders, and various other gradations in relationships.

Relatives and close friends are often the most important segment of this source of finance. They are distinct from other private financiers in that their ability to evaluate creditworthiness and willingness to provide funds are both enlarged by the prior existence of a close relationship between the financier and recipient. They are also distinct in that their terms of financing are often very liberal. Finance from friends or relatives is, however, sometimes encumbered by increased obligations to employ possibly unqualified or poorly motivated dependents of the supplier of funds. The funds extended by friends and relatives are thus both in advantages and defects much like internal funds.

The *moneylender* or private financier who lends for business reasons rather than with the purpose of assisting friends and relatives is, on the other hand, a clearly external source of financing and one which has often been criticized. The two main criticisms of private financiers have been that they (1) charge high rates or, more specifically, the maximum each recipient can afford and (2) seek to utilize their position to take over the firm in a moment of weakness. The second criticism is particularly serious, since where financiers are more interested in acquiring control than in profitable return on their funds, their allocation of finance may be the opposite of desirable development criteria; they may seek to finance failure rather than success.

However, moneylenders clearly must have, or appear to have, some offsetting advantageous characteristics, since they are frequently used by small industrialists, even where regular bank facilities or special small-industry financing programs are an effective alternative. The commonly stated reasons for use of private financiers, aside from the lack of other alternatives, are: (1) the promptness and informality with which requests are met and (2) the flexibility of terms. A third reason, less frequently stated but usually implicit in the foregoing, is that such funds are often provided on a risk basis (whether explicitly in the form of equity or not), and risk financing is often what the small industrialist needs.

It is not surprising that some entrepreneurs have found private financing advantageous, while others have found it an extremely costly or hazardous source of funds. Aside from the broad differences already noted between financing by friends and relatives and that by others, there are inevitable great differences among the latter financing arrangements, depending upon the personal relationships, character, and bargaining strength of the particular individuals involved. These transactions are less subject to the standardizing influence of laws, since they are usually small and numerous, informal and unpublicized. Tradition sets some standards, but in many communities *caveat emptor* still governs business relations.

Often the first step in bringing about more productive arrangements for channeling private finance to small industry and increasing the volume of such financing is to recognize that both the financier and the small-industry borrower are engaged in potentially productive activities, and both are interested in maximizing their income. It is necessary to think in terms of fostering a more productive and mutually attractive relationship between private financiers and industrialists rather than in terms of merely improving the income of industrialists at the expense of the private financiers.

The popular view that private financiers make no contribution to development and should be eliminated does not seem to be correct, at least if applied indiscriminately to all types of finance from individuals outside a firm. Rather, what is needed is an active approach to increasing the volume of finance from such sources and to improving the nature of the relationship. Despite their well-known shortcomings, moneylenders are not easily and completely replaced by a better source of finance. It is usually easier to make them a constructive element in the economy than to replace them entirely. Developing other channels of finance is, of course, also desirable both in itself and as a means of improving the operations of moneylenders.

The first problem which must be dealt with in order to make private financiers a more useful source of finance is the usual high and unstandardized charges for their services. The cost of private finance is certainly a problem where interest exceeds the rate of inflation by more than 1 or 2 percent per month, as it sometimes does.[10]

A realistic approach to the cost problem, however, needs to be taken. Where an industrialist borrows only a small proportion of his total finance for a short period from a private financier, even a fairly high rate may have only a modest effect on the overall production costs of the enterprise. At the same time, the basic costs of lenders when related to very small short-term loans result in a minimum sound lending rate much above conventional bank rates. Moreover, such loans are often made on a very flexible unsecured basis, exposing the lender to all the risks—and giving the borrower all the benefits—of equity capital. Where this is the case, the cost must be expected to approximate the average cost of equity.[11] In

---

[10] A Bank of Korea survey, for example, reported that private funds in 1960 were normally lent at 4 to 5 percent per month, although ranging as high as 30 percent per month. (See *Far Eastern Economic Review*, Dec. 8, 1960, p. 563.) The rate on private funds in Taiwan is reported to have exceeded 40 percent per month in June, 1949, although falling to around 40 percent per year in 1960. (See Tenenbaum, *op. cit.*, p. 60.) The average rise in prices in both Korea and Taiwan in 1960 was somewhat less than 2 percent per month.

[11] Not only are private loan funds very similar to equity, they are sometimes in fact equity reported as loans by the entrepreneur, since interest payments are

countries where it takes a reasonable expectation of 30 percent or more per year to induce equity investments, the rate on loans having little more protection than nonvoting preference shares cannot be expected to be a great deal less.

The most fruitful approach to reducing the charges for private finance is to open it to increased competition and to reduce the risks and expenses of extending such finance.[12] Equally or more important than reducing the normal charges is to standardize them in a way that they relate to costs rather than to what the market will bear.

Greater availability of finance through more easily supervised channels, such as banks, is one way to increase competition. It may be possible simply to expand banking facilities and the volume of credit, though the cost and possible inflationary implications of this approach may limit these possibilities.

It is often possible to divert to banks some of the funds on which private lending is based by raising the rate paid to bank depositors. The very low savings rate paid by credit institutions as compared with the effective market rate of interest virtually compels private savers to become money-lenders in many developing countries. Many savers would prefer the security and simplicity which saving through institutions is supposed to provide, but they cannot afford to ignore major differences in returns on savings—particularly if there are also risks involved in institutional saving. It is sometimes objected that any increase in savings rates will add greatly to inflationary pressures. This need not be so. In many cases the spread between savings and lending rates is already excessively large so that no rise in lending rates is required. Moreover, moderate increases in lending rates do not in practice seem to have much influence on the general level of prices in less-developed countries. It is also possible to counteract any inflationary pressures stimulated by higher lending rates through fiscal and other measures.

Better regulation of banks may also help to increase the volume of direct lending to small industry. In some cases, banks utilize moneylenders as a go-between to permit them to evade interest-rate regulations. One of the more clever arrangements of this type has been described with some irony by Tenenbaum:

> However, at least one more scrupulous bank, whose legal adviser is an expert in Talmudic Law, has been careful to avoid charging illegal interest. Even

---

usually deductible from business income as an expense but dividends on equity are not. (See Tenenbaum, *op. cit.*, p. 64.) Cases of this practice were also observed in field work in Japan and some Latin American countries.

[12] For an interesting but somewhat pessimistic discussion of ways to reduce the administrative costs in private moneylending to agriculture, which involves some of the same problems, see A. Bottomley, "The Cost of Administering Private Loans in Underdeveloped Areas," *Oxford Economic Papers,* July, 1963, pp. 154ff.

within the books of its subsidiary company, time deposits are accepted at customary rates of interest . . . through certain outside brokers. In return for bringing in deposits, these brokers are allowed to "recommend" borrowers, who receive loans at legal rates of interest. . . . If the broker chooses to charge a heavy "commission" to the depositors who accept his advice about where to deposit, that is not the bank's business. If the broker fails to report all these confusing payments to the income tax authorities, this is not his business. If the broker happens to be the uncle of the bank's manager, that is nobody's business. . . .[13]

It is not always easy to differentiate between legitimate and constructive financial arrangements between banks and private lenders and those which serve no purpose but to raise the price which the ultimate borrower must pay for funds. Some private financiers normally derive a major part of their funds from banks. This relationship can contribute to small-industry financing where private financiers, by their guarantee and knowledge of clients, can enable bank funds to be channeled to small enterprises which banks would not otherwise be able to serve. However, a large part of the cases where the moneylender serves no constructive purpose can be eliminated by the establishment and enforcement of bank regulations keeping the actual profitability of bank loans to moneylenders in line with the profit on comparable loans to industrial borrowers. Where there is an interest-rate ceiling and a large unsatisfied demand for financing, setting higher rates on smaller and riskier loans may be essential to motivate banks to lend directly to small industry.

A further way of increasing competition for private financiers of small industry without increasing the national volume of credit is to provide advisory services which will keep small industrialists informed of alternative financing arrangements both among private financiers and from banks and other sources. Advisory services can do much to standardize rates in relation to costs, as well as to lower them by spreading information designed to intensify competition. Even in highly industrialized countries, a major part of the financing problem of industrialists is that the latter do not know how to go about obtaining finance, what the alternative sources are, what it should cost them, and how to calculate the actual cost of funds offered them. Rubenstein, speaking of the generally highly educated heads of research-based New England companies of a generally larger scale than our definition of small industry, notes: "Many entrepreneurs confessed complete ignorance and lack of information on how to go about raising money."[14] The problem of raising funds from individuals is particularly difficult. "Such

---

[13] Edward A. Tenenbaum, *Israel's Industrial Finances: A Second Look,* report to the Government of Israel and the United States International Cooperation Administration, Continental-Allied Company, Inc., Washington, D.C., 1960, p. 98.
[14] Albert Rubenstein, *Problems of Financing and Managing New Research-Based Enterprises in New England,* Federal Reserve Bank of Boston, 1958, p. 43.

persons [private financiers] keep in touch with investment houses, brokers, but they do not advertise and do not want a line of investors at their door. They are not technical people but want to be satisfied that the entrepreneur is competent. They do not want a marriage, although some are looking for an employment opportunity."[15] In less developed countries the problem of raising funds from private sources on a satisfactory basis is similar but often made more complex by the lesser industrial experience of both parties and by the greater social barriers that tend to separate them.

Because sources of private funds are hard to identify, their terms not well known, and because they can afford to reject an application and wait for another, they tend to be in a very strong bargaining position. The entrepreneur, on the other hand, because of his lack of knowledge and uncertainty about how to obtain funds, often puts off seeking outside funds until the need becomes critical; then his bargaining position is even weaker than it would be normally. Entrepreneurs can be helped through advisory services to resolve their uncertainties and appraise their opportunities so they will seek finance before emergencies arise. They can also be guided through such services as how to support their applications so as to obtain the best possible terms.

There have been few efforts to try to organize better channels of communication between private financiers and entrepreneurs, although there has been some recognition of the need. The Medium Industry Bank in Korea has recently reported plans for a consultation office to bring industrialists and private financiers together.[16] Banks in many countries put applicants in touch with private lenders, although usually more by way of serving the financier than the applicant. In Israel, for example, banks which have fully lent their own funds often assist a borrower to obtain from private lenders, normally at the legal rate of interest plus a brokerage fee and possibly a charge for a bank guarantee.[17] Stockbrokers, attorneys, accounting firms, and various individuals sometimes assist applicants to locate finance in return for a fee, but like private financiers they have the drawback that they tend to charge what the market will bear.

What entrepreneurs need is an impartial source of information and assistance which will serve them at easily ascertainable and reasonable costs. Even in the United States one author has concluded:

---

[15] *Ibid*, p. 37. See also Federal Reserve System, *op. cit.*, p. 62. For a discussion of similar difficulties by British cutlery, pottery, and other growing firms in locating and satisfactorily negotiating with private sources of funds see Duncan Burn, "Retrospect," in Burn (ed.), *The Structure of British Industry: A Symposium*, Cambridge University Press, London, 1958, vol. II, chap. 20, p. 455.

[16] Korean Medium Industry Bank, *Annual Report*, 1962, p. 27.

[17] See *International Financial News Survey*, Apr. 19, 1963, p. 1, and Tenenbaum, *Israel's Industrial Finances: A Second Look*, pp. 97, 98.

Small growth companies are badly in need of competent counseling services on financing, programming and planning. This function should be assumed by the State Government. The latter could and should provide the funds— whether with or without federal subsidy—for such services by competent members of the state's university faculties. The scope and nature of such consultation would be basically analogous to the services provided by the county (agricultural) agent. The result would be beneficial to both the business community and those engaged in teaching.[18]

To increase private financing and make these relationships more productive, it is often necessary to think in terms of assisting the financier as well as those financed. It is sometimes forgotten that financiers are deceived by industrial promoters as well as vice versa and that financiers' consciousness of this and their lack of knowledge of industry causes many of them to confine their financing to real estate, speculative transactions, and other fields with which they are more familiar. Also, the higher rates of interest which detract from these funds often reflect high costs as well as high bargaining strength. The financier's high cost may stem from several sources. He may not know how to evaluate the creditworthiness of industrial finance applicants, so that risks involved in good and bad applications must be averaged rather than the good being taken separately. This is particularly true of those who invest or lend as a sideline to their regular occupation, but may also be true of professional financiers who, despite versatility in financial and legal matters, may be little equipped to understand the technical and economic complexities of industry. As Tenenbaum noted in Taiwan:

> Many small lenders, unfortunately, have no basis for their choice of borrowers, other than rumor or external appearances. Thus at one time there was much talk about the favorable future of the textile industry and many lenders sought to put their money into textile mills (thereby exacerbating the tendency for overexpansion in this field). Similarly, many lenders considered that the Tang Eng Ironworks was a desirable borrower because the owners gave an expensive wedding party for their son, and because the large smokestacks, bustling activity, and constant expansion gave an appearance of prosperity which later turned out to be deceptive.[19]

Educating private financiers in sensible ways of evaluating applications and assisting them with appropriate information can do much to lower lending costs. Identifying interested borrowers is expensive where the smallness of operations, laws, bargaining strategy, or other factors keep the lender from publicizing his operations. Where an industrial extension service exists

[18] Salomon J. Flink, *Equity Financing of Small Manufacturing Companies in New Jersey,* Rutgers—The State University, for the New Jersey Department of Conservation and Economic Development, Trenton, N.J., 1962. Flink is referring to owner-managed companies of the general size range that makes public stock issues of less than $300,000.

[19] *Taiwan's Turning Point,* p. 64.

which can draw larger numbers of promising applicants to financiers' attention, this can help to lower lending costs.[20]

An advisory service which undertakes to bring together mutually satisfactory partnerships will often be of special value. The owners of small enterprises, particularly in less-developed countries, often have only part of the knowledge and part of the finances needed for a successful venture. They thus need to join in partnerships with others having complementary skills and funds.

The problem is not always one of simply enlarging capabilities by joining two fairly similar entrepreneurs with comparable contributions to make to the joint venture. It is often necessary to link persons who have the ambition and knowledge to launch enterprises but very little finance with others who have funds or access to them but very little entrepreneurial capacity. These groups are frequently further separated by different social and educational backgrounds. Each may rightly feel that the other has a unique power over the enterprise and may fear that the power might be misused in a partnership. In most less-developed countries, there is a group of wealthy persons who, as a result of their long landed-gentry status, possess few entrepreneurial qualifications and little contact with persons outside their own small social group; at the same time, there are usually immigrant groups, often of Levantine, Chinese, Indian, or European extraction, who by their international connections, culture, and personal drive to advance can productively utilize more funds than they possess, but who tend to be socially isolated from other sources of finance. The difficult but important task that needs to be undertaken in these cases is to find means by which the funds of one and the entrepreneurial abilities of the other can be combined in one enterprise on a basis satisfactory to both.

Partnerships within families are more readily formed and more lasting than other types, because family and community ethics and pressures provide a favorable framework for resolving differences. A substitute for these is needed in circumstances where these cannot be drawn on. Legal regulation of partnerships is of some value, but its limitation should be recognized; litigation of differences is too expensive for small enterprises, and the laws do not provide much protection where most entrepreneurs have little understanding of their provisions. An industrial advisory service which is impartial and well versed on aspects of industrial ventures might, however, through information, advice, and mediation do much to facilitate sound partnership arrangements. Some countries have begun to provide services along these lines for fairly large ventures involving foreign partners as

[20] Some financiers who have formed small business investment companies in the United States have reported that the main attraction of this arrangement was that the SBIC organizational form gave the private financier publicity and public status sufficient to attract worthy applicants, whereas good applicants tended not to know and to be suspicious of individual financiers.

shareholders, but little attention has yet been given to facilitating domestic partnerships.

In stressing the value and possibility of encouraging partnerships, however, we do not imply that the task will be easy or that any two persons having complementary resources and abilities, even of the same social background, should necessarily be encouraged to form partnerships. At least a part of the entrepreneur's usual aversion to partnerships is well based. An example from Nigeria illustrates the problem of some partnerships everywhere:

> Distrust of other businessmen is the most important block to the pooling of experience and resources by Nigerians in business. "If three people join and incorporate a business, one of them will be a crook." This statement by an Enugu chemist typifies the feelings widespread in much of Africa today. . . . The Enugu businessman provides an example of the situation in which many African entrepreneurs find themselves. In each case the firm's difficulties arose from dishonesty: each experience served to further underline the man's wariness in entering into business relations with others.[21]

McCrory reports similar problems in India:

> The partnership, where the craftsman's skill and the merchant's capital might normally be expected to meet in small industry, does not appear to work. It has an exceedingly bad name among craftsmen. It is distrusted by the merchants. . . .
>
> On general testimony, partnerships as such are said to work badly "because people just don't trust each other." Nor do they find it easy, it would seem, to resolve differences of opinion between the partners except by dissolution of the partnership.[22]

The author has heard many similar accounts of ill-matched partnerships leading to the failure of the business or the exploitation of one partner by the other. On the other hand, a great many cases of successful partnerships could also be cited, some involving partners of very different social and cultural backgrounds. A great many partnerships clearly fail, but this is not to say that this needs to be so.[23] Selectivity in the partnerships that are encouraged as well as provision of sound partnership planning advice and impartial mediation should encourage the more rapid formation of partnerships of a fruitful and durable type.

---

[21] Nyhart, "Notes on Enterprise in Africa," Harvard University, Center for International Affairs, Cambridge, Mass., 1961, pp. 26, 27. (Mimeographed.) A survey of Nigerian business also reports general distrust of partnerships. See Sayre P. Schatz and S. I. Edokpayi, "Economic Attitudes of Nigerian Business," reprint no. 1 from *Journal of the Nigerian Economic Society, vol.* IV, no. 3, 1963, p. 262.

[22] McCrory, *op. cit.,* p. 26.

[23] For a discussion of some of the difficult problems which often have to be resolved in partnerships between merchants and craftsmen, see McCrory, *op. cit.,* pp. 26–28.

Interbusiness Finance

Interbusiness credit commonly ranks close in importance to finance from private parties as an external source of small-industry finance in newly developing countries. Yet interbusiness credit does not seem to be nearly as important a source of funds in less developed countries as it is in more industrialized countries.[24] Moreover, as this section will bring out, interbusiness credit in less developed countries tends to be characterized to a lesser degree by some of the major merits interbusiness credit commonly possesses in industrialized countries and to a greater degree by some of the major drawbacks associated with interbusiness finance. This suggests that the full potential of interbusiness credit is far from being realized in less-developed countries. Thus in such countries, measures to stimulate a larger or more productive volume of interbusiness credit may be an important means of improving the financing available for small-industry development.

The General Characteristics of Interbusiness Credit

Interbusiness credit refers to all financing between independent, nonfinancial firms. The most common type is *supplier credit,* particularly credit by suppliers of materials and components.

Open-book credit, which is supplier credit in its simplest and usually cheapest form, is merely the trusting of a customer for payment of goods ordered and shipped. The period is usually short, sometimes a matter of days, and allows for the time involved in transmitting the goods, the bill, and the payment.

More formal arrangements are sometimes made involving trade acceptances, trust receipts, or notes signed by the recipient. Much greater use is made of these arrrangements and less use is made of open-book credit in developing countries than in more industrialized ones. The credit period varies greatly, usually allowing time to cover the period of transfer, but may extend beyond this to include the normal period the goods will be carried in inventory, or even longer.

A supplier may also send goods on consignment where he, in effect,

---

[24] These comparisons are necessarily based on impressions from field experience, since there have been few national and no international comparative quantitative studies to the author's knowledge. The following data are illustrative of the general importance of interbusiness credit. A 1962 survey in Colombia found that nearly half of the manufacturers with assets less than $50,000 and over three-fourths of larger enterprises received some supplier financing. [*Small and Medium Industry in Colombia's Development,* report of an inquiry organized by the Banco Popular, aided by a team of consultants from Stanford Research Institute, Banco Popular, Bogotá, 1962 (English and Spanish editions), p. 111.] Supplier credit was found to be somewhat less common and much more expensive in Brazil. (See Davenport, *Financing Small and Medium Manufacturing Enterprises in Latin America, op. cit.,* Chap 4. Interbusiness credit in India is discussed in Chap. 2, and in Japan in Chap. 13.)

bears all the risk as well as the financing costs of the period goods are in transfer and inventory.

Credit by equipment suppliers is usually distinguished from normal supplier credit by a longer period of credit, ranging up to several years. Thus, although the volume of such credit is much smaller than that for materials and components, it is of special importance. Arrangements for equipment credit are typically quite different from credit for materials and components. Equipment is usually provided under installment contract or lease arrangements. Installment sales usually require a minimum down payment of around one-third to one-fourth of the amount with monthly installments for the balance over a period ordinarily not in excess of one-fourth of the estimated life of the equipment. The financing period is thus commonly as short at two to three years, although it may extend up to four or five years or more in some cases. The terms of equipment financing vary greatly around these typical terms, depending on such factors as the characteristics of the equipment, state of competition, earning prospects of the customer, and the general credit conditions. In less-developed countries, supplier equipment credit to small firms is much less common than in more industrialized countries and the terms less favorable. In northeast Brazil, only one-fifth of the firms surveyed reported having received equipment on supplier credit and, in most cases, for periods of only 5 to 10 months.[25] In Nigeria, the repayment period for equipment credit from suppliers is reported as one to three years.[26] In many other countries, particularly those where equipment is largely imported, supplier credit is virtually unavailable to smaller firms.

Interbusiness finance may also take the form of direct loans or advances between two enterprises or of guarantees by one on loans to the second from third parties. Such financing is usually extended by customers rather than by suppliers, and, in the former case, is commonly tied to a contract for the delivery of future production. Financing of suppliers by customers is much less common than supplier credit.[27]

[25] See Davenport, op. cit., chap. 4. For a detailed discussion of equipment financing in the United States based on an investigation in 1940 but still generally valid, see Raymond Saulnier and Neil H. Jacoby, Financing Equipment for Financial and Industrial Enterprise, National Bureau of Economic Research, Haddon Craftsmen, Inc., Scranton, Pa., 1944.

[26] Indigenous Industry in Nigeria Robert R. Nathan Associates, Inc., Washington, D.C., 1964, p. 27. Much shorter periods were indicated in an earlier report: Report of the Advisory Committee on Aids to African Business, Federation of Nigeria, Lagos, 1959, p. 53.

[27] In the United States, where such services are generally more common than in most countries, a survey of 275 large corporations indicated that less than one in five extended credit to small suppliers and usually in very limited amounts, whereas all of them extended credit to customers. Federal Reserve System, op. cit., pp. 484, 493.

Equity financing is another type of interbusiness finance sometimes extended to an independent enterprise by suppliers, particularly in the case of equipment, and occasionally by customers. Where the recipient is genuinely independent, the share of equity provided by individual sources of this type will usually be relatively small and commonly in exchange for nonvoting preference shares.

Besides financial relationships between independent firms, financing is sometimes combined with other interbusiness relationships which together are so extensive, exclusive, long-term, or otherwise of a quality that the smaller firm, although nominally independent, is basically controlled by the larger one. While all interbusiness relationships involve some loss of freedom by one or both firms, the nature of the relationship tends to be fundamentally different when the loss of freedom is great and one-sided. In the latter case, interbusiness credit ceases to be so much a means by which recipients may finance their growth as a means by which the extender can control, to his own advantage, the business policies of the recipient. One of the major deficiencies of the interbusiness credit that is available in less-developed countries, particularly between large and small firms, is that it frequently tends to be employed in a way which weakens the independence of small firms. As a result, it often cripples rather than facilitates the realization of the growth potential of small firms.

Factors Encouraging the Growth of Interbusiness Credit

Through these various types of interbusiness financing, but primarily through the simplest type, open-book credit, business firms have become more important than banks as a source of finance to other business enterprises in at least one industrialized country, the United States. The total interbusiness credit extended in the United States in 1962 is estimated to amount to $112 billions, or more than twice the volume of bank credit.[28] United States manufacturing corporations with assets of less than $250,000 obtained about 40 percent of their external credit, or 20 percent of their total resources, from interbusiness finance. This is about three times the proportion of the finance which these corporations obtain from banking sources.[29] Why and how they have become so in a country with an advanced and flexible banking system merits some explanation. An understanding of this will help clarify the extent and the ways in which interbusiness finance might be improved in other countries.

[28] Martin H. Seiden, *The Quality of Trade Credit,* National Bureau of Economic Research, Occasional Paper 87, 1964, p. 10. See also Robert T. Hungate, *Interbusiness Financing: Economic Implications for Small Business,* Small Business Administration, Washington, D.C., 1962, p. 14.

[29] See Federal Trade Commission-Security and Exchange Commission, *Quarterly Financial Report for Manufacturing Corporations;* data are for 1958, the latest year for which data for the indicated scales have been published.

Interbusiness financing is, for the most part, not thought of as a financing operation by the source, but as an inseparable or sometimes unintentional part of marketing. As one prominent United States manufacturer has stated: "To us, credit is a sales tool. We provide it because we must. In doing so, it is neither our wish nor purpose to compete with banks."[30] It is thus a product of competition, custom, and the state of some customers' finances—maximizing sales requires in many cases shipping the goods first and waiting for payment. Once this general procedure is set in motion, the supplier is to some degree at the mercy of the buyer as to how long a period of credit this may be. He can, of course, establish financial penalties for delays, sue, or refuse future orders except for cash. The first however, is not always effective as a credit control, the second is costly, and the third may result in serious loss of customers. The weakness of cash discounts as a curb on payment delays is illustrated by the comment of an Israeli manufacturer on the subject: "My customers would take the discount, and insist on credit anyhow."[31]

The state of competition is a major factor influencing the extent to which a supplier will grant credit. It depends not only on how much competition there is but the kind of competition. Credit competition is often preferred to price competition, since terms can be more easily concealed from competitors. Also, it enables discreet favoring of some customers over others.[32] It tends to be extended by well-financed firms, particularly where their competitors are unable to extend a similar service. Also, it tends to be extended when this is an important consideration to a major group of potential customers.

There are a variety of other reasons which help to account for the large volume of interbusiness finance in the United States. Essentially these are: (1) the presence of an unfulfilled demand for finance by creditworthy firms, (2) the presence of firms with sufficient internal resources and easy access to external finance that they can extend financing with little strain on their own financial resources, (3) the ability of some firms to extend credit to their customers on a more economical basis than banks can achieve, (4) more aggressive promotion of financing services by firms extending

[30] Speech by the president of Deere & Company to the American Bankers Association in 1958, cited in Federal Reserve System, *op. cit.,* p. 364.

[31] Tenenbaum, *Israel's Industrial Finances: A Second Look,* p. 82. A similar view was expressed by numerous manufacturers interviewed in field work in Latin American countries. Controlling customers' use of interbusiness finance is somewhat less difficult in the United States, where credit rating services are widespread and heavily relied upon. A firm's credit rating is impaired by a reputation as a "slow payer," or even by a record of failing to take discounts. The effect of this on the general availability of credit to the firm is sufficient that most firms in the United States do not abuse supplier credit privileges.

[32] For an excellent brief statement of this use of interbusiness credit, see Federal Reserve System, *op. cit.,* p. 26.

interbusiness finance than by banks, and (5) a desire for this form of finance by some firms having alternative sources. These may be briefly elaborated.

Many firms which are creditworthy cannot readily demonstrate this fact to banks. The latter tend to reject requests from applicants whose credit-worthiness cannot be established by standard low-cost screening methods. For example, growing firms may be rejected because they have not kept conventional bank liquidity standards; new firms may be rejected because they have no past credit record. At the same time, there are often other well-financed firms which are interested in selling their products to, among others, firms of the above types with unfulfilled credit needs.

Suppliers, by their relationship to customers, are in a position to screen at little special cost the creditworthiness of customers whom banks may not be willing to investigate. Suppliers can do this by gradually building up such information through their sales activities. The credit-evaluation cost to the supplier is thus small, the major part of it being a prepaid byproduct of sales activity. Firms unable to obtain bank credit may also be served by suppliers, because suppliers can better afford and are commonly willing to accept a higher degree of risk.[33]

Threats of recession, which set bankers to eliminating riskier clients from their portfolio, set suppliers to worrying about stimulating sales. Losses on credit to customers may be less serious—at least to the department that incurs them—than the alternative of losses due to low sales. Similarly, tight credit, which causes banks to increase their rejections, brings increased customer demands on suppliers for credit, which suppliers are less in a position than banks to refuse. Further, what will constitute losses to a bank may not be losses in the same degree to a supplier. The latter, by the nature of his organization, may be able to repossess and resell materials or equipment on which the credit was extended at a smaller loss than could the bank. For the same reason, he may be in regular direct contact with the customer and may be able to help prevent or avoid the conse-quences of developing difficulties better than a bank.[34]

Farsighted large firms, finding their expansion blocked by the failure

[33] For a comparison of the relative rewards to be obtained by banks and suppliers in risk taking in the United States, see Pearson Hunt et al., *Basic Business Finance*, Richard D. Irwin, Inc., Homewood, Ill., 1961, pp. 180, 182. The loss ratio on credit suffered by suppliers in the United States is many times higher than that of banks, being about 1.6 percent of the volume of credit outstanding in 1960, and over 1 percent in all but one year in the preceding decade. There is, however, a wide variation between enterprises. The above loss ratio does not take into account expense incurred in collecting from delinquent or defaulting debtors. See Seiden, *op. cit.*, p. 17.

[34] A great many suppliers, of course, do not have direct contacts with at least some of their customers and thus may be less informed about these customers' creditworthiness than banks are. We refer here only to those who have, or for sales reasons should have, staff regularly calling upon customers.

of small suppliers or customers to grow or modernize, sometimes actively promote the use of finance and other credit assistance to encourage the more promising of them to expand. One of the classic cases of this type has been the activity of Sears, Roebuck and Company in encouraging the local manufacturing of products in Mexico and other countries where their distribution operations have been restricted by the cost or unavailability of imports and the inadequate quality and supply of local products. Another is the activity of large United States automobile manufacturers in assisting the establishment of able distributors of their products. A common practice has been for the automobile company to put up as much as three-fourths of the approximately $100,000 required to operate a dealership; the dealer supplies the remainder with the right—and often the obligation—to buy out the total equity from the company from profits.[35] A further example of farsighted promotion of interbusiness finance is the case of suppliers of basic materials, such as steel, who sometimes not only extend credit on materials which they supply, but also assist customers to obtain credit for equipment processing their materials.[36]

Interbusiness finance also seems to have spread because many business enterprises prefer it to bank finance, at least for some purposes. An important reason for this is that entrepreneurs, particularly in small firms, are reluctant to undertake the planning and positive action required to get bank loans when supplier credit can be obtained simply by not paying bills. This reluctance in some cases may be merely a lack of initiative or planning ability or a lack of time and resources to plan. In some cases, the greater difference in the social or professional background of bankers and entrepreneurs than between the latter and their suppliers may be an important psychological factor. This is often intensified by the difference in screening methods: the supplier tends to ask fewer questions because of his greater understanding and direct knowledge of the business, his continuous contact with it, and his reluctance to offend the customer; he is often assisted in being discreet by his ability to get information from his clients' bankers. The banker, on the other hand, often lacks the specialized knowledge needed to understand the applicant's business and thus feels the need for very detailed information in order to evaluate creditworthiness; moreover, in order to save time he may open his investigation by a questionnaire which in effect seeks to extract a complete confession from the applicant of possible financing dangers. As a result, enterprises attaching a great importance to business secrecy tend to feel more comfortable dealing with suppliers.

[35] Chrysler, which has had more difficulty in obtaining suitable dealers, has accepted new dealers who put up as little as $5,000 or about 5 percent of the initial finance required. *Business Week*, August 18, 1962, pp. 54–56. See also Federal Reserve System, *op. cit.*, pp. 119, 492.

[36] See case study of steel industry in Hungate, *op. cit.*, pp. 130ff.

A further reason why firms often prefer supplier finance is that it tends to foster a greater interest by the supplier in their success. Suppliers are sometimes in a position to extend valuable informational assistance and will often do so at no cost, whereas financial institutions are rarely so equipped. The supplier's capacity to supply assistance arises in part from his experience with his product; an aggressive supplier will build up a great deal of knowledge about everything related to his product, particularly on technical and marketing matters relating to its use. He is often in direct contact with a wide variety of customers in the same industry and by this comparative view tends to be aware of what the latest and most success- ful methods are.[37] If he is a medium or large manufacturer, he often has better resources than banks for solving technical and management prob- lems.[38] Sales interest alone may stimulate a supplier to extend informational assistance to customers, although where financing is extended he tends to know more about his customers and to have a greater vested interest in seeing that their operations are profitable.[39]

Merits of Interbusiness Finance

Many of the merits of a good interbusiness credit system have been suggested by the preceding discussion. Some enterprises which banks find it very difficult to finance can be relatively easily financed by suppliers or customers. Moreover, many enterprises, including some with access to

[37] A good example of the capacity of a supplier to assist his clients through his knowledge of a wide variety of firms is the report of an automobile dealer: "If I turn in a statement showing I lost money, Chevrolet sends down a team of experts immediately—and automatically—to find out why. They want me to grow and earn money." (*Business Week,* Aug. 24, 1963, p. 96.) Assistance of this type is also extended to clients who are manufacturers rather than distributors, but distributors appear to be far better served.

[38] The capabilities of suppliers as a source of technical information is testified to by the frequency with which customers depend upon them for such assistance. An OEEC survey on how firms solve problems when they are unable to solve them internally found suppliers as a body were the most frequently named source of assistance in all countries. In the United States, the figure was 58 percent, Germany 58 percent, United Kingdom and Norway, 50 percent, Austria 36 percent, Italy 24 percent, and Belgium 21 percent (OEEC/EPA, *Technical Information and the Smaller Firm,* Oct., 1958, p. 47). For examples of the great variety of assistance extended by suppliers, which ranges from simple information to specific research, see OEEC/EPA, *Technical Services to the Smaller Firm by Basic Suppliers,* 1960, p. 14. See *ibid.,* pp. 19ff.

[39] Buyers of "turnkey plants" from foreign suppliers, for example, appear to receive rather more guidance on plant installations and operations where the supplier is to be paid out of the profit of future years. An example of how credit relationships stimulate supplier assistance is the establishment by American Machine and Foundry Company of a consulting service for clients using its bowling equipment on a lease or installment purchase basis in response to the increasing difficulty of clients in maintaining profits (see *Business Week,* Jan. 12, 1963, p. 58).

bank finance, find that some access to interbusiness finance is helpful in facilitating quick small changes in their net credit position. It adds to the flexibility of a firm's finances, simplifies planning, and enables greater risk taking. Because it permits a firm to change its credit position by a very small amount for a very short period of time, it is, under some circumstances, the most economical source of finance, even though the rate of interest charged may exceed that of alternative sources with less-flexible lending procedures. A firm must consider not only the interest rates, but also the period through which it must maintain credit outstanding and indirect costs, such as time spent preparing the application. Moreover, interbusiness finance is often—although not always—a more dependable source, since credit decisions are based on considerations less likely than bank financing to be affected by temporary difficulties of the firm or changes in business conditions. This is of particular importance since small firms tend to be affected first and most severely by tightening of bank credit, making banks a risky source of finance, especially where sharp changes in bank credit availability are common.[40]

Interbusiness equipment finance is of special importance where it is extended on a medium-term basis. In many countries, banks and other institutions are often not prepared to make this type of loan, particularly on the security of machinery and for relatively small amounts of funds. Equipment-supplier credit in its most developed state meets just such needs.[41] Equipment financing reduces the initial capital outlay required of an entrepreneur and diminishes his risks. It is therefore of special value to new and growing enterprises where risk and size of capital requirement are often major obstacles.[42]

[40] Hungate's study of interbusiness financing (*op. cit.*, p. 30) concludes:

The data gives [sic] us reason to conclude that interbusiness financing is counter-cyclical to some degree in making credit available during periods of business slump, when commercial sources of credit tend to assume the conservative viewpoint and act to diminish the supply. In this situation, interbusiness financing complements monetary policy, for both are actively striving to offer more credit. On the other hand, when monetary policy is set in motion to put on the brakes during periods of prosperity and the credit supply declines due to a period of tight money, interbusiness financing opposes monetary policy and once again increases in volume to meet the need created by the shortage in credit. In this latter situation, interbusiness financing acts to relieve some of this monetary pressure and equalize its effects by giving the small businessman a source of funds that will fill the resultant gap.

[41] A survey of 169 United States equipment manufacturers and distributors revealed that in the case of over 50 percent of these, most sales on installment contracts amounted to less than $1,000, and in the case of another, 30 percent to between $1,000 and $5,000. (Saulnier and Jacoby, *op. cit.*, p. 5.)

[42] The importance of this type of financing is brought out by a study in the United Kingdom showing that over 50 percent of the firms having a high rate of growth used hire-purchase finance. In the case of declining firms, on the other

In less-developed countries, interbusiness credit has a special importance because better sources simply are not available. As McCrory observed in his investigation of the use of such financing by small machine industries in India:

> Whatever the defects of the wholesale trader, however unsatisfactory and undependable he may be as a source of credit and finance, he has been to date the Chopur craftsman's *only* source. Beyond this, the merchant middleman is the only person performing, for the small entrepreneur, a host of other necessary service functions that in other countries, perhaps in other parts of India, are performed by the local banker, trade associations and journals, technical societies and Government agencies.[43]

Limitations of Interbusiness Financing

Among the disadvantages of interbusiness finance, the most common one is a high cost to the recipient. Interbusiness credit, however, is not always costly and sometimes involves no direct costs at all. It is common to offer a discount for cash payment and to allow payment within a short period after shipment to be treated as cash; credit during this period is thus free of cost. In the case of seasonal products, the period of free credit for shipments made in advance of the main season may be as much as several months.

Beyond such periods, interbusiness credit tends to be available only at relatively high interest rates not only in newly developing countries, but also in more advanced ones. In the United States, open-book credit is commonly offered up to 30 to 60 days, and sometimes longer, subject to the loss of the cash discount. The effective interest cost for credit beyond the cash period is commonly higher than bank rates, and, where suppliers wish to discourage such credit, may be much higher. It is not uncommon for terms to require payment within 30 to 60 days, with a cash discount of 2 percent if paid within 10 days; the implicit interest rate in these cases would be over 14 percent per annum for the last 50 days where payment is required in 60 days and over 36 percent per annum for the last 20 days of the credit period where payment is required within 30 days.[44]

Considering the usual charges for supplier credit in United States, a

---

hand, less than one-fourth used hire-purchase. *Hire-purchase* is the British term for a form of installment finance which may be extended by suppliers or by special finance companies, often with recourse to suppliers in case of collection difficulties. (See James Bates, "Hire-purchase in Small Manufacturing Business," *Bankers' Magazine,* September, 1957, pp. 275–279.)

[43] James T. McCrory, *op. cit.,* p. 24.

[44] A Federal Reserve Bank survey found discounts by suppliers ranged from one-half of 1 percent for some primary metal products to as high as 8 percent in the apparel industry, but the most common discount was 2 percent. The credit period also varied greatly, although 30 days was typical. Federal Reserve System, *op. cit.,* p. 486.

charge of 1 to 2 percent per month for supplier credit in a country such as Brazil is surprising only in its close comparability to the lending rates of banks in Brazil.[45] While there is very little information on the cost of supplier credit in developing countries, the situation in many countries may not be greatly different from that in Brazil.[46] Fairly high rates are to be expected. It is particularly important to suppliers in countries where there is a general shortage of finance to set credit limits and some penalty rates to prevent unexpected increases in credit demands by customers. Even for a normal period, where some financing is a part of the regular service to customers, rates higher than bank rates may be essential to ease the cost of the service in view of the higher risks such financing may involve.

Besides the formal charges for credit, another cost may be involved—a higher price for the product than the price of alternative products. Antitrust laws, public opinion, standard, publicly known prices, and the general availability of credit from other sources discourages major abuses of this type in the United States, although the liberality of credit from some particular suppliers may enable them to obtain somewhat higher prices than their competitors. In less developed countries where these restraining influences on concealing the charges for supplier credit in the price of the products purchased are not generally operative, the hidden charges may be much greater.

Interbusiness sources more frequently extend credit to unsound business ventures than banks normally do, which is another drawback to this credit channel. Although suppliers of interbusiness credit undoubtfully prefer sound and prosperous clients, the financing of possibly unsound enterprises may be worth risking where the credit losses are well guarded against by collateral. Credit extension is normally a minor activity of business enterprises, sometimes casually administered, and the urge to expand sales may outweigh sound credit considerations. Such credit practices may have an undesirable effect on the general economy during business downturns and dissipate national resources in unsound ventures.

In less industrialized countries it is widely believed, although not easily verified, that interbusiness credit is liberally extended by some sources for the purpose of enlarging the recipient's dependency on the supplier and of enabling the latter to take over or to otherwise exploit the recipient

[45] See Davenport, op. cit., chap 4.

[46] A study in Nigeria, however, reports that it is not unusual for hire-purchase contracts on equipment to charge £150 to £200 in interest per £1000 on loans repayable within 12 months. This would be equivalent to 2.5 to 3.3 percent per month. Indigenous Industry in Nigeria, Robert R. Nathan Associates, Inc., Washington, D.C., 1964, p. 31. The author's survey of small manufacturers in Colombia in 1962 indicated that discounts of 3 to 5 percent for cash within 10 days were commonly offered but not often taken by customers; in a few cases, discounts as high as 10 percent were offered, and these reportedly were successful in inducing most, but not all, customers to pay cash.

in time of weakness.[47] Many cases were observed in field work where suppliers had taken over firms because of interbusiness debts. The circumstances occasionally suggested that financing was deliberately and successfully used as an instrument to capture weak firms, but the proportion of such cases, out of the total contacted, was very small. Such use of interbusiness credit may nevertheless be a significant threat to small entrepreneurs, particularly when they are unable to correctly appraise their financial needs or financing costs.[48] Bank credit, which can be more easily regulated against such malpractices, thus may be preferable to interbusiness finance in some circumstances.

The possible costs and risks of heavy and exclusive dependence upon another firm apply not only to interbusiness finance, but also to all fundamental interbusiness relationships. Thus, an exclusive dependence by a firm on a particular supplier or customer for key materials or sales may enable the latter, whether or not he extends financing, to exploit the firm. Indeed, in such cases the financing may flow from the dependent to the dominant firm, this being another aspect of the exploitation.[49] Typically, however, the flow of finance is in the other direction, simply because firms in a dependent position usually lack the financial resources to be a significant source of finance. The special importance of interbusiness finance in *dominant-dependent* types of interbusiness relationships is that when finance is extended by the dominant to the dependent firm, it may compound an already serious dependency and eliminate a previous possibility of the weaker firm regaining independence.

Dominant-dependent types of interbusiness relationships are often regarded as undesirable on the grounds of social justice, since the dominant firms tend to absorb most of the benefits from the relationship. Where the dominant firm is shortsighted, it may also prevent the dependent firm from accruing the necessary funds to achieve improvements, to lower production costs, or to improve quality. The controlling firm in an interbusiness relationship, however, is not always—and need not be—shortsighted in this way. In England, for example, the retailing chain of Marks and Spencer,

---

[47] See International Labour Office, *Services for Small-scale Industry*, Geneva, 1961, p. 116; Baljit Singh, *The Economics of Small-scale Industries*, Asia Publishing House, Bombay and New York, 1961; and Martin S. Klein, *African Trade in Kenya*, United Research Inc., Cambridge, Mass., 1962.

[48] Such problems are not unknown in more industrialized countries although, again, it would be difficult to establish that credit policies were designed to exploit the weakness of smaller firms. Hungate (*op. cit.*, p. 153), for example, comments: "Extensive financing, particularly in low profit margin situations, can be a distinct disservice to the small businessman involved. If this financing makes entry into the industry very easy, all kinds of unqualified people will be attracted who will, in the normal course of business turnover, lose whatever equity they put into the business. . . . In essence, the larger supplier in this case is buying customers with financing and making a profit out of the business failures of others."

[49] See the problem in Japan, discussed in Chap. 13.

Ltd., is reported to obtain its merchandize by contracts with producers which specify "every production detail. . . . Thus M & S ties its suppliers' hands up tight" and allows "a profit margin admittedly lower than normal." In return, however, M & S offers a guaranteed market and the assistance of its 300-man Technical Service Group free of cost.[50] Japan has had some success in reducing undesirable characteristics of dominant-dependent types of interbusiness relationships, while utilizing them as a channel for increasing financial and technical assistance to smaller enterprises.[51]

A further possible drawback to interbusiness finance is that it may become an important element in monetary expansion outside the direct control of the monetary authorities. Credit extension by one firm creates pressure for credit extension by other firms. A shift of emphasis in competition from prices to credit terms under inflationary conditions could adversely affect stabilization measures. It may also have the undesirable effect of eliminating constructive competition in industries in which there are one or two enterprises capable of extending credit on liberal terms, while other equally efficient—although often smaller—firms in the industry lack the financial resources to compete on this basis.

The usefulness of interbusiness credit as a means of financing small-industry development is limited in other ways besides its susceptibility to the above-cited problems. It is not easily channeled to some uses or types of enterprise. For example, it can easily be directed to firms needing to purchase raw materials but not to firms that need funds principally to employ labor or to hire professional services. In general, where supplier credit for equipment is available and loans for working capital are not, the tendency will be to substitute machines for labor. The problem of improving interbusiness credit is also more difficult for some types of enterprises than for others, because of a less favorable general structure of business relationships characteristic of that type of enterprise. Thus clothing manufacturers often receive an important part of their funds from interbusiness financing, whereas fruit and vegetable canners commonly do not.[52]

Measures to Improve Interbusiness Financing

In many less-developed countries, improving interbusiness finance is made difficult by fundamental conditions which are not easily altered. Whereas direct interbusiness relations between manufacturers of equipment and basic materials and independent customers often provide the best base for productive types of interbusiness financing, these possibilities are limited in many countries by the dependence on imports for many types of equipment and

[50] *Business Week,* Sept. 22, 1962, p. 118.

[51] See Chap. 13.

[52] Further illustrations of how the availability of interbusiness credit tends to vary from industry to industry is given in Chap. 13 and also in Charles L. Merwin, *Financing Small Corporations in Five Manufacturing Industries, 1926–1936,* National Bureau of Economics Research, New York, 1942, p. 68.

materials. The business structure and general business environment and attitude in less developed countries are often not conducive to close business relations between independent firms having a supplier-customer relationship. Prices may be customarily negotiated on a case-by-case basis, so that those desiring interbusiness credit cannot easily evaluate interbusiness credit terms. Even large concerns may not have adequate staff to permit them to combine the extension of informational assistance with interbusiness finance. Credit rating services to assist firms in extending credit are often unavailable. Competitive sources of finance to serve as a regulator on interbusiness finance may be limited by the general shortage of finance and inadequacies of other institutional arrangements. Although, for these reasons, many of the possible improvements in interbusiness financing can be achieved only gradually and through long-term efforts, there are some institutional changes which can be helpful in bringing about more immediate improvements.

Interbusiness finance usually depends in part upon banks. Thus, appropriate bank credit policies may influence the allocation of interbusiness credit. Bank policies on the discount of trade bills often need improvement. In some countries, banks are not accustomed to extended credit against bills. In others, there are sometimes policies of not accepting bills of over 30 days or some other period which may not permit adequate supplier credit to cover shipping time for some enterprises but may be more than adequate for shipping and inventory purposes for others.[53] The relatively good access to credit of small enterprises in Japan is in part explained by a well-developed system of interbusiness credit on the basis of bills and of bank lending against the security of such bills.[54]

The elimination of transaction taxes and documentation duties may be important in facilitating the development of supplier credit. Where these taxes are substantial but not well enforced, the practice of cash transactions, through which these taxes may safely be evaded, may impede the development of trade acceptances and other types of supplier credit. Lack of credit information and other problems tend to retard the development of open-book credit in many countries, so that encouraging trade acceptances is often important.[55]

Measures to encourage establishment of nondiscriminatory pricing practices may also be helpful. Where prices of products are reasonably standard to all customers and publicly known, users of interbusiness credit are much less likely to be deceived as to the real costs involved.

[53] For an example of this problem in Brazil, see Davenport, *op. cit.*, chap. 4.
[54] See Chap. 13.
[55] An equivalent of open-book credit—sales against postdated checks—has developed in Taiwan and Israel, despite the impeding conditions of less-developed countries, and despite even legislation to curb this credit practice (see Tenenbaum, *Taiwan's Turning Point*, p. 73 and *Israel's Industrial Finances*, pp. 55–59). This form of credit is also used to some extent in several Latin American countries, but it meets only a minor part of the supplier credit need.

Special credit and other incentives may be used to induce larger companies to increase both their financial and technical assistance to smaller firms. There is often a need to educate suppliers concerning the advantage which they may derive from extending finance. Bills which are interest-bearing and readily discounted as trade acceptances and installment papers often provide a good form of liquid reserves which suppliers do not always fully appreciate. Surveys may be useful to demonstrate to large companies the extent of markets which can be tapped by improving arrangements for customer financing. Studies indicating the cost and returns to suppliers in extending finance may help induce companies to consider extending useful forms of supplier credit.

Improving bank and finance company services so that firms extending interbusiness credit may rely on specialized institutional assistance in such matters as credit information and routine procedures for handling the paper work involved is frequently valuable.[56] Encouraging the development of commercial credit insurance may also be useful.[57] The establishment of a good system of interchange of credit information among banks and between banks and suppliers and other sources of credit, so that reliable and inexpensive credit information on most firms in the economy is readily available, may also be needed. Without such specialized services, a great many concerns will not be capable of extending supplier credit to their small-industry customers, even when they have adequate finance.

Providing adequate bank funds to equipment manufacturers so that they can extend medium-term credit to their customers is another useful measure. In many less developed countries, domestic machinery manufacturers are often small or medium-sized firms which have difficulty in obtaining credit for normal production purposes, let alone for the extension credit to customers. Domestic equipment producers may require bank assistance to compete effectively with the terms being offered by foreign suppliers. The manufacturer has often greater motivation than banks to assume the normal risks of equipment financing and to actively promote greater use of credit to add new equipment, but he may require bank support in order to do so.[58]

---

[56] Even large United States companies extending finance to customers, such as motor vehicle manufacturers, have found it advantageous to establish separate companies where specialized financial services can be organized on an efficient basis (see *Business Week,* Nov. 18, 1961, pp. 31–34). Similarly, most equipment suppliers in United States draw on special finance companies to administer the financial aspects of their interbusiness financing transactions, as well as to provide most of the finance, even though the supplier must still normally carry the risk. (See Federal Reserve System, *op. cit.,* p. 27, and Saulnier and Jacoby, *op. cit.,* p. 3.)

[57] For a detailed description of the commercial credit insurance services of one United States finance company, see Clyde W. Phelps, *Commercial Credit Insurance as a Management Tool,* Commercial Credit Corporation, Baltimore, 1961.

[58] A number of countries have started programs in recent years for discounting installment sales bills for equipment, including Brazil and Finland, but no analysis

Small industrialists in lines other than equipment manufacture may in some cases also merit additional bank credit intended to facilitate their extension of credit to customers. Credit extension may be essential in order to widen markets and to permit growth to a more efficient scale. The sale of durable goods, particularly exports, may be especially dependent on credit extension. Before measures of this type are taken, however, studies may need to be made of the extent to which and the circumstances in which extension of credit by small industry is desirable.

Measures facilitating interbusiness technical-assistance relationships can in some cases open the door to improved interbusiness financing. Foreign licensing and patent agreements, for example, are much more easily arranged (particularly in the case of small firms) than foreign finance. Satisfactory licensing arrangements not only enlarge internal resources by improving production and marketing techniques, but also may bring about a relationship on the basis of which foreign finance may be obtained.

In some situations, measures to reduce the need of small factories to extend credit may be an important means of improving their financial position. For example, small factories, particularly in durable consumer goods lines, are often under pressure to match the liberal credit terms offered by better-financed competitors.[59] If the credit periods offered by competitors are excessive from the point of view of sound business practices or of national monetary stability, the most appropriate measure may be to discourage such credit competition through regulating or taxing undesirable types of sales credit. In other cases, excessive credit extension by small enterprises may result from customers—such as government bodies and larger firms—being in a strong bargaining position and delaying payments. Better financing of small industry, conditional upon reduced credit extension, may both aid and encourage small industry to resist pressure from customers for unreasonable credit terms. Also, sometimes arrangements

---

of their operations is yet available. In several countries where supplier credit for equipment is not available because equipment is largely imported, attempts have been made to fill this need by establishing government corporations to buy the equipment from manufacturers or other suppliers and resell it on installment terms to small enterprises. On India's experience, see Chap. 2. On the Burmese program, see Joseph E. Stepanek "Hire-purchase Loans for the Mechanization of Small Industry," *Industrialization and Productivity,* no. 1, April, 1958, pp. 49–55. The Indonesian program is analyzed in great detail by Eric Manning in *The Loan Project for Mechanization of Privately Owned Factories,* United Nations Bureau of Technical Assistance, New York, 1960.

[59] The danger that excessive credit competition may arise when foreign suppliers or other well-financed firms are permitted to make unrestrained use of credit as a sales tool in credit-short economies is well illustrated in Edward A. Tenenbaum, James Taylor, and H. Kirkpatrick, *Helping Honduran Industry: A Diagnostic Study,* Continental-Allied Company, Inc., Washington D.C., 1961, pp. 32–33, and in Tenenbaum, *Israel's Industrial Finances: A Second Look,* pp. 78, 83–89, 175, 180.

can be worked out with banks and such large customers, enabling the small supplier to borrow against such claims. Bringing the nature and the consequences of the problem to the attention of such customers and the general public may often be helpful in reducing delays.[60] Where the "large customer" is a government body, legislation may be necessary to enable banks to lend against claims for goods sold.[61]

Improving the quality of interbusiness finance and related assistance is often as important as increasing the volume. It is difficult in practice to regulate the terms of interbusiness financing. Thus, improvement in the quality of interbusiness credit is primarily dependent upon creating a degree of competition among the main suppliers of interbusiness finance or between these and other sources of finance. In part, this implies widening the sources from which small enterprises can obtain finance and improving the terms available from sources which can be directly regulated to some degree, such as banks. In part this is also an educational task. Advisory assistance on general financial planning can be helpful. Often a firm's difficulties stem not so much from the credit terms or motivation of the supplier as from bad financial management on the part of the recipient that has led to an excessive dependence on or inappropriate use of such finance. Advisory assistance which helps make recipients aware of the costs and other implications of the various alternative sources of finance may also improve their bargaining capacity and thus the terms on which they receive financing.

Improving the quality of interbusiness finance in some cases is as much in the interest of the source of finance as of the recipient, so that education may need to be directed toward both parties. Large companies, for example, often overlook the possibility that relatively simple and low-cost informational assistance may more than pay for itself by reducing credit losses and expanding sales.

Finally, progress in improving interbusiness financing relationships can sometimes be made simply by focusing the attention of the various parties involved on these problems: for example, by joint discussions between members of the shoe and tannery industry, or of the iron and steel machinery and metal-fabricating industries, or of the textile and garment industries. An impartial mediating organization, well equipped with the relevant facts, can often assist the two parties in working out programs for enlarging interbusiness credit and other relationships to their mutual benefit and to the benefit of the general economy.

[60] For Japan's experience with legislation prohibiting large companies from delaying payments due to small subcontractors, see Chap. 13.

[61] The problem of slow collections from government is common in many countries. See Chap. 2 for the problems in India. In Colombia, a firm manufacturing supplies for a government hospital reported payment delays of 5 to 6 months; another selling to a government power company reported delays of 3 months. Similar problems in Nigeria are cited in *Indigenous Industry in Nigeria*, Robert R. Nathan Associates, Inc., Washington, D.C., 1964, p. 33.

Chapter 7
Mobilizing Commercial Banks
and Savings Institutions

Commercial Banks

Commercial banks are the largest source of institutional finance in most countries, regardless of stage development. However, in less-developed countries, commercial banks often do not contribute greatly to the financing of small-factory growth, or at least do not contribute so much as the performance of advanced commercial banks suggests they might, and are not nearly so important as the noninstitutional sources previously discussed.

In Korea, for example, only 27 percent of bank loans outstanding to industry in December, 1961, went to small enterprises, even though these enterprises accounted for about 55 percent of industrial production.[1] In India, the relative neglect of small enterprises by banks is even greater, as has been indicated in Chapter 2. Similar problems confront small enterprises in Puerto Rico, Colombia, and Brazil, although some banks in all these countries provide much more extensive services to small factories than others.[2] The impressions from field work in other countries in Latin America and Asia reinforce the view that commercial banks in a great

---

[1] The Medium Industry Bank, *Annual Report,* 1962, Seoul, Korea, p. 25. The data cover the lending of the Korean Reconstruction Bank as well as of the five commercial banks. As the result of the creation of the Medium Industry Bank, which focuses its services on small enterprises, the share of small enterprises in total bank lending to industry rose to 37 percent in September, 1963. (The Medium Industry Bank, *Quarterly Statistical Review,* October 1963.) *Small industry* is defined as manufacturing enterprises employing between 5 and 100 workers and mining enterprises employing between 5 and 200 workers, in both cases with total assets of less than 20 million won (about US$154,000).

[2] See Chaps. 3 and 12 and R. W. Davenport, *Financing Small and Medium Manufacturing Enterprises in Latin America,* Inter-American Development Bank, Washington, D.C., 1962 (English and Spanish editions).

many developing countries have important potentialities for financing small-factory growth which are not being fully realized.

If the experience of banks in industrialized countries is any guide, then it should be possible for banks in developing countries to contribute more to the financing of small-factory growth. In Japan about one-fourth of their total resources are derived from banks. About four-fifths of such units—as compared with one-fifth in India—make some use of bank finance.[3] In the United States, small manufacturers generally make some use of bank finance but are much less dependent upon it than in Japan. United States manufacturing enterprises with assets of less than $250,000 obtain on the average about 7 percent of their resources from banks, as compared with an average of less than 5 percent for all United States manufacturing enterprises.[4]

The need of less-developed countries is not merely to enlarge the volume of finance extended by banks to small factories, but also to improve the quality of bank services so that the financing extended will have a greater impact on small-factory development. The experience of banks in industrialized countries is suggestive of ways in which both the quality and quantity of bank financing in less-developed countries might be improved. It will therefore be drawn on when it appears appropriate in the following discussion.

Basic Characteristics of Commercial Banks

Two distinguishing characteristics of commercial banks are their high dependence upon deposits as a source of funds and their ability to create checking deposits. A ratio of deposits to capital of 10:1 is not uncommon, and higher ratios prevail in some countries. Commercial banks depend primarily upon demand deposits, but savings and other time deposits are of major importance in a number of countries.

Commercial banks are typically privately owned, although part or complete government ownership of important commercial banks is not uncommon in Europe (e.g. France, Austria) and in less developed countries, (e.g. India, the Philippines, Brazil, and Nicaragua.)

In practically all countries, commercial banks have various public responsibilities and are subject to special regulations. Regulations have been directed primarily toward protecting the general public as depositors, maintaining monetary stability through influencing commercial banks' activity, or protecting borrowers from "usurious" lending rates or from the misuse by banks of their fiduciary position. In recent years, increasing stress in

[3] See Chap. 13.

[4] FTC-SEC, *Quarterly Financial Report for Manufacturing Corporations*, Fourth Quarter, 1958, p. 23. The relatively low dependence on bank credit of United States manufacturers generally is explained by the relative ease with which they can obtain funds from other sources.

regulatory efforts has been placed on banks' responsibility to serve equally and impartially all members of the community requiring financial services, or even to give special attention to segments unable to meet standard qualifications. Commercial banks have not, for the most part, been given public responsibility for allocating loans on the basis of development criteria, other than those relating to monetary conditions, although experimentation in this direction has begun in some countries.

Commercial banking principles at one time prescribed that banks engage only in extending short-term, self-liquidating loans. Although the concepts of commercial banking have greatly changed since, bank legislation and tradition in many countries still restrict commercial bank lending to the discount of trade bills or other well-secured short-term loans. In some of the more advanced countries, banks have greatly expanded their forms of lending, increasing their ability to serve the diverse needs of industrial enterprises. Acceptable security has been enlarged to include real estate, industrial buildings, equipment, inventories stored on the firm's premises as well as in special warehouses, and guarantees by other creditworthy individuals or organizations. Unsecured lending has long been important in the United States, depending heavily upon bankers' judgment of the character and capabilities of borrowers and, in recent decades, also upon detailed analysis of a firm's financial record.[5] Other important forms of credit sometimes extended by commercial banks are lines of credit under which the bank agrees in advance to extend credit up to a certain amount during the client's main borrowing season or some longer period. This is of great value in diminishing an important business uncertainty—the availability of additional funds if needed—and in facilitating business planning.

In addition to short-term financing, commercial banks have entered into financing for longer periods. In most countries commercial banks have in practice allowed some borrowers to renew short-term loans repeatedly or to remain permanently in debt to commercial banks by shifting their short-term obligations between several banks. *Term loans* (loans for a period of over one year) are of increasing importance in a number of countries. In the United States, where term lending by commercial banks first became important, term loans now constitute a major part of commercial bank loans and extend in some degree to small as well as large enterprises.[6]

[5] See Neil H. Jacoby and Raymond J. Saulnier, *Business Finance and Banking,* (Financial Research Program, National Bureau of Economic Research, E. L. Hildreth and Company, 1947) for the unique background of United States banking which facilitated the adoption of advanced financing techniques.

[6] Term loans of United States Federal Reserve member banks in 1957 amounted to 38 percent of their business loans. Term loans were even more important as a share of total bank loans for the smallest (as well as the largest) size category of enterprise for which data are available, the proportion being 46 percent in the case of enterprises with less than $50,000 assets. (See Federal Reserve *Bulletin,*

Term lending by deposit banks has become substantial in a number of European countries in the postwar period, although it is not commonly extended to smaller enterprises.[7]

Commercial banks tend to regard themselves as department stores of banking services and thus, besides extending loans, commonly engage in such operations as draft or note collection, issuance of letters of credit and guarantees, provision of credit or related information, foreign exchange transactions, purchase and sale of securities, trustee functions, safe deposit box services, and many others. In the United States, two large banks have even recently begun equipment leasing. Most of these services are usually minor functions performed primarily to assist the building up of the volume of deposits and loans, although some are highly profitable; the bulk of bank income is derived from the return on loans, with an important share in some countries also being derived from securities. The varied interests of commercial banks, however, are often broader than their sources of income would indicate. In many countries they own or are closely linked with finance companies, insurance companies, and various other types of financial institutions.

Merits

There are a number of advantages in involving commercial banks in development financing of small industry, aside from the obvious fact that they are one of the substantial repositories of financial resources and that every additional source that can be drawn on is of value.

The offices and staff of the total commercial bank network tend to be widespread, reaching most centers of industrial enterprises. Bank staffs are thus in a position to maintain regular personal contact with enterprises and to build up a knowledge of local conditions and long personal relationships with businessmen, which are often essential to loan evaluation and administration. As Beckhart has put it:

> The contact between client and bank is seldom, if ever, confined exclusively to that of borrower and lender. In most instances there are other dealings between the two. The debtor normally is also a depositor of the bank and more often than not enjoys other relationships with the bank.[8]

Apr., 1958, p. 402.) Bank term loans accounted for 2.9 percent of the total resources of manufacturing enterprises with less than $250,000, as compared with the average for all manufacturing enterprises of 2.2 percent (FTC-SEC, *op. cit.,* pp. 22, 23). These averages reflect, of course, the fact that data for many enterprises which receive no term loans are combined with others which have substantial dependence on term loans. It is estimated that around one-fifth of the total mining and manufacturing enterprises had term loans in 1957.

[7] OEEC/EPA, *The Supply of Capital Funds for Industrial Development in Europe,* Paris, 1957: Summary Volume, "Commercial banks and 'banques d'affaires.' "

[8] B. H. Beckhart (ed.), *Business Loans of American Commercial Banks,* The Ronald Press Company, New York, 1959, p. 36.

The possible importance of commercial banks' networks of offices and credit relationships to a small-industry program is perhaps best illustrated by Japan's experience. Japan's Small Business Finance Corporation, after 12 years of existence and steady expansion, still administers over 60 percent of loan volume—principally its smaller loans—through agency arrangements with commercial banks and related institutions because they have offices in many places and credit relations with many clients which the SBFC is not yet capable of serving.

Banks do not always fully exploit their potential of knowing clients or possible clients. A system of branch banking and a high centralization of decisions, together with a practice of rotating local staff, may greatly reduce the local knowledge of banks. Customary lending procedures may confine a banker's business contacts to meetings in bank offices, and his knowledge of a client's operations to deposit and loan repayment records and the value of the security offered against loans. The social and intellectual orientation of a banker may further isolate him from major sections of the business community, particularly small industrialists. In large cities especially, physical presence of a bank unit does not by itself guarantee local knowledge—and banks in less developed countries sometimes possess surprisingly little—but it does provide commercial banks with a foundation upon which local knowledge can be economically built up.

Banks lend to a large number and wide variety of enterprises and are thus in a position to have a comparative view of enterprises, a broad knowledge of economic conditions, and easy access to information on credit conditions. This contributes to their ability to judge the soundness of loans accurately and efficiently and also to extend financial and economic information and assistance to borrowers. This possession of information is, of course, truer of the banking system as a whole or of large bank networks than of individual unit banks. Where there is little exchange of information between banks—as is the case in a great many countries—much of their potential knowledge on credit, financial and general economic conditions remains unfulfilled. The potential is further qualified where bankers are isolated from real contact with business. This knowledge and access to information is nevertheless an important contributor to the industrial financing capabilities of the more successful commercial banks in industrialized countries.

The opportunity banks have to keep in touch with a broad range of enterprises and to obtain a comparative view of similar enterprises may also equip them to extend advisory assistance to their clients. They have, so to speak, their hand on the pulse of the total economy as well as on that of competitors of individual clients. In practice, their capacity to perform advisory functions tends to be overrated. Besides the problem common in less developed countries already cited that banks sometimes do not actually have much information about the firms they finance, even in more advanced countries banks rarely have the specialized staff to enable them to understand much of what they have the opportunity to know.[9] There is the further problem that extending advice may conflict with their financing functions. Clients must feel assured that the knowledge the bank acquires of them is kept confidential; also they must not feel that the bank can in any way be held responsible for mistaken operating decisions. Thus whatever their knowledge, bankers tend to keep their advice to clients on a fairly general level.

Banks are enabled by their long experience and large volume of lending to standardize many procedures, so that much of the routine paper work can be carried out economically and reliably. The larger the volume of lending, the easier it is to extend special types of loans or other financial services. Again, much remains to be done to fully exploit this bank potential, particularly in less developed countries. Few studies of bank costs have been made, although competition and the recent trend toward automation is resulting in increased attention being given to bank costs analysis, at least in the more industrialized countries.

Banks' relations with their clients are subject to regulation and supervision. This tends to check any abuse of the fiduciary position banks acquire as lenders. Banks normally cannot hold a controlling position in industrial or commercial companies and must dispose of all enterprises acquired in lieu of loan repayment within a reasonable period. Their charges are relatively standardized, publicly known, and are subject to public regulation. In less developed countries, however, the regulation of banks' relations with clients is sometimes deficient or, more commonly, deficiently administered. Such inadequacies, where they exist, are, for the most part, not difficult to correct.

Banks are less subject to some of the major biases which tend to influence some of the other sources of finance and thus may extend financing to sectors not served by other sources. Internal finance, for example, tends

[9] In the United States, larger banks have begun to maintain a few economists and industrial specialists, but even in these cases they are too thinly staffed to undertake any extensive informational assistance. A survey of firms in the United States indicated that only one-fourth of those with assets between $1 and $9 million consulted their banks before important financial decisions and that somewhat less than half of larger firms did. The primary reason for not turning to banks for specific advice seems to be summed up in the statement from one company, "Banks don't know enough about anything to give advice to anyone." Most firms did turn to banks for some advice but primarily of a general sort. As one of those interviewed stated, "When I am talking to bankers I want to get from them their best appraisal for a year or two in advance of what we can expect of business activity, interest rates, and the availability of money." George Katona, *Business Looks at Banks,* University of Michigan Press, 1957. See chap. 4, "Views About Advice from Banks." Companies also turn to banks for specific information they are prepared to provide such as credit information, information on government regulations affecting business, and so forth.

to be reinvested in the enterprise from which the income is derived; thus enterprises without a past high-profit record have little access to this source. Interbusiness finance is more commonly extended in some lines of industry than others. Government lending agencies may be subject to political pressures and biases of those in political power. Whatever biases or favoritism in loan decisions banks may have—and every source tends to have some— these will at least be somewhat different from those of other lending units. Moreover, in matters of personal judgment—of which there is a large element in loan decisions—the biases of individual commercial banks will tend to differ, which further opens the system to a broader range of borrowers. The differing judgment of individual banks is, of course, more important in countries where there are many independent banks, including small banks with a natural local small-business orientation, than where commercial banking consists of a few highly centralized branch networks.

Banks may have funds at a time when funds are difficult to obtain from other sources or of a type unavailable elsewhere on as attractive terms. The seasonal and cyclical availability of funds tends to differ from individual enterprises because of the offsetting influences of banks' wide variety of depositors and because banks often have access to funds from other financial institutions, particularly from the central banking authority. This is, of course, more important in countries where economic activity is highly diversified and financial institutions highly developed, although it is generally of significance even in less developed countries.

Banks, by their access to low-cost funds and by low-cost lending procedures, are able to extend some types of financing on more attractive terms than alternative sources. Competition or regulations are also necessary, however, to ensure that these economies are fully reflected in lending rates.

Limitations

The limitations on the usefulness of commercial banks to small-industry development financing stem mainly from the nature of three characteristics of banks: (1) their sources of funds; (2) their basic orientation to financing; and (3) their traditional lending procedures and staffing patterns.

The major source of bank funds are depositors. Depositors, for the most part, are willing to make funds available only on the assurance of unquestionable security and a high degree of liquidity. Since those who do not require the same degree of security or liquidity can place their financial savings with other institutions which offer a greater return, it is appropriate that banks should be able to meet these depositor requirements. Banking laws in many countries limit the types of financing commercial banks may undertake in order to protect the liquidity and security interests of depositors.

In less developed countries, the need to assure depositors of complete safety and liquidity poses special problems for using banks as a channel for development financing. The nature of the economies and the low confidence of the public in banks tend to reduce deposit stability. Central bank and government measures to protect depositors are also generally less common. As a United Nations' study put the matter:

> In many underdeveloped countries, confidence in banking institutions of all types is a tender growth, and development must suffer serious setbacks if such confidence is undermined. The principle of safety of savings deposits should be paramount, and should govern the investment policies of public depositories of savings, as well as government policies in relation to private depositories. In particular, governments should not, in trying to utilize commercial banks as instruments of economic development, induce or compel the banks to involve themselves in risky or less liquid investments without taking appropriate measures to safeguard savers and depositors.[10]

Thus, while it is possible under some conditions for commercial banks to engage in term lending or short-term financing of a more risky type, obligations to depositors tend to rule it out under present conditions in many less-developed countries. Corrective measures sometimes important in enabling commercial banks to engage in term lending are considered below.

The dependence on depositors for the bulk of bank funds places another important limitation on commercial banks as a channel for small-factory financing, particularly where small industrialists are not a major source of deposits. A bank's income depends as much upon attracting deposits as on making loans. Depositors may be attracted by the convenience of offices and special services relating to deposits, but usually regulations prohibit interest payments, except in the case of time deposits, where normally a uniform rate to all depositors applies. Attracting depositors, particularly large demand depositors, tends to depend heavily on according them priority in loan considerations. Interviews with bankers in less-developed countries confirm the applicability there of Hodgman's comment: "Anyone who troubles to inquire of commercial bankers will discover that the deposit relationship of a loan is a primary consideration in determining the cost and availability of bank credit to that customer."[11]

Large merchants, by their individual size, their aggregate importance in the economy, and the nature of their business, tend to be the major sources of bank deposits in less-developed countries. Banks have, therefore, had sound economic reasons for channeling a large part of their loans to merchants and for standardizing their lending forms and procedures in terms of those best suited to merchants. Bankers in a number of newly industrializing countries echoed the statement and query of a Honduran

---

[10] *Domestic Financing of Economic Development,* United Nations, New York, 1950, p. 2.

[11] Donald R. Hodgman, "The Deposit Relationship and Commercial Bank Investment Behavior," *The Review of Economics of Statistics,* August, 1961, p. 257.

banker: "Furthermore our clients are mostly merchants. They give us deposits, remittances and foreign draft business. If we transfer our limited resources to industry, cattle-raising and agriculture, which don't make deposits, where would we get depositors?"[12]

Small industrialists, on the other hand, are usually of minor importance as depositors, lacking individual bargaining power with banks and being of minor importance in the aggregate either as depositors or borrowers of immediate potential. Banks thus tend to extend them financing only to the extent that funds are not required by the primary customers and to the extent that financing can be arranged without special risk or problems of departing from standard procedures. The form and amount of such residual financing is often not well adapted to small-industry needs. Its fluctuating availability makes it a risky source of funds to depend upon.

Merchants are not the only group that by their importance as depositors tend to reduce the interest of commercial banks in extending development financing to small industry. Deposits are required from all sectors of the economy, from consumers as well as producers. It is thus generally helpful to the generating of deposits for banks to create the public impression of extending loans and other services to all sectors by at least token services to the important groups. The smaller industrialist with development financing needs thus normally has to share the residual funds after the bank has met the needs of major enterprises whose deposits and goodwill commercial banks may be interested in maintaining. Token service tends to forestall the establishment of larger and more constructive financing programs.

A second group to which commercial banks are responsible are shareholders, who provide the risk capital for which they are accorded basic policy control. Where shareholders are private, their influence can be expected generally to direct financing to clients of the most remunerative types. The structure of interest-rate regulations and traditional bank lending practices in many countries results in a substantial part of small-industry financing falling in the low-profit or unprofitable category. Under these circumstances, little small-industry financing can be expected from commercial banks.

Even profitable small-industry loans may be neglected where other important gains are dependent upon emphasizing loans to other sectors. Banks, as department stores, have many services to sell; the small industrialist may seek only loans, but merchants may require other services, such as collections or exchange services, which may have high profit margins. Banks

---

[12] Edward A. Tenenbaum, James S. Taylor, and Henry Kirkpatrick, *Helping Honduran Industry: A Diagnostic Study,* Continental-Allied Company, Inc., for the ICA, Washington, D.C., 1961, p. 34. Or as a banker in Taiwan reported: "Taken as a whole, therefore, industry wants to borrow rather than deposit." (Edward A. Tenenbaum, *Taiwan's Turning Point,* Continental-Allied Company, Inc., Washington, D.C., 1960, p. 90.)

must consider a client's business as a whole, both the deposits he brings and the services he buys, and when loanable funds are in short supply even profitable clients may be neglected in favor of more profitable ones. A further problem is that owners of private banks sometimes are more concerned about assuring service to particular clients than about minor variations in profits. Thus even opportunities for profitable small-industry lending may not induce them to serve this sector. Bank ownership is sometimes sought less from concern for the rate of return that will directly accrue from bank shares than from a concern for easy access to bank finance. As a result, important commercial banks are sometimes controlled by various closely knit business groups. The structure of banking in Mexico, which is not greatly dissimilar to that in many other developing countries, is a good illustration of this:

> Each of these big entrepreneurial groups—Garza Sada, Banco Nacional de Mexico, Banco de Comercio, Banco Comercial Mexicano, Carlos Trouyet, Raúl Bailleres, Aarón Saéna, Elías Sourasky and Sociedad Mexicana de Credito Industrial—has expanded in similar organizational form: establishing or tying in with one or more banks, one or more finance companies, one or more mortgage institutions, tens of industries, tens of commercial businesses, a few real estate developments, and, in three cases, a mutual fund. Each of the nine, which together control financial institutions possessing a majority of the nation's private bank capital, by and large finances its own industrial and commercial promotions. Inasmuch as the big nine utilize their banking capital to become owners of new promotions, other entrepreneurs can acquire credit from them only at relatively high interest rates. Two sets of rules thus govern much of Mexico's private bank credit: financial institutions of the big nine extend credit on easy terms to companies within their respective empires but charge the maximum which the traffic will bear in making credit available to outside parties.[13]

In Korea a similar problem is reported:

> The banks are not always able to furnish these larger industrialists with the needed money in time. So, they [larger industrialists] invest money in banking businesses or buy up stocks of commercial banks with a view to directly or indirectly taking the control of them so that they may be able to run them in such a way as to comply with the financial needs of their enterprises. In fact, large businessmen have taken the control of city banks

---

[13] Frank Brandenburg, "A Contribution to the Theory of Entrepreneurship and Economic Development: The Case of Mexico," *Inter-American Economic Affairs*, Winter, 1962, p. 22. For similar comments on commercial banking in Mexico, see Sanford A. Mosk, "Financing Industrial Development in Mexico," *Inter-American Economic Affairs*, vol. 1, no. 1, 1947, and Margaret G. Myers, "Mexico" in B. H. Beckhart, *Banking Systems*, Columbia University Press, New York, 1954. On similar relationships in Honduras, see Tenenbaum et al., *op. cit.*, p. 44.

in many cases, and as a result, the loans to them . . . amounted to far more than 30 percent of the total loans advanced by the banks.[14]

The primary purpose of the bank, in the eyes of such shareholders, is to assure funds as required to the controlling business group. Shareholders may also utilize their influence over loan allocations as a pawn in bargaining with other businessmen or a reward to others for past or future favors. The commonness of this situation in some countries tends to result in banks not being regarded by major shareholders—and sometimes by banking authorities—so much as a public service facility (as it tends to be in most advanced countries) as just another private enterprise or private possession. Since small industrialists are not usually influential bank shareholders, they tend to be excluded from bank financing by such shareholder attitudes. In some cases, major owners and their friends may even have a substantial part of their business in importing and other merchandising activities, giving them a special bias against the development of many types of small industry.[15]

Foreign banks still play a major role in the banking systems of many less developed countries. These have been traditionally oriented primarily to financing foreign trade and foreign-controlled enterprises. Banking regulations also often restrict the activities of foreign banks in ways which reduce their ability and interest in financing local business, particularly in local currency or on a term basis. The social and cultural background of their management may further isolate them from close relationships with the local business community, particularly the less cosmopolitan smaller industrialists. Thus, it has been a common complaint in many countries that foreign banks are difficult to interest in financing local industry. This situation, however, appears to be rapidly changing in many parts of the

---

[14] *The Profile of the Medium Industry Bank,* The Medium Industry Bank, Seoul, Korea, 1962, pp. 11, 12. The access of smaller firms to banks in Greece is similarly reported to be restricted by the close relationships between banks and the largest business concerns. Howard S. Ellis et al., *Industrial Capital in Greek Development,* Center of Economic Research, Athens, Greece, 1964, p. 197. The practice of shareholders utilizing their control over banks to serve their other business interests is more common in less-developed countries but occurs everywhere: "In Texas, they call it 'buying balances.' As an example, one Houston builder normally borrows about $900,000 from local banks in the course of his operations, of which some $200,000 has to be kept on deposit as a compensating balance. Now, he has raised $120,000 (using stock as collateral) to buy a small country bank that has $270,000 in cash that he can deposit at a bigger bank whenever he needs a compensating balance to cover banking there. As a result of this ploy, the price of small banks in Texas has risen sharply, and some businessmen are looking out of the state." (*Business Week,* Nov. 3, 1962 p. 110.)

[15] Salaried employees, as well as shareholders, may be influenced by the advantages of securing the favor of large enterprises. Aside from direct rewards, such as bribery, the friendship or favorable opinion of a client with large resources is always more worth attaining than that of a client with small resources.

world. In a few countries—such as El Salvador—foreign banks are showing more active interest in adapting their services to meet the needs of the small industrialist than is shown by many locally owned institutions.

There is a further problem in channeling development financing through banks noted for cliquishness or simply managed by persons unlikely to be able to acquire the confidence of small industrialists. Development considerations require banks to have a substantial knowledge of the enterprises to which they lend. Enterprises, however, are often reluctant to trust information to closely held banks for fear they may not safeguard confidential details provided them. Commercial bank standards must, moreover, be high enough to make it possible for them to interchange general credit and other information important to development financing. Partially or wholly government-owned commercial banks tend to have at least as much difficulty as private banks which are known to be controlled by particular business groups in achieving the confidence of borrowers needed for development financing.

A third group upon whom banks are dependent is monetary authorities. As a result of banks' ability to create checking deposits and to enlarge the money supply, they are in most countries subject to the regulations of the monetary authorities, who have the power to alter the volume of their resources, the liquidity of their assets, and sometimes the form and allocation of their loans. The power of monetary authorities can be—and normally is—applied in ways which are helpful to channeling commercial bank funds toward development purposes. The major problem which arises from monetary regulations in utilizing commercial banks for financing of development of small industry is that monetary authorities often have a single-minded focus on the money supply, wihout considering the fact that changes in the quality may affect the form of financing, its allocation, or the volume of output.[16] Because small industry is normally at the bottom of the scale in terms of bank lending priorities, a curb on bank credit may have great effect on credit availability to small industry long before it has any perceptible effect on the total money supply. In economies where monetary policy sharply fluctuates, this adds to the hazard of small firms relying upon banks.

The problems stemming from the nature of the sources of bank funds and tending to impair the usefulness of commercial banks as a channel for financing small-factory development may be briefly summarized. Banks have responsibilities to several groups which reduce their flexibility and tend to increase their conservativeness. Some of these responsibilities tend to conflict with requirements for small-industry development financing. Commercial banks, moreover, are not generally development-oriented. They

[16] For an example of this in Israel, see Edward A. Tenebaum, *Israel's Industrial Finances: A Second Look.* Continental-Allied Company, Inc., Washington, D.C., 1960, p. 178.

are reluctant to incur the expense—or displeasure of clients—that may be involved in determining whether finance is productively used. Indeed, aside from this problem, financing such activities as consumption or commodity speculation is in some cases more closely in accord with their interest than financing activities clearly of more productive value to the total economy.

A further impediment to utilizing banks as a channel for small-industry development financing is the nature of traditional bank lending procedures and staffing patterns. Many banks are accustomed to making only short-term loans on the basis of trade acceptances or heavily secured notes. Operating such lending services requires established routines but very little special knowledge, except possibly for that of one or two key persons. Development financing, even where it involves short-term credit extension, requires a knowledge of industries and of the ways industries use finance—a knowledge which commercial banks do not always possess. Most countries lack the tradition of unsecured lending based on a bank's knowledge of an applicant's management capabilities and the nature of his operations; it is this tradition which has given commercial banks in the United States some preparation for undertaking some productively important and complex types of financing. Banks which in screening applications focus exclusively on the supporting guarantees tend not to build up the knowledge, the staff, or the procedures necessary to apply development lending criteria or to appreciate the possibilities of sound lending programs being created for small enterprises.

It is particularly with regard to extending medium-term credit that commercial banks are handicapped by a lack of knowledge about economic trends in general, the fundamentals of various industries, and the financial details of specific enterprises. Such knowledge is important not merely to screening loans, but also to the giving of subsequent advice and supervision normally essential to sound, medium-term financing. Especially in the case of medium-term loans, collateral is an unreliable protection against unsound lending. Knowledge, aside from its importance to assuring the repayment of medium-term loans, is also very important to evaluating and supervising the development contribution of financing.

The only substitute for economic, industrial, and financial knowledge—and it is often an essential complement rather than a substitute—is an intimate knowledge of the industrialists themselves. Lending procedures focusing primarily on collateral, however, contribute little to either type of knowledge. While banks utilizing such procedures also tend to lend primarily to persons they know well, they will not necessarily know well the small industrialists and other minor borrowers to whom they make well-secured short-term loans from residual funds.

Many of the previously cited characteristics of banks add up to making them very conservative institutions. Their resistance to change is often heightened because bank regulations and monopoly positions strengthened by a general shortage of funds permit their present practices to be quite profitable. Inducing change may also be made difficult by the need for other simultaneous changes over which banks have no direct control. Under these conditions, there can arise what one study called "an amazing paradox—a classical example of starving in the midst of plenty," noting that "while on one hand, commercial banks cannot find sufficient borrowers on short-term, the African businessman on the other hand, is unable to find sufficient lenders."[17] The problem is that these clients cannot even meet the banks' standards for short-term funds. Remedying these difficulties to permit productive needs for funds to be met by banks on a reasonably safe and profitable basis may require changes not only in lending methods, but also in legislation, in other institutional services, and in the way borrowers conduct their business.

Measures

The possibility of a greater involvement of commercial banks in small-industry financing and of improved commercial bank services to such enterprises has been envisaged in many countries and measures taken to help bring about this prospect. While many of these programs have not been very successful, this appears to have been a result not so much of faults in the measures taken but of the absence of other important supporting measures. Both measures with which there has been some experience and new types of measures that also appear to be needed will be considered here.

Much of what is wrong with commercial banking in less-developed countries and of what needs to be done to make them more useful to small-industry development financing is identical with the deficiencies of United States banking and the remedies suggested by the American Banker's Association at the end of World War II:

> Accepting only gilt-edge loans that come in voluntarily might have been a satisfactory method of operation years ago, when banks had a virtual monopoly on credit, but times have changed and will continue to change. Creditwise, banks may be both aggressive and sound. Today there is a growing demand for bank credit on a more diversified scale, and logically it is expected that modern banking will provide such service to deserving people. This emphasizes the need for banks to explore ways and means of making a greater variety of credit applications bankable.[18]

A part of what is needed to improve banking in many countries is simply a general banking reform aimed at modernizing banking operations and

---

[17] *Report of the Advisory Committee on Aids to African Businessmen,* Federation of Nigeria, Lagos, 1959, p. 13.

[18] American Bankers Association, *Installment Loans to Small Business,* New York, 1947, p. 3.

banking philosophy to achieve the efficiency, breadth of services, and pub-
lic-spiritedness found in advanced banking systems. Aside from such reforms,
measures useful in inducing and enabling banks to give greater service
to small industrial enterprises are of four broad types: (1) those increasing
or setting aside funds for loans to such enterprises, (2) those increasing
the profitability of such financing, (3) those reducing the risk or complexity
of such financing, and (4) those increasing the development orientation
of such financing.

ENLARGING BANK RESOURCES. A part of small enterprises' problem is
that banks lend them only their residual funds after the demands of larger
enterprises, commercial firms, and other favored clients are served. In capi-
tal-short economies, the residual may be small and transitory. As was earlier
indicated, higher interest rates on deposits and other measures increasing
banks' ability to attract deposits would be useful in many countries to
increase the incentives for private savings and to divert funds from private
lenders into banking channels.

Because of the extent of banks' other, more attractive lending opportunities, increasing banks' resources in the above fashion may not be adequate
to induce loans to small enterprises. As was noted earlier, its resources are
usually mainly short-term deposits which may not be suitable to the types
of financing desired. Changes in central bank regulations can often correct
at least the limitations arising from liquidity problems, as has been
illustrated recently in France.

A more direct measure is to provide either government or bank funds for
small-industry financing or to earmark a portion of normal bank resources
for small-industry financing. In the Philippines, the Industrial Development
Center makes funds available to commercial banks for approved loans to
small enterprises. The Fondo de Garantia y Fomento a la Industria
Mediana y Pequeña in Mexico and the Development Board in Singapore
similarly have arrangements for extending funds to commercial banks which
provide approved loans to small enterprises. Special rediscount facilities
are among the measures taken in India to encourage commercial banks
to finance small industry. Special funds for financing small industry have
been established by the United States Aid program in commercial banks
in such countries as Jordan, Greece, Iran, Israel, India, Korea, and Taiwan.
The United States Export-Import Bank has provided funds for financing
the purchase of United States equipment and services by small and medium
enterprises to commercial banks (sometimes indirectly through a central
or development bank) in such countries as Chile, Japan, Guatemala, Spain,
and India. In Japan, commercial banks allocate and administer a large
part of the Small Business Finance Corporation loan funds. Cooperative
small-enterprise banks with special access to public funds have been established in many countries such as France, Belgium, Holland, Italy, Germany,
Colombia, and Brazil.

ENLARGING THE PROFITABILITY OF SMALL-INDUSTRY FINANCING. Where the possibility of return from special funds is small, banks may not use them, even though they may constitute a net addition to profits. Banks tend to be conservative about changing their lending habits and may be able to forego the small profit possible. To overcome this resistance, funds have sometimes been provided at special rates to provide a wider margin of profit. The Iran-American Industrial Guarantee Fund, for example, makes funds available to commercial banks for lending to smaller industry at 4 percent which may be relent at 10 percent.[19] The Central Bank of Colombia permits banks to rediscount loans to small industry at one percent lower than the normal rediscount rate.

Even where special discount rates have been offered for small-industry loans, the margin has usually not been adequate to induce much lending of the desired type. This has been in part because of an underestimation of the real costs in undertaking such financing. Another reason, however, has sometimes been that the procedures involved in obtaining special funds for small-industry lendings have greatly added to operating costs. Where, for example, every loan must have prior approval of the central bank or some other agency—and particularly if this cannot be obtained without considerable delay and further demands upon bank staff time in providing information—the costs and psychological objections to using such funds may be great. The administrative costs in utilizing these funds must be kept in reasonable proportion to possible returns.

Lending costs differ greatly for different types of financing and for different types of applicants. The margin allowed must thus be adjusted to the costs involved in the particular type of financing expected of banks. In addition, there will be special costs where banks are expected to undertake types of financing which they are not already equipped to provide in terms of staff, organization, and past experience. If banks have not yet acquired experience in term lending to large enterprises, it may be too much to expect them to participate in a program of term financing for small enterprises.

Where term financing is feasible, experiences in more developed countries suggest efforts will usually be best concentrated on loans of two to three years, since the various obstacles to term financing tend to rise sharply for longer periods. Only in the United States have commercial banks so far engaged in much term financing to small business, despite various, not very successful, attempts in a number of countries to induce banks to extend term financing to smaller enterprises. Most term loans to small business in the United States are for relatively short periods. A study in

[19] For a description of these operations, see Nathaniel Engle, *Industrial Development Banking in Action; A Study of Organization, Operations, Procedure of Private Development Banks in India, Iran, Pakistan, Turkey,* Pakistan Industrial and Commercial Investment Company, 1962 p. 78. (Mimeographed.)

1957 based on interviews with banks reports that maturities on unsecured term loans to small business averaged two and a half years, and loans secured by equipment had average maturities of a little over two years. Only in the case of loans secured by real estate were periods longer than five years common.[20] In the usually less stable environment of developing countries, anticipating capabilities of management, costs, competition, technological and market changes, and other such factors for more than two or three years is often not possible.

Banks may also be deterrred from serving small enterprises by high costs which arise from their reliance on procedures adapted to financing large firms but unsuitable for small ones. Loan-handling costs, rapid loan processing, and the decentralization of loan decisions tend to be much less important in the case of large than small firms. It thus may be important to provide banks with assistance which will reduce transitional costs and the uncertainties involved in instituting new lending arrangements.

In many cases profit margins can only be widened sufficiently to make small-industry financing attractive by permitting higher rates to be charged on such loans than on other types of financing presently preferred by banks. The level to which it is practical to raise rates depends on what small enterprises can afford, but it is often far higher than the rates at which small-industry funds are usually lent. In Korea and Taiwan, small-industry loan programs were established under which banks provided one-fifth of the resources, and the other four-fifths were derived from the special funds which the government made available. The interest rate charged on the special funds was fixed at about 7 percent, and banks were permitted to charge about 22 percent on the portion derived from their own funds, giving an effective rate to the borrower of about 10 percent.[21]

The importance of adequate incentive is well illustrated by the way higher rates obtainable through installment arrangements have stimulated commercial bank term lending to small enterprises in the United States.

> In many areas of the country, usury laws and banking tradition prevent nominal or stated rates from going above six percent. . . . Most affected by these limitations are loans, particularly short-term loans, on which the effective rate is close to the nominal or state rate subject to the ceilings. On installment loans with interest calculated on original amount of the loan, however, effective rates generally are close to twice the nominal or stated rates. In many jurisdictions, the applicable ceiling on such loans is the nominal rate rather than the effective rate.[22]

[20] Federal Reserve System, "Commercial Banks," *Financing Small Business,* chap. III.

[21] *Information Relating to Selected Investment Loan Fund and Industrial Development Projects, China (Taiwan), Korea, Panama, Philippines, ICA,* Office of Industrial Resources, Technical Aids Branch, Washington, D.C., 1957.

[22] Federal Reserve System, *op. cit.,* p. 390.

An alternative approach to increasing lending rates for loans to small factories is to reduce the profitablility of other types of lending through taxation or other means. In Taiwan, Tenenbaum concluded: "Ultimately, the only way to shift loans to more productive employment may be by reducing the profitability of loans to commerce."[23]

Profit incentives depend upon the potential volume of lending as well as upon profit margins. If the volume of funds provided is small or possibly temporary or if lending opportunities to small industry are inherently limited, banks may not consider it worth the initial effort required to establish or enlarge their small-industry financing services. Funds which may appear insignificant to very large banks, however, may appear substantial to smaller ones; similarly, funds spread over many banks may not be of significance to any one of them, but if concentrated on a few may be enough to command attention. Thus a small volume of financing may be made more significant by concentrating it in selected banks. Against this consideration must be balanced the value of spreading funds among institutions to obtain a broader, more diversified service and a healthy degree of competition between lending institutions.

Reducing Lending Risks

Risk is a separate obstacle which cannot simply be offset by enlarging profits. In many cases banks, being unfamiliar with the risks involved, have exaggerated notions as to the extent of risks. Also, risks may be higher than they need be because banks are unfamiliar with the most suitable ways of extending such financing. Whatever the causes, and whether real or imagined, measures must often be taken to reduce estimated risks to acceptable magnitudes in order to obtain the effective cooperation of banks. Selectivity among applicants is a basic method of minimizing risks. This permits the lender to concentrate on financing only those applicants which can be served on a reasonable risk basis. Reducing risks through selectivity however depends upon the lender's knowing how to make such evaluations and upon his being able to obtain on an economical basis information reliably indicating the extent of the risks involved. Improving banks' ability to screen applicants may be fundamental to the constructive use of commercial banks in small-industry financing, particularly if term financing is involved.

The risks and costs of serving borrowers are much less where reliable information is available on an economical basis on the credit history of applicants. The affairs of large enterprises may be public knowledge in the social circles in which bankers move, but this is much less often true for the more numerous small enterprises. Where lenders do not maintain adequate credit files, the first step needed may be to assist them in improving these. As one authority has stressed:

[23] Tenenbaum, *Taiwan's Turning Point*, p. 90.

The importance of adequate credit files cannot be overemphasized. Credit information in someone's head is fragmentary at best, subject to the whims of memory, unavailable if the person is out of the bank, and lost forever or replaceable only through costly repeated investigation in the event of death.[24]

Improving the credit records of banks and improving the interchange of credit information among banks and other lenders is needed in most developing countries. According to a banking consultant with experience in Argentina and other relatively advanced Latin American countries, credit records of banks in these countries are highly inadequate and sometimes completely unreliable. Bankers in several Latin American countries have told the author that much of the information relevant to credit evaluation is regarded as so confidential that it is rarely recorded. Nevertheless some developing countries have found it possible to make progress in these matters. Colombia and India are taking steps to establish a system of exchanging credit information between banks. In Israel, an arrangement of this kind was suggested by a recent banking study:

> In addition [to establishing a credit rating company], the banks should set up a system for the exchange of information on their customers' accounts, so as to reduce the possibility of playing one bank against the other. This system should be developed voluntarily, through the new bankers' association. . . . Each bank should report to the association at least monthly on loans made to every customer (and possibly other basic information, such as the balance of the customer's account, total debits to the account, etc.). Ideally, such information should be entered on punched cards, or might even be processed by one of Israel's underemployed electronic computers. Banks could obtain information concerning any client, but would not be given details on the client's relations with individual competing banks.[25]

Another way of facilitating risk evaluation is to introduce the practice among potential applicants of maintaining reliable accounts. Encouraging the establishment of professional accounting and auditing firms and improving their standards is frequently of value. It may require considerable time and effort to make progress in these respects in many countries, but making a start is nevertheless generally important. In the United States, the practice of using audited accounts evolved over several decades and was aided by a number of favorable circumstances.[26] Many small but modern enterprises still cannot provide banks with audited accounts.

[24] B. H. Beckhart (ed.), *Business Loans of American Commercial Banks,* The Ronald Press, New York, 1959, p. 63.

[25] Edward Tenenbaum, *Israel's Industrial Finances: A Second Look,* pp. 186, 187.

[26] On the United States experience, see Beckhart, *op. cit.,* p. 60.

A broad knowledge of the critical elements in various industries, of the general trends of industries, and of comparative performance standards of competitive enterprises may be required for evaluating risk. Making industrial survey information available to banks at a moderate cost is useful for this purpose. Beyond this, however, the staff of banks must have enough fundamental knowledge about small industrialists and their operations to utilize information from surveys, specialists, and other sources. Banks may need assistance in acquiring officers with appropriate training. Further specialized training such as industrial survey experience may also be important in providing these officers with a practical insight into the overall operations of a variety of enterprises, and with personal knowledge of how specialists analyze and evaluate industrial operations.

Bank management often needs to be educated on the necessity of loan officers' maintaining direct contact with small industrialists and their operations. "Loan officers in the more progressive banks no longer sit at their desks waiting for customers to come in. They go out to see present and prospective customers at their place of business."[27] Inducing bankers to build up both formal and informal contacts with small industrialists is important in enlarging both their interest in financing small enterprises and their judgment capacity for screening and administering loans.

Direct assistance to banks by a supporting agency in screening or supervising loans can be of value and may be essential. Commercial banks' lack of appropriate staff to evaluate and supervise term loans and the difficulty of integrating the required staff in the commercial bank type of organization are usually serious obstacles to their entering into this type of financing on a reasonable risk basis. Where a supporting agency possessing industrial specialists and close contacts with business operations has been established, it may, as we have indicated in Chapter 5, be capable of carrying out technical and economic evaluations for individual lending institutions.

Risk involved in financing some applicants may be reduced by improving the protection available to lenders in the event of default. Collateral is one method of reducing loss in such cases. However, many types of assets such as inventories, equipment, or sometimes even real estate may not be acceptable as collateral because of deficiencies in legal or institutional arrangements or because lenders are unacquainted with the possibilities or advantages in accepting such collateral in support of loans. Reducing the legal barriers to the acceptance of a wider variety of collateral is often possible. Introducing lenders to practical arrangements for utilizing a broader range of collateral arrangements may also be helpful. For some types

---

[27] *Ibid.,* p. 309. An example of a progressive bank which practices this is the Bank of America, whose president some years ago on joining top management laid down the rule that all officers spend at least one day a week outside the office servicing accounts. (*Business Week,* Nov. 11, 1961, p. 114.)

of collateral, such as field warehouse receipts, broad assistance to establish new types of institutional arrangements may be necessary.[28]

Credit insurance, credit guarantees, and risk-sharing arrangements of various types are other measures of possible value. The experience with these types of arrangements has, however, been mixed, being generally more satisfactory in countries such as the United States, Canada, the Netherlands, and Japan.[29] Guarantee, insurance, or risk-sharing arrangements have failed to have a significant impact on lending operations in a number of less-developed countries, including the Philippines, India, Ghana, and Liberia.[30]

Part of the problem with these measures, particularly in less-developed countries, is that too much tends to be expected of them. Guarantees may induce lenders to undertake unfamiliar or otherwise more risky types of financing if risk is the only obstacle. However, if such financing requires different staffing patterns or new techniques—as is often the case—banks may require other types of assistance to overcome these. In the United States banks themselves developed after a couple of years of experience, including a high default rate, better techniques for extending the type of loans the guarantee program was intended to stimulate—term loans to veterans starting new small businesses.

In the Netherlands, several circumstances have contributed to the success of the guarantee program. Responsibility was delegated entirely to one semiofficial bank of moderate size but with a national network of branches—the Netherlands Middleclass Bank (Nederlandsche Middenstandsbank, N.V.). The bank was motivated by this exclusive responsibility,

[28] See Neil H. Jacoby and Raymond J. Saulnier, *Financing Inventory on Field Warehouse Receipts,* National Bureau of Economics, The Haddon Craftsmen, Inc., Scranton, 1944. Problems and measures relating to collateral are further discussed in Chap. 10.

[29] The nature of the operations and problems of guarantee and insurance programs for veterans in the United States, which has been one of the more successful programs dealing with small loans, is analyzed in detail in R. J. Saulnier et al., *Federal Lending and Loan Insurance,* Princeton University Press for the National Bureau of Economic Research, New York, 1958, appendix C. The Canadian program started in 1961 is described in *Financing Canadian Industries,* Government of Canada, Department of Trade and Industries, Ottawa, Canada. On the Netherlands, see E. J. Tobi, "Financial Structure of Small Scale Industries," International Course on Small Scale Industries, Technological University of Delft, the Netherlands, ca. 1957, pp. 4, 5. (Mimeographed.) On Japan, see Chap. 13.

[30] The Philippine program, which was started in 1952, has achieved little volume. For a description, see *Information Relating to Selected Investment Loan Fund and Industrial Development Project: China (Taiwan), Korea, Panama, Philippines,* International Cooperation Administration, Washington, D.C., 1958. See also the Philippine Industrial Development Corporation, *Annual Report.* On India, see Chap. 2. For a description of the nature of the Ghana program and the practical problems experienced, and for a proposed scheme for Nigeria, see *Report of the Advisory Committee on Aids to African Businessmen,* pp. 19–22, 27–29.

as well as by the limited lending alternatives imposed by competition from larger banks, to devote the time and effort required to develop suitable lending procedures for smaller enterprises. A simple system of automatic guarantees which contributed to the program's efficiency was facilitated by the well-established reputation of the bank and by its quasi-official status.

In Canada, a substantial volume of loans (around $25 million a year) is being made by chartered banks under an automatic guarantee program. It has worked well, in that losses have so far been small. However, the program is only five years old and has not yet been tested by unfavorable economic conditions. Banks also appear to have participated more out of a desire to please the government than from a serious interest of their own in the program. The volume of loans made annually has shown no tendency to increase since the programs first started. It seems doubtful that banks are taking much advantage of the experience to develop better techniques for extending term loans to small enterprise.[31]

In Japan, experience with its rather different type of guarantee program also suggests that something more than a simple assumption of risks by government is required to make guarantee programs an effective means of stimulating banks to greater small-industry financing, even in industrially advanced countries.[32] In less-developed countries, the extent of innovation required will often be much greater and the environment less favorable for inducing banks to undertake term lending for small manufacturers, even with guarantees, if otherwise unassisted.[33]

Care in designing satisfactory administrative arrangements is also important to stimulating lending by guarantee arrangements. Delays were a serious problem in the United States program initially, until simplified procedures were worked out. In Sweden, guarantee arrangements have not greatly enlarged lending, in part because the lengthy delays involved discourage both borrowers and banks.[34]

Mutual guarantee arrangements through industrial associations or similar arrangements have been utilized in Europe and in Japan to strengthen guarantee arrangements. The underlying premise of these arrangements is that association officials will have the knowledge of members to judge their creditworthiness or will be in a position to assist them in the case of diffi-

[31] This opinion may prove to be unduly sceptical, but it seemed to be confirmed by brief discussions with several charter bank officials, as well as knowledgeable bankers or officials of other institutions in Montreal and Calgary in 1965.

[32] See Chap. 13.

[33] See, for example, India's experience in Chap. 2. In Jordan, attractive guarantee arrangements appear to have stimulated loans but without altering bank lending techniques, with undesirable results. See *The Economic Development of Jordan,* The Johns Hopkins Press, Baltimore, for the International Bank for Reconstruction and Development, 1957, p. 230.

[34] Brian Wickremesinghe, *Financing of Small-scale Industrial Development in Sweden,* Företagsekonomiska Institutionen, Uppsala Universitet, 1962, p. 21.

culties. Borrowers may also feel a greater sense of obligation through their various ties with the group to repay debts guaranteed by it.[35] The main problems with efforts to apply these principles have been that (1) the groups have not always had, in practice, a community sense, (2) admission has been made in some sense automatic rather than selective on the basis of creditworthiness, (3) credit has been sought by members and granted to them as a right without adequate consideration as to the wise use of such credit, or (4) the group leaders have used their ability to influence the allocation of credit in a partial manner.

Another approach to reducing the risk of lenders is to facilitate arrangements for supervising the operations of borrowers sufficiently to detect problems in their early stages and for providing the assistance needed in overcoming them. Improved accounting and reporting on operations by loan recipients is important for this purpose as well as for screening applicants. Field visits to clients may be important to supplement such information or to take its place when the latter is unavailable. It may be possible for a supporting service agency to provide such services for banks on a reasonable cost basis, as has been suggested in Chapter 5.

The risk obstacle to small-industry development financing might also be reduced by inducing banks to extend financing involving some degree of risk. A system of deposit insurance would reduce one objection to risk-taking. Lending rates which provide some incentive for risk taking can also be helpful. Better regulation and supervision of banks may reduce the undesirable types of risks banks sometimes undertake in extending financing to important clients, thus leaving more scope for risk taking of a more productive type. Even with such measures, commercial banks probably at best can be expected to assume only a very modest degree of risk.[36]

---

[35] On Japan, see Chap. 13. A great expansion of small-industry credit associations is reported in Germany. See "Small industry credit associations in Germany" (in German), *Deutsches Handwerksblatt,* Bonn, Apr. 10, 1962. See also G. Weissner and B. Fassnacht, "Cooperatives as an Aid to Small Business in Germany," *Law and Contemporary Problems,* Winter, 1959, vol. XXIV, no. 1, pp. 208–221. For a review of mutual credit associations for artisans in several European countries, see *Le Crédit Artisanal en France et à l'Etranger,* Institut de Droit Comparé de l'Université de Paris, Centre International d'Etudes de l'Artisanat, Sirey, Paris, 1958. The helpful role of trade associations in Sweden in guaranteeing credit is described in Wickremesinghe, *op. cit.,* pp. 19–21.

[36] The possibility of banks assuming even modest risks is challenged by some banking authorities. (See Samuel B. Chase, Jr., "Credit Risk and Credit Rationing: Comment," *Quarterly Journal of Economics,* vol. LXXV, no. 2, May, 1961, p. 326.) Most authorities, however, are inclined to the view that banks can and should take at least a small amount of risk. See Howard D. Crosse, *Management Policies for Commercial Banks,* Prentice-Hall, Inc., Englewood Cliffs, N.J. 1962, p. 58, and Beckhart (ed.), *Business Loans of American Commercial Banks,* p. 59; Hunt (*Basic Business Finance,* Richard D. Irwin, Inc., Homewood, Ill., 1961, pp. 181ff.) stresses the limited risks banks can afford in view of the usual return open to

Increasing the Development Orientation of Financing

A final measure of general importance is increasing the development orientation of commercial banks. In most programs utilizing commercial banks, there have been complaints that funds are not used for development purposes, that recipients do not qualify as small enterprises, that interest rates exceed the limits established, or that banks deviate from the intended program in various other ways. Assisting commercial banks in evaluating the development merits of financing and in actively seeking out development financing opportunities through arrangements such as those discussed in Chapter 5 may be useful. Supervision of a type which does not interfere with regular lending operations is important to assure that financing is being administered in a way to give the results intended. Periodic public review and evaluation of commercial bank contributions to small-industry development financing by banking and legislative authorities may be useful in reaffirming the broad public responsibilities of banks in the thinking of bankers, public officials, potential borrowers, and the general public. This creates the kind of climate of public opinion which encourages banks to accept and fulfill these responsibilities. It also provides reliable specific information on how well banks are serving small-industry development needs, what the exact natures of obstacles to better service are, and what legislative or other major changes might be desirable.

Detailed qualitative credit controls have been tried by a number of countries to achieve greater development orientation, but the limited success obtained suggests that this approach should be applied cautiously and only if the staff and organization capable of administering such controls efficiently have been assured.[37]

An Adequate Set of Measures

The list of measures for increasing banks' participation in the financing of small-factory development is long, but it should not be assumed that they must all be accomplished at once, or that they are all needed in every situation. Progress can be achieved on a step-by-step basis. Yet it must be admitted that, starting with the commercial banking system of

---

them. A Swedish writer underlines the importance of commercial bank risk taking in his country (see Lars-Erik Thunholm "The Commercial Banks and the Financing Problems of the Sixties," *Skandinaviska Banken,* Quarterly Review, vol. 4, no. 1, 1963). It is the author's impression that banks in less-developed countries take a greater amount of risk than they are usually credited with; the problem thus appears to be one of redirecting rather than increasing risk taking.

[37] France's experience with qualitative controls, which is a good indicator of the problems and achievements to be expected under favorable conditions, is described by J. S. G. Wilson in "France," Chapter 1 in R. S. Sayers (ed.), *Banking in Western Europe,* Oxford University Press, 1962. On Colombia's experience see Chapter 12 below.

a good many developing countries, a major increase in the contribution of banks to small-factory development cannot be expected until a combination of a number of these measures has been effectively applied. A practical means for achieving this in many countries, in the author's view, is through a program of the type which was recently suggested for activating greater participation by banks and other institutions in financing small-industry development in Peru:

> Our brief appraisal of Peruvian conditions suggests that lending institutions in Peru, as in a great many other countries, generally lack the organization, staff, and knowledge of lending techniques required to meet the development financing needs of small and medium factories, particularly in locations outside of Lima. There are, moreover, special cost and risk considerations that deter realistic financing organizations from attempting to provide development financing services under prevailing conditions, which offer few, if any, special incentives or compensations for entering into this field.
>
> To remedy this situation, an approach is needed which can cope with all major facets of the problem more or less simultaneously. . . .
>
> In our judgment, a Development Fund equipped to provide incentives, assistance, and guidance to credit retailing institutions and to other organizations providing industrial extension and related supporting services offers the most promising means for increasing the flow of development financing to small and medium industrial enterprises in Peru. . . .
>
> The Development Fund approach is not new. It has been employed with varying degrees of success in such Latin American countries as Colombia and Mexico, as well as in other parts of the world. The particular type of fund recommended here, however, is markedly different from those elsewhere in its capacity to support its lending operations through other activities. . . .
>
> The Fund, to achieve its ends, will need three main types of policy instruments:
>
> > *a.* Capacity to provide funds to credit retailing institutions on an incentive basis. . . .
> >
> > *b.* Staff equipped to guide and supervise credit retailing institutions and institutions providing supporting services. . . .
> >
> > *c.* Special resources for contracting essential supporting services.[38]

Savings Institutions

Savings banks, insurance companies, trusts, mutual funds, and similar institutions may be briefly treated, since they are normally of minor importance to small-industry development financing programs. The low level of income restricts the spread of these institutions in many countries. Also, in some countries, many of the functions of savings institutions are carried out by departments of commercial banks.

[38] For complete details, see Robert W. Davenport and Peter D. Duncan, *A Regional Program for Channeling Development Financing to Small and Medium Industry,* Instituto Nacional de Promoción Industrial, Lima, 1964.

To the extent that separate savings institutions exist, their unique values as channels for financing small-factory development rests primarily upon their aggregation of funds which may appropriately be used for medium- or long-term purposes. Savings banks are similar in many ways to small commercial banks. They often have a local community orientation and are accustomed to serving clients in the lower-income scales. However, like small banks, they tend to be ill-equipped to take risks or to evaluate complex risk situations. For uses within small communities, however, their capabilities of judging local character and competence may be important in helping them extend financing in traditional lines. Their funds tend to be more expensive than those of commercial banks so that lending rates may be expected to be higher.

Savings banks have been used as a channel for small-industry financing, usually with government guarantees, in a number of countries. In Uganda the government-owned Credit and Savings Bank utilizes both savings and special development funds to finance firms which cannot qualify for commercial bank loans, giving special attention to local persons. It has, however, been handicapped by the scarcity of borrowers with suitable collateral, by high lending costs, and by the shortage of suitable staff.[39] In Sweden some term loans to small firms against security of real estate, government and private guarantees, and reliable bonds are made by savings banks, but the total volume of such financing is of relatively minor importance.[40] In Spain the possibility of according savings banks a special role in small-enterprise development has been under consideration.[41] In other European countries most savings are restricted to investments primarily in government securities, although they become available to industry in some degree through government or central bank industrial financing measures.

Although the risks involved in financing small-factory development pose special problems for savings banks, it is easy to exaggerate this problem. As an Organisation for European Economic Co-operation (OEEC) study has commented, "depreciation of trustee securities has brought to many savings banks in Western Europe far heavier losses than some element of industrial risk in the composition of their investment might conceivably entail."[42] With adequate guarantees, savings bank funds might be channeled through other institutions better equipped to administer small-industry loans.

[39] IBRD, *The Economic Development of Uganda,* The Johns Hopkins Press, Baltimore, 1962, pp. 75, 76, 286, and *Public International Development Financing in East Africa (Kenya, Tanganyika, Uganda),* Columbia University School of Law, New York, 1962.

[40] Wickremesinghe, *op. cit.,* p. 16.

[41] IBRD, *The Economic Development of Spain,* The Johns Hopkins Press, Baltimore, 1963.

[42] OEEC/EPA, *The Supply of Capital Funds for Industrial Development in Europe,* Paris, 1957, p. 103.

They might also be utilized for financing industrial estates where the source of funds has smaller risk and loan administration responsibilities.

Insurance companies are important sources of term finance in some countries. Only a small part of insurance funds, however, can normally be used for purposes involving risk. A further problem is that they are ordinarily not equipped to allocate or administer very small loans. An exception to this, however, is the relatively small loans made to policy holders against life insurance policies. In Colombia, some loans from insurance companies have been channeled to moderately small industrial enterprises under an arrangement by which risks and administration are assumed by a government-mortgaged bank. Although the volume of these loans has been small because of administrative difficulties, similar but better design arrangements appear to be feasible.[43]

Insurance companies can assist the financing of small industry in a number of other ways: They may extend funds to other institutions which have the facilities for administrating industrial financing. Loans to finance companies, investment banks, development corporations, and industrial estates may be of substantial importance. Participation loans with commercial banks are being experimented with in the United States.[44]

A further way insurance companies can be helpful to small-industry development financing programs is by insuring some of the risks involved. Life insurance on management is of particular value in the case of small industry where one man is often the key element in an enterprise's future. Insurance on collateral is also an important service which insurance companies are in a position to provide. Insuring other risks is likely to be feasible only where the number of enterprises to be covered is large and sufficient experience has been acquired to determine loss probabilities.[45]

Pension funds are another source of increasing importance in many countries. Like savings and insurance funds, they require relatively secure investment outlets, since they involve funds of small savers who cannot afford risks. Pension funds have somewhat greater flexibility as to use than funds

---

[43] See Chap. 12.

[44] For example, a major insurance company in the United States has had a special small-business loan division since 1950 which issues term loans through, and in participation with, commercial banks. Loans have ranged upward from $6,000. Insurance company loans through commercial credit corporations and state, county, and municipal industrial development agencies are estimated to have amounted to about $2 billion since 1950 (*The New York Times,* Dec. 2, 1962). The Nacional Financiera in Mexico has also received a large loan from a United States insurance company; the Financiera in turn makes funds available to finance corporations extending finance to small industry.

[45] United States insurance programs recently established for export credits are suggestive of what might be done. The problem in applying the underlying concept of these arrangements to small-industry financing programs in some developing countries is that the total small-industry population is relatively small.

depending on voluntary savings. Pension fund administrators, unlike voluntary savings organizations, need not be concerned that the risk involved in individual loans will result in a decrease in available funds—by frightening their more cautious contributors—so long as the overall security of the portfolio is not in danger. Pension funds, however, tend to be managed by institutions which are not better equipped for loan administration than are insurance companies. In general, they tend to be suitable for contributing to small-factory financing in the same ways as insurance funds.

Investment trusts and mutual funds differ from the preceding in that they are normally funds from persons in the upper income brackets capable and interested in undertaking risks where the reward is adequate. These funds tend to go to larger enterprises in part because of the absence of the appropriate administrative facilities to extend funds directly and in part for the same reason many commercial banks prefer financing large enterprises. Although there has been little experimentation in ways of drawing upon such resources for small-industry financing, it should be possible to devise arrangements for channeling a portion of these funds through institutions equipped to administer small-factory financing.

Chapter 8
Encouraging Finance Companies

FINANCE COMPANIES ARE defined here broadly to include a very hetero-
geneous but related category, ranging from commercial finance companies
to various types of private term and equity financing organizations. Their
significance for small-industry development financing programs lies not so
much in their present volume of financing as in their capabilities for extending types or terms of financing which are not so readily extended by other
sources. Finance companies are rapidly expanding and multiplying in many
countries, and they are already of substantial importance in some countries,
such as Mexico and the United States.

Increasing the usefulness of finance companies to small-industry development financing programs can be achieved in part through some of the
measures suggested in Chapter 7 in the case of banks. The following, to
avoid repetition, is primarily concerned with what additional or special
measures may be needed in view of the special characteristics of finance
companies. The broadly distinguishing characteristics of finance companies
in general are first considered, followed by a brief examination of major
types of finance companies.

General Characteristics of Finance Companies

Finance companies can be separated roughly into two groups: (1) the
older and relatively unregulated forms such as commercial finance companies; (2) the newer special finance companies shaped by government
assistance and regulatory measures. The older types of finance companies
still provide by far the greater volume of finance. The more recent government-assisted finance companies however are of special importance for the
qualitative characteristics of their financing. There is a third group which
will not be dealt with here: private-venture capital organizations which
are relatively little regulated or assisted by government bodies. The latter
have been omitted in this discussion since the possibility of their extending

assistance to companies in the size range which we are considering is relatively small.[1] The special finance companies as well as private-venture capital organizations shade into development banks, which we will be discussing in the next section.

Finance companies are in a sense merely enlarged versions of the various types of individual financiers and moneylenders, but they are more formally organized and have more standardized operating methods. These differences, although primarily a matter of degree, are significant, since they result in finance companies operating more in the public eye and being more easily subject to public control. At the same time, their operations are in some ways similar to those of commercial banks. Their major operating differences stem in large part from the different nature of their financial resources. Debt capital is less dominant in their capital structure and is usually in longer-term forms than in the case of banks. Debt to equity ratios vary greatly, sometimes approaching those of commercial banks but generally being around 4:1 or 3:1, and occasionally lower. Unlike most commercial banks, finance companies often can draw a large part of their debt capital from bonds and term loans; also in contrast to banks, they are not usually permitted to accept demand deposits or to create checking deposits. Many finance companies obtain a large proportion of their funds through bank loans, so they do indirectly draw in part on the same sources of funds as commercial banks. Bank loans to finance companies may be short-term or demand loans, although lines of credit or term loans are common in the United States. Some types of finance companies also compete with commercial banks for time and savings deposits. High interest rates and sometimes guarantees of liquidity tend to be used to attract such deposits.

[1] There are a few interesting cases where purely private venture capital firms have financed small factories. Of the greatest significance are managing agency firms in India (and in many other formerly British areas) which the author analyzed in some detail during 1954 and 1955. Despite well-known deficiencies in some managing agency arrangements, the operations of a number illustrate the possibility that extending financing together with good management services to relatively small enterprises can be profitable to the financier and useful to small-factory development. Long-term management contracts were a key element making it possible for them to finance small enterprises. These provided a fairly certain minimum return; they permitted the managing agency to hold a minority share position over a long period—needed to gain maximum appreciation—without worry that majority shareholders might, through unsound or unfair policy decisions, prevent the realization of this potential; and they made it possible for the public to take shares in a relatively new or small company because of its confidence in the agency holding the managing contract. Under these arrangements, the usual danger in financing small enterprises of being locked in low profit or unprofitable ventures for long periods was greatly reduced. Another key to the success of operations of this type was the fairly extensive interests of the agencies, permitting them to afford industrial specialists and also to spread risks through a degree of diversification.

Government is an important source of funds for one type of finance companies—designated here as *special finance companies* and often called *development finance companies.* Government funds are normally conditional upon concentrating financial activities on purposes deemed to be of high development importance, particularly uses requiring medium-, long-term, or equity financing. Government funds have been provided in a variety of ways, but normally on a long-term and low-interest-rate basis, and sometimes sharing the risk with equity capital.

The equity capital of finance companies tends to an even greater degree than that of commercial banks to be closely held. In many cases the major shareholder is a commercial bank. Thus, through loan and sometimes equity relationships, finance companies are often linked to commercial banks. In the case of some special finance companies, no stockholder may own more than a small percentage of the total shares, although even in such companies the commercial banking community is usually a major shareholder.

Because of the capital structure of finance companies and because they are newer and of smaller aggregate importance, their financing activities have been less subject to formal regulations and less limited by tradition and outside pressure than those of commercial banks. In recent years, it has been increasingly recognized that finance companies, even though they cannot create deposits, can have an important influence on monetary conditions both by increasing the circulation of funds and influencing their allocation among activities having different productive or inflationary effects. The recent experience of Argentina with finance companies provides a good example of how unregulated activities of finance companies can disrupt monetary policies.[2] As Warren P. Hogan has stressed:

> The effect of the growth of non-banking financial intermediaries is to thrust the burden of adjustment to their activities upon the banking system. The trading banks suffer losses of reserves as a result of lending activities outside their control; they are therefore forced to limit the amount of credit provided by the banking system. By itself, such action may only swell the fringe of unsatisfied borrowers, who will turn in greater numbers to other financial intermediaries. An effective control of the financial system is not possible when monetary policy is directed solely toward controlling the liquidity of the banking system. It is necessary to devise techniques affecting the liquidity of the entire financial structure. Otherwise, financial assets can always be transferred between intermediaries to circumvent the authority of the Central Bank.[3]

[2] See O. Jones, H. W. Laurant, A. R. Beckwith, and H. J. Robinson, *Sources of Capital Investment Funds for Argentine Industrial Development,* Stanford Research Institute, for Comisión Nacional de Administración del Fondo de Apoyo al Desarrollo Económico, Buenos Aires, 1962.

[3] Warren P. Hogan, "Monetary Policy and Financial Intermediaries," *The Economic Record,* vol. XXXVI, no. 76, December, 1960. p. 528.

Because of this, finance companies may be subject to increasing limitations on their operations as their volume of lending becomes substantial; finance companies utilizing government funds are already subject to some special regulations. Nevertheless, finance companies generally have and are likely to continue to have a flexibility in choosing the forms, procedures, and conditions of financing which they extend that commercial banks do not ordinarily possess.

Finance companies have very little in common with savings institutions, although the latter sometimes provide them with funds through loans or bond purchase. The organization and staffing of finance companies (somewhat in contrast to that of savings institutions and commercial banks) usually are more oriented to the extension than to the aggregation of finance. Like savings banks, however, they depend heavily on interest rates to attract the funds they require. Often, but not always, they must operate with smaller staffs and fewer branch offices than commercial banks or savings institutions. Where finance companies are affiliated with commercial banks, they may make use of bank staff and branches. This has been of some importance in the case of Australian commercial finance companies, Mexican *financieras*, and small business investment companies in the United States.

Commercial Finance and Related Companies

Commercial finance companies are a type of institution which is just beginning to spread to the less-developed countries. However, since this process is likely to continue, those responsible for financing programs may find an awareness of their basic characteristics useful. An understanding of how commercial finance companies operate may also be helpful to the understanding of what can and cannot be achieved through the similar but more complex operations of government-assisted development finance companies to be discussed later.

Most of what can be said about commercial finance companies must be based on the experience with them in the United States, where they have been primarily concentrated. A few large and many small companies of this type have operated in the United States for several decades engaging primarily in providing finance and collection services for credit extension on company sales. In 1956, United States commercial credit companies had around $2 billion credit outstanding to some 20,000 clients and were continuing to expand rapidly. In the postwar period, such companies have also multiplied in Europe, particularly England and France, and in several other countries, including Australia, Argentina, and Peru.[4]

---

[4] The literature on finance companies in the United States is extensive, although their role in financing small industry has been summed up in a study by Francis R. Pawley, "Survey of Commercial Finance Companies and Factors," *Financing*

Services may be for normal short-term accounts receivable or for longer-term credit on durable goods and may include sales to consumers as well as sales to other business enterprises. About half of the loans outstanding of 30 companies in the United States at the end of 1956 were for short-term receivables and about one-third for equipment financing. The small remaining share went to inventory financing or to other types of seasonal or emergency finance; this was often extended to regular clients utilizing sales financing and was in most cases secured.[5]

Normally sales financing is extended against the security of bills, up to around 70 percent to 80 percent of their value, with the collection risks being borne by the seller, not the finance company; in operations known as factoring, however, the finance company purchases the bills outright. Large diversified finance companies offering all of the above types of services and others, such as leasing, account for most of the credit extended by finance companies in the United States. Smaller companies tend to specialize in factoring equipment, in sales financing, or along other lines.

Finance companies have been able to flourish, utilizing in part bank funds, because they have developed techniques for extending types of financing which banks for various reasons have not extended in adequate volume to meet demand. Their techniques tend to involve elaborate credit investigation and supervision procedures, specialized knowledge, and also engagement in a higher degree of risk—although still small—than banks are accustomed to undertaking. Unlike bank loans secured by receivables, the receivable financing of finance companies provides credit on a revolving basis with daily adjustments as bills are collected or new invoices added. This greatly simplifies the client's financial management problem as well as reduces the volume of credit he requires. Finance companies have extended not merely finance, but also collection services, advice on credit risks, budgeting, financial management, and often informal advice on merchandis-

---

Small Business, Federal Reserve System, Washington, D.C., 1957, pp. 449ff. For their role in Europe, see OEEC/EPA, *The Supply of Capital Funds for Industrial Development in Europe,* Summary Volume, Paris, 1957, pp. 129ff. On finance companies in Australia see Margaret G. Myers, "The Control of Consumer Credit in Australia," *The Journal of Finance,* vol. 16, no. 3, September, 1961. A rapid expansion of sales companies is taking place in the Philippines according to *The Philippine Industro-Economic Survey,* Industrial Development Center, Manila, 1963, p. 80. On Argentina, see Jones et al., *op. cit.* On Peru, see Robert W. Davenport and Peter D. Duncan, *A Regional Program for Channeling Development Financing to Small and Medium Industry,* Instituto Nacional de Promoción Industrial, 1964. The Mexican finance companies are discussed below.

[5] Federal Reserve System, *Financing Small Business,* report to the Committees on Banking and Currency and the Select Committees on Small Business, 85th Cong., 2d Sess., 1958, p. 451. The 30 companies surveyed by Pawley were estimated to provide about three-fifths of the volume of United States finance company financing. The 30 companies included most of the large companies and some of the numerous smaller companies.

ing, production, personnel, and other aspects of business operation.[6] An important reason why finance companies have been able to use such techniques is that they have been able to assess higher charges for their services than regulations and traditions have permitted banks to charge.

Among the major merits of finance companies is that they have been aggressive in seeking out credit extension opportunities without being limited by fixed preconceptions as to the procedures that might be used, expenses that might be incurred, or risk that might be taken. Because of this tendency to introduce new types of financing and through their general competition, they have stimulated banks to offer broader services also. Their innovation in equipment financing has been particularly important and is one of their more rapidly growing services. They have enabled manufacturers to extend credit for periods of usually one to three years with limited direct involvement in the management of credit operation. Finance companies' ability to provide this service on an efficient basis has been explained in the following way:

> Equipment financing is an example of a well developed trend in lending practices, namely mass financing on a relatively routine basis. In this respect, it can be interpreted as more than a parallel to consumer installment financing; equipment financing, in fact, grew out of the latter type of lending. The individual contracts are frequently of relatively small size and the financing agency must acquire a large number of them in order to develop sufficient volume to make the operation profitable. Under these circumstances it is essential that the unit transactions be handled through established routines, and that credit appraisal procedures be standardized. Credit standards must be such that they can be applied to individual contracts without incurring considerable expense in individual investigations. It is necessary, of course, to make a very careful investigation of the source from which the contracts are being acquired, and to arrive at an over-all appraisal of the individual credits that are to be offered for discount, but once this has been done individual contracts must be passed upon promptly as originated, with only routine appraisal.
>
> There is an element of insurance against loss in equipment financing resulting from this mass basis of operations, but this aspect is not as prominent as in the installment financing of consumer durable goods where both debtors and goods are more standardized and contracts are smaller and more numerous. Nevertheless, it is substantially true that the success of equipment financing must be judged not by reference to individual contracts but by credit

[6] For a detailed description of finance companies' procedures and services in extending financing on accounts receivable, see Raymond J. Saulnier and Neil H. Jacoby, *Accounts Receivable Financing,* The National Bureau of Economic Research, The Haddon Craftsmen, Inc., Scranton, Pa., 1943, especially pp. 91, 110–119. For a description of their procedures in extending finance on equipment, see Saulnier and Jacoby, *Financing Equipment for Commercial and Industrial Enterprise,* The National Bureau of Economic Research, The Haddon Craftsmen, Inc., Scranton, Pa., 1944, pp. 73–78. Also, on finance company services see the Federal Reserve System, *op. cit.,* pp. 449, 452.

experience over a period of time with a large number of contracts. This characteristic of equipment financing is important both for credit administration and bank supervision. For example, the problem of establishing appropriate reserve and maintaining proper control over balances is obviously different in a mass financing operation of this type than it is in the extension of single credits such as are encountered in conventional short-term business lending and also in term lending.[7]

Another important service which financing companies have helped to introduce is equipment leasing. The volume of capital equipment leasing contracts in the United States has risen from less than $10 million in 1952 to an estimated $600 million in 1962.[8] Equipment leasing is rapidly spreading to other countries; Britain's first equipment-leasing firm was established in 1959. Since then equipment leasing has spread to other countries in Europe and Mexico, and plans are being made to introduce it into other Latin American countries.[9] Equipment leasing now extends to a wide variety of equipment from fluorescent lights to giant computers, although vehicles remain the most common item. The advantages of this type of financing depend in part upon the nature of tax laws in many countries. Aside from this, however, it permits financing of firms which are in a financially weak position, since the financier can recover leased property quickly and inexpensively in the case of delinquency. Short leases may permit the user greater financial flexibility, although long leases may reduce flexibility even more than equipment purchased with borrowed funds. Financially embarrassed companies also are undoubtedly attracted to leasing because this obligation may not need to be entered on the balance sheet and thus does not impair possibilities of obtaining additional credit from other sources.[10]

[7] Saulnier and Jacoby, *Financing Equipment for Commercial and Industrial Enterprise*, pp. 87, 88.

[8] A little over half of the total equipment contracts were extended by companies engaged primarily in manufacturing and most of the remainder by specialized leasing organizations or other finance companies. In 1963, two commercial banks also began equipment leasing, and other banks are expected to follow suit. The entrance of banks into this field again illustrates the role finance companies have played in the United States in stimulating broader banking services. On bank leasing, see Warren A. Law and M. C. Crum, *Equipment Leasing and Commercial Banks*, Association of Reserve City Bankers, Chicago, 1963, and Lester Mason, "Banks Scan Opportunities in Equipment Leasing," *Burroughs Clearing House*, September 1963.

[9] See *Business Week*, July 20, 1963, pp. 61, 62; *The Economist*, Aug. 3, 1963, p. 455; and *Review of the Economic Situation in Mexico*, June, 1963, pp. 10, 11.

[10] For a discussion of the advantages and disadvantages of equipment leasing, see Pearson Hunt et al., *Basic Business Finance*, Richard D. Irwin, Inc., Homewood, Ill., 1961, pp. 378ff., and Robert T. Hungate, *Interbusiness Financing: Economic Implications for Small Business*, Small Business Administration, Washington, D.C., 1962, pp. 93ff.

Other important contributions of finance companies are their provision of advisory, collection, and other services that simplify management problems. This is of particular value to small firms. They also tend to be willing to extend a larger amount of credit in relation to the equity of individual concerns than banks will consider. This is particularly helpful to concerns entering rapidly expanding markets.

Among the important drawbacks of finance companies is that they have been exempt from monetary and banking controls in most countries. The way they may contribute to monetary problems when unregulated has already been indicated. Finance companies may also contribute to banking problems where they are important borrowers from banks and engage themselves in high-risk lending.[11] These problems can be reduced where finance companies are not permitted to accept deposits and where bank lending activities to finance companies are properly regulated. If the extent of consumer financing could be limited without impairing their total operations this would increase the value of finance companies' services in inflation-prone countries.[12]

The relatively unregulated way in which finance companies have been permitted to operate has resulted in some extending their activities into manufacturing and other nonfinancial operations. This is generally undesirable, since other functions may conflict with their responsibilities as financiers, just as the mixed functions of private moneylenders sometimes do.

The value of finance companies' services to small enterprises is limited to some degree by their concept of the minimum volume of credit required to make services to clients possible. Although services in the United States are extended to firms with a net worth as small as $10,000 or less, minimum annual sales required tend to range upward from $50,000; the average receivables outstanding per client in 1956 were around $100,000 for equipment financing and around $150,000 for factoring. The average client was estimated to have total assets of between $350,000 and $650,000.[13] Much smaller companies have often benefited from finance companies' services indirectly, however, as buyers of equipment or other products from companies able to extend credit as the result of finance companies' services.

A further limitation of finance companies' services is that the use of them often reduces a client's ability to obtain credit from other sources.

---

[11] Recent failures of finance companies in the United States have caused banks to tighten up lending standards (Edward Cowan, "Lenders' Credit Short," *The New York Times,* July 10, 1963, and *Business Week,* July 13, 1963, pp. 93ff.)

[12] Under regulations established in Argentina in 1962, finance companies are no longer permitted to accept deposits or borrow from banks; they may issue one-year certificates in blocks of about $400 or more and may borrow from abroad. The Central Bank is authorized to regulate reserves and to apply selective regulations to the financing of particular products (see Jones et al., *op. cit.,* p. 107).

[13] Federal Reserve System, *op. cit.,* p. 455.

Because financially weak concerns often turn to finance companies and have not always fully revealed this dependence in applying for credit from other sources, banks and suppliers are inclined to regard the use of finance companies as evidence of financial weakness.[14]

A final handicap associated with finance companies' services is their relatively high interest charges. In the United States charges have ranged from 8 to 24 percent (with a medium of around 14 percent) for both accounts receivable and equipment financing.[15] Although account needs to be taken of the greater services extended by finance companies than banks normally provide and also of the lower volume of credit often required when finance company services are used, these are still substantially higher rates than banks charge to small firms. It is doubtful, however, whether there are any practical ways of reducing finance company charges other than by making as widely available as possible alternative competitive sources of credit based on less expensive lending procedures.[16]

Special Finance Companies

In many countries there are now privately owned and managed institutions constituted to engage primarily in term and equity financing. Most of these institutions have been established within the past decade, and others are just coming into being, although a few date from the prewar period. They have been created largely as a result of special government measures and usually with substantial direct assistance. Their policies, as a result, tend to reflect in some degree the objectives of the initiating governments.

The objectives of governments, although often vague, have centered around a desire that institutional term and equity financing should be available for some portion of the long-term capital needs of firms too small, new, or otherwise unable to sell shares or bonds to the general public.

[14] A United States finance company has sought to overcome general bank prejudice against users of finance company services by advertisements in banking journals which stress the complementarity of the services of finance companies and banks, noting that finance company assistance enables financially weak companies to achieve bank standards of creditworthiness whereupon the clients often transfer to banks. In the interim, banks obtain the clients' deposits and build up an acquaintance with his operations, thus receiving other benefits from the finance company's assistance to the firm's survival.

[15] Federal Reserve System, op. cit., pp. 460–462.

[16] Interest-rate regulations are another alternative, although effective enforcement is very difficult, as Peru's regulation efforts in recent years well illustrate. Nevertheless, the rapid growth of finance companies was halted in Peru following the establishment of interest regulations, which suggests that regulations may have had some influence on lending rates. See Robert W. Davenport and Peter D. Duncan, A Regional Program for Channeling Development Financing to Small and Medium Industry, Instituto Nacional de Promoción Industrial, Lima, 1964.

Governments, by general measures to stimulate private finance companies, have achieved a degree of control over the nature of these services while at the same time inducing private investors to provide risk funds and to assume the operational responsibilities.

In many cases the urgency for establishing these organizations was increased by a dissatisfaction with other types of existing institutions intended to provide such services. Particularly in Europe, government action was stimulated by the desire to clearly separate deposit and investment banking in view of a failure during the 1930s of important banks in which these activities were mixed.

In many less-developed countries, the limitations of government development banks revealed in the early postwar period provided an important stimulus to the creation of more politically insulated and more highly profit-motivated services.

Some of these organizations are sometimes classified as *development finance corporations* or *private development banks*. Their mixture of private and public resources and objectives varies considerably within this category and shades into semigovernmental, predominantly governmental, and wholly governmental development financing organizations. In this section we are primarily concerned with those in which government influence is limited and indirect.

The financing operations of special finance companies vary from organization to organization but primarily consist of term lending. In some cases, their financing has profit-sharing or other equity characteristics. However, they usually do not seek the management rights normally associated with equity financing, nor do they obtain permanent holdings in companies. They are essentially transitional sources of finance permitting client companies to utilize these funds while the client achieves the capacity to draw upon conventional equity or debt sources.

More specific characteristics of special finance companies can best be brought out by examples from various countries illustrating the major differences among these organizations.

The Financiera of Mexico[17]

The Mexican type of *financiera* or finance company probably provides the closest link between companies in this category and commercial finance companies previously discussed. As these have served as a prototype for private development finance corporations in many other countries, particularly in Latin America, they are worth considering in some detail. The

[17] This section is largely based on information gathered by the author while collaborating with the Mexican Fondo de Garantia y Fomento a la Industria Mediana y Pequeña in 1961 in an investigation of a program for stimulating small-industry development in Mexico.

legal framework for finance companies in Mexico was established by bank reform laws in 1932; however, only a few were established until their functions were broadened in 1941. By 1961 there were over 100 finance companies in operation. Their total resources of 11 billion pesos (Mex$)— or approximately US$900 million—were two-thirds as large as those of commercial banks. Finance company offices spread to many areas, although the majority are still in Mexico City and most of the remainder are in five or six other centers.

Mexican finance companies have been formed by a wide variety of groups: most of the large finance companies are subsidiaries of commercial banks; some companies however have been formed by closely associated groups of industrialists and still others by foreign venture capital concerns.

Mexican finance companies have typically operated with high debt to equity ratios, often not greatly different from those of commercial banks. Their debt funds are primarily derived from loans, including term deposits, which under Mexican laws are treated as loans. In 1961 over one-third of these were obtained from abroad, another one-fifth from domestic banks, and the remainder from local individuals and concerns.[18]

The rapid growth of finance companies is partly explained by their ability to attract term deposits and loans through paying high interest rates, ranging up to a maximum of 12 percent.[19] Term deposits may be for periods as short as 90 days. Reserve requirements and other restrictions on deposits, especially those in foreign currency, have in recent years caused finance companies to draw more heavily upon bonds as a source of funds; however, by 1961 these were still only 13 percent of resources. Bonds have been sold in part, especially in earlier years, to the Bank of Mexico, although a public market for finance company bonds has been created by the general willingness of finance companies to repurchase them at par value.

Government measures encouraging the establishment of finance companies were intended to foster industrialization. However, the finance companies were given no specific responsibilities in this regard, and they have been criticized in past years for their limited contributions to this end. Myers, for example, reported:

> These companies were expected to revive capital funds for new industry, but they have not done so. Many of them were organized by a bank or business enterprise in order to facilitate obtaining credit for itself, so that the financieras were in many cases merely affiliates of an established concern. Their bonds were largely held by the Bank of Mexico. Moreover,

[18] For data on the growth of finance companies up to 1961, see O. Ernest Moore, *Evolución de las Instituciones Financieras en Mexico,* Centro de Estudios Monetarios Latinoamericanos, Mexico, 1963, chap. VIII.

[19] "High" is, of course, relative; in Argentina, where both inflation and banking restrictions are more severe, finance companies are reported to have paid 17 to 20 percent for funds in 1961 (Jones *et al., op. cit.,* p. 108).

a large part of the credit extended by them was at short maturity more appropriate to commercial than to investment banks.[20]

Their major activities continue to be lending for fairly short periods. Loans accounted for 69 percent of their assets in 1961, with almost half being for periods of six months to one year.[21] Loans for a period over one year made up only 42 percent of total loans or 28 percent of assets in 1961. Investments and company securities, although increasing in absolute amount, have declined as a percent of assets during the 1950s, being less than 10 percent in 1961. Interest rates have been high, frequently 15 to 18 percent and occasionally higher. Loans have normally been secured by collateral at twice or more the value of the loan.

The Mexican government has sought to direct financieras toward a greater financing of small-industry development through conditions imposed on rediscounting loans.[22] In 1954 a special organization, the Fondo de Garantia y Fomento a la Industria Mediana y Pequeña, was established by the government-owned Nacional Financiera, S.A., in order to provide a rediscount service in the case of loans to industrial enterprises having the total capital of between Mex$50,000 and Mex$3,500,000 (approximately US$4,000 and US$300,000).[23] Loans to be eligible for rediscount must ordinarily be for one to two years for working capital loans and two to five years for purchases of fixed assets. As of June, 1961, over 70 percent of the total amount discounted was for periods of one to three years. Lending rates are fixed (currently 12 percent). The rate of discount leaves the lending institution a margin of 4 percent. Lending institutions are responsible for all loan risks and for normal loan administration.

The Fondo's services have indirectly made available credit to nearly 2,000 enterprises, which may amount to 5 to 10 percent of the enterprises in the eligible size categories in Mexico.[24] Financed enterprises had

[20] Margaret G. Myers, "Mexico," in B. H. Beckhart (ed.), *Banking Systems,* Columbia University Press, New York, 1954, p. 597. Similar criticisms have also been made by Sanford A. Mosk, "Financing Industrial Development in Mexico," *Inter-American Affairs,* Institute of Inter-American Studies, Washington, D.C., vol. 1, no. 1, June, 1947.

[21] Moore, *op. cit.,* p. 286.

[22] Financieras in Mexico are also subject to regulations of the Bank of Mexico and the National Banking Commission on many aspects of their operations including requirements or incentives intended to influence how some of their resources are to be used.

[23] In converting these and subsequent figures to dollars from foreign currency, very roughly rounded figures have been given, since figures converted into United States dollars can at best provide only an approximate measure of the actual amounts.

[24] There were approximately 20,000 enterprises in Mexico in 1950 in the size category eligible for Fondo assistance. However, enterprises in the scales which the Fondo appears to have given primary attention to—those with assets between US$40,000 and US$300,000 with an average employment of around 60—numbered

an average of Mex$1 million (about US$80,000) in capital and 37 employees. Through the Fondo's services they received on the average nearly two loans apiece, each averaging Mex$175,000 (about US$15,000).[25] Over three-fourths of the volume of loans have gone to enterprises in the federal district, another one-fifth were in seven other states, and 5 percent in the remaining 13 states.[26]

Over a hundred finance companies and banks have discounted some loans with the Fondo, but the major use of its facilities has been by a few finance companies. The most important of these is the Financiera de las Industrias de Transformación, S.A. This company was established in 1949 by the Cámara Nacional de las Industrias de Transformación, which for many years has been a leading supporter of the interests of smaller and newer types of manufacturing concerns. It was the result at least in part of the campaign of the Cámara for more and cheaper credit for these enterprises that the Fondo was created in 1934.[27]

The achievements of the Fondo have been modest but significant. Its services have not been sufficient to influence lending rates of financieras, generally, and, although the volume of its financing is increasing, it is not likely to achieve such a volume in the immediate future.[28] They have, nevertheless, made less expensive credit available to a substantial number of enterprises. They have introduced the practice of installment payments and of requiring balance sheets and profit and loss statements. These are steps toward better financial management and planning by enterprises and better loan criteria by lending agencies.

The activities of the Fondo staff, however, have so far been primarily concerned with analyzing records to assure that loans go to profitable firms with adequate security. The addition in recent years of several engineers and economists now enable Fondo staff to visit a small portion of enterprises applying for loans and further evaluate creditworthiness. However, assistance to firms either in preparing loan applications or in other ways is

---

only 4,000, so possibly a large part of the enterprises in these scales received financing (*Fondo de Garantia y Fomento a la Industria Mediana y Pequeña: Antecedentes, Experiencia, Resultados,* Nacional Financiera, S.A., (see above) Mexico, D.F., 1958, p. 28).

[25] Of the total loans, 15 percent were in amounts of Mex$100,000 (US$8,000) or less; 73 percent were in amounts between Mex$100,000 and Mex$600,000 (US$8,000 and US$48,000) ; and 12 percent over US$48,000.

[26] Data supplied by the Fondo. The regional location as well as the scale of enterprises served depended on the applications submitted to the Fondo by banking institutions, since the Fondo does not initiate loans and, according to Fondo staff, has probably rejected less than 5 percent of applications received.

[27] For a brief digest of information on individual financieras, see *Anuario Financiero de Mexico,* La Asociación de Banqueros de Mexico, D.F.

[28] The Fondo's discounts outstanding in 1961 were equivalent to a little over US$10 million, or between 1 and 2 percent of total finance company loans.

to the financiera or bank issuing the loan. Since the Fondo does not field-check enterprises after loans are made, the extent to which loans actually go to eligible types of enterprises and are utilized for prescribed purposes depends upon the degree to which lending institutions can be relied upon to adhere to these purposes and to supervise their clients to do likewise.[29] The Fondo's discount criteria, being confined primarily to size and financial soundness of enterprises, appear inadequate in any case to assure that financing will be channeled primarily to small-industry development purposes.

Another limitation on the Fondo's services is that the paper work involved in discounting causes some delay in processing loans. Although part of this is essential and has some educational effect upon lending institutions and loan recipients, it seems doubtful that this is the most economical or effective way of achieving the Fondo's intended goals. Despite these limitations, the Fondo's activity has made a positive contribution to small-industry financing in Mexico. Moreover, it continues to make periodic evaluations of operatons and to enlarge and improve upon them.

The United States Small Business Investment Companies (SBICs)

In the United States, efforts to combine government assistance and regulation with private resources to improve small-industry financing has resulted in a rather different kind of finance company, the small business investment company. The SBIC program, enacted in 1958, was intended to be experimental and is still undergoing modifications.

Great improvements have already been made in the original regulatory framework by the responsible authority, the Small Business Administration (SBA), through its efforts to keep closely informed on the practical working of the regulations and its readiness to revise or interpret them flexibly wherever this appeared to further basic program objectives. The program is worthy of study by others contemplating financing programs for this policy approach alone, if for no other reason.

Government assistance to SBICs has been of two main types: tax concessions and government loans. Tax concessions are primarily designed to make investments in SBICs attractive to persons in higher income tax brackets and to induce risk taking by giving especially favorable tax treatment to SBICs in the case of losses on loans and also to shareholders in the case of losses on the sale of SBIC shares.

---

[29] An evaluation of the Fondo's operations in 1963 made the very constructive suggestion that the Fondo should establish regional offices staffed by a trained banker, auditor or economist who could assist in evaluating credit applications. It also suggested that loans might be made conditional upon the acceptance of technical assistance from the Productivity Center. *Survey of the Institutional and Financial Requirements of Medium and Small Industry in Mexico,* report to Centro Industrial de Productividad, Arthur D. Little, Inc., Mexico, D.F., 1963, p. 30.

Government financing is available in the form of 5 percent 20-year subordinated debentures, treated as a part of capital, in amounts matching paid-in-capital and surplus up to a maximum of $700,000.[30] This is helpful in initial formation of SBICs. However, government subordinated debentures must normally be retired as the SBIC raises funds in excess of $1 million from the sale of equity securities to the public.

The SBA may, in addition, make long-term, low-interest rates (currently $5\frac{1}{4}$ to $5\frac{1}{2}$ percent) loans to the SBICs. An SBIC may borrow from the SBA up to 50 percent of the amount of paid-in capital and surplus, or up to $4 million, whichever is less. The SBA initially made these loans for a period of five to six years, renewable for another four years, with the apparent intention of utilizing the lending authority as a means of encouraging strict adherence to SBA regulations. In 1965, the loan period was increased to 12 to 15 years. SBICs are also permitted to borrow from private sources in an amount up to four times their capital and surplus.

Government regulations establish licensing and reporting requirements for SBICs and restrict the scale of enterprises to be served and the forms of financing to be extended.

Financing must be for a period of at least five years, but may be amortizable at the rate of 20 percent per year. Financing may be in the form of a loan, a convertible debenture, or other debt or equity securities. Convertible debentures and the more recently authorized debentures with attached warrants giving rights to purchase additional shares have been the most popular. The latter provide the SBICs interest income from the outset to cover operating expenses, assure the SBIC of first claim against a firm's assets in case of failure, permit the sale of the debenture to more conservative investors (if and when the enterprise establishes a sufficient profit record), and enable the SBIC to participate as long as it may choose in the profits through its warrants. Twenty percent of an SBIC's assets, exclusive of SBA or short-term loans, may be invested in loans of less than five year maturity under new regulations issued in 1965.

The charges for SBIC financing are largely left to negotiation between the client and the SBIC. Interest rates are subject to state and, in some cases, SBA regulations, with the maximum ranging up to about 15 percent per annum. Where interest is supplemented by equity participation rights, interest has commonly been between 6 and 9 percent. In addition to this, there are often legal, auditing, and other fees which may amount to $1,000

---

[30] The limit was raised from $400,000 to $700,000 in February, 1964. The provisions governing the formation of SBICs are summarized clearly in a brochure, *The SBIC*, Small Business Administration, Washington, D.C., 1962, and a report by the Select Committee on Small Business of the House of Representatives, *How to Obtain Financing Under the Small Business Investment Act of 1958*, 85th Cong., 2d Sess., Washington, D.C., 1958.

or more. The prices fixed for converting debentures or warrants are subject to general regulations but have been flexibly interpreted. Most SBICs provide funds on a basis which ensures some equity participation rights with the expectation of making most of their income out of the profit-sharing provisions. They are thus depending on their capacity to select enterprises with a high profit potential and to negotiate favorable conversion terms. A few SBICs have engaged partly or largely in ordinary loan operations, lending at interest rates of usually 10 to 12 percent.

SBICs are not normally permitted to acquire indefinite control of an enterprise through ownership of voting shares or by other means; nor are they permitted to assume management functions, although exceptions to all of the foregoing provisions may be granted by the SBA. SBICs are encouraged to provide advisory services to their clients and are permitted to charge reasonable fees for such services.[31]

With regard to the scale of enterprises that may be financed, these have been very broadly defined as companies with a maximum gross asset of $5 million, net worth of $2.5 million, and net income after taxes of $250,000; companies may also qualify if they are *small businesses* as defined in the Small Business Administration loan program, which generally established the maximum size for most manufacturing concerns as 250 employees or for other enterprises as a sales volume which varies, ranging up to $5 million. In addition, an SBIC cannot extend financing to a single enterprise in amounts of over 20 percent of the SBIC's capital and surplus.[32]

The formation of SBICs was initially slowed by the need to adjust regulations to overcome various unanticipated practical problems, but by 1961 SBICs were being rapidly formed. Their growth has been greatly slowed since by a general lull in the stock market for new shares and by a tendency for accumulating experience to deflate some of the more optimistic expectations. By 1964 numerous weaker companies were being liquidated or merged. Data for March 31, 1965, indicated that 645 reporting companies had $536 million outstanding in 11,184 loans and investments.[33]

Over three-fourths of the SBICs are of minimum size, each having not over $325,000 capital. These, however, account for only about a quarter of a total capital in all SBICs. Twenty-three large public companies account for nearly half of the total capital and individually range in size from a capital of about $5 million to $25 million.

[31] Although the limit on fees is very generally stated, the SBA has indicated its intention to police these fees through its announcement in November, 1961, that some SBIC fees were too high and should be reduced. See *Business Week,* Nov. 11, 1961, p. 140. One instrument for supervising these fees is a regulation requiring SBICs to keep a record of all staff time spent consulting with clients and of all charges for these services.

[32] Originally loans in excess of $500,000 were prohibited, except with SBA approval, but this limitation was lifted in February, 1964.

[33] Small Business Administration.

Banks are shareholders in about 11 percent of the SBICs, although this includes shareholding in half of the larger public companies. In three-fourths of the cases of bank participation in SBICs, banks are minority shareholders, with their shareholdings rarely exceeding 10 percent of the total. In the remaining one-fourth of the cases, banks are the sole owners of SBIC subsidiaries.[34] Besides banks, SBICs are in some cases affiliated with real estate and construction companies, commercial finance companies, security specialists, management consultants, and other firms. Approximately half are unaffiliated with other business or financial concerns.[35]

It is too early to judge the possibilities of SBICs. A few have been highly successful, but the overall record has been at best mixed and so far has disappointed earlier high expectations. A survey in 1963 covering 218 SBICs found that 95 percent of those in operation since 1959 had achieved less than 10 percent appreciation in their portfolio.[36] Losses, however, have also been small, with about one in 10 reporting a liquidation of an investment at a loss. Eighteen of the forty-two public SBICs showed a profit during 1964, fourteen showed losses, and 10 broke even. This understates their actual financial performance, however, since many of the SBICs were still in the process of building up a required reserve against losses equivalent to 10 percent of the value of their investments, and many also were accumulating capital gains which would not show up on profit records until investments were liquidated. The investing public continues to take a dim view of their prospects, with 37 of the 42 public companies being valued in the market at less than their book value, in many cases at less than two-thirds of book value.[37] Stockbrokers, however, by 1965 were suggesting that a number of SBICs represented good buys.

The SBICs have been fairly slow in investing their funds, although by 1965 it was estimated that they had 70 percent of their resources invested and at the present rate would be fully invested by the end of 1966.[38] New legislation, therefore, is under consideration for creating a capital bank for SBICs and for providing other means of enlarging SBIC's access to financial resources.[39]

[34] For a detailed analysis of the role of commercial banks, see S. J. Flink, *The Role of Commercial Banks in the SBIC Industry,* The American Bankers Association, New York, 1965.

[35] For more detailed information about individual SBICs, see Richard E. Kelley, *The SBICs, Supplier of Venture Capital,* Keyfax Publications, Inc., Sherman Oaks, Calif., 1961, and Samuel Hayes and Donald Woods, "Are SBIC's Doing Their Job?" *Harvard Business Review,* March, 1963.

[36] Hayes and Woods, *op. cit.,* p. 188.

[37] "On the Bargain Counter   Small Business Investment Companies are Selling at Big Discounts," *Barron's,* Nov. 22, 1965, pp. 3ff.

[38] U.S. is Changing S.B.I.C. Approach," *The New York Times,* Aug. 1, 1965.

[39] For a description of these proposals, see "Proposed Capital Bank to Double SBIC Resources," *The Commercial and Financial Chronicle,* May 20, 1965, p. 22.

Approximately 10 percent of the SBICs so far licensed have been subsequently dissolved, and over a hundred are reported to be virtually inactive. Among those giving up their licenses were two very large companies which apparently concluded that greater or more easily identifiable profitable opportunities could be found in financing larger-scale enterprises, even without special benefits accorded to SBICs.

The SBICs which have experienced the most serious difficulties have been the smaller ones, particularly those with capital of less than $1 million. The above-cited 1963 survey indicated that many of these were considering mergers, syndicates, affiliations, and other arrangements to achieve economies of scale and to obtain larger enterprises as clients. New regulations in 1964 permitting as many as five small SBICs to share the same management were designed to encourage mergers of smaller companies.[40] Minimum private capital requirements were also increased from $150,000 to $300,000 in 1964.

Few SBICs with a capital of less than several million dollars are equipped to seek out or to screen opportunities, much less extend advisory assistance. A possible exception to this is an SBIC which is owner-managed by a person with the training, experience, and wide connections in the business world needed for identifying potential opportunities, scientifically evaluating them, and generally guiding the firms financed. Even a minimum-size firm in this case might prove a constructive source of finance and a profit-making business. Attracting persons with these exceptional abilities to start SBICs may thus be essential to successfully fostering small SBICs. Unfortunately, the present incentives to start SBICs are directed primarily to attracting funds rather than to attracting operating capabilities. The capabilities required for this type of operation are difficult to hire and use efficiently until an operation is achieved of large enough scale to permit hiring at least several different types of specialists.[41]

Even the largest of the existing SBICs operate with a professional staff of 2 to 15 persons. Consultants may be used to supplement staff capabilities, although frequent use is not commonly made of them by even large companies. A survey of SBICs in which banks are shareholders indicated that most provided some advisory services often free, although in the case of wholly bank-owned SBICs, less than half provided such services[42] Services

[40] "SBA Aims to Spur Mergers, Curb 'Raiding' of Small Business Investment Companies," *Wall Street Journal,* June 1, 1964.

[41] In Flink's view, an SBIC might start with a minimum staff of a full-time executive officer and a part-time cost accountant, a part-time lawyer and $500,000 in financial resources. He also assumes an exceptional manager, although not necessarily an owner-manager. Flink, *op. cit.,* pp. 128–130. Another *caveat* should be added to this, in the present author's view. The part-time lawyer needs to be both well-versed in the peculiar legal aspects of this type of operation and substantially interested in his business relationship with the SBIC. Legal advice of a casual sort is likely to prove highly hazardous for this type of operation.

[42] Flink, *op. cit.,* pp. 104, 105.

are, however, usually quite limited and, particularly where they are free, may be extended only after a portfolio company has gotten into difficulties. A few SBICs have special wholly owned subsidiaries to extend advisory services, and some require clients to enter into consulting contracts. Where charges are made for these services, they vary greatly, ranging from flat annual charges of $1,000 up to as much as $9,000. Some SBICs charge rates ranging upward of from $50 to $100 daily for such services.

The largest of the SBICs, which is a part of a $90 million complex of companies, has two subsidiaries, one to advise it on what investments to make and the second to provide management consulting services. Its consulting subsidiary serves 21 clients with 15 consultants, who are also the executive staff of the SBIC. It occasionally also hires outside consultants. Its capacity to extend these services is greatly enhanced by the fact that it specializes in a relatively narrow type of company, electronics concerns. For advisory services it charges its clients a flat fee averaging about $9,000 a year. It attributes much of its success to its ability to help its clients overcome unexpected problems as they arise through its advisory staff.[43]

Whether or not smaller or more diversified SBICs will be able to extend useful advisory assistance is uncertain, although a number are experimenting with such services. Aside from the capabilities of SBICs, there is also a question of how many small-growth companies will be willing to permit their financiers to become directly involved in management matters.

Despite problems, the outlook is for SBICs to continue expanding, particularly after capital market conditions improve sufficiently to facilitate further security sales. One study estimates a future expansion of 16 percent per annum.[44] Even at this rate, however, it is clear that it will be many years before the volume of SBIC financing becomes significantly large in relation to the total sector they are intended to serve.[45] Moreover, it seems likely that banks will now refer many less-profitable or riskier term-loan applicants, which they might otherwise have assisted, to affiliated SBICs, where these exist. Although this may be appropriate, it suggests that a part of the SBIC financing does not represent a net increase in availability of finance to small enterprises.

Not all—and probably a declining portion—of these funds is going to

[43] See *Business Week*, Nov. 17, 1962, pp. 114–116, and Apr. 9, 1960, pp. 49–52.
[44] See Hayes and Woods, *op. cit.*, p. 182.
[45] In 1953 there were over 400,000 manufacturing and mining enterprises alone with assets of less than $5 million and with total assets aggregating to $47 billion; even for the category of assets from $50,000 to $1 million, there were over 100,000 enterprises with $22 billion in assets. See the Federal Reserve System, *op. cit.*, p. 167. Since SBICs are not restricted to manufacturing and mining enterprises but may finance almost any type of business enterprise within the size limitations, the number and assets of eligible firms is far larger than the data just cited. SBIC financing outstanding in March, 1965, was $536 million.

what is defined in this study as *small enterprises*. Even the smaller SBICs
are reported to extend financing usually in amounts of $25,000 to $40,000.[46]
The larger SBICs, which have the most future promise, are seeking primarily opportunities over $100,000. One reason for this is that SBICs
fear that investment in small companies, even when profitable, may have
to be held for long periods. Companies with half a million dollars or more
assets have a much better prospect of reaching a size permitting public
flotation of securities within five years or less. This problem may become
less critical for SBICs once they are firmly established and income is flowing
in from successful ventures.[47]

Another explanation of the concern over size is the high minimum screening costs involved.[48] It seems likely that more systematic, less costly, and
more productive methods of identifying investment opportunities might
be employed by a great many of the SBICs if their volume of financing
were sufficiently large to afford appropriate staff for this purpose.

SBIC regulations provide few specific development criteria for the allocation of loans. However, they do permit SBICs to compensate for higher risks
and expenses by charges for their services and to a certain extent by participation rights. Thus the regulations do provide a strong incentive to select
enterprises with a high growth potential. Many SBICs nevertheless have a
more marked preference for safer types of investment than supporters of the
program had hoped. In an effort to limit the amount of money going into
real estate, a 1964 regulation restricts real estate investments to one-third of
an SBIC's portfolio.

Many of the SBICs, particularly the smaller ones which are more dependent upon low-cost government funds, may find it difficult to increase their
share of the more risky types of financing. For one thing, SBIC regulations
provide that a company's capital will be regarded as impaired—and the
SBIC subject to special supervision or possibly liquidation—if losses exceed

---

[46] Flink, *op. cit.*, p. 72.

[47] The problem of SBIC being locked into their investment in firms for long
periods of time is made more serious by the fact that they are minority shareholders.
A 1965 amendment to SBIC regulations reduced this problem somewhat by permitting
an SBIC to require a client to buy back the SBIC's equity holding after a minimum
period of five years at a price based on a set formula. The client also has the right
to buy back the shares voluntarily on the same terms.

[48] One SBIC reports that it costs a minimum of $3,000 to make a full investigation
of an opportunity and that four such investigations are normally required to turn
up one acceptable client (see Hayes and Wood, *op. cit.*, p. 192). Another SBIC
interviewed during this study has indicated screening costs borne by the SBIC
were probably nearer $1,000. Another recent study indicates that the costs of investi-
gation and final negotiations on loans usually ran well over $1,000 (Flink, *op.
cit.*, p. 72). Screening costs may be expected to vary greatly, depending upon
the extent to which the SBIC specializes in a particular area or a particular line
of industry and how thoroughly it investigates its opportunities.

50 percent of its capital and surplus, excluding subordinated government debentures. A small SBIC using the maximum leverage in government financing and fully invested could thus have its capital impaired with a loss of less than 17 percent of its total investments.

Perhaps a more important reason why many SBICs have not been more venturesome and have not given as much emphasis to the growth potential of firms as would be desirable is that the management of many SBICs does not have the professional skills and temperament required for objectively evaluating the outlook of an enterprise, even though applicants often provide extensive information on the economics of their enterprises and the qualities of management. Although SBIC officers normally have had previous experience in financial institutions, managing a venture capital operation requires a combination of talents rarely needed in other types of financing operations.[49] Where SBIC staff lack the specialized knowledge needed to appraise the outlook of enterprises, they tend to place greater reliance on the judgment of friends who are supposed to know the enterprise or the entrepreneur or who have friends who do. As useful as these informal channels sometimes are, a heavy reliance on them tends to encourage loose thinking rather than closely reasoned investment evaluations and procures rather haphazard advice.

There has been some recognition of this problem by regulatory authorities. Since October, 1964, regulations have required all new SBICs to have not only a full-time manager, but also one with at least five years experience in business financing. This, however, does not really get at the heart of the problem, since experience in business financing can be extensive without necessarily assuring the knowledge and skills required for *venture* capital operations.

Screening methods, the practice of negotiated prices for SBIC financing and other services, and a wide variation in SBIC capabilities suggest that the availability of economical and impartial service which could assist potential small-industry clients in establishing sound relationships with SBICs might improve services to smaller enterprises. The SBA, so far, has taken the position that loan negotiations are a matter for the SBICs and their clients to arrange without intervention or direct supervision by the SBA.[50] The SBA has a staff of examiners which is rapidly expanding. So far these have been primarily concerned with assuring that financing does not go to types of enterprises and purposes which are not eligible under the act. Much greater policing of the relations between the SBICs and their clients may become necessary.

[49] For a brief statement of the skills essential to operating an SBIC and a discussion of why most SBIC officers believe experience as a loan officer in a commercial bank is highly inadequate for the task of operating an SBIC, see Flink, *op. cit.,* pp. 61, 62.

[50] See Small Business Administration, *The Small Business Investment Corporation,* Washington, D.C., pp. 11, 12.

Private Investment and Term-lending Institutions in Europe[51]

In Europe wholly private term-lending institutions financing smaller enterprises are less important than official institutions and often rely on special government funds for this purpose. A brief description of a few private European institutions which have given some attention to smaller enterprises will illustrate the nature of these operations.

In Germany, the Industriekreditbank was formed in 1949 by reconstituting the previously existing private but government-supervised industrial bank.[52] Government loans from Marshall Plan foreign aid funds constituted most of its resources during its early years, but it now depends principally on bonds sold to the public. It is the largest German bank specializing in medium- and long-term lending. In 1964, it had eight branches, a total staff of 382 persons, and loans outstanding in excess of US$430 millions.

During its first decade of operations, loans of less than 300,000 deutsche marks (DM) (US$75,000) constituted about half the volume of its loans. This was primarily because it received special public funds which were earmarked for loans to small enterprises requiring loans up to DM100,000 (US$25,000) and to medium-sized enterprises requiring loans up to DM300,000 (US$75,000).

Small loans have declined in importance in recent years as dependence on government funds has declined. The average size of loans granted in 1964 was more than double the average size of loans granted during the first 10 years of operation. Although the average loan in 1964 was still less than US$80,000, many of these were supplementary loans to existing borrowers. The ratio of amount of loan to net assets is also usually quite low, so that borrowers of sums less than $125,000 were typically firms with net assets of around $1 million and several hundred employees.

The bank began with a staff already well experienced in term lending. In evaluating loan applications, its principal concern is to select able and trustworthy management. It relies primarily on financial specialists to evaluate and supervise loans and makes very little use of engineers or other technicians. It draws upon its extensive loan files and information assembled by a small economics staff from published sources to help assess the prospects of an applicant. Applicants and borrowers are expected to be able to provide detailed accounts and reports on their current operations.

Comparatively simple evaluation procedures, combined with conservative loan criteria and prosperous postwar conditions, have made it possible for the bank to spend an estimated average of no more than two weeks of all types of professional staff time on evaluating a loan application. Annual

---

[51] See Chap. 13 for information on Japan's small business investment companies.

[52] This description is based on information obtained from the annual and special reports published by the Industriekreditbank and from discussions with members of its staff in 1965.

expenditures on staff are equivalent to only 0.4 percent of its loans outstanding.

In Italy, several private term-lending institutions were formed in the postwar period: Medio Banca (Banca di Credito Finanziario) was formed by three large commercial banks and draws the bulk of its resources from one-to-five-year time deposits; EFI (Ente Finanziamenti Italiani) was formed by banking, insurance, and industrial companies and derives most of its resources from one-to-five-year bonds; and Centro Banca (Banca Centrale di Credito Populare) was formed by the popular banks (local and regional commercial banks, originally cooperatives). Other similar private institutions have been formed during the last few years. Centro Banca is of particular interest in that it may lend only to small and medium firms. Its capital and reserves are relatively small, being equivalent to a little over US$3 million in 1960. However, it obtains its additional resources from time deposits, loans from other banks, rediscounts with a government credit agency, and allocations of special public funds. Its volume of loans has increased rapidly in recent years with loans outstanding at the end of 1960 being equivalent to a little over US$42 million.[53]

In France, private regional development companies have been stimulated by special tax exemptions, dividend guarantees, and other provisions enacted in 1955. By 1962, there were 15 regional development companies with a share capital totaling about US$20 million. Over 1,300 enterprises had received financing equivalent to over US$150 million at the end of 1962.[54]

In Denmark, the Manufacturing and Manual Industries' Finance Corporation was established in 1958. Its major shareholders are banks, insurance companies, and other private organizations, although the central bank is among its shareholders and assisted in its establishment. Its resources have rapidly expanded, amounting to nearly US$39 million in December, 1964, about 60 percent of which was raised from debentures and most of the

[53] For a description of Italian term-lending institutions, see Giovanni Landriscina and Francesco Accardo, "Rapport sur l'Italie," *The Financing of Industrial Development in Europe and the United States,* Supplement I, European Productivity Agency, 1958. See also Centro Banco, *Annual Report.*

[54] Although the Regional Development Companies are designated in France as "wholly private" companies, nearly one-fifth of their shares are held by nationalized banks, and they are closely supervised by the government. See *Bulletin SEDEIS,* Société d'Etudes et de Documentation Economiques, Industrielles et Sociales, Dec. 20, 1959, no. 740 supplement, "Les Sociétés de Développement Régional," and "Inventaire et Bilan de l'Action des Sociétés de Développement Régional," *Journal Officiel de la République Française,* May 26, 1962. Other recent institutional innovations in France which promise to give important support to the operation of regional development companies are technical and financial advisory companies organized jointly by industrial associations and private and public banking institutions. See *Bulletin d'Information de la Caisse Nationale des Marchés de l'Etat,* nos. 12, 14, 15, 1963, and "TEFICA Aide les Entreprises de la Mécanique," *Entreprise,* Mar. 9, 1963.

rest from share capital. It has made 805 loans averaging around US$60,000, each for periods ranging generally between three and eight years.

In 1965, it had a total staff of 20. It employs only financial specialists in analyzing applications and supervising loans, even though about one-fifth of its clients are new enterprises. It may spend anywhere from 1 to 10 man-days in evaluating an application, including a visit to the plant, a study of records and plans, and checking with industrial associations, banks, and other sources of information. Because it is closely linked through its shareholders to many organizations, it is able to do much checking quickly by telephone. Its principal concern is to select able management.[55]

A final example of this type of institution in Europe is the Industrial and Commercial Finance Corporation (ICFC) of the United Kingdom. The ICFC was established in 1945 as a result of official initiative, and a small portion of its equity is held by the Bank of England, which participates in its board of directors. Its major shareholders are private banks, who also provide most of its other resources through loans. In recent years it has issued debentures. The ICFC engages primarily in long-term lending (over 10 years) which permits sharing in the profits of borrowers through coupling loans with preference shares. It does not seek to control or to participate directly in a borrower's management, although it may ask for a membership on a borrower's board of directors. It nevertheless maintains a close relationship with borrowers utilizing a small group of specialists who keep closely informed on the operation of the borrowers and extend advice and information. It concentrates its services primarily on medium-scale enterprises and has an upper loan limit of 200,000 pounds sterling (£) (approximately US$560,000). It has no formal lower limit, but, as it has found loans of less than £15,000 (about US$45,000) ordinarily show no profit, loans of less than this amount have been restricted to a small percentage of its total financing. Its total loans and investments outstanding are in excess of US$100 million.

Development Finance Corporations in Other Countries

Organizations intended to concentrate primarily upon extending term and equity financing have been established under private ownership and management in a variety of newly industrializing countries in recent years. These include: The Industrial Credit and Investment Corporation of India, Ltd. (ICICI), established in 1955; in 1957, the Pakistan Industrial Credit and Investment Corporation (PICIC); in 1958, the Industrial Development Finance Company of Colombia (IDFCC); in 1959, the National Finance Corporation of Colombia (NFCC), the Industrial and Mining Development Bank of Iran (IMDBI), and the Industrial Finance Corporation of Thailand (IFCT); in 1963, the Private Development Corporation

[55] Information based on the *Annual Reports* of the Finansieringsinstituttet for Industri og Handvaerk A/S and discussions with staff of the corporation in 1965.

of the Philippines (PDCP) ; and in 1964, the Honduran Finance Company, the Costa Rican Industrial Finance Corporation (COFISA), the Industrial Development Corporation of Panama, and the Development and Investment Finance Corporation of El Salvador.[56]

There are also a number of closely similar institutions which differ only in having semiofficial organizations among their shareholders, such as: the Development Finance Corporation of Ceylon (DFCC, 1956); the Valle Finance Corporation (1960) and the Finance Corporation of Caldes (1961), both in Colombia; the Industrial Development Bank (1950) and the Industrial Credit and Investment Bank (1963), both in Turkey; the New Zealand Finance Corporation (1963); and the Nigerian Industrial Development Bank (reorganized, 1964).

A clear line is not easily drawn between private and official institutions—or, as examples have already indicated, between commercial and development finance companies. Institutions in which governments are direct holders of a minority of shares do not, in some cases, reflect the typical characteristics of official institutions more or of private institutions less in their practical operations than many wholly privately owned but government-assisted development financing corporations. Indeed, the ICICI of India, which was orginally wholly private, now has a major government shareholder as a result of the nationalization of life insurance companies, but this has not had any perceptible effect on the ICICI's operations.

Because the following discussion focuses upon lending institutions which are clearly privately owned and operated and which clearly concentrate on term or equity financing important to national development, three examples of similar but less easily categorized finance companies may be useful to illustrate the varying characteristics of companies often known as private development finance companies.

The first example are the many small lending institutions known as *private development banks* which have been established in the Philippines since 1958 under the sponsorship of the government-owned Development Bank of the Philippines (DBP). The large direct role which a government institution (the DBP) plays in these organizations distinguishes them from

[56] For an analysis of some of the older of these private or quasi-private development finance corporations, see William Diamond, *Development Banks,* The Economic Development Institute, for International Bank for Reconstruction and Development, The Johns Hopkins Press, Baltimore, 1957; Shirley Boskey, *Problems and Practices of Development Banks,* for International Bank of Reconstruction and Development, The Johns Hopkins Press, Baltimore, 1959; Robert W. Davenport, *Financing Small and Medium Manufacturing Enterprises in Latin America,* Inter-American Development Bank, Washington, D.C., 1962 (English and Spanish editions) Nathaniel Engle, *Industrial Development Banking in Action; A Study of Organization, Operations, Procedure of Private Development Banks in India, Iran, Pakistan, Turkey,* PICIC, 1962 (mimeographed) ; and George Nebolsine and Allen H. Russell, *Certain Aspects of Private Development Banks,* Coudert Brothers, New York, 1957, 17 pp. (Mimeographed.)

our definition of private development banks, although the DBP's role is intended and may prove to be transitory. At present it provides about half of their resources, primarily through the purchase of preference shares which are accorded voting rights; it has representation of their boards of directors, helps select and train staff, and in general takes an active role in stimulating their formation and guiding their operations. These private development banks are also distinct in being quite small and locally oriented, none of the 20 formed up to June, 1963, having a capital over 1 million pesos (about US$25,000). Although the participation of foreign banks or other foreign investors in these institutions is not entirely ruled out, all directors must be Philippine citizens and preferably local residents.[57]

A somewhat different case is the Nicaraguan Investment Corporation, formed in 1964. The majority of its shares are held by local private financial institutions and three foreign banks. However, its formation was sponsored by INFONAC, a government development agency which became one of the few major shareholders. Its objectives and initial operations, however, have given such emphasis to short-term receivables financing that it has had difficulty gaining recognition as a *development* finance company eligible for loans from international development agencies.[58]

A final example is Peruinvest, a private finance company established without local-government assistance or special regulations but which reflects in a part of its operation some of the characteristics most desired in development finance companies. Peruinvest was established in 1960 by a consulting firm and a Peruvian bank. Its shareholders have since been broadened so that now approximately one-third of the shares are held by Peruvian organizations, nearly 60 percent by European and American financial institutions, and the remainder by individuals. In volume, its operations have been predominantly short-term foreign exchange transactions. However, it has by an effective use of its relationship with a substantial, well-staffed industrial consulting firm and by its active exploration of the possibilities of financing new enterprises, small industry, industrial parks, and other projects considered of high development priority, won at least partial local and international recognition as a development finance company. In 1963, it received a $750,000 loan from the Inter-American Development Bank, which it has agreed to lend, together with matching funds of its own, to small- and medium-sized industries.[59]

[57] See Development Bank of the Philippines, *Guideposts on Private Development Banks,* Manila, ca. 1963, and *Fifth Annual Report, 1962–1963,* Manila, 1963. The Private Development Corporation of the Philippines, cited earlier, is not one of the PDB sponsored "private development banks" described above. It has most of the characteristics of our definition of a private development finance corporation.

[58] Based on discussion with the manager of NIC in 1964 and NIC reports. The United States Agency for International Development approved a loan on highly favorable terms to the NIC in May, 1965.

[59] R. W. Davenport and P. Duncan, *op. cit.*

Turning to lending institutions which can be more firmly categorized as *private development finance companies,* it should be clear that the very concept of private development corporations implies some hybridization of private and official structure and purposes. Thus the organizations considered here are much more of an official nature than their designation as private corporations may suggest. Government is at least a silent partner in all the organizations in this group. It typically provides a major share of the funds on a heavily subsidized basis or guarantee of similar financing from international development agencies. As a result of this, governments sometimes have the right to appoint a member or observer on the board of directors.

A blending of public and private points of view also stems from the major role which national and international development agencies such as the IBRD, the United States Agency for International Development (AID) and the Commonwealth Development Finance Corporation have played in establishing and funding these organizations. These agencies are guided by specific responsibilities for facilitating local development but, at the same time, are relatively immune to local political pressures. Like private bankers, they tend to be highly concerned with maintaining operations on a sound financial basis, although less concerned than many private bankers about the level and immediacy of profits. Their participation is usually accompanied by experienced professional assistance on the establishment and operation of a development financing institution, which adds to the special qualities of the private development finance corporations. In most cases, they exercise a degree of continuing supervision over operations, although this is necessarily limited by the distance from which it must usually be exercised.

The terms on which international development agency funds have been available have also greatly assisted the development finance corporations. The International Bank for Reconstruction and Development and the Inter-American Development Bank have been the most conservative, providing funds only on a medium- to long-term loan basis, normally repayable in hard currency at 5 to 6 percent interest. The International Development Association has made a few loans to governments on a very long-term, low interest rate basis for relending to industry through development finance companies, although the government recipients have not been permitted to pass these special terms on to finance companies, at least directly. The International Finance Corporation has provided funds in the form of equity investments or convertible debentures. This has in many ways been a more helpful form of financing in the early years of these organizations when interest payments can often not be afforded and funds are needed which can absorb possible losses without forcing a liquidation of other sound investments. The United States Agency for International Development has also provided funds on very advantageous terms, often very long term loans at very low interest rates and, in some cases, with provisions for repayment in local currency. Similar agencies in other countries such as the Commonwealth Development Finance Corporation, Ltd. and Kreditanstalt für Wiederaufbau (the German Development Aid Corporation) have been other important sources of funds, often in the form of equity or otherwise advantageous terms.

The participation of international development agencies in sponsoring the development finance corporations has had the further effect of leading to the participation of private foreign banks and investment companies, which adds another dimension to the development finance companies. The participation of foreign banks and investment companies is intended to bring extensive banking experience and a private point of view, tempered by a willingness to accept a moderate and long-maturing return on investment. Such participants, although profit-motivated, tend to be less concerned with the direct return on their investments in development financing corporations than with opening up other, much larger loan and investment opportunities through the closer relationships with national and international organizations arising from participation in development finance companies. Unfortunately, the constructive influence of foreign shareholders on the operations of development finance companies appears to be much less in practice than its theoretical possibilities. Their individual holdings are often not large enough to give them a real concern with the affairs of the private development corporation. Their own staff shortages and the demands of other investments of much larger significance has kept them from making major contributions to the staffing or training of staff in most cases. Their participation has nevertheless helped to encourage private domestic investment in the development finance corporations and has generally contributed to development financing capacity and outlook.

The staffing, as well as the capital structure, of development finance companies is intended to enable them to undertake financing involving greater risks and slower-maturing returns than conventional banking institutions. The unavailability of qualified personnel, however, has to some extent prevented them from obtaining optimum staffing levels. One of the oldest and best-staffed institutions is the Industrial Development Bank of Turkey. The IDBT, with loans of about US$25 million outstanding, and new approvals in 1964 for nearly as much, operates with 65 technical, managerial, or other professional staff and 95 accounting, clerical, and other supporting staff. Although such staffing compares favorably with that common in industrially advanced countries, it is in many ways inadequate for the needs of less-developed countries.[60] Some indication of this is the 13 additional

[60] The Industrial Development Bank of Canada, which is a fairly comparable institution set in an advanced economy, had a staff of 504 in 1964, of which about half were professional. It operated 25 branches, made 2,083 loans for $88 million in Canadian dollars and had Can$224 million in loans outstanding.

professional positions which the IDBT has budgeted for but which it has not yet been able to fill. It would also have to budget for a much larger staff if it were to serve the two or three next most important centers outside Istanbul with local, largely self-sufficient branches. It has only recently opened its first two offices outside Istanbul, each operating with only one officer and clerical staff.

Staff inadequacies are also believed to be the reason why the IDBT cannot extend as much accounting and other informational services to potential clients and aftercare to loan recipients as would be desirable.[61]

Another of the better-staffed institutions is PICIC, which is reported to have 111 staff members, of which 90 are in the head office at Karachi and 21 in the branch offices at Dacca and Lahore. A great many of these are accounting staff, junior assistants, and clerical employees. The central office, however, includes a technical division of five engineers, a loan analysis division of six financial analysts, an end-use division of four financial analysts, an economic research division including four officers with advanced degrees, and various other professional staff in its legal and general departments. The branch offices have additional professional staff.

The ICICI is similarly staffed with around 100 employees. IMDBI has around 60 staff members, including seven professionals from foreign countries.[62] Development finance companies, which are newer than the foregoing and have much smaller financial resources, necessarily have much smaller staffs, but even the newest and smallest normally have, besides a manager, a financial analyst, an engineer, an accountant, and a full- or part-time legal adviser. A great many have been assisted and required by the terms of financing from international development agencies to employ initially one or more experienced loan officers from abroad.

Development finance companies have been intended to serve primarily needs for term and equity financing. Term loans in foreign exchange have constituted a major part of their operations. Some development finance companies also extend limited amounts of short-term financing. There has been considerable interest by the private participants in some of the new and proposed development finance companies in Latin America in undertaking receivable financing along the lines of Mexican and United States finance companies. To what extent they will be permitted to do so remains uncertain.

As a channel for financing small-factory development, private development finance corporations tend to have a number of handicaps. A major

---

[61] One clear indication of this is its current small but significant problem of defaults, now being remedied by changes in procedures and organizational responsibilities and some staff additions. (Information based on reports of the IDBT and discussions with IDBT staff in 1965.)

[62] For further information on the staffing of PICIC, ICICI, and IMDBI, see Engle, *op. cit.*, pp. 12–14, 47, 91.

one is that the ownership of these organizations is primarily in the hands of very large financial, industrial, and commercial organizations which tend to be biased both by knowledge and interests toward financing larger enterprises. Many of the measures that are useful in inducing commercial banks to undertake small-factory financing are also applicable to these organizations—for example, the earmarking of special funds exclusively for small-factory financing. Because of the much greater influence of domestic and foreign development agencies upon these institutions than upon banks, such measures often will be much easier to apply.

Another common handicap of private development corporations is that their operating methods, as well as their interests, tend to be geared to the financing of large projects. This usually means that offices and staff are highly centralized, elaborate and costly screening procedures are followed, relatively little direct supervision or technical assistance is extended, and controls are applied which involve large amounts of paper work, standard collateral, or other requirements which the small enterprises may not be able to meet. Thus, their operating procedures suffer many of the deficiencies of those of official development banks, although they may on the average be administered with a greater efficiency.[63] Applicants must ordinarily submit detailed technical and financial operating plans. Once these are prepared, the applicant must await their evaluation by the lending institution. Engle estimates that it takes PICIC approximately three months to screen a loan application and another four months to receive the approval of the International Bank. Other delays, including those relating to the import of financed equipment, resulted in the usual period from application submission to the first withdrawal being about fifteen months.[64] Follow-up procedures once loans are made are also ill-adapted to the requirements of smaller enterprises. Thus, in the case of ICICI, which is one of the older and better-staffed development finance corporations, the end-use check program is only two years old and "largely a matter of record keeping. There is very little field work utilized. It is recognized that this will be necessary, but the ICICI so far has not been geared to do this."[65]

Given the basis on which these institutions presently operate, financing small factories is likely to be administratively difficult as well as unprofitable. Additional special subsidies might overcome the objection of profit-oriented concerns to such operations, but unless small-factory financing is organized on a more economical basis, the very large subsidy required would make this approach impractical. This problem has caused some students of development institutions to despair of utilizing profit-motivated institutions as a channel for small-industry financing. An A. D. Little investigation team in Argentina, for example, recommended that the Industrial Bank of Argen-

[63] See Chap. 9 for the deficiencies of official development banks.
[64] Engle, *op. cit.*, p. 105.
[65] *Ibid.*, p. 16.

tina should not be converted into a private bank, despite its history as a government institution of contributing little to small-industry financing. The team explained: "Moreover, if, by government or international aid, such a private bank were set up to operate on purely business criteria, it would still need to favor the larger industrial borrowers to safeguard the interest of its shareholders and would thus be almost certain to neglect the medium and smaller firms most in need of development loans."[66]

In the present author's view, this deficiency of private development banks can often be remedied sufficiently to make them useful for small-industry financing, even though there is probably no country in which their services will not need to be supplemented by various other types of institutions. Direct assistance to these institutions in adapting their procedures and in supplementing their capabilities to screen, supervise, and assist enterprises at distant locations, however, will often be essential if they are to serve small factories on a satisfactory basis.

Development finance corporations will frequently find it in their own interest to give some attention to financing small-factory development, even though this may require some special effort. As indicated in Chapter 1, there are important advantages to serving small firms with growth potential that are not reflected in the immediate return on such lending activity It helps generate more profitable business, both in attracting other, larger clients and in helping small clients grow up. It contributes to a corporation's reputation as a public service institution, which can be of great value to organizations heavily dependent on government assistance. It helps train staff and stimulates them to seek more economical and effective financing methods which will help improve operations generally.

Finally, experience in serving smaller enterprises helps to keep a staff of specialists aware of the importance of the human element and of the interrelation of various aspects of industrial operations in the success of a venture. These considerations are fairly obvious and unavoidable in evaluating the potential of smaller enterprises but may be lost sight of in the more elaborate and specialized analysis of larger enterprises.

Private development corporations have already undertaken in a number of cases to assist small enterprises, although the volume has so far been small and the enterprises primarily in the upper size ranges of our definition. The Colombian finance companies have been particularly active. The Industrial Development Finance Corporation of Colombia received a million dollars from the Inter-American Development Bank in 1961, one-half of which was earmarked for loans in amounts less than Col$300,000 (about US$35,000) and the remainder in amounts of less than Col$600,000 (about US$70,000). Although the IDFCC and other Colombian finance companies are undertaking to finance some relatively small companies, these

---

[66] *Industrial Development in Argentina,* Arthur D. Little, Inc., Cambridge, Mass., 1961, p. 120.

activities are still a minor part of their finance; they have also been treated as such, with little consideration being given to the economics of this activity or the special requirements of these enterprises.[67] Other development finance companies have followed a similar course. "PICIC's endeavor has been to assist small and medium-size industries in addition to financing the requirements of large industries."[68] However, loans of less than US$100,000, although large in number, have accounted for a very small part of the total amount of PICIC's financing. Clearly, if the small-industry financing of private development banks is to reach a significant volume and become a continuing activity, special assistance will be required to put this activity on a sounder basis.

[67] For further details see Chap. 12.

[68] Statement by the chairman of PICIC at the Fourth Annual Meeting of May 10, 1962.

Chapter 9
Utilizing Official
and Quasi-official
Organizations

THERE ARE FEW countries in the world that do not have a wholly or partially government-owned development bank or other official agency with industrial financing responsibilities. Not all these are concerned with small industry, but most are expected to serve small as well as larger enterprises. A great many, moreover, are intended to serve primarily enterprises described as small and medium scale, and a considerable number have special or exclusively small-enterprise responsibilities. We are concerned here with all official agencies which might directly finance small factories, whether as a primary or secondary activity, although particular attention is given to organizations with a major interest in financing them.

The broad category of official institutions of concern to us is obviously made up of highly diverse elements. Among official institutions, there are major differences as to the extent of government participation, organizational form, scope of financing responsibilities, degree of attention to small industry, and nature of financing activities. Moreover, the local environment and the specific personalities involved often have a major influence on the nature of official financing agencies. The general and summary treatment we must give official agencies leaves out of account often important individual differences. There is thus a hazard that the general points worth making about this category may be misunderstood. It should be stressed, therefore, that our purpose in generalizing about this group is not to delineate universal characteristics of official institutions but rather to provide guidelines concerning the aspects of official institutions meriting careful appraisal when these types of organizations are being considered for channeling finance to small enterprises. Also, our characterizations are, for the most part, intended generally to be more descriptive of: (1) wholly government-owned institutions than those with a substantial degree of nongovernmental participation; (2) specialized term and equity financing organizations than those engaged in general banking or other financing activities; and (3) institutions in less industrialized countries than those in more advanced ones.

In newly developing countries, official development financing institutions are, with few exceptions, postwar creations. In industrialized countries, many of them originated during the depression of the 1930s, and a few date from an even earlier period. The most common type of development financing organization, private or official, is that which is wholly government-owned. Even wholly government-owned agencies with development financing functions take many forms; they include government-operated development banks, special official corporations with nonfinancial as well as financial functions, central banks, state-owned commercial banks, and offices of government ministries. Wholly government-owned agencies with important financing functions are found in countries at all levels of development and in all regions of the world. They include, for example: the Small Business Administration in the United States; the development banks of Canada, Australia, and the Union of South Africa; the Central Institute for Medium-term Credit to Small and Medium Industry of Italy; the Small Business Finance Corporation of Japan; the National Small Industry Corporation in India; the Rural Industrial Development Authority of Malaya; the Industrial Bank of Iraq; the Government Development Bank and the Industrial Development Company of Puerto Rico; the Industrial Development Corporation of Jamaica; the Industrial Bank of Argentina; the Economic Development Corporation of Chile; the National Development Institute of Nicaragua; the Industrial Development Corporation of Kenya; the Federal Loans Board of Nigeria; the Development Bank of Ethiopia; and dozens more.

Government financing activities are primarily administered through autonomous corporations, but this organizational form is not always used. Financing in some cases is directly extended by government ministries, e.g., financing extended under the State-Aid-to-Industry Act Fund in India, the Nyasaland Industrial Development and Loan Board, the Norwegian District Development Fund, and the Development Area Treasury Committee funds of the United Kingdom.

Official and quasi-official institutions are here defined to include also organizations in which governments share in the ownership and control with private organizations or individuals. Development financing organizations with this type of mixed ownership have been increasing in relative as well as absolute importance in recent years, although they remain less numerous than wholly government-owned financing institutions. They are also quite widespread and include some long-established organizations in

Europe, such as the Netherlands Middle-class Bank, the Industrial Credit Company of Ireland, the Swedish Industrial Credit Bank, and the Norwegian Bank for Industry, as well as more recently established institutions in other countries, such as: the Industrialization Finance Corporation of Finland, the Artisan Bank of Israel, the Bank of Northeast Brazil, the Industrial Bank of Bolivia, the Popular Bank of Colombia, the Industrial Bank of Peru, some state finance corporations in India, the Korean Small and Medium Industry Bank, the Industrial Development Finance Corporation of Viet-Nam, and many more. In most cases, private shareholders have a minority position, and in some cases, their participation is largely nominal. In a few organizations government is a minority shareholder, such as the Industrial Development Bank of Israel, the China Development Corporation, the Liberian Development Bank, the Malayan Industrial Development Finance Ltd., the C. A. Venezolana de Desarrollo (Sociedad Financiera), and the Moroccan National Bank for Economic Development.[1] Government shareholding, however, does not always measure the degree of direct government influence; the latter is occasionally smaller but more often is much greater than the government's share in the equity of the organization.

The scope of responsibilities of official and quasi-official development financing organizations is varied. Some are responsible for all sectors of the economy; others are limited to particular sectors. None are limited exclusively to manufacturing, and only a few are limited to manufacturing and mining. Manufacturing is usually a major activity, but it is sometimes a relatively minor one; it is minor as compared with agriculture in the case of the Commonwealth Development Bank of Australia, the Agricultural and Industrial Credit Corporation of Ceylon, and the Development Bank of Jordan; or as compared with hotels in the case of the Industrial Development Corporation of Kenya; or with utilities, as in the case of the Development Bank of Brazil.

Not all these institutions have nationwide responsibility. Quite frequently, in moderately large or industrially advanced countries and occasionally in smaller and less industrialized ones, special regional, state, or local institutions supplement others with nationwide responsibilities. Such organizations include the state and community development organizations in the United States, provincial development funds in Canada, and state or regional corporations in such countries as Italy, France, India, Nigeria, and Peru.

The degree of emphasis on small enterprises also varies widely among these organizations. Most do not have specific restrictions on the scale of enterprise to be financed, although a number do. It is common, however,

[1] Government shareholding in the Moroccan Bank was reduced to a minority position by new share issues to private banks and the International Finance Corporation in 1962. Institutions in which government has a minority shareholding are often grouped with the private finance corporations previously discussed, particularly since they fall within the World Bank and IFC's ownership standards of eligibility for financing as "private" banks.

for their general policies to indicate a primary or, more vaguely, a special interest in a usually undefined scale labeled small and medium enterprises. Small enterprises, broadly defined to include all businesses employing less than 100 workers, are numerically the predominant type of borrower from these institutions. The volume of financing to such enterprises is nevertheless not usually of great significance. Not many official financing organizations have extended a major share of their financing to small industry, and in even fewer instances have they become a major source of finance for such enterprises. A few institutions, such as the Small Business Finance Corporation in Japan, the Small and Medium Industry Bank of Korea, and the Middleclass Bank in the Netherlands, have become a major source of financing for small factories and other enterprises of comparable size. Some others, such as the Indian National Small Industries Corporation and the Danish Ministry of Commerce and Industry small-enterprise loan program, although not of major importance as a source of small-enterprise finance, have extended most of their loans to enterprises in this scale.

Most official financing organizations, particularly those with specific development responsibilities, have extended financing primarily in the form of term loans. A few have provided some equity financing, but few have attempted to extend equity financing to their small-enterprise clients.[2] A

[2] Two organizations which have experimented unsuccessfully with equity financing of small enterprises in developing countries are the Orissa State Finance Corporation and the Salvadorean Finance Company for Small Industry. The Netherlands has also been experimenting with two equity financing companies since 1960. One, administered by the Middleclass Bank, takes minority participations in companies on a temporary basis in amounts up to US$27,000; the second, administered by the National Investment Bank, takes participations ranging from US$27,000 up to about US$700,000. These operations are based on rather ingenious arrangements. The two financing companies obtain their funds from long-term deposits of financial institutions. Both the depositors and the financing companies are guaranteed against any loss by an Industrial Guarantee Fund of about US$8 million, established by the Netherlands government. The financing companies purchase shares in firms at values determined on the basis of the firms' assets and earnings. The firms have an option to repurchase such shares within a certain period at par plus 10 percent annual appreciation less the amount of dividends paid in the period on the shares. Thereafter, the financing companies may sell the shares at market value or at an "appraised fair market value" determined by two auditors, one appointed by the financing company and one by the firm. Although these provisions would appear to meet most of the usual objections to financing small firms on an equity basis, neither the potential recipients nor the bank administrators of the Dutch equity financing operations have shown much enthusiasm for the arrangements. Up to October, 1965, the company administered by the National Investment Bank had made ten investments, while the other company does not seem to have made any.

The foregoing draws upon discussions with officials of the lending institutions in 1965. For further details see "Financing Possibilities in the Netherlands for Increasing Owner's Capital (Equity Capital)," Research Institute for Management Science, Memorandum No. 3187 (mimeographed), and The National Investment Bank of the Netherlands, *Annual Report*, 1964.

substantial number of official financing organizations extend short-term as well as long-term financing, including such organizations as the Artisan Bank of Israel, the Small and Medium Industry Bank of Korea, the Bank of Northeast Brazil, and the Institute of National Development in Nicaragua. Short-term financing has even been a primary activity of some institutions in this group, such as the popular banks in Colombia, France, Italy and other European countries, and the government-owned commercial banks with special small-industry programs in India, Indonesia, and other countries.

Merits

The literature on financial institutions contains extensive listings of common weaknesses in official institutions but makes little mention or explanation of what, if any, special merits they may have. Defenders of government financial institutions can be found both in and outside them, but they have been much less articulate than critics and generally have not gone beyond cataloguing accomplishments to explain the special capabilities of official institutions.[3] Yet the large number of official institutions and the continued formation of new ones in such a wide variety of countries requires some explanation.

A major reason that governments establish supplemental official development financing institutions, even in private enterprise economies having a variety of private financial institutions, such as the United States, is that it takes time and experimentation to work out incentives and regulations which will induce private institutions to allocate finance to particular objectives which government may regard as meriting priority. In the interim, these objectives may be neglected. Moreover, the means available for guiding the financing activity of private institutions can usually influence only the broad directions of private lending and tend to be slow acting and inefficient for achieving quite narrow and specific objectives. When government policy makers are seeking very specific action and quick results, there is much to be said for the directness of implementation which official institutions permit. Many of the official financing institutions in the more industrialized countries have arisen in depressions or in other critical times when prompt

[3] Marquez, however, has pointed out that "the general contribution which government financial institutions have made to development cannot be denied. . . . They have undertaken investments which require more funds and yield lower and/or slower returns than private enterprise requires. . . .

"Their outlook has been broader than that of private enterprise. Considerations such as the short- and long-run balance of payments situation have had a great influence on their operations, and their work has frequently been coordinated with investments made out of budgetary funds. They have taken more risks than private financial institutions and have carried out basic research." (Javier Marquez, "Financial Institutions and Economic Development," in H. S. Ellis (ed.), *Economic Development for Latin America*, Macmillan & Co., Ltd., London, 1961, p. 187.)

and specific action was required. Federal lending programs for business in the United States, for example, "were designed hastily to meet dire emergencies, when there was neither the opportunity to create institutions of the federally sponsored type (as agricultural cooperative banks) nor the practical possibility of inducing an increased flow of private investment funds under the protection of loan insurance."[4] Official institutions have, moreover, generally better justified themselves by their level of performance when under the public pressure for results which emergencies engender than they have after high public interest in their success has passed.

In less developed countries, the directness of action possible through official institutions has a special appeal, since administrative means of influencing private institutions through incentives and regulations are much weaker. At the same time, private financial institutions in many of these countries tend to be much less ready than their counterparts in more advanced countries to accept public responsibility. This reflects not merely the general orientation and philosophy of different bank managements, but also differences in the general environment in which the various banks operate. There is a great need under these circumstances for simple and direct ways of implementing policy measures which an official bank might provide.

Also in less developed countries, governments have access through foreign and international lending programs to substantial resources for development financing purposes. Because government guarantees are usually required for loans from abroad and thus government is to a degree directly involved whether the loan allocation is privately or publicly administered, there is a tendency for governments to favor official institutions in these cases. Thus the flow of funds from abroad to developing countries has tended to contribute to the spread of official development financing institutions.[5]

A demand for official financing organizations also arises from the commonness, particularly in developing countries, of important needs for particular types of financial services or needs for financing by particular types of enterprises, which private institutions cannot be easily induced to provide.

---

[4] R. J. Saulnier et al., *Federal Lending and Loan Insurance,* Princeton University Press, Princeton, N.J., for the National Bureau of Economic Research, 1958, p. 60. And as another banking authority, who indicates that the need for government lending institutions in the United States today is at best debatable, comments: "Few fair-minded observers will argue the necessity for the creation of government lending agencies at the time of the banking crisis which had its inception in 1929." William G. Price, "Why Business Firms Borrow from Commercial Banks," in Benjamin Beckhart (ed.), *Business Loans of American Commercial Banks,* The Ronald Press Company, New York, 1959, p. 56. Urgent and critical conditions had a similar role in the creation of many European official lending programs.

[5] A counterinfluence in recent years has been the tendency of international sources of finance to prefer private or mixed institutions to wholly government-owned ones in establishing credit relationships.

A major function of official institutions in most countries has been to meet demands of this type. For example, when existing institutions are primarily engaged in short-term lending, they often cannot be readily induced to meet needs requiring term financing, particularly when there are ample opportunities for their present types of services. It may be difficult to overcome the objections that term financing involves special risks or depends on specialized staff and procedures which existing institutions cannot easily acquire or integrate into their present operations. A different but also common situation is where there is a possibility of changes which would drastically revise the economics of investment opportunities (such as the overthrow of an existing government). Even fairly large special incentives may not be enough to induce private sources to undertake financial commitments not easily and quickly liquidatable. Where such uncertainties exist, governments are in a better position to take a long-term view or to spread risks than are private institutions.

Official institutions are often essential for types of financing programs which are highly experimental. Because it is difficult to know what the risks and results will be, it is not always possible to establish a framework which will induce private institutions to carry out such experiments. Official agencies, such as the United States Reconstruction Finance Corporation (1932–1953), have carried out important pioneering work in new types and forms of financing.[6]

Official institutions may also be needed to a limited degree in some countries to set competitive standards for similar private institutions. Although excessive or unequal competition holds the danger of discouraging private institutions altogether, moderate and discreet use of official institutions may—particularly by providing specific, reliable, and detailed information on financing costs and problems—be an important supplement to regulatory efforts where the administrative mechanisms for regulating private institutions are inadequate.

Many developing countries are confronted with various circumstances, such as the foregoing examples. For all the limitations of official organizations, which are discussed below, it seems likely that the conclusions of a study in East Africa are applicable to a number of areas at a similar level of development:

> It is the desire to see development corporations act in accordance with sound economic and commercial principles that has . . . induced the World Bank to give its aid mostly to privately owned and operated development companies . . . . But it is clear that, in East Africa, at any rate, the development corporation must for some time to come be exclusively or predominantly a public agency, supplied mainly by public funds and managed in the public interest.[7]

[6] See Saulnier et al., *op. cit.*, pp. 250–259.

[7] *Public International Financing in East Africa (Kenya, Tanganyika, and Uganda)*, Columbia University School, of Law, New York, 1962, p. 113.

In most countries, however, official financing organizations need not be the exclusive channel of development funds, even though there are few countries where they may not prove to be one important channel.

Limitations

That serious deficiencies have characterized the operations of many official development banks is clearly indicated by the number that have been liquidated or reorganized because of serious financial problems in the postwar period. These include banks in such countries as: Honduras, Thailand, Argentina, Bolivia, Ecuador, Paraguay, Korea, Guatemala, Colombia, Vietnam, Ghana, and a great many others.[8] In addition, there are many institutions with poor loan recovery records which have so far escaped liquidation or reorganization, and there are still others with impeccable balance sheets but little evidence of significant contributions to accelerating development.

The record of official lending institutions has been no doubt disappointing to those seeking through them simple solutions to complex problems. But it is easy to exaggerate their failings or the generality of deficiencies which have marked various official institutions.

In particular it is not true that all official institutions which have gone bankrupt or required subsidies are necessarily failures. The value of many of the contributions of these institutions to the economy does not show up in their balance sheets, but the cost of providing them inevitably does. Official development banks are usually lenders of last resort. Having ascertained, at some expense, that some project or type of client can safely and profitably be served, they must often allow private lenders to take over the repeat business and move on to financing which private lenders still find too risky or unrewarding. In recent years, for example, the Industrial Development Bank of Canada has found its successful pioneering of term lending rewarded by the loss of not only some of its most attractive accounts, but also some of its experienced staff to newly-formed private term-lending institutions.

Contributing to private institutions in this way is no doubt a part of its development functions, but such costs should not be lost sight of when private and official institutions are compared. Official institutions are also much more restricted than private institutions in charging as much for their services as the market will bear. Thus the inability of an official lending institution to operate on a budgetarily sound basis raises suspicions but by no

---

[8] One consulting firm with a long acquaintance with development banks in Latin America reports that: "In Latin America, for example, the preponderant majority of government-sponsored development banks have gone bankrupt (although their bankruptcy is sometimes concealed for political reasons.)" Edward Tenenbaum and Louis Thompson, *Tanganyika Five Year Industrial Plan,* vol. I, Continental-Allied Company, Inc., Washington, D.C., 1964, p. 20.

means convicts, particularly in an environment where subsidies and other distorting influences on the price system are common.

Finally, in considering the record of official institutions, it should be recognized that not all the limiting traits which have characterized them are really inherent in their organizational form. Therefore, in assessing the potential of official banks as a channel for financing small-industry development, it will be important to distinguish remediable deficiencies from less tractable ones.

A major limitation common to many official agencies, which need not characterize them, is that they tend to have wide responsibilities much beyond their total capacity, and often responsibilities ill-suited to their special capabilities. In such circumstances, no matter how well the institution utilizes its resources, it can never be a success in terms of what it has been chartered to do. At least a part of the misallocation of financing and inefficiency attributed to official institutions stems from such mischartering of their responsibilities, rather than from their organizational form per se. An institution directed to accomplish the impossible inevitably tends to fritter away much of its energies in token effort and in shifts in direction. Also, intentional misdirection of activity is easily camouflaged under such circumstances. Private institutions, when similarly burdened, have similar problems.

A basic merit of official institutions previously cited was that such institutions when properly organized and provided adequate and appropriate resources offer an immediate and fully controlled means of implementing given objectives with specified priorities. In many cases, however, this is not the way official institutions are established. They often are established largely because policy makers have not been able to resolve objectives and priorities, because of either a lack of information or basic disagreements among themselves; institution creation gives the semblance of action and temporarily relieves the pressures on policy makers to resolve difficult issues. Agreement on establishing an institution is reached by incorporating most or all of the varying objectives advocated by different policy makers, by omitting priorities on debatable issues, and by keeping the appropriation for resources sufficiently small in order not to arouse opposition from the economy-minded or other claimants on resources. Although compromise is inherent in the democratic process, many of the compromises in creating official financing institutions have been unnecessarily bad. The conduct of basic investigations of the type indicated in Chapter 4 before programs are established would do much to resolve these issues.

Other serious limitations to which official institutions have sometimes been subject are the related effects of political opportunism, favoritism, and corruption in the allocation of financing. Official banks have often found it difficult to appraise objectively or to follow the objective evaluations of their economic and technical specialists in the case of large politically popular projects. Such financing has been the cause of many of the development bank failures and has weakened others to an extent that they have been unable to bear the normal costs and risks of development financing. In other cases, politically popular projects have been sound but so large in scale as to tie up most of the bank's resources. In such cases, official banks at best are able to extend only token financing to small manufacturers. In such financing, little attention is likely to be given to achieving economical methods for serving small enterprises or to allocating funds in a way that maximizes development results.

Government institutions have special problems with favoritism in loan allocation, because frequently no one managing or supervising these institutions will lose personally from such practices, whereas in private institutions the owners of the funds involved are usually in a position to check such practices where they threaten the security or profitability of the organization. Government organizations have special favoritism problems also because large sections of the influential public in many countries accept or tolerate the use of political office for enriching the officeholder or his friends. Thus, the managements of official institutions are subject to pressures and temptations which the managements of private institutions are less likely to experience.

Official institutions tend to be under great pressure to favor not only politically influential individuals, but also politically influential groups, such as small farmers, artisans, and lower-income groups generally. Petty loans made for political or social reasons are usually not expected to be self-supporting, and, as a result, little attention may be given to the efficiency with which they are administered. Even though the volume of such lending is not high, where the number of such loans is large, the total administrative costs of such loans may make up a large part of the total administrative costs of the organization. The Development Bank of the Philippines, for example, in 1961 extended about two-thirds of the number, although only about 1 percent of the amount of its loans, in sums of 2,000 pesos or less (roughly US$500 or less) to graduates of technical schools.[9] Similarly the Industrial Bank of Argentina had in 1960 almost two-thirds of its loans in amounts of less than 100,000 pesos (roughly US$1,200), and 10 percent were less than (M$N) 10,000.[10]

Where official institutions are burdened with petty loan programs of

[9] Development Bank of the Philippines, *Annual Report,* 1926.

[10] Arthur D. Little, Inc., *Industrial Development in Argentina,* Cambridge, Mass., 1961, p. 121. See also the petty loan problems of the Banco Popular discussed in Chap. 12 and of the Bank of Northeast Brazil discussed in R. W. Davenport, *Financing Small and Medium Manufacturing Enterprises in Latin America,* Inter-American Development Bank, Washington, 1962 (English and Spanish editions), Chap. 4.

the above types, they also tend to drift into slack collection procedures. There are usually too many loans to supervise well. Moreover, repayment responsibilities become vague where loans are intended to serve social or political objectives.

Once the institution is known to tolerate poor repayment records on these loans, collection difficulties on all loans generally increase, and its capacity for sound development banking may be seriously impaired.[11]

The problems stemming from political influence, favoritism, or corruption in loan allocation are serious enough for official institutions. The extent to which they are associated with the official organizational form, however, is easily exaggerated. The actual or alleged shortcomings of official institutions are more quickly drawn to the public's attention than those of private banks, since official institutions are more frequently caught up in political debates in which unfounded or exaggerated—and also sometimes accurate—charges of corruption and favoritism are common.

The degree of favoritism and related problems may in official institutions reflect the standards and customs of the country, plus fairly universal human tendencies in seeking or allocating commodities and services in short supply. A development bank's task of serving the business community or satisfying public institutions' standards is inevitably complex in countries where the standards of the business community differ sharply from public concepts of the standards government institutions should maintain.

Private as well as public institutions often favor friends, although rarely to the point of endangering bank solvencies.[12] Bribery also occurs in private institutions, although it is usually less of a problem than in official institutions, since the financing charges of private institutions are more likely to approximate the maximum the market will bear.[13]

[11] Two prime examples of institutions whose operations have suffered from problems of this type are the Rural and Industrial Development Authority in Malaya and the Rehabilitation and Development Council of Arequipa in Peru. The problems of the former are described by Gayle Ness, "Letter from Malaya," *Institute of Current World Affairs,* June 1, 1962, and in more detail in *Report of the Loan Programme,* Review Committee of the Rural and Industrial Development Authority, Kuala Lumpur, Malaya, 1963. The Arequipa operations were analyzed in detail by the author and briefly reported on in Robert W. Davenport and Peter D. Duncan, *A Regional Program for Channeling Development Financing to Small and Medium Industry,* Instituto Nacional de Promoción Industrial, Lima, 1964.

[12] See the discussions of commercial banks and finance companies.

[13] A study referring to banks generally in Taiwan, including the essentially private commercial bank, reports: "Small borrowers sometimes have to make expensive presents, offer entertainment, or in some way provide bank officials with 'payola' (to use an expression which has been adopted by many English-speaking Chinese). The initial cost is said to be roughly 10 percent of the interest payment." Edward A. Tenenbaum, *Taiwan's Turning Point,* Continental-Allied Company, ca. 1961, p. 62. The extraction of payments from loan applicants by private bank managers occurs occasionally even in the United States (see *Burrough's Clearing House,* December, 1962, p. 83).

Official institutions also sometimes have to contend with greater problems of bad faith from borrowers, despite a high standard of loan administration, than private institutions might have to contend with in similar circumstances. In some cases, this problem arises with very small borrowers with little to lose and a strong conviction that they are entitled to anything they can get free from government. In other cases, it is a case of borrowers so economically and politically powerful that they often believe official institutions incapable of forcing repayments. One gathers the impression from discussions with bank officials who have experienced this problem that this difficulty arises less commonly with small manufacturers operating on the scales of primary concern here, being particularly rare in the case of enterprises with a strong urge to grow and a continuing need for outside financing.

The special necessity of official institutions to avoid not only favoritism but also all appearance of favoritism handicaps their operation in a number of ways. Maintaining an unquestionable posture of strict impartiality tends to impair a lending organization's ability to be selective among applicants, particularly where differences are not easily proven. The problem of official institutions in this respect has been aptly put by de Block:

> Another principle of government policy is that identical cases must be treated in an identical way. However, many shades of differences are possible in the grant of credits and guarantees. For example, identical credit or guarantee applications can still represent different cases, if only because of the different personalities who are involved. While the possibility of public criticism on the one hand will tend to result in great caution, in order to prevent the danger of losses, the necessity of equal treatment may, on the other hand, result in the granting of unwarranted credits and guarantees.[14]

Official institutions are inhibited not only in being selective about whom they finance, but also in the terms that may be accorded to different recipients of finance. Interest rates, in particular, have tended to be standardized for all borrowers, irrespective of differences in lending costs. Official institutions have usually also been expected to lend at less than market rates. Where loans are bargains but are in very limited supply, any allocation is likely to be the subject of controversy. At the same time, improper pressure is more likely to be brought to bear on those making the allocation. Smaller enterprises become less attractive to lending authorities, both because with uniform rates of interest they are inevitably less profitable and because they are less able to exert pressure. Despite the below-market rates, moreover, the loans may not be as much bargains for small enterprises as for large ones, since the indirect costs that commonly accompany the lending

[14] L. de Block, "The Relationship Between Government Credits and Guarantees and the Credit Policy of Commercial Banks: An Evaluation of a Possible Trend," in Nederlandse Bankiersvereniging, *Trends in Bank Credit and Finance,* Martinus Nijhoff, The Hague, 1961, pp. 160, 161.

procedures of official institutions tend to be much more burdensome relative to the amount of loan in the case of small loans than large ones.

Official institutions frequently do not prove to be as venturesome as their founders had expected. Indeed, too often there is little to distinguish their operations from those of private banks except more laborious procedures. Such institutions may not encounter financial difficulties, but as development institutions they may fail to justify their existence any better than those which lose their resources. A common reason why official institutions fail to make any unique or net contribution to financing development is simply that they have not been provided with the proper staff and other resources to enable them to depart from conventional concepts of sound financing. Another circumstance that tends to contribute to this type of deficiency is that the staffs of official institutions may not be in the position to protect themselves from unjust criticism should losses occur. In circumstances where opponents of the government in power tend to seize upon any case of loss as evidence of incompetence or impropriety, and where the general public has little detailed information or understanding of an official financing institution and is generally suspicious of official entities, it is understandable that the staff of official financing institutions will be reluctant to undertake inherently risky types of financing. As de Block has commented, probably referring to the Dutch experience:

> The competence of government officials to evaluate credit worthiness and their ability to calculate long-term prospects, although probably better than is generally believed, is limited. A government official is inclined to be cautious because a correct decision raises no public attention, while a wrong decision may have the most unpleasant repercussions, particularly if it becomes a political football.[15]

Even though adequate special reserves have been set up to take care of expected losses, and though profits will at least ultimately offset losses, this may not solve the problem of the staff's vulnerability to criticism when normal losses occur. McCrory has described this problem as it affected lending programs in India in the following terms:

> Whatever the dimensions of actual corruption, fear of it and a willingness to suspect it bulk large enough to make the public servant, on one hand, hesitant to exercise his discretion and government, on the other, prone to leave him as little room as possible to do so. The difficulties this presents are obvious in a small industrial loan program where loans are based on discretion and errors not recoverable through security.[16]

Another general deficiency of official institutions is a variety of characteristics resulting in what the public labels bureaucratic inefficiency and red

---

[15] *Ibid.*

[16] James T. McCrory, *Small Industry in a North Indian Town*, Government of India, Ministry of Commerce and Industry, Delhi, 1956, p. 49.

tape. These have an important effect on the types of financing which official institutions are able to undertake. Delay, a major by-product of this characteristic, is less a handicap when the financing constitutes a large part of the borrower's resources, when it is being extended to new enterprises or for fairly long-term purposes, and when the economics of the purpose for which funds are borrowed is not likely to be greatly modified with the passage of time by such influences as inflation, the action of competitors, or other changes in the general environment. Red tape and inefficiency, apart from the delay element which they involve, are more tolerable when the applicant has regular staff and procedures for complying with the requests for information and for following up on applications and information submitted to assure that they will keep moving through official channels. In general, these limitations more seriously restrict the usefulness of official institutions in financing small than large enterprises.

The time taken to process applications depends on a great many factors, but some examples of the time required in various official institutions may illustrate the seriousness of the problem. One writer discussing the United States Smaller War Plants Corporation states:

> The process involved a considerable lapse of time; Chairman Maverick indicated that, in early 1945, the Corporation needed from six weeks to two months to make a loan. On top of this, long delays were common in the actual execution of a loan after it was authorized because of complications in arranging the mortgages and other documents often required.[17]

The same author cites a quotation of Howard Markel on the RFC:

> My own feeling as a result of this experience is that the present routine in handling small loans through the Reconstruction Finance Corporation is so cumbersome that the average small concern cannot wait for the final result. In addition, it is so expensive because of all the documents involved, usually including special legal and accounting fees, that the small firm feels it cannot afford to make an application on a speculative basis. The net result of both these conditions is that unless there is some definite feeling that the loan will be consummated, most small borrowers are discouraged at the outset.[18]

After the RFC's operations were decentralized, some of the delay was eliminated.

The same kind of problem exists in many other countries and often to a much greater degree with official institutions. The delay problem in the Swedish Industrial Credit Corporation is described as follows:

> The average time, measured from the day of receiving application to that of granting a loan, may vary from between 3–5 months. This time factor

---

[17] Douglas R. Fuller, *Government Financing of Private Enterprise,* Stanford University Press, 1948, p. 153.
[18] *Ibid.,* p. 112. The RFC operated from 1932 to 1953.

is a serious setback to the borrower, as to the availability of the loan, and secondly, the borrower may sometimes have to make temporary arrangements with other sources to tide over the period, and thereby incur extra expense or effort.[19]

A study in Argentina comments on the Argentine Industrial Bank as follows:

> Of those interviewed, many had previous contact with the Banco Industrial. . . . We were told that it normally takes eight months to obtain a loan from the bank. This is in remarkable contrast with the speed with which commercial banks normally make loans, generally within one week. Many industrialists said they would not attempt to deal with the bank because of the long delays and complicated procedures necessary to obtain loans.[20]

The problem in Ecuador has been summed up in the following way:

> Equally frustrating and costly are the procedures for obtaining industrial credit through the complex of the National Development Banking System, the National Board of Economic Planning and Coordination, and the National Securities Commission. Applicants have reported delays as long as two years in processing loan applications.[21]

Problems are equal or greater in developing countries elsewhere.[22]

The exceptionally attractive terms offered by official institutions are often both a direct and indirect cause of their various administrative problems. Many more applicants tend to be attracted than can be efficiently served. Moreover, "fair allocation" becomes an important and complex question.

Much of the red tape in official institutions is the result of efforts of the founders to protect the organization from its susceptibility to favoritism and the result of efforts of administrators to protect the organization from its vulnerability to criticism on this account. The remedies normally applied, however, tend to result in authority and responsibility being divided. This produces delays and cautiousness in decisions. It results in requirements that applicants provide detailed written information, and it also results in officials having to write down their analysis and judgment at each stage of action on the application. This creates good archives in case a review

[19] Brian Wickremesinghe, *Financing of Small-scale Industrial Enterprises in Sweden,* Företagesekonomiska Institutionen, Uppsala University, 1962.

[20] Arthur D. Little, Inc., *op. cit.,* p. 119.

[21] Checchi & Company, *Expanding Private Investment for Ecuador's Economic Growth,* ICA, July, 1961, p. 13.

[22] For the similar problems in India, see Chap. 2; in Indonesia, see Douglas Paauw, *Financing Economic Development,* The Free Press of Glencoe, New York, for the Center for International Studies, Massachusetts Institute of Technology, 1960, p. 140; Tudor Engineering Company, *Report on Industrial and Loan Programs in Indonesia,* Washington, D.C., 1957, pp. 52, 53 (mimeographed); and Eric Manning, *The Loan Project for the Modernization of Privately Owned Factories,* United Nations, New York, 1960, pp. 24, 25 (mimeographed).

should be necessary, but requirements that all information and judgments should be put in writing produce great cautiousness and vagueness as well as delays. Standard procedures, moreover, tend to be closely adhered to since individual officials often lack the authority or incentive to modify or waive procedures, even though they are not appropriate to particular cases.

To avoid the appearance of partiality, some official institutions have relied heavily on quantitative types of analyses in screening loan applicants. However, complete reliance on quantitative analyses is impractical, since judgments on character and abilities, which are not subject to quantitative measurement, are crucial elements. The necessity of official institutions to give the appearance of depending largely on quantitative analysis is particularly burdensome in developing countries, where complete and unquestionable information even on quantitatively measurable matters is often unavailable. There is often a tendency in such cases to construct elaborate procedures which appear to provide quantitative measures related to loan application but which are really little related to loan decisions. Because these elaborate quasi-analytical procedures may be beyond the comprehension of applicants and politicians alike, they may have the beneficial result of discouraging improper efforts by outsiders to influence loan decisions, but they may also greatly add to operational expenses. Such pseudoscientific arrangements tend, moreover, to result in the lending institutions' officers themselves becoming confused as to what is essential in making loan decisions.

The procedures which official institutions tend to follow and the delays and red tape that tend to be involved are not entirely a result of the nature of the institution. The type of financing they are expected to extend and the types of clients they are expected to serve often are a contributory element. Term financing, which makes up a large part of their financing, is not quickly or simply arranged even by private institutions.[23] The development responsibilities of official institutions complicate their screening task particularly where an attempt is made to operate in accordance with very elaborate development priorities.

Another cause of the time taken by official institutions to screen loans is that they tend to be lenders of last resort meeting the needs of those most difficult to serve. Delays in part originate with applicants' failure to submit proper information; in some cases applicants do not understand what is required, in others they have difficulty in meeting informational requirements, and in still others they are simply seeking to avoid these requirements even at the risk of delay or refusal.

[23] See the discussion of term lending by commercial banks and finance companies. Small business investment companies in the United States appear to require a minimum of two months to arrange financing of enterprises which submit well-prepared projects.

Personnel policies of official institutions commonly neither attract staff of exceptional abilities nor motivate exceptional performance, which further contributes to the tendency of official institutions to be characterized by slow-moving, unimaginative operating procedures. The limitations imposed by such personnel policies are particularly serious handicaps in developing countries, where the shortage of qualified staff results in there being a very wide gap between the capabilities of the few well-qualified and those of the much larger group who barely meet minimum standards. The general characteristics of personnel in official institutions make it more difficult to overcome staff shortages through such techniques as increasing staff effort in bottleneck areas or utilizing simpler and more flexible procedures. In countries where there is a general shortage of staff, personnel policies which inhibit the effective operations of an institution become a much more serious handicap than in countries where qualified staff is relatively abundant. In circumstances where the staffing of official institutions is likely to be heavily influenced by political considerations, this alone can be fatal to the solvency or usefulness of the institutions. Political influence on staff selection tends to result in insufficiently motivated and frequently unqualified staff. It may also result in a vast overstaffing, to the detriment of operating costs and efficiency, as appears to have been the case of the Industrial Bank of Argentina at the time of the author's visit in 1961.[24]

The special staff problems of official institutions are particularly serious for types of lending where advisory assistance is important. Counseling staff must, for the most part, consist of persons of exceptional rather than ordinary abilities and must be motivated to make exceptional efforts periodically with shifts in work requirements and generally to display initiative.

Official institutions are commonly short not only of staff of the right caliber for counseling, but, moreover, of adequate personnel even to service normal lending functions aside from counseling. Only a few official institutions find it possible in practice to extend any counseling assistance of real substance. Most do not even make field visits to loan recipients after loans have been issued unless and until borrowers get into difficulties and behind in their payments. Most official institutions analyzed in this study indicated a need for at least greater contact with the actual operations of clients but explained their incapacity on the basis of a lack of staff. This has been true not only of official development banks in less developed areas, such as Nigeria and Northeast Brazil, but also of more advanced countries such as Japan, Sweden, and the United States. While some critics may argue that official institutions do not use the staff they have as effectively as possible, normally the staff shortage is much too severe to be overcome by improving efficiency, and it is usually unrealistic to expect great improvements in efficiency without basic changes in these organizations.

Official institutions are handicapped by their official capacity in extending

[24] Information reported by a banking consultant reorganizing the bank's operation.

counseling in other ways. Counseling is a complex and delicate task. Entrepreneurs often do not really want counseling—or are at least ambivalent about it—particularly if it is likely to suggest fundamental changes in management policies and practices. Even though they may be anxious to improve their businesses, they may be reluctant to face up to their failures or deficiencies or to accept the discomfitures of change. Good counseling thus requires not merely knowledge, but also persuasive abilities and a setting conducive to good rapport between the counselor and the counseled. The traditional feeling of rivalry and suspicion which entrepreneurs hold for government officials provides a particularly poor climate for counseling from official agencies.[25] In a great many countries, few enterpreneurs would be surprised to learn that at least some aspects of their operations might be termed illegal if laws were fully enforced or if some possible interpretation of a law were to be enforced. It is not surprising, therefore, that businessmen wish to minimize contact with official agencies and are particularly averse to receiving counseling from them. Entrepreneurs fear that the salaried staff of official institutions not only may lack the practical experience required to understand or solve their problems, but, moreover, may be unsympathetic to common business practices or may be unreliable in keeping business secrets. These difficulties tend to be enormously enlarged when official financing organizations are closely associated with other government agencies and appear to be expected to assist other government agencies in carrying out such functions as the enforcement of tax and labor legislation. Under these circumstances, the staff of official institutions has difficulty in merely obtaining from the entrepreneur information needed to check the soundness of loans, let alone obtaining the intimate knowledge required to counsel him on ways of improving the enterprise.

Although the present operations of the vast majority of official institutions suffer in some degree from the foregoing types of limitations, there are ways of overcoming or reducing a great many of them. It is to measures which will contribute to these ends that we now turn.

Maximizing the Effectiveness of Official Organizations

Much of what has been said about measures for increasing the contribution of private institutions to the financing of small-factory development

[25] A Small Business Administration official in the United States has commented that one of the merits of SBA participation loans with private banks is that the private bank can inform the applicant of steps he must take to put his enterprise in order if he is to qualify for a loan. Such advice from an SBA official, on the other hand, might be interpreted as undue interference by government in the affairs of private enterprise. While there is no doubt a greater tendency in the United States than in other countries for an applicant to write his Congressman about alleged official infringements on the rights of private enterprise, entrepreneurs in most newly developing countries have equally low receptivity to advice of official institutions.

is applicable in some degree to official institutions, particularly to those whose main failings are cautiousness, limited and ill-adapted types of lending services, neglect of small-factory requirements, inadequate or unclear development orientation, and other deficiencies common also to private banks. Thus, much of what needs to be done to increase the usefulness of official organizations can be briefly indicated by reference to measures already discussed.

Official institutions need appropriate resources, both funds and staff, for the types of financing they are expected to undertake, just as other financial intermediaries do. It is usually essential for achieving this to keep their functions limited and their efforts sharply focused, since they are normally endowed with but modest resources. It is equally essential that the difficult nature of the type of operations they are commonly called upon to perform be recognized in initial staffing and budgeting. To extend the exceptional types and qualities of financial services usually desired and to be adequately staffed to do so—particularly within the framework of an official organization—official lending institutions cannot be expected to be low-cost operations. Setting very low lending rates may therefore be budgetary suicide. Subsidies are, of course, possible, but unless provided on a well-designed basis, they may reduce motivations for good bank administration. Exceptionally low interest rates in any case greatly complicate lending operations when the lender is intended and equipped only to supplement existing suppliers of finance.

The financial resources of official development banks must be suitable to the risks they are expected to undertake. If they are to assume high risks, adequate loss reserves must be provided. Those supervising such institutions must, moreover, be prepared to expect that such reserves may in good part be expended over time in covering losses. As McCrory has put the matter:

> If such loans were not risky there would be no need for government to undertake them. Because they are risky there will be errors and losses—and very likely political capital out of them, parliamentary questions and demands for inquiries. These risks go with such a program just as surely as the prospect of a percentage of bad loans and unless government is plainly willing to accept its share, its servants cannot be expected to accept theirs and there will be no program. The condition of accepting responsibility is freedom to make honest mistakes.[26]

Governments find it difficult to accord the management of official banks the "freedom to make honest mistakes," because it is not always possible to distinguish with certainty between honest and dishonest mistakes, between errors of incompetence and errors arising from the assumption of reasonable

[26] McCrory, *op. cit.*, p. 49.

risks. Such distinctions, however, can be made more quickly and accurately, thus preventing rumors from getting out of hand, if lending programs are regularly supervised by an impartial agency with the professional competence and time for reviewing loan operations in detail and keeping the public informed on them. Unless those supervising official loan programs have the capacity to keep directly and fully informed, supervision may simply add to the red tape and cautiousness in loan operations without providing much assurance of honest or intelligent loan administration. Able monitoring of loan operations is also important to stimulate and guide policy-making authorities in making the modifications in programs which become necessary from time to time. Otherwise official organizations, even when well designed initially, tend to lose their initial dynamism and become more conservative and bureaucratic and may even slip gradually into unsound lending practices. Organizational arrangements through which a creative monitoring service might be provided for official as well as other development lending activities have been discussed in Chapter 5.

Official institutions usually lack both the resources and the organizational capacity to encompass all the specialized services required to give full effectiveness to their lending operations. It is nevertheless important that they have access to services such as industrial surveys, credit information, training, and counseling. Assistance from an independent agency with specialized industrial competence in making appraisals of industrial applicants for finance is frequently necessary to enable official institutions to screen applications on a rapid, low-cost, and impartial basis. Supporting services which help identify financing opportunities and provide counseling assistance to those financed are useful in enabling important types of financing to be undertaken that might otherwise tend to be neglected. Supporting services which help applicants deal with official institutions can be valuable in cutting red tape, delays, and favoritism.

Measures to assure that the forms and terms of financing which official institutions offer are appropriate to small-factory development needs are essential. Such measures are just as important for official as for private financial institutions, even though the particular deficiencies that needed to be guarded against in the two cases tend to be quite different. As we have noted, official institutions tend toward overelaborate procedures to assure funds are developmentally used and may provide little assurance of development results. Also, official institutions tend to concentrate on equipment financing, which may be just as inadequate as private banks' concentration on short-term financing if there is an urgent need for medium-term working capital. Those operating official institutions need to be kept thoroughly and currently informed on the exact nature of the financial requirements of small factories, the relative importance of particular financial requirements, and the kinds of problems and benefits involved in meeting them. On the basis of complete information on these matters, it will normally be possible to design forms of finance and financial procedures tailored to meet the primary financing needs of small factories. The basic problems of official organizations stemming from their official status, the nature of their personnel, and other basic characteristics must be taken into account in formulating new approaches. Usually screening procedures which are much simpler and less costly, both for the lender and the borrower, than the project evaluation procedures commonly followed at present should be possible. Detailed investment planning requirements often can be replaced by greater emphasis on direct evaluation of character and capacity of the applicant and on monitoring his subsequent performance by the provision of counseling to the extent practicable. These and other possible innovations in lending procedures of official institutions will usually increase the importance of there being separate but coordinated organizations for performing some of the new services required.

The capacity of official institutions to contribute to small-factory financing is also influenced by the general way in which official institutions are constituted, both in organizational structure and responsibilities. Policy makers have considerable latitude in deciding on these aspects in the case of official institutions, particularly in initiating new ones. The remainder of this section is therefore devoted to considering how official organizations are best constituted for the purpose of serving small-factory development.

Organizational Measures

The autonomous corporation is generally regarded as the most useful form of organization, since it facilitates official agencies in operating at arm's length from the political pressures in normal government operations. Although this may increase the problems of coordinating activities with regular government bodies and may tend to perpetuate an official institution beyond its necessary lifetime, these are usually relatively minor drawbacks compared with the advantages in extricating financing activities from the stultifying influences and responsibilities that tend to devolve upon them when they are too closely associated with regular government activities.

Some participation in the management of official agencies at the broad policy level by groups from outside government is also useful for similar reasons. It helps reduce inappropriate political influences on operations and, equally important, increases public confidence in the integrity of official institutions. The desirable degree and form of participation by representatives of nongovernmental groups will depend on such factors as the vitality and maturity of the government and of the groups from which representatives may be selected. The inclusion of representatives from organizations representing small industrialists is particularly important if the lending agency is to command their confidence and keep well posted as to their needs. Representation of international development agencies in the directorate of official banks can also be useful. Because of the basic outlook of such agencies and because they occupy a position as major sources of development funds, they tend to be public-welfare oriented and influential advocates of this point of view. Representatives of international development agencies may not always be acquainted and identified with local needs, but the representation of a wide variety of local groups can make up for this deficiency.

The participation of nongovernmental groups often needs to involve more than merely membership on a board of directors having policy and review responsibilities. Participants frequently need an immediate and tangible interest in the success of the institution in order to spur them to the required degree of participation in policy making and supervision. Ownership of shares provides this kind of interest in some degree, although it tends to concentrate attention on profitability which, though necessary, may not by itself assure the success of a development institution.

Securing shareholding by outside private groups in government financial institutions has usually been difficult. Government guarantees of a minimum return on investment have commonly been necessary but not always adequate. Legal obligations or informal pressure have sometimes been used to induce private financial institutions, small industrialists, and others to take shares in development financing organizations initiated by governments. Requirements that clients of such institutions become shareholders by devoting a small percentage of loans received to share purchases have been tried in a number of cases. It was successful in the case of the Federal Land Banks established by the United States government in the 1920s to improve agricultural financing (where the idea may have originated) but has been less successful for small-industry financing organizations in less developed countries.[27] Small-industry associations are commonly too weak financially to purchase shares in official organizations established to finance small enterprises, but governments have sometimes made them grants enabling such organizations to become shareholders.

Sharing policy-making and review authority in an official organization with nongovernmental shareholders has its disadvantages; it may reduce policy flexibility, slow decision making, and increase the conservativeness of a possibly already overcautious approach to financing, but these may be acceptable limitations in view of the contribution which outside shareholding can make to reducing the usual defects of wholly government-administered organizations. Too much, nevertheless, should not be expected of bringing representatives of private groups into sharing the control of official banks. The problems of official institutions stem in part from the general level of business standards. Where the leadership of business and

---

[27] See, for example, the experience of the Artisans' Bank in Israel in Edward Tenenbaum, *Israel's Industrial Resources—A Second Look,* Continental-Allied Company, Washington, D.C., 1960, p. 173.

government is drawn from essentially the same small group of individuals, private participation in an official bank may not bring much real change in its operations. Also, where the value of private shareholders' stake in the institution is for them a relatively insignificant amount, they may not be spurred to be concerned with the efficiency or soundness of the bank but may use their position as shareholders to influence the official institution's policies in a direction favorable to their particular interests. Private commercial banks, for example, as shareholders have in some cases been more concerned with preventing development institutions from encroaching on their business than with encouraging sound and constructive lending activities. It thus may be important to be selective in accordance with local conditions concerning how many and which particular types of unofficial shareholders should be attracted to official institutions.

It is equally—and perhaps much more—important that operational responsibilities be delegated to an able and courageous manager and that he be given the authority and resources to surround himself with a staff of equally exceptional character and abilities. Political pressure will inevitably be brought to bear upon an institution utilizing public funds, even in the most politically advanced society and when the most ingenious organizational techniques are used to insulate the institution against political authority.

The history of two of the more successful development banks relying heavily on public funds—the Industrial Development Bank of Canada and the Industrial Development Bank of Turkey—demonstrates how valuable the selection of an able professional manager to whom operations may be entrusted can be in protecting the institution from outside pressures.

The Industrial Development Bank of Canada, as a recent Minister of Finance has said, has a 20-year history of operating independently of the government and "has earned the respect and esteem of the business community."[28] This is not because elected and appointed officials in Canada have always refrained from representing views which differ from those of the Bank, but rather because the Bank's managers have given firm support to their staff's professional judgment in response to such representations. In doing so, they have built the Bank's reputation for integrity. An official or quasi-official institution will frequently be subjected to pressures of various types and degrees. It is therefore especially important that the original management of such an institution be capable of establishing a clear tradition of the inviolability of its professional judgment, recognizing that in banking even the most skilled and impartial judgment will occasionally be proven wrong by events. Once a tradition of relying on professional judgment is established, succeeding managements will find it easier to maintain.

[28] Speech to the Canadian Institute of Actuaries by the Honourable Walter L. Gordon, then Minister of Finance, Ottawa, Sept. 20, 1965.

Unless such a tradition *is* established and maintained, an official bank will quickly lose its usefulness as a development institution.

A further important organizational question is to what extent and in what way official institutions should specialize. Specialization in some degree is employed by most official development financing organizations, if for no other reason than to prevent direct competition with private institutions. It also assures minimum attention is accorded to the specified needs or specified types of financing by excluding other needs or types of financing from its responsibilities. It provides a high motivation for the staff of the specialized organization to develop the most economical and satisfactory means of meeting these particular needs by making achievements in this respect the primary measure of success or failure.

Specialization requires careful planning if it is not to involve several possibly serious drawbacks. If the boundaries of specialization are too broadly defined, financing may go primarily to enterprises which, though within the definitional boundaries, have little in common with the central group—financing institutions naturally give first attention to the less difficult or more familiar types of financing. This may result in just another institution offering the same kind of services as existing banks. Resources may be wasted by unnecessary duplication or by the creation of an organization which is badly designed for what prove to be its ultimate activities. The results at best may not justify the effort expended in creating the new institution, and the process may delay the initiation of more useful institution-building efforts. Institutions too narrowly specializing, on the other hand, may lose important operational economies that depend on large volume or partial complementarity of diverse activities. Excessive specialization may lead to a proliferation of institutions which absorb more scarce personnel and other resources than the country can afford to devote to these activities.

There are four major types of specialization which usually need to be considered: line of enterprise, period or type of financing, geographical coverage, and size of enterprise or general level of wealth of applicants. The variety of choices facing those designing official institutions is, of course, much wider; each type of specialization may be applied in various degrees. Also, specialization may involve not merely a single type, but various combinations. Specialization by size of enterprise is obviously of greatest interest here. However, the other three types of specialization need to be discussed first to show their bearing upon this matter.

Some specialization by line of industry is commonly important to the effectiveness of development institutions. Agricultural financing, for example, tends to involve staff skills, office location patterns, and general approaches different from those important to financing manufacturing; where both activities are of substantial importance, separate organizations may make for better administration of both.[29] Commerce, consumption, and certain other activities are sometimes excluded from the services of development banks on grounds that sufficient financing is available to them through interbusiness credit, commercial banks, and other private sources. Fine specialization by line of industry is seldom practical and of no importance so far as small-factory financing is concerned. Even separating agriculture and industry may not be practical in small countries or in the case of regionally specialized institutions where the total volume of finance to both sectors is not large. On the other hand, where specialized agricultural financing institutions exist, even these may be of some usefulness to small-factory financing. As the Colombia case study suggests, a small manufacturing firm located in a rural village or selling largely to farmers or utilizing largely agricultural products as raw materials may in some cases be more easily financed by an agricultural bank with a local branch and a knowledge of agriculture and local conditions than one specializing in industrial financing. Usually, however, institutions primarily concerned with financing agriculture will require more external guidance and supporting assistance in order to contribute effectively to small-factory financing than financial institutions more used to serving the needs of industrial enterprises.

Another widely practiced type of specialization is achieved by excluding short-term financing from the functions of the financing institution. Short-term financing requires financial resources, staff, and operating procedures generally different from those required by longer-term financing and also involves different risks. Although it is possible to equip an institution with the various requirements of the two generally different types of financing, it is important to recognize that such an institution will also require a much higher level of top-management skill than if it were only concerned with one or the other of these activities.

Another argument for this type of specialization in official development institutions is that the primary need not being met may be for term financing. There may also be strong opposition from commercial banks and finance companies—whose cooperation is often needed—where official lending institutions attempt to compete in the field of short-term financing. There may be the further danger of term financing being neglected if incorporated in a general lending institution. Not only is there less experience to draw on in the case of term financing, but also its requirements for resources, staff, and other aspects are much harder to meet, particularly in less devel-

[29] Checchi, for example, supports the separation of agricultural and industrial financing on the grounds that: "These require entirely different types of management attitudes and abilities and involve different administrative problems." (Vincent Checchi, "Development Banks," *U.N. Conference on the Application of Science and Technology for the Benefit of the Less Developed Areas,* vol. VIII, 1961, p. 141.) For a similar argument see James R. Brooks and William C. Ladd, *A Liberian Bank for Industrial Development and Investment,* Office of Private Enterprise, International Cooperation Administration, Washington D.C., 1960.

oped countries. The higher-risk element in term lending further diminishes lenders' interest in it. Inflationary conditions create additional obstacles to term financing. The possibility of higher returns offsetting these disadvantages may be barred by interest-rate controls. Thus, without institutions specializing in term financing, little financing of this sort may be possible.

Excluding short-term lending and other types of deposit banking from the responsibilities of the official development financing organization has a number of other advantages. Government institutions appear to have the least competence in deposit banking types of operations. They have not proven to be very successful in attracting the deposits on which short-term financing must usually be based, and they tend to lack the speed and flexibility important to short-term financing and other commercial bank services. The problems arising from overemphasis of short-term financing are well illustrated by comments on the activities of the Artisans' Bank of Israel:

> Purely banking functions, such as the receiving of deposits, do not seem to provide benefits commensurate with their cost. There are ample checking deposit facilities in the private commercial banks, and artisans have not shown any serious preference to deposit in their own bank. On the contrary, lacking the widespread network of branches that other banks have developed, the Artisans' Bank deposit and checking facilities are substandard and are likely to remain so. It might therefore be desirable for the Artisans' Bank to give up its deposit business to some other bank or banks, and to concentrate on medium and long-term lending.[30]

Aside from the foregoing considerations, the responsibilities of deposit banking tend to distract from management's ability to follow policies and procedures important to maximizing the development results of financing.[31]

There are, nevertheless, disadvantages in confining official development institutions to term and/or equity financing. These must be either accepted or in some way overcome, if such specialization is to be adopted. For one thing, the exclusion of commercial-type banking activities reduces the geographic areas which the organization can afford to serve directly with local branches, since short-term financing might be expected to support branches in some areas where the volume of term financing is small.[32] Short-term financing operations, moreover, build up relationships and information of considerable value to other types of financing. In a country where the accounting records and other information are inadequate, the insight into a firm's economic condition provided by the commercial bank account

[30] Tenenbaum, *op. cit.,* p. 198.

[31] For further elaboration, see the discussion of the influence of deposit banking on the development orientation of the Bank of Northeast Brazil, Davenport, *Financing Small and Medium Manufacturing Enterprises in Latin America,* loc. cit. See also the discussion in Chap. 12 on Colombia and Chap. 7 on commercial banks.

[32] For an early discussion of this problem, see *Domestic Financing of Economic Development,* United Nations, New York, 1950, pp. 64, 65.

is of great value. The Netherlands Middleclass Bank is reported to place great reliance in its loan operations, on this source of information even in the very favorable environment in which it operates.

Term-lending institutions which have commercial banks as shareholders may have no problem in obtaining access to the information and branch facilities of these shareholders. It is also possible for term-lending institutions to engage the assistance of unrelated banks, but in practice these arrangements are often not very satisfactory. The United States Small Business Administration, which specializes in term lending, seeks to supplement its relatively limited number of branches by cooperative arrangements with commercial banks. However, its capabilities of serving many areas are limited by this dependence, and its services are not well known. The Japanese Small Business Finance Corporation similarly depends on collaboration with other institutions in serving a great many areas, but these arrangements in the view of some staff members have important deficiencies as a means of extending development financing. In less developed countries, the problems in establishing satisfactory agency arrangements for an official bank would usually be much greater.

The inclusion of deposit banking as a function of official institutions has also sometimes been favored when the institution is new, since short-term lending operations associated with deposit banking provide a more immediate source of income than term or equity financing. Also, short-term lending has the advantage of being a simpler type of financing operation, which may be important at a stage when new staff are acquiring experience and a knowledge of clients. Although there is some merit in this reasoning, a major difficulty with it is that in practice it becomes difficult to shift over to term lending after a heavy investment has been built up in the kinds of staff and facilities required for deposit banking but which are largely superfluous for term financing.[33]

There are two other possibly important reasons for considering the inclu-

---

[33] Banks such as the Industrial Bank of Argentina, the Development Bank of Honduras, the Popular Bank in Colombia, and, to some extent, the Bank of Northeast Brazil seem to have been retarded in entering upon term financing by their heavy commitment to short-term financing. On Colombia, see Chap. 12; on Brazil, see Davenport, *loc. cit.* See also A. D. Little, Inc., *op. cit.*, pp. 118ff., and Edward Tenenbaum, James Taylor, and H. Kirkpatrick, *Helping Honduran Industry: A Diagnostic Study*, Continental-Allied Company, 1961. Recommendations for a development bank for the Ivory Coast also stressed the need to avoid these problems. "Particular care should be taken to keep the Bank's activities limited to the purposes indicated in our 'Report and Recommendations' and its Annexes—so as to prevent the occurrence in the Ivory Coast of such controversial action in other countries as tends to create Development Banks of a mixed type with no small emphasis on commercial and deposit banking activities." Richard Quandt, *Ivory Coast: Report and Recommendations on Proposed Establishment of an Industrial Development Bank and Industrial Development Center*, Agency for International Development, Washington, 1961, p. 2.

sion of short-term financing in the activities of development banks concerned with small industry. First, this may be a major type of need not being adequately met. In Korea, for example, short-term financing appeared, when the Small and Medium Industry Bank was formed, to be the most urgent need of small enterprises. In many less developed countries, increased short-term financing may be needed for at least some types of small enterprises. Secondly, there are sometimes advantages in being able to meet all the financing requirements of clients, not merely their term needs. Thus, despite the problems arising from the mixing of the two activities and the usual possibilities of increasing the short-term financing of other institutions, some official financing institutions such as the Nicaraguan Institute of National Development have found it advantageous to be able to provide some short-term financing.

The geographic coverage undertaken by an institution and the degree to which staff and authority are dispersed are important factors influencing the costs of operations as well as the extent and nature of the services that can be provided. The usual approach has been to centralize staff and offices in the main industrial center. This often permits close contact with the majority of the small manufacturers, making it possible to give them the best available service at lowest cost. Nevertheless, it has an attendant disadvantage. If service is extended solely or primarily to those in the principal metropolitan center, this is likely to increase the tendency of small firms to agglomerate there, which may be undesirable since excessive concentration of industry in the large metropolises is already a serious development problem in many countries. The trend may be reduced by spreading services to other areas. There are several alternative ways of doing this with differing impacts on costs and services.

The most common approach is to attempt to serve other areas from the main industrial center by means of transportation and other communication facilities. This creates several problems. Time and travel costs involved can add substantially to the cost of making the size of loans required by small manufacturers. Moreover, lack of knowledge of the locality and absence of local connections decreases the reliability of evaluation and supervision. For the same reason, supervision of loan recipients becomes more costly, less reliable, and more likely to be neglected. This compounds the already greater risk problem of enterprises in smaller urban and rural areas. There is the further drawback that many promising industrialists are unlikely to apply for financing since, because of lack of regular contact, they are not sufficiently informed of services or given the necessary guidance to submit acceptable applications.

Another method is to establish branches in important regional centers. The main problem here is that unless the centers are industrially advanced enough to provide a certain minimum volume of business, branch operations may be costly. Costs may be minimized where the branch is able to obtain the assistance of specialists and other services from the central office. The existence of other local supporting services, described in Chapter 5, will also help reduce branch operating costs. Such support, and continuous close review of branch operations by the central office, will also contribute to the quality of services. This type of assistance, plus greater immunity to local pressures, usually makes such branch operations more efficient and developmentally useful than completely independent local development institutions. However, their value will be greatly diminished if they do not have the authority and ability to evaluate and decide upon most local loan applications. Too often the usefulness of branches is marred because they are reduced to serving as little more than mailboxes for applications.

A loan program which is less specialized with regard to the type of enterprise it finances or the type of financing it extends will, of course, be able to afford to operate in smaller centers. The Industrial Development Bank of Canada has been able to support an expanding network of branches, partly because it has broadened the field of applicants eligible for financing to include service, commercial, and agricultural enterprises, although the size of its branch network is also in part explained by the willingness of the IDBC to subsidize the operations of some branches. Commercial banking functions help support the branches of such institutions at the Netherlands Middleclass Bank, the Bank of Northeast Brazil, and Colombia's Banco Popular. The advantages of narrower definitions of eligiblity and functions described above must, of course, be weighed against the advantage of being able to afford more branches in less industrialized areas if functions and eligibility are broadened.

Some of the benefits of branches can be obtained by other means in centers where branches cannot be afforded. Many institutions, such as the Small Business Finance Corporation in Japan, use the agencies of commercial banks, credit cooperatives, and related institutions. Although the capabilities and motivations of agencies are often less satisfactory for administering development financing, agency arrangements may nevertheless be of sufficient value to warrant their use.[34] Another method, used by the Industrial Development Bank of Canada, is to have loan officers make regular visits, well publicized in advance, to towns remote from branch offices. Where repeated visits have been possible, good results have been obtained in the form of an increased volume of desirable applicants.[35]

The extent to which it is desirable to extend financial services to less industrialized areas deserves careful consideration. Fund limitations, as well as cost considerations, may make it desirable to concentrate on financing centers with substantial industrial growth prospects in the immediate fu-

[34] On Japan's experience, see Chapter 13. For some shortcomings in the operation of the SBA's comparable program of participation rights, see *Burrough's Clearing House,* March, 1964, pp. 54–55.

[35] Discussions in 1965 with IDBC staff.

ture. If funds are not adequate to meet all the requirements of the most important secondary centers, then development priorities would probably not be served by attempting to extend services to even smaller towns and villages.

Scale specialization also has important merits, but, as the preceding discussion has sought to indicate, whether or to what extent it may be practical depends in part upon how essential other types of specialization are and, of course, on the extent and importance of small enterprises. There are three main reasons for favoring specialization by scale in official development financing institutions. Firstly, small enterprises tend to be a neglected sector, and it may be necessary to have an institution concerned primarily or exclusively with serving them to overcome this neglect. Very large units tend to be favored by both private and official sources of financing, since financing large units tends to be economically more attractive. Also, the size and often the ownership of large units tend to give them a great deal of influence over lending decisions. Even artisans and craftsmen, because of their politically influential number, and very small merchants, because of their special access to interbusiness and commercial bank finance, may fare better than small manufacturing enterprises. A second reason for having an official lending institution concentrate its services on small factories is that there appear to be many fewer problems of improper influences and of default or diversion of finance to nonproductive uses with enterprises in this general scale than with either much larger or much smaller units. A small-factory focus thus may simplify the management and operating problems of official financing institutions. The third argument in favor of some scale specialization is that the nature of financial needs and of appropriate financing methods tends to change with scale. Specialization encourages the discovery and adoption of methods and forms of financing better suited to particular scales.

The major limitation on scale specialization is one of cost. Unit financing costs tend to rise sharply as the volume of an institution's financing declines below a certain level. In countries where factories, large or small, are not numerous, this may well be a critical consideration.

Another important consideration is that where the demand for term loans greatly exceeds the supply, a well-managed official institution will have opportunities to make some very simple, safe types of large loans, and the profit from these loans can be used to support most of its overhead costs or, in effect, to subsidize smaller and riskier loan operations. Such operations have, no doubt, contributed to the ability of some institutions, such as the Industrial Development Bank of Canada, to serve small firms at relatively low interest rates. Whether large borrowers of the gilt-edged type should be financed depends, of course, on such factors as their use of the funds, alternative sources, and the adequacy of the official institution's resources. It is usually possible to assure that small firms remain the focus of the program by establishing regulations setting aside a major portion of funds for such loans.

The organization and operations of official institutions designed, at least in part, to finance small-factory development must be practical in terms of costs, but there is also a danger of exaggerating the extent and significance of these costs. The principal objective is a financial service that will produce the results desired at some acceptable cost. A rise of 50 or even 100 percent in the administrative costs of lending might be worthwhile if, as a result, better credit facilities for small manufacturers could be provided in cases where—as is frequently the case—administrative costs amount to only 2 to 4 percent per annum of the value of loans outstanding.

Part Four
Some Operational Problems

Chapter 10
Allocating Finance

THE IMPROVEMENT OF allocation procedures is one of the underlying purposes of having a special program concerned with small-industry development financing; the other major purpose, to improve the effective use of funds allocated to small enterprises, is considered in the following chapter.

Four Basic Approaches to Screening

Allocation procedures (or those used in selecting or screening applicants) commonly employ one or more of the following four basic approaches: (1) evaluating the capacity, motivations, and other characteristics of the individuals responsible for the proposed fund use or repayment; (2) forecasting the earning prospects and repayment possibilities—and in some cases the probable development results—from the project for which the funds are used; (3) evaluating collateral or other recourse in the event of repayment difficulties; and (4) testing actual performance in the use of credit through credit extension on a trial basis.

The usefulness and particular limitations of possible approaches to screening vary greatly, depending upon the way and the combination in which these basic techniques are applied, how suitable the circumstances are for the particular approach adopted, how well equipped those conducting the screening are for carrying out the adopted approach. Previous chapters have considered the particular approaches commonly applied by various suppliers of funds and possible measures to improve them. This discussion should have made evident that there is not one ideal approach to screening which is equally suitable to every supplier of funds, to every type of financing, or to the various other differences in circumstances. Later sections of this chapter will examine some of the circumstances that influence which method or combination of methods are likely to be most practical and what might be done to render screening methods presently applied more useful in the allocation of development financing to small manufacturers. First, however, it will be useful to summarize the essential nature of each of the screening approaches and the major values and deficiencies commonly associated with them.

Management Evaluation

The characteristics of those who have the responsibility for use and repayment of funds are usually a major and sometimes the sole element evaluated in making financing decisions. The characteristics which financiers are most concerned with are capabilities and motivations. Capabilities refer not only to knowledge and experience important to the undertaking contemplated, but also to mental ingenuity and dexterity in dealing with the unknown or unexpected, physical energy, emotional balance, and related qualities important to success. Motivation includes the nature and kinds of objectives which influence the applicant and the degree or intensity with which they stimulate action. Whether or not the project—and the financing—is a success depends thus not merely upon the capabilities of the applicant; it depends also on how hard he strives for the success of a project and for the fulfillment of his obligations to the financier, how compatible his objectives are with those of the financier's, and how frank, cooperative, and amenable a relationship can be created between the applicant and the financier.

Management evaluation remains a basic criterion utilized by suppliers of term and equity funds in such industrially advanced countries as the United States, Canada, Germany, the Netherlands, Denmark, and Japan, despite more favorable circumstances for utilizing other screening methods than exist in less developed countries. The emphasis put upon management evaluation in developed countries may be in some degree deceptive, as lenders in these countries are in a better position to take balance sheets showing profits and the availability of reasonable collateral for granted; lenders in the most advanced countries do, nevertheless, focus most of their screening efforts on assessing management.

The importance of management evaluation in the making of loan decisions is obvious to anyone who has participated in a survey on a number of enterprises in the same industry. One finds, as the author has in such diverse countries as Brazil, Colombia, Guatemala and India, repeated examples of firms of similar type and resources competing for part of essentially the same market but with markedly different results. One can find examples also of firms which have been progressively declining over several years but suddenly begin to prosper when there is a change in their owner-managers. It was observations of this kind also that lead a prominent student of small enterprises in the United States to conclude that "management has, on the whole, been the most decisive factor influencing the success or failure of the small enterprise."[1] The factor of management is much more important in developing countries where the quality of management tends to be, on the average, lower and in general much more varied.

The need of financiers to give special stress to management evaluation in smaller firms is heightened by two factors: (1) management in the smaller firm consists of one or two persons, so that weaknesses at the top have no chance of being remedied further down the line, as they sometimes are in larger companies; and (2) there is not the possibility in financing the smaller firm that often exists when the recipient is a large company—that of changing management should the initial evaluation prove incorrect. A misjudgment of management capabilities—or its tasks—in granting loans to small companies can in some cases be corrected by advisory assistance. This remedy, however, depends not only on the lender being able to extend or arrange such assistance, but also on prior screening which selects applicants with such personal characteristics as cooperativeness and willingness to learn. The ability and willingness to utilize even excellent advice is not necessarily a characteristic of otherwise creditworthy owner-managers of small factories.

In types of enterprises and environments where uncertainty is high (which is more common in the case of smaller enterprises and in less developed countries) the qualities of management are of special importance. Fluctuating availability of supplies, changing technology, volatile prices, shifting tastes, and competition often confront the small enterprise in less developed countries, enlarging the role of management decision in success. In such an environment, moreover, information is not adequate enough and conditions are not stable enough to be relied upon as heavily as might be in an industralized country in making an evaluation of the earning prospects or of the recourse value of collateral.

Particular qualities of management become of special importance in the case of smaller enterprises in less developed countries: energy and dexterity because planning is more difficult; ability and willingness to learn because the general level of know-how is low; initiative and capacity for self-improvement because of the limited availability of good sources of information and assistance; and cooperativeness and amenability because difficulties requiring special assistance are more likely to occur and because there are fewer other checks against the misuse of funds. A former chief adviser to the Industrial Finance Corporation of Thailand stressed closely simi-

[1] A. D. H. Kaplan, *Small Business: Its Place and Problems,* McGraw-Hill Book Company, New York, 1948, p. 103. A recent study of 270 manufacturing concerns in the state of Washington similarly concluded that positive management action to promote growth was *the major factor* explaining the more rapid growth of firms showing the greatest expansion. See Joseph W. McGuire, *Factors Affecting the Growth of Manufacturing Firms,* University of Washington, Bureau of Business Research, Seattle, 1963.

lar management characteristics when he said that the task of screening in development banks was one of identifying *trustworthy* individuals with *drive* and *clear ideas.*[2]

What standard of business ethics other than integrity in honoring financial obligations should be insisted upon is a difficult question. In environments where there are many uncertainties as to what is legal and where there is lax or uneven enforcement of laws, obviously the same standards of business ethics cannot be applied as are applicable in more advanced countries. Even in the United States, some bankers reportedly would, if forced to make a choice, "rather deal with an able and dubious management than with an honest but stupid management."[3] Where the development of entrepreneurial leadership is a central objective of a financing program, obviously the ethics of applicants may be an important criterion. But the standard applied will not necessarily be the one commonly used in a more ordered society.

Evaluating management is subject to difficulties, because many of the judgments, particularly as to motivation, must be qualitative and subjective. Character and capacity judgments based on a brief interview, the reports of persons with whom the applicant has done business, and standards derived from those common to the screener's social circle may be highly misleading. Nevertheless, a great many banks in less-developed countries do no more than this, to the extent that they consider management capacity and character at all in loan decisions. The need for a special effort to acquire such knowledge, particularly in term-lending institutions, is just beginning to be fully understood in countries with larger industrial lending experience. The British Industrial and Commercial Finance Corporation has had problems with this aspect of evaluation according to Brian Tew:

> With regard to human data, the major difficulties are the strictness of the British law of libel, and the natural desire of possible informants to keep well clear of any avoidable unpleasantness. In consequence the I.C.F.C. (or

[2] Interview with Oliver P. Wheeler, May 7, 1963. Quite different views, however, have been expressed by others with equal experience. H. Faivre, the late loan adviser to the Nicaraguan Institute of National Development, held that management evaluation was of little importance in less developed countries, since applicants' capabilities were uniformly mediocre or poor. A development bank's main task was therefore—in his opinion—to identify sound projects and then to accompany financing with sufficient advice and supervision to assure a minimum standard of management. The author would agree that sound projects and counseling are often important and recognizes that the possibility of exercising selectivity among applicants tends to be small in little-industrialized areas. Often, however, development banks could be more selective on the basis of character and capacity if they were less selective as to the applicants' ability to offer security.

[3] Drake in reporting his having heard bankers express this preference notes: "While I do not subscribe to this thinking, there is a kernel of truth in it" (Milton J. Drake, "How a Banker Evaluates a Credit Risk," *Robert Morris Associates Bulletin,* October, 1955, p. 35.)

any other lending institution) has in practice to rely mainly on the judgment of its own staff. However, though the I.C.F.C. has opportunities of meeting applicants at its head office (or at its branches in Birmingham, Manchester and Edinburgh) and also of visiting them on their own premises, it is not always easy to make up one's mind quickly about people who are studiously on their best behavior.[4]

The lender needs to know not only how an applicant performs at his best but also how he *usually* performs and how he *might* perform under the stress of an unexpected streak of bad luck. For such knowledge the lender must have more than a formal acquaintance with the applicant and his operations.

Character and capacity evaluations require an active and extended effort to know potential applicants through informal as well as formal contacts. The importance of this is underlined in an advertisement of the Foundation for Commercial Banks in the United States which advises potential customers to "get to know your banker before you need him" to build a deposit relationship with him and to borrow a little money, pay it back, borrow more and establish a record with him.[5] Lenders as well as prospective borrowers can and should take the initiative in building up these relationships.

Among helpful means of evaluating the character and capacity of an applicant is the study of his business and financial record and reputation as compared with others in the same line of activity. This requires, of course, the creation of a system for accumulating such comparative information. Visual inspection of an applicant's enterprise and operations and comparisons with other similar ones can reveal a great deal about an entrepreneur, provided the viewer has a broad technical and business background and the knowledge of competitive firms needed to make such comparisons. A problem sometimes remains nevertheless—as the Chief Executive of the Malayan Industrial Development Finance Ltd. has noted—because management which has performed well in past operations may not necessarily be competent for the greatly expanded or perhaps quite different operations that may be contemplated.[6] The applicant's personal exposition of his future plan of action and objectives is a further guide to his capabilities and motivations, although again primarily to one well familiar with the nature of the applicant's type of business.

The main limitations on management evaluation as a criterion for financing lies not so much in the difficulty of making an accurate overall evaluation as in quantifying each element in the evaluation. Where the function of screening must be delegated and is not closely supervised, reviewing

[4] Brian Tew, "The I.C.F.C. Revisited," *Economica,* new series, vol. 22, p. 11.

[5] *Business Week,* Nov. 3, 1962, p. 115.

[6] Dermot O'Regan, "Financing Malayan Industries," *Far Eastern Economic Review,* Aug. 31, 1961, p. 394.

authorities will find it difficult to evaluate screening judgments or to detect intentional misallocations. Thus there may be danger of favoritism in this type of screening unless persons of unquestionable integrity administer loan allocations and unless suitable reviewing procedures are employed.

Another important limitation is that the conclusions on one important characteristic—the possibility of a close cooperative relationship—depend upon the personality and other characteristics of those extending as well as those receiving financing. Where those administering financing are seriously inhibited by their lack of knowledge, social background, personality, or other factors from developing relationships of mutual confidence with small industrialists, then management evaluation by itself is likely to be an unsatisfactory basis for loan allocation.

Enterprise Evaluation

Enterprise evaluation involves an analysis of the enterprise in which financing will be used and the environment in which it will operate in an effort to forecast earning and capacity to make scheduled repayments. The analysis may also attempt to determine to what extent such financing will contribute to development objectives. In its most elaborate form, this approach is commonly termed *project analysis* and may include physical and financial plans intended to reflect realistically the probable consequences of the contemplated use of funds. However, enterprise evaluation may be carried out on a much simpler level and often is because of the cost and other difficulties in carrying out complete project analyses.

This approach, in its simplest form and under the most favorable conditions, may involve little more than a quick review of past balance sheets and profit and loss statements. Account analysis can tell a great deal about a firm in a matter of minutes, or at most a few hours, where good accounts are available and the appraiser has comparative data over time or on the operations of similar firms. Unfortunately, in less developed countries both are often lacking. In such cases, screening procedures dependent upon account analysis may result in useless paper work for borrowers and also provide an unsound basis for loan decisions. Although account analysis is thus not always immediately practical as a screening method, it will usually be desirable to ensure that recipients of loans institute adequate accounting practices, for reasons indicated in Chapter 5.

Where accounts are available but of uncertain accuracy or completeness, other investigation will be essential if enterprise evaluation is to be a major element in screening. Accounts are abstractions and generalizations which at best leave out many possibly important details and are easily misleading. Profits, for example, may vary greatly depending upon how depreciation or the sale or purchase of assets are recorded. Under conditions of inflation, particularly, there are not always clear rules concerning the most meaningful ways of recording such changes. To take another example, the degree to which current assets may include accounts due but not collectable, or inventory valued at cost but not saleable, is often not readily ascertainable from accounts but is a fact of great importance in evaluating the findings suggested by conventional balance sheet analysis. Verification of accounts by checking internal consistency is simple but is rarely adequate, particularly for uncovering intentional deception. Field checks, such as plant visits to check inventories or appraise the value of assets visually are essential in most countries and are commonly employed in the case of term loans or new clients, even in countries with relatively advanced accounting practices.[7]

Field checking adds to the screening costs, as it usually requires, at a minimum, several hours or more. Where applicants are geographically dispersed or distant from the lender's office and/or where specialists are required to carry out field checking, costs are especially likely to be far more than those involved in the types of screening that can be carried out in the lender's office. To omit field checking, however, may render account analysis of little value in many countries. This is particularly true where development criteria are to be applied, since important elements of information for this purpose are not ordinarily supplied in regular accounts. While supplementary information can be and often is requested, there are usually fewer easy checks on the accuracy of such information than there are in the case of account information.[8]

Much more can be told from a firm's record when the evaluator has comparative records of other firms. Banks with a large clientele able to file detailed financial reports have a good source of comparative information. They may compare the firm's operations with both its own past performance and the performance and trend of other enterprises on the basis of various financial ratios.[9]

[7] The recently publicized case in the United States of loans on warehouse receipts allegedly covering stored vegetable oil where, because of the prominence of the borrower and other factors, field checking was not employed, promises to prove costly to the lenders. See "Scandal in Salad Oil Gets Bigger Every Day," *Business Week,* Dec. 14, 1963, pp. 32ff.

[8] Where accounts are used by an enterprise for internal control purposes and where they are carefully supervised for accuracy by government revenue or other authorities, lenders can usually place more faith in information from firms' accounts than in specially prepared information. On the other hand, accounts sometimes are prepared primarily to deceive tax authorities, who may be ill equipped to prevent this. In such cases, banks commonly, and quite rightly, make little use of accounts, relying instead upon such information as that which the entrepreneur is willing to provide orally and confidentially, his deposit history, and visual evidence of the growth of the enterprise or of the owner's wealth.

[9] Some of the ratios used are receivables to net sales, inventories to net sales (or cost of sales), net fixed assets to net sales, working capital (net current assets) to net sales, current assets to current liabilities, cash and receivables to current liabilities, current assets to total debts, net fixed assets to tangible net worth, total debt to tangible net worth, net profit to sales, and net profit to tangible net worth.

A further step which may be used in appraising the outlook of an enterprise is to assess the trend in its general line of industry. The usefulness of this type of analysis depends, of course, upon the accuracy of the assessment, the cost and problems in assessing industry trends, and the way such assessments are applied. Knowledge that the brick industry is in financial trouble due to the ending of a housing boom and rapidly expanding production of competitive concrete building block may not provide definitive guidance for handling all loan applications from brick producers but if the information on the brick industry's plight—and on conditions in other industries—is accurate and detailed, it can greatly simplify the screening task.

The inherent limitations of information about broad industrial trends as a screening guide are enlarged where the generalizations are not derived from recent quantitative data gathered and analyzed through reliable methods but are based upon such information as the impressions from an individual's accumulated experience or from traditions handed down by supposedly knowledgeable persons. Information and conceptions of this type, however, are often in practice a significant element in the allocation of financing. Drake, in commenting on the degree of subjective judgment in loan allocations in the United States, reports:

> Bankers will also be found to have confidence in certain lines of business and a lack of confidence in other lines of business. There is no question that his experiences in some lines have been unsatisfactory and that he is likely to look upon those lines with a certain disfavor. Bankers, being human beings, are also influenced in making a loan decision by their confidence in the general economic outlook.[10]

The same tendency of bankers to overgeneralize from personal experience is equally common to developing countries. Of particular relevance to this discussion is the frequency with which faulty or exaggerated conceptions about the costs and risks involved in financing small factories appears to impede small-factory financing. The consequences of such misconceptions in developing countries tends to be more serious, since there is not the same corrective pressure as is exerted in industrialized countries by the existence of competitive nonbanking financial services and of reliable basic data from which more accurate assessments can be made. Thus faulty conceptions once given wide currency tend to perpetuate themselves. It is particularly important in these circumstances that objective studies of industrial trends be made.

A detailed study of the industry to which an applicant firm belongs can be of great value in appraising not only general trends, but also the competitive capabilities of the applicant. Detailed knowledge of markets and marketing relationships in an industry and the competitive strengths and weaknesses of the various members are essential to an accurate assess-

[10] Drake, *op. cit.*, p. 33.

ment of the prospects of a particular firm. The industry may be expanding, but a shift to mass-production technology may make the prospects poor for a smaller firm; or entrance may be closed to new firms by the nature of the marketing relationships. In less developed countries, information of this type is usually available only where well-trained specialists are employed in conducting field surveys.

A more elaborate approach to enterprise evaluation is project analysis. This differs from account analysis in usually making use of: more specific and comprehensive quantitative data which interrelate the physical and financial aspects of operations, instead of merely financial data measuring capacity and operations; various types of qualitative information; an analysis of markets and the environment of the firm; and budgets, or estimates of future operations.

Project evaluations are a relatively new approach to making loan determinations. They were designed originally for very large investment decisions but have gradually been extended to evaluating requests for smaller amounts of term and equity financing. It is a method which has very important advantages, particularly for development-oriented financing, but it is also one with major disadvantages, particularly for allocating loans of smaller amounts and in the general circumstances prevailing in newly developing countries. This section summarizes both the advantages and disadvantages of project evaluation as it has so far been applied in screening small-factory loan requests for developing countries. In the final section of the chapter, we will consider what might be done to enable more effective use to be made of project evaluations methods in financing the development of small factories.

Projects enable the supplier of finance to check the adequacy and accuracy of the facts on which the applicant's plans are based, the reasonableness of the assumptions as to the future or other unknowns, the internal consistency of plans, and the nature and certainty of results forecast. Perhaps as important, they force entrepreneurs, who tend to be optimists and often rely excessively on intuitive judgments, to carefully check out their own plans against the facts available.

Projects provide helpful information on planning and related abilities of entrepreneurs as well as information on the characteristics of the proposed operation. They normally indicate how and when repayment is expected to be generated. The possibilities they suggest of future capacity to repay can be of great importance. Where past records provide little or no guidance concerning future earnings, such as in the case of new enterprises or major expansions in existing ones, plans may provide the only possible guidance. In the latter case, unfortunately, plans also tend to be much less precise and reliable guides to future action.

Projects provide the means of a more detailed and direct calculation of development benefits likely to accrue from an enterprise than do most other screening methods. They make it possible to analyze the total sources and uses of funds in the enterprise over the period of financing (and possibly longer) in order to ascertain the extent to which such funds constitute an essential net addition to the productive capacity of the enterprise. The detailed examination which project analysis permits may reveal, for example, that a profitable enterprise may desire, and may be easily able to afford, to use loan funds which do not increase production, productivity, or profits, but which permit the withdrawal of part of equity funds for nonproductive purposes or which permit the substitution of machinery for labor. As reasonable as these objectives may be from the point of view of management, this use of development funds may have a low priority.

Project analysis is also favored by some as a screening device on the grounds that the data projects bring together when modified by "accounting prices" will provide a corrected profit figure, which is useful as a guide to the development importance of a project.[11] Although theoretically possible, in practice such efforts appear to complicate an already complicated, costly, and time-consuming procedure and thus are not recommendable, at least for screening smaller enterprises.[12]

Projects screening, as it is commonly applied in practice, has a number of important weaknesses, particularly as a method of determining financing allocation to smaller enterprises. One of these is that the time, scarce skills, and general cost involved in formulating and evaluating projects can easily exceed benefits derivable from this type of allocation procedure, particularly for loans of less than US$10,000 to $20,000. This, of course, depends upon the degree of detail employed in project procedures. In any case, however, costly and time-consuming data collection and verification procedures tend to be involved, because in many countries there are no organized arrangements for efficient and reliable collection of even the most general data required.[13]

---

[11] Accounting prices are estimates of the real social values involved, which are used in place of market prices. See the *Manual of Economic Development Projects,* United Nations, New York, 1958, pp. 203ff., and Jan Tinbergen, *The Design of Development,* The Johns Hopkins Press, Baltimore, 1958, pp. 39, 40.

[12] Shirley Boskey, concludes that the problems of estimating shadow or accounting prices are "formidable," not only in the case of small enterprise, but also for projects generally, and gives several good reasons why this is so. See *Problems and Practices of Development Banks,* International Bank for Reconstruction and Development, Washington, 1959, p. 50.

[13] The time and cost requirements of detailed projects has given rise to complaint even in the case of loans amounting to several million dollars or more. See for example, Wolfgang G. Friedmann (ed.), *Public International Financing in Chile,* Columbia University School of Law, New York, 1964, p. 43. In the present author's opinion, cost and delay objection to projects is much less likely to be valid in the case of large projects. The burden of delay and costs is relative to the amount and life of the investment being considered; it is when the ratio of project screening time and costs to investment life and amount began to exceed 5 percent that they became a serious problem, regardless of the absolute amounts involved.

In some countries, there are simply insufficient data and insufficient stability in conditions to draw up meaningful plans, particularly for periods of more than one or two years. Project preparation may take several months and possibly much longer; evaluation time varies over the same range. Thus, such planning as may have been useful when begun may be no longer valid by the time implementation becomes possible.

Project analysis requires technical and other specialized staff and knowledge which most suppliers of finance in developing countries do not possess and cannot afford to employ on a full-time basis. Specialists, moreover, if they lack much business experience in making investment decisions, tend to be overly concerned with the fineness and logical consistency of past or future technical and economic operations and to neglect elements not readily susceptible to abstract technical analysis, such as the energy, ingenuity, and organizing abilities of management. Where desk methods or unsophisticated staff are used in project analysis, the central dynamics of the firm tends to be lost sight of in an effort to interlink a maze of details, many of which are unrealistic, being poor estimates or assumptions rather than fairly certain facts.

Entrepreneurs in less developed countries frequently do not possess the knowledge or disposition to formulate projects or to benefit much from projects prepared for them by outside specialists. Moreover, the bonds of confidence between lenders and borrowers are often much too weak—and sometimes rightly so—for entrepreneurs to provide lenders in the form of detailed projects information revealing the keys to their business success and the paths for capturing their future opportunities.

A major part of the value of projects lies in the guidance they may provide to the lender for supervising subsequent implementation. Suppliers of finance, however, do not always have staff with sufficient knowledge to supervise implementation constructively. Supervision of projects by staff not able to appreciate the fixity or flexibility with which plans should be implemented may jeopardize the soundness of the financing by straining client relations, increasing operating costs, and preventing or delaying required changes in plans.

Projects often foster—although they need not—the mistaken notion among both lenders and applicants that the results of investments can be scientifically predetermined, that only enterprises whose success can be preplanned are worth undertaking, and that once the feasibility of an enterprise has been determined, its financing and management can be reduced to a mechanistic routine. These misconceptions of what is scientifically possible are obstacles to constructive development action. They overlook the fact that a large part of development is based on action by entrepreneurs with sound instincts as to the key elements and accurate knowledge of these and a willingness to venture ahead without insisting on certainty about less important aspects.

Not all the limitations commonly associated with projects stem from the basic approach of project analysis, which is essentially to make a well-rounded evaluation of the prospects of an enterprise. Many of the deficiencies stem from an imperfect knowledge of the degree to which this approach is useful and of the most useful methods for applying it in the circumstances of less developed countries. Another factor explaining some of the difficulties that have been experienced in using project analysis is that the organizations commonly applying the method in less developed countries have frequently been official institutions. As has been previously indicated, official institutions tend to follow elaborate, mechanistic, and highly documented procedures, whatever the particular screening method used. Delay problems, for example, have also been serious in some cases, where official institutions have screened applications primarily on the basis of collateral offered.[14]

A part of the problem with projects arises from difficulties in developing countries of effectively mobilizing the specialized industrial knowledge required to make sound project evaluations. There is both a shortage of industrial specialists and a lack of knowledge in lending institutions of how to utilize such staff. The consequences of trying to apply project procedure without appropriate staff are illustrated by the experience of the Finance Corporation of the Western Region of Nigeria: "Lacking the staff for technical planning and evaluation, the Corporation seeks to protect itself by tightening the procedure for loan approval, which has the effect of requiring each applicant to go through a series of paper and interview presentations in themselves as much tests of endurance as of industrial capacity and financial need." Screening was estimated to require about 14 months. "Given the power to evaluate technically what can actually be done by and with an applicant," it was suggested, " the need for excessive paper and contact will simply go away."[15] Without being quite so optimistic as to what technical competence can achieve, we would stress the need for staff with a thorough knowledge of industrial operations. This requires more than technical competence. It also requires, as has been elaborated elsewhere, an organizational approach which will permit competent staff under the circumstances of newly industrializing countries to develop the knowledge needed for making decisions in a rapid and efficient manner.

Collateral or Recourse Evaluation

Perhaps no screening method is so widely used—or so widely deprecated —as that of evaluating applications on the basis of the adequacy of

---

[14] See, for example, the experience with the Central Mortgage Bank in Colombia (Chap. 12) and with the National Small Industries Corporations in India (Chap. 2).

[15] *Agricultural and Industrial Credit for Expanded Production in the Western Region of Nigeria,* International Development Services, Inc., New York, July, 1960, p. 38.

collateral or other recourse in the event repayment difficulties arise. Practically all allocations of financing in less developed countries are based in part, perhaps largely, on this criterion. Collateral is commonly required in Europe and the United States also in case of small-industry borrowers, particularly for term loans.[16] The important differences between countries or institutions lie not so much in whether collateral is required but the way in which these requirements are applied. The major deficiencies in this approach to screening tend to arise when: (1) it is the sole or primary criterion applied; (2) collateral ratios are high; and (3) the types of assets acceptable as collateral are narrowly limited.

The reliance upon collateral as the sole criterion for loan decisions is in a sense at the heart of the difficulties, since this contributes in good part to the necessity for high collateral ratios and high selectivity in the type of assets accepted. Apart from these objections, conservative collateral requirements may, from a practical banking point of view, be equally unsatisfactory as sole loan criterion in other respects. Collecting from collateral is often subject to some legal uncertainties. There is also the possibility that, unless closely supervised, collateral will lose value or be unavailable because of fraud or other reasons when the need arises to have recourse to it. Even conservative collateral requirements thus do not always eliminate risk: "No amount of collateral security can provide a substitute for competence and honesty. As the finance companies have long ago learned, a poorly managed company, or one that is run by untrustworthy persons, is a bad risk on any terms."[17] The numerous defaults experienced by the small-industry loan program administered by commercial banks in Taiwan has been attributed to their almost complete dependence on collateral to assure repayment. Collateral ratios in this case were relatively low as compared with the usual practice in less developed countries but not low from the borrower's point of view. Ratios ranged upward from 100 percent; however, imported equipment was valued at 60 percent of its foreign price and land at 50 percent of market value, giving an effective ratio of 180 percent or more. A subsequent increase in collateral ratios only added a further problem—available funds could not be fully lent.[18]

[16] A study in 1957 found that practically all United States Federal Reserve Bank member loans for more than five years to borrowers with assets of less than $1 million were secured, and 66 percent of the short-term loans to borrowers with assets of less than $50,000 were also secured (*Financing Small Business,* Federal Reserve System, Washington D.C., 1958, p. 384. Discussions with selected European and Japanese lending institutions in 1965 indicated that even special lending programs generally require loans to be fully collateralized.

[17] H. Felix de C. Pereira, "Risk Protection," in Beckhart (ed.), *Business Loans of American Commercial Banks,* The Ronald Press Company, New York, 1959, p. 96.

[18] Tenenbaum, *Taiwan's Turning Point,* Continental-Allied Company, Washington, D.C., n.d., 1961?, pp. 41ff. British hire-purchase companies making loans secured

Collateral may be inadequate protection even with good management when adverse changes occur in economic conditions or in public attitudes toward collateral claims. United States banks learned from the depression of the 1930s that not only can economic conditions greatly change the value of even standard collateral, but they may also change the climate of public opinion, inducing general client resistance to surrendering collateral and public support for such resistance. Banks in Nicaragua seem to have had a similar experience at the end of a boom in cotton growing a few years ago. Government banks sometimes find it difficult to enforce their collateral rights at any time, particularly in the case of large and politically influential borrowers and in the case of collateral such as houses and other vital personal property.

Besides the possibility of losses, an exclusive dependence on collateral raises problems which are troublesome to any lender. Collecting funds through the liquidation of pledged collateral is an unpleasant business at best. It provides bad publicity for the lender and tends to damage relationships with the borrowing public generally.

From a development point of view, a serious criticism of relying on the criterion of collateral in making loan decisions is that it does not differentiate between finance used for development and non-development purposes. If applied conservatively, it tends to allocate financing according to applicants' relative wealth or even their relative liquidity. In practice, this is likely to give a poor allocation for development purposes. Property ownership does not necessarily imply entrepreneurial drive and capabilities; indeed, the wealthier borrowers are often more lacking in these qualities. Heavy collateral requirements in practice tend to keep growing firms and small firms generally from obtaining the finance they require for major improvements in production.[19]

---

by equipment are reported to have realized the limitations of exclusive reliance on collateral only recently: "Hire purchase was lending on security of goods—the preserve of the dealer. So indeed the hire purchased companies thought—until they discovered that the security of the goods was an illusion and that they, too, were in the lending business, with the uncomfortable difference that they were unequipped for it in organization, in staff and even in the legal basis of their contracts." ("Has Banking a Future?" *Economist*, Jan. 26, 1963, p. 332). See also Chap. 3 on the loss ratio of the Government Development Bank in Puerto Rico on loans secured primarily by equipment. Such problems are more serious in countries where the resale market for machinery is more limited. A somewhat more exotic case of the dangers of depending exclusively on collateral is that of a lender to a Farmingdale, New Jersey zoo which later went bankrupt and left the lender confronted with the problem: What do you do with a yak received in lieu of repayment?

[19] Kilby has made the same observation in regard to the problem of collateral requirements in Nigeria: "Nevertheless the requirement of security valued at 150 percent of the loan sought effectively screens out the great majority of those who

Where collateral ratios are high, there is a further objection to these requirements in that they increase the risk of the venture to the entrepreneur—by increasing penalties in the case of failure. This will discourage ventures whereas the purpose of financing is usually to stimulate more, not less, venturesomeness.

The collateral approach to screening has additional drawbacks when there are narrow limits to the types of collateral which are acceptable. For many banks, the short-term trade acceptance is still a primary type of collateral required. Even these may be restricted to those relating to a narrow range of easily marketable commodities. If most credit is dispensed on the basis of the availability of trade acceptances, this procedure favors concerns which utilize a large part of the resources in credit extension—and concerns in a position to utilize supplier credit—and may be of no assistance to firms which do not extend or receive trade credit. Many small firms, because of the nature of their clients and suppliers or because of the smallness of individual transactions with them, will be among those excluded. Moreover, where this is a primary form of credit, it encourages enterprises to solve sales problems by credit extension rather than by expenditures improving the product or production techniques. Under conditions where there is a general excess of productive capacity, this type of credit allocation may result in unsound forms of credit competition hazardous to the economy as well as to individual enterprises.

Widening the range of assets acceptable as collateral permits a greater variety of enterprises to draw on financing allocated on a collateral basis. Other types of collateral, however, sometimes involve additional problems. Where real property is used as collateral, there is the additional time and cost involved in appraising it. A visit to the property is normally required, the cost of which may be high for more remote locations. The appraisal costs also rise when less-standard items are involved, such as used machinery and some types of inventory. There are often substantial legal fees, taxes, and other expenses involved in establishing claims against some form of

---

could productively utilize additional finance. Unhappily there is no correlation between the ownership of real estate, on one hand, and entrepreneurship and industrial skills on the other." (*Measures to Promote the Development of Indigenous Industry,* a report to the Federal Ministry of Commerce and Industry and the Western Nigeria Ministry of Trade and Industry, 1962, p. 13.) In Spain also a World Bank Mission found a need for more unsecured loans, noting: "The dynamism of an economy depends more on personal initiation than on personal possessions." (International Bank for Reconstruction and Development, *Economic Development of Spain,* The Johns Hopkins Press, Baltimore, 1963, p. 133.) In Malaya, an evaluation of operations of the Rural and Industrial Development Authority found that overemphasis on collateral was resulting in the dissipation of its efforts on enterprises with little potential for development. (*Report of the Loan Programme Review Committee of the Rural and Industrial Development Authority,* Kuala Lumpur, Malaya, 1963, p. 10.)

collateral.[20] In other cases, it may not be possible under existing laws to establish claims which can be enforced with reasonable certainty, promptness, and economy in the event of default.[21] There is the further problem of assuring the supplier of funds control over the collateral during the period of financing and of assuring that the value of the collateral is maintained. This poses special difficulties where the collateral is costly to store, where it easily loses value in storage or use, and where it must be utilized in the course of business but at the same time is difficult for the financier to supervise when left in the borrower's use. The controls necessary to protect the lender in the case of inventories or light equipment may add directly to financing costs and also indirectly by restrictions and delays resulting from controls. Some types of equipment are expensive to repossess, may be too specialized to be easily resalable, or may be subject to rapid or unpredictable obsolescence. Even in the case of buildings, there may be important additional insurance requirements or restrictions on remodeling or particular uses. Moreover, the future liquidation value of an industrial building when located outside major industrial areas is often low in relation to cost, so that relatively little may be lent against it.

In cases where cosigners are a necessary collateral, acceptable cosigners may charge a substantial fee for this service. Where the requirement of a cosigner in effect shifts the financial dependency of a borrower from a regulated institution to unregulated cosigners, this tends to create problems similar to those discussed in Chapter 6, which arise when financing is derived directly from unregulated lenders.

Cosigners may also be unsatisfactory guarantees from a bank's point of view, even when the cosigner is unquestionably capable of meeting the obligation should the borrower fail to do so. Cosigners do not always realize the full implications of the responsibility they are accepting. They are thus apt to be resentful about being called upon to meet these obligations when it is necessary, and as a result the bank may lose the cosigner's business The bank thus may rightly conclude that it is not worth risking a good client's business to gain the business of a questionable one.

Collateral has important advantages as a basis for allocating finance, despite the limitations that hamper its use in various forms. Even where

[20] For problems of this type in Brazil, see Robert W. Davenport, *Financing Small and Medium Manufacturing Enterprises in Latin America,* Inter-American Development Bank, Washington, 1962, chap. 4.

[21] The absence of clear real estate titles, for example, is a barrier in many African countries. See, for example, International Bank for Reconstruction and Development, *The Economic Development of Uganda,* The Johns Hopkins Press, Baltimore, 1962, p. 74 and, *Report of the Advisory Committee on Aids to African Businessmen,* Federation of Nigeria, Lagos, 1959, pp. 17, 18. Problems of this type also exist in India, Peru, and many other developing countries. The general leniency of courts toward delinquent borrowers has been cited as a serious problem in Nigeria: *Indigenous Industry in Nigeria,* Robert R. Nathan Associates, Inc., Washington, D.C., 1964, p. 31.

credit is allocated primarily on the basis of the volume of trade acceptances applicants can offer as collateral, there is the merit of this being a relatively quick, simple, and economical means of allocating credit in small amounts without involving the lending institution in significant risks. For concerns which must regularly extend credit on sales, it provides a source which normally can be expanded or contracted with variations in production and sales. Where the extension of financing against trade acceptances includes the sales of equipment on medium-term credit, small enterprises of all types often become major beneficiaries through the increased availability of supplier credit for equipment purchases. Many types of equipment, moreover, are produced on a small scale and must frequently be sold on credit whether or not bank financing is available for this purpose. The willingness of banks to extend credit against bills for equipment sales thus can be very important to such enterprises.

Collateral standards can be a valuable supplement to other requirements applicants must meet. This reduces the degree of certainty which other approaches need to achieve in evaluating the probability of repayment and other consequences of financing. It does this not so much by assuring an alternative way of recovering funds when evaluations of management or the enterprise prove inaccurate, but by providing a lever for improving performance in the event of difficulties. Collateral, by its penalty on failure to repay, discourages fraud. This is important where it is costly or impossible for lenders to evaluate the character of a large part of the applicants in great detail. As Tenenbaum has observed in Taiwan: "It is easy to criticize Taiwan's banks for being too conservative, but less easy to suggest how they could relax their [collateral] requirements in a society that condones default, and tolerates bankruptcies . . . . Financial statements are usually incorrect . . . . The law tends to protect borrowers at the expense of lenders . . . . "[22]

Bad faith by borrowers is not the only good reason for having collateral requirements. Collateral creates a strong incentive for entrepreneurs to make the maximum effort to solve problems threatening repayment capacity. Failure to do so comes to mean not merely lost opportunity but also a loss of present resources. Since the success of an enterprise varies greatly with the intensity as well as the quality of management effort, a high motivation may be important in overcoming problems that arise. Collateral thus may serve to make enterprises more productive, even though using collateral as an allocating guide is not directly related to productive possibilities. Because this incentive effect of collateral depends not so much upon what the liquidation value of collateral is to the lender as on its value to the

---

[22] *Op. cit.*, pp. 75, 76. Tenenbaum also later notes that Taiwan's banking laws are another barrier to eliminating collateral requirements, since they specifically restrict the bank's ability to make unsecured loans, as they do in a number of other countries.

borrower, collateral of little or no liquidation value may still be useful. A suggestion by Klein that coconut trees, because of their economic and social importance in some parts of Kenya, can provide useful security for small loans may not be farfetched, if forfeiture can really be enforced.[23] Where collateral has little liquidation value, there is sometimes a problem that borrowers simply do not believe foreclosure is a real possibility. In the case of small loans, this can be overcome by a demonstration of a willingness to take losses rather than tolerate excessive delinquency.[24]

Collateral can serve a further important purpose. Where a firm is being extended all the external finance it appears capable of using wisely, collateral requirements are useful as a control, being easily administered and preventing additional borrowing likely to jeopardize the soundness of the enterprise or its capacity to repay the first loan. By the same token, collateral requirements which prevent further borrowing when financing extended is inadequate for sound operation may themselves be the cause of failure. It is thus a use of collateral which must be administered with care.

Ceylon's Development Finance Corporation handles this problem by taking a comprehensive lien on assets but giving its own guarantee to enable applicants to obtain working capital from others. Pakistan's PICIC frees a portion of assets to use as collateral against bank loans for working capital as the need arises.[25] A major criticism of the Bank of Brazil raw material and equipment loans by some borrowers was that all their assets were tied up for relatively small loans which cut them off from other lending institutions.[26] The dangers in comprehensive collateral requirements if improperly administered are illustrated by experience in Israel:

> The floating charge takes precedence over all other claims against the enterprise, other than mortgages on real property. It thus makes it very difficult for the enterprise to borrow from other sources later on. In theory the IDBI [Industrial Development Bank of Israel] is willing to make arrangements to share the floating charge pari passu with other lenders, or to exempt raw materials or other assets that have been purchased with short-term credit from other sources. However, this requires very complicated legal arrangements and a substantial administrative burden on the banks that wish to lend to IDBI borrowers.[27]

[23] Martin S. Klein, *African Trade in Kenya,* United Research, Inc., Cambridge, Mass., 1961, p. 68.

[24] Where loans are individually so large that the institution cannot afford to foreclose when there is any hope of repayment, collateral with little liquidation value may not serve any useful purpose. This is a frequent problem in loans to large enterprises but is of course much less likely to be one in lending to smaller enterprises.

[25] Boskey, *op. cit.,* pp. 84, 85.

[26] See Davenport, *op. cit.,* Chap. 4.

[27] Tenenbaum, *Israel's Industrial Finances—A Second Look,* Continental-Allied Company, Washington, D.C., 1960, p. 159.

In case borrowers do get into insoluble difficulties, collateral has the final value of assuring the lender priority over other claimants. It helps reduce the losses, even though it cannot usually be depended upon to prevent losses altogether. Particularly for a development financing organization serving small new or growing enterprises where some failure must be expected, collateral, to the extent it can be provided, is an important means by which the financing organizations can reduce unnecessary risks or losses, making it possible for it to enlarge its assumption of more productive risks.

Performance Testing

What is designated here as *performance testing* is perhaps not screening in the usual sense. However, it is a method of selecting applicants which can be used in place of more thorough screening by the preceding methods. Performance testing differs from the preceding methods in that it places less emphasis on attempting at one point in time to forecast the results to be expected from financing over some future period. Performance testing also involves some effort to predetermine what performance may be expected, but it goes about it in a different way—by establishing a pilot experiment. Nevertheless, as compared with management and enterprise evaluations, it involves less forecasting until a considerable body of direct experience with the client has been built up.

Basically, this approach involves the extension of some initial provisional financing with a minimum of investigation but usually on terms of above-average stringency. The opening of a financial relationship is utilized to enable the lender to acquire an intimate practical knowledge of the applicant's operations. The accumulating experience provides an increasingly reliable basis for judging creditworthiness and, where the evidence is favorable, permits the credit relationship to be enlarged and liberalized.

The theoretical outline of performance testing in the preceding paragraph may not closely resemble the way this approach is applied in practice, since it is rarely applied without being accompanied by other screening measures to some degree. A few examples where it has been almost the only approach used, however, may provide a more concrete image of the fundamentals of this approach. In the case of interbusiness credit, finance is sometimes extended largely on a trial and error basis with delinquent and defaulting clients being eliminated as they fail to meet repayment standards and as more desirable types of clients are identified. Collateral in the form of the commodity being sold is utilized, but no screening is required in this case. Another example of almost pure trial and error is an approach which has been widely used by credit institutions in developing a clientele for credit cards: applicants are accepted on the basis of signing a simple agreement; new accounts are carefully supervised and cards cancelled at the first sign of substandard performance. The concepts underlying this procedure are that losses and supervision costs will be less than the costs involved in other types of screening. Moreover, the delay involved in other methods is avoided, reducing the cost and inconvenience to clients in obtaining credits and permitting a large volume of business to be developed quickly.[28]

The more common use of this approach is to rely upon it to permit the reduction of the strictness of other screening standards. Since certainty as to results can never be achieved by other screening methods, one may say that performance testing is to some extent always relied upon. However, it only becomes significant as a method when an effort is made to substitute it for other screening approaches in order to reduce costs, delays, or limitations on the type of applicant that can be screened or to avoid other defects in other screening methods. It may also be used in conjunction with other methods to improve overall results. For example, in both the United States and Japan, banks, in making term loans, not only employ extensive evaluation of management and its enterprise, and frequently require collateral in the case of smaller enterprises, but they also generally restrict these loans to clients with whom they have had a long experience in short-term financing and deposit relationships. Although this is a very conservative use of the performance testing approach, it reflects banks' appreciation of the special value of direct financing experience with a client and his enterprise as a basis for determining whether broader or riskier types of financing can be extended.

The possible merits of the trial and error approach, summing them up briefly, are four: (1) it can widen the population from which applicants are to be drawn, improving the selection and enlarging the volume of financing by permitting less stringent application of other screening methods; (2) it helps economize on screening costs; (3) it can provide a degree and kind of knowledge about an applicant and his enterprise important to evaluating future financial results, which other screening methods in themselves are not capable of providing; and (4) it can greatly reduce the delays involved in making allocations. The general merits of coupling this approach with other screening methods tend to be particularly important for the extension of development financing to small factories where the cost, delays, and informational or collateral requirements tend to be major obstacles.

The successful application of this approach tends to depend upon: (1) an ability to arrive at a generally creditworthy group of applicants on the basis of, at most, quick and simple investigation; (2) a reliable

[28] Prof. Leonard Marks of Stanford University Graduate School of Business has noted, in commenting on a draft of this chapter, that some who have tried this approach in developing a credit card business later abandoned it as being too expensive—in terms of the resulting bad debts. The example is intended to illustrate the kinds of merits which this approach tends to have; they are not of course realizable under all circumstances.

knowledge of the average loss probabilities; (3) a sufficient number of borrowers to permit reliance on actuarial principles; (4) the establishment of appropriate loss reserves; (5) a monitoring system capable of providing fairly advanced warning of changes in the creditworthiness of clients; and (6) lending arrangements permitting financing to be quickly modified or terminated, particularly in the case of relatively new credit relationships.

Monitoring, which is the heart of this approach, must be carried out in such a way and financing must be sufficiently attractive that desirable applicants will accept monitoring as a reasonable accompaniment of financing. Where applicants do not maintain reliable accounts, there must be arrangements under which they are willing and able to establish accounts. Usually this implies that accounting assistance will enable the establishment of accounts which are not only useful to monitoring, but also of direct and apparent value to the borrower.

It is often useful to couple this approach with the capacity to advise, influence, or regulate the borrower in the event of difficulties. This will require a staff which can competently and economically supplement account analysis with periodical plant visits and related field investigations. The type of staff required tends to be scarce. Their economical use often depends upon organizational arrangements permitting them to perform several closely related functions, each partly supporting the overall costs. This is not always easy or possible to work out. Where this approach to screening can be combined with counseling and other postfinancing efforts to improve upon screening results, this approach becomes much more attractive and economical.

Essential Considerations in Choosing Screening Techniques

Which one or more of the basic screening approaches might best be applied and in what degree or combination will vary greatly with: (1) the form and type of financing; (2) the major types of applicants, enterprises, or purposes to be financed; (3) the nature of the environment; (4) the capabilities and objectives of the financing agency; and (5) the nature and extent of post-allocation supervision, counseling, or control contemplated. The way these factors influence the desirability of different screening techniques is briefly illustrated below.

Form and Type of Financing

The importance of screening techniques' being adapted to the form and type of financing extended is fairly obvious. Techniques suitable to long-term financing, for example, may be ill suited to short-term financing and vice versa; or techniques suitable to large amounts of funds or large increments to an applicant's resources may be less appropriate where smaller amounts of increments are involved. In general, the smaller the amount and the shorter the term, the less elaborate screening procedures need to be to provide a given level of results, the less costly or more easily corrected screening errors are likely to be, and the more important it is from several points of view for screening to be rapid, simple, and low in cost.

Types of Applicants, Enterprises, or Fund Uses

Allocation procedures also need to be adapted to the major types of applicants, enterprises, or uses which financing is intended to serve. In screening small enterprises, for example, greater attention usually needs to be given to evaluating management than to evaluating the economics of the enterprise as compared with techniques appropriate for large enterprises. The attention that needs to be given to the economic and technical soundness of plans in financing the establishment of new enterprises (and especially in cases where management is relatively inexperienced) may be in large part wasted if applied to screening financing for moderate expansion of well-established enterprises. Collateral as an allocation determinant is more useful for types of enterprises and fund uses where relatively large amounts of easily evaluated collateral are involved. Allocation procedures intended to serve a wide variety of types of applicants, enterprises, or fund uses must be sufficiently flexible to provide a reasonable test of eligibility for all categories.

Environment

The environment in which financing is extended is an important determinant of what types of screening procedures are economical and effective. In small communities where social ties are strong and very little is secret, screening on the basis of character is likely to be more useful than in large metropolitan cities. Or again, the appraisal of the long-range outlook of enterprises is much more meaningful in economies with relatively stable prices, steady growth, and an abundance of easily available data on competitors, markets, supplies, and so forth than in other types of economies.

Capabilities and Objectives of the Financing Agency

Not every supplier of funds is in an equally strategic position in applying different screening approaches. A commercial bank, through its branches, may be sufficiently in touch with the finances and activities of leading industrialists in small towns to be able to evaluate loan repayment possibilities adequately at little direct expense. A special term-lending institution or insurance company operating primarily from a central office in the capital may find the same evaluations much more difficult. Or again, a major supplier of basic materials, in financing customers, may rely on its knowledge of the competitive outlook of large numbers of enterprises and its ability to recover materials in the event of default as adequate assurance of repayment. A bank, on the other hand, may lack the supplier's detailed knowledge of the industry and his comparative knowledge of the enterprises in it, and as a result he may be less able to evaluate the outlook of such enterprises. At the same time, a bank is likely to be much less protected by a claim on the materials, as it does not have the supplier's marketing facilities and the knowledge of the value of the material.

Screening capabilities often depend upon usual staffing of different types of lenders. Different approaches require different staff capabilities. The evaluation of the outlook of enterprises in particular requires specialized capabilities. As discussed in Chapter 5, financing agencies are not always able to staff appropriately for particular screening methods.

The objectives as well as the capabilities of financing agencies may influence their approach to screening in a number of important ways. Screening which provides a high degree of certainty concerning results tends either to be rough and simple but so conservatively based as to exclude many eligible borrowers or to require detailed investigation involving expense and delay. Private banking agencies seeking a high degree of certainty and profits, as most do, tend to favor the first type of screening—simple, low in cost, and conservative. This is particularly true where lending rates are fixed and the demand for financing is far in excess of supply. Where screening involving more detailed investigation is employed, a concern for profits encourages financing agencies to shift the burden of expense to the applicant insofar as possible. Beyond a certain point, expense and delay arising from screening methods tend to exclude eligible borrowers, particularly among small enterprises and others requiring funds in relatively small amounts or for short periods.

The problem of achieving near certainty as to financial results through screening becomes more complex when the results sought are not simply repayment of funds with interest but some definite contribution to national development. Thus, the appropriate screening method also depends on how important allocating funds according to national development procedures is to the objectives of the supplier of funds or to agencies regulating them.

The Extent of Post-allocation Measures Contemplated

The need to identify in advance whether a given allocation of finance will produce the results desired is reduced if the lender is willing and able to influence results forthcoming after allocations have been made. Not every lender has the same willingness or capability to engage in post-allocation supervision or counseling, as we have already indicated. This also gives rise to differences in the extent and type of screening appropriate for each.

Measures to Improve Screening

If the screening methods commonly employed in newly developing countries are taken as a whole, five major deficiencies can be identified which impede the extension of development financing to small enterprises:

1. Screening relies too heavily on easily evaluated and liquidatable collateral, on traditional rules of thumb, and on very limited personal impressions about what is financially sound or developmentally useful.
2. The absence of sufficiently comprehensive, economical, and rapid information collection frequently makes it difficult to supplement these admittedly inadequate methods.
3. Screening tends to be too predominantly a negative and passive process.
4. There is a general overreliance on achieving certainty of results through screening and inadequate emphasis on risk taking and post-allocation efforts to improve results.
5. The development consequences of financing are not adequately taken into account, and efforts to do so have for the most part been of a type sharply increasing the cost and delays involved in small-industry financing without greatly improving the developmental results.

The general types of measures that can be taken to reduce these deficiencies will be considered below.

Creating Informational Foundations Essential to Better Screening Methods

One of the most obvious, although initially expensive, ways of improving screening methods in newly developing countries is to create some of the informational foundations which render screening a simpler and more useful process in advanced countries. Good accounting practices in the enterprises of potential clients are usually one of the first informational foundations that need to be created.

Even good accounts provide only a starting point in evaluating the capabilities of management and the potentialities of an enterprise, but they are major time-savers for screening authorities and enable a preliminary screening of types of enterprises that it might not otherwise be practical to consider. Good accounting is also fundamental to post-allocation efforts to improve or evaluate results. Thus, even though costs and difficulties in introducing accounting are often considerable, the value of so doing must be appraised in terms of the large overall contribution of good accounting to sound industrial growth.

A second informational foundation that is badly needed is a pool of credit and financial records. A simple exchange of information on repayment performance and outstanding obligations of potential applicants by banks and other suppliers of finance through a central credit information bureau would be a valuable first step in many countries.

The extensive interchange of credit information in industrialized countries, particularly in the United States, however, has only become possible because of mutual confidence between banks and other organizations engaged in the pooling of such information. The latter has been facilitated by a widely accepted explicit code of ethics.[29] There is a great need in developing countries for a similar consensus or a code of ethics among those engaged in credit work and for other active steps to create a firm base of mutual confidence. A pool of credit information not only reduces the cost of individual investigations but, more importantly, provides more complete and reliable information than may otherwise be obtainable. Moreover, once such a system is widespread and well established, it encourages much higher standards of repayment performance.[30]

[29] The ethical standards adopted by the Robert Morris Associates in the United States provide:

> *The first and cardinal principle in credit investigation is to respect the confidential nature of the information received.*
>
> *The name of the inquirer, in whose behalf the inquiry is made, should not be disclosed without permission.*
>
> *In answering inquiries, the source of the information should not be disclosed without permission.*
>
> *Any betrayal of confidence stamps the offender unworthy of future consideration.*
>
> *Each letter of inquiry should indicate specifically the object and scope of the inquiry.*
>
> *When more than one inquiry on the same subject is sent simultaneously to banks it should be indicated that information from their own files is sufficient as other checkings are being made.*
>
> *All letters, including form letters, should bear the manual signature of the inquirer to establish responsibility.*
>
> *The recipient of a credit inquiry is negligent in his duty if he does not read carefully each letter of inquiry and answer frankly, to the best of his ability, its specific questions.*
>
> *In answering inquiries, it is advisable to disclose all material facts bearing on the credit standing of the subject, including the basis upon which credit is extended.*
>
> *Indiscriminate revision of files, when there is no real need for information, is wasteful and undesirable.*
>
> *Where periodic revision of file information is made, it may be desirable to give your own experience in the letter of inquiry, in order that duplication and unnecessary correspondence may be kept to a minimum.*
>
> *In soliciting accounts, it is not permissible nor the part of good faith for the soliciting bank to make inquiries from a competitor without frankly disclosing the nature and object of the inquiry.*

(Cited from Lawrence T. Knier, "Organization of Lending Activities of Commercial Banks," in Benjamin Beckhart (ed.), *Business Loans of American Commercial Banks,* The Ronald Press Company, New York, 1959, p. 64.) The above code was first adopted in 1916 and has had a major influence on the interchange of credit information. "The fact that credit information flows throughout the banking fraternity is due in no small part to uniform acceptance and adherence to these rules." (*Ibid.*)

[30] Another type of information which has been used in the United States but which it may not be possible to develop immediately in less industrialized countries is composite financial data measuring the overall detailed aspects of the performance of different types of enterprise. Composite financial data is helpful not only in

A third important informational foundation is general survey reports on various lines of industry describing the nature and trend of competition, markets, supplies, technology, and other aspects important to appraising the outlook of an industry as a whole and of individual applicants planning to compete within it. Survey information is valuable because it provides much broader information, including important qualitative evaluations, than can be obtained from composite financial data previously described. It is useful in itself and essential as a supplement to comparative financial standards in evaluating the outlook of individual enterprises or of industries. Moreover, survey programs providing at least important general information can often be more quickly established than those collecting financial data, since the latter depend more on the existence of good accounting and a high level of cooperation. Industry surveys periodically updated are much more economical and often more reliable ways of gathering much of the information needed for project evaluation than leaving the entire task to individual applicants, particularly in the case of small enterprises and especially where a large number of concerns make up the industry. Industry surveys facilitate the evaluation of applicants relative to their competitors, which is the only really meaningful standard for judging outlook in competitive industries.[31]

---

screening individual applicants, but also in following the trend in various industries and in guiding clients as to particular aspects of their operation that might be improved. In the United States, an organization of commercial bank credit officers, Robert Morris Associates, compiles a variety of ratios measuring performance from composite financial statements and earning reports of 170 types of manufacturing and commercial enterprises, subdivided in some cases by scale of enterprise. See Harry B. Odle, "A Banking Association that 'Sticks to its Last,'" *Burrough's Clearing House*, August 1963, pp. 52ff. Ratios for many lines of business are also compiled in the United States by Dun & Bradstreet.

[31] The need for wider recognition of this has been stressed recently by United States banker, H. L. Jenkins, who suggests that competition should be added to the banker's traditional criteria of character, capacity, and capital (or capability and collateral, as the last two are sometimes labeled). (*Burrough's Clearing House*, July, 1963, pp. 10, 11). Lenders in industrially advanced countries, possibly lulled by the general postwar industrial prosperity, have, in the author's view, given surprisingly little attention to analyzing comparative competitive ability, marketing trends, and related factors. However, there has been more and recently growing recognition of the value of industry surveys for the purpose of evaluating individual units. The 1962 annual report of the Industrial Credit Company Ltd. of Ireland in its discussion of a new industrial development financing program noted, for example:

> In considering applications for special loans, it will be necessary to have regard not only to the circumstances of individual applicants, but also to the structure, plans, and prospects of industries as a whole. . . . In addition to consulting with the Department of Industry and Commerce we shall of course have regard to the reports of the Committee on Industrial Organization on particular indus-

Stimulating a More Active Approach to Screening

There are a number of reasons why not only banks but most other suppliers of finance in less developed countries maintain a rather passive approach to screening. Demand for finance from good credit risks often runs far in excess of the supply of finance, so that little initiative is required to maintain a profitable financing business. The more active approach we are suggesting is clearly more demanding in terms of expense, energy, and imagination, and if a more active approach is to be introduced, these will somehow have to be provided.

Efforts to introduce a more active approach to lending must take into account several other factors which explain the present banking policies. There is a long—but now very much outdated—banking tradition that bankers should be aloof, unapproachable, and reluctant lenders, a tradition still held by some bankers in the most advanced countries.[32] The bankers who hold these traditions may have sound reasons why this approach serves their own interests, even though there may be better approaches, particularly from the point of view of national interests. The stance of the traditional lender is widely believed by those who practice it to be essential to warding off in a quick and inexpensive way applications from a hoard of undesirable applicants who tend to apply for credit on the slightest encouragement even though their possibilities of repaying are poor. The traditional bankers' stance may also tend to help to pave the way psychologically for rejecting unacceptable applicants or for enforcing repayments from clients in financial difficulties. There is likely to be less argument, ill will, and general disappointment in such cases if the banker has appeared reluctant to lend from the start. Also important is the fact that an apparent reluctance to lend greatly strengthens the lender's bargaining position vis-à-vis the borrower, since the borrower in applying acknowledges the need for funds, whereas the lender acknowledges no need for clients. Bargaining has always been a very important element in setting financing terms. It is also true in many cases that at least those screening applications are in a sense often truly reluctant lenders. Particularly in less developed countries, there are many elements that might affect the soundness of loan decisions which the screening officer is unable to evaluate with certainty, while at the same time

---

tries. These reports, which provide for the first time a comprehensive picture of the industries surveyed, are a valuable source of information for those who, like the Industrial Credit Company, are engaged in providing capital for industry as well as for industrialists, who must now plan to meet the most competitive conditions of the future.

(Industrial Credit Company, Ltd., *Annual Report,* 1962, p. 5).

[32] On the persistence of defensive or passive lending attitudes among many bankers in the United States, see Howard D. Crosse, *Management Policies for Commercial Banks,* Prentice-Hall, Inc., Englewood Cliffs, N.J., 1962, p. 228.

near-perfect decisions are usually expected of him. Honest misgivings thus tend to retard approval on many very good loans.

The problem with the traditional banking approach is that bankers get isolated from the activities and the managements they are intended to serve. They do not build up the intimate knowledge that arises only from close and informal contact and, lacking this, are greatly handicapped in screening applicants or in designing terms that will prove mutually satisfactory. This often becomes translated in the minds of businessmen, particularly small businessmen, into a reputation for haughtiness, impracticality in setting terms and procedures, and merciless use of a strong bargaining position. Such reputations discourage the best types of applicants from applying for finance. Where applicants are reduced largely to those in desperation, which is a particularly strong tendency in the case of government institutions having slow and laborious procedures and of unregulated lenders charging very high rates, even the best of the applicants are not likely to be very promising ones.

An active approach to screening usually does not require a publicity campaign soliciting clients, but rather depends upon an adequate knowledge of the sectors to be served. As Crosse has very aptly summed the matter up:

> The essence of loan development lies, first, in a willingness to examine carefully every request for credit and to try conscientiously to make it "bankable"; and second, to search actively for opportunities to promote the growth of the community and the individual businesses therein with sound credit. The two go hand in hand, and the bank which has an established reputation for constructive lending will not have to do as much searching. Nevertheless, a major objective of visits by bank officers to their customers' places of business, be it farm or factory, should be to find new ways or additional productive purposes for the customers' use of credit.[33]

Crosse's further advice on ways of coping with the overly conservative bias of lending officers in the United States is also pertinent to less-developed countries:

> A further sound policy, not exercised enough, is to require a review of loan applications of substantial amounts which have been *denied* by the lending officers. It is particularly important in branch banking organizations operating over fairly extensive areas for senior management and the directors to assure themselves that branch managers or loan department heads are not turning down legitimate requests for credit merely to protect their records of "safe" lending. If directors wish to encourage imaginative lending that is "sound" in the broadest sense, they must encourage their lending officers to make sound loans out of some weak-looking applications, and must expect and be tolerant of occasional mistakes.[34]

[33] Crosse, *op. cit.*, p. 229.
[34] *Ibid.*, p. 215 (italics added).

An active approach depends on lenders being well informed. Industry and area surveys are an important source of information. How surveys can lead to an active selecting of promising applicants is illustrated by the results of an informal survey of the cattle industry which a bank made in Panama in 1950. Having concluded from the survey that modernization of the cattle industry was a promising field and that suitable terms could be worked out to interest cattlemen, a financing program was begun which in 12 years reached the volume of $6 million outstanding to 1,500 ranchers.[35]

Individual suppliers of finance may not be able to afford to make such surveys themselves, but it is important that some organization in the economy provide them. It is equally important that suppliers of finance have the benefit both of the findings and of frequent informal discussions with those engaged in such investigations. An effort by those engaged in surveys to bring to the attention of suppliers of finance possible clients of great promise and to make the latter aware of the possibilities of external finance can be of great value in improving the results of development financing programs.

Those allocating finance require some direct and personal knowledge of small industrialists and their enterprises. This usually requires that decisions in large institutions with branch offices be decentralized to the local level.[36] Training programs which provide the staff of banking institutions with at least brief experience in surveying the outlook of industries can be extremely valuable in widening their understanding of how to evaluate industrialists and the information on industry. Equally useful are organized efforts to assist and stimulate bankers to attend industrial association meetings and to establish other informal contacts with small industrialists. Encouraging lenders themselves to visit enterprises in arriving at loan decisions is also important. Even where assistance from economic and technical specialists is available, the latters' appraisals are not an adequate substitute for the visit of the loan officer himself. Without his own direct impressions, a loan officer is not equipped to evaluate the advice of specialists and to make his own final judgment.

[35] See Oscar Schisgal, "Banks That Build New Businesses around the World," *Reader's Digest*, February, 1963. For a discussion of the value of surveys and direct knowledge of the various potential borrowing needs of a community for even sound commercial bank operations in an advanced economy, see Crosse, *op. cit.*, pp. 139ff.

[36] This may also contribute to staff development and good customer relations, as Crosse has indicated (*op. cit.*, pp. 211, 212). The value of decentralized operations is also confirmed by the experience of the Industrial Development Bank of Canada, which has placed great stress on decentralized but supervised operations. In 1962, 72 percent of the total loans were approved by the office at which application was made, another 14 percent by a regional office, and only the remaining 14 percent referred to the head office for approval. *Submission by the Industrial Development Bank to the Royal Commission on Banking and Finance,* Ottawa, Canada, 1962, p. F-2.

Banks and other suppliers of finance, with the possible exception of trade creditors, cannot be expected to be staffed with specialists in all the types of activity they finance. In order to finance industry on an informed basis, banks need to be able to draw on outside professional staff who are trained and regularly engaged in more specialized aspects of appraising industrial operations. This is particularly true in countries where lenders cannot rely on the guidance of financial statements or on entrepreneurs in general being highly experienced in their line of operations.

Besides access to outside specialists, lenders will usually require on their own staff one or more persons who are sufficiently grounded in the fundamentals of industrial operations that they are able to interpret and evaluate the information from specialists.[37] It is important that banks be assisted in building up such staff.

Other obstacles to drawing upon the services of outside specialists which must be overcome are the scarcity and cost of such specialists, difficulties in assuring their availability when needed, and competent performance of tasks assigned. To cope with these problems, careful organizational arrangements are essential. It must be possible to utilize specialists with efficiency so that costs are kept reasonable in terms of the value of loans. The subdivision of work between bank staff and outside specialists must be done in such a way that it does not increase screening time substantially or result in diminished bank control over the quality of some parts of the evaluation process. The ability to draw upon specialists to make technical and economic appraisals of an enterprise and of the special abilities and credit reputation of management must not in any way diminish the lender's basic responsibilities or capacity to make loan decisions. On such critical and subjective matters as character, moreover, the major part of the evaluation must be made by the bank loan officer. Not only does the responsibility rightly belong here, but, as previously indicated, there are often serious obstacles to getting others to perform this type of evaluation satisfactorily. The banker must judge the quality and relative importance of more narrowly specialized evaluations and integrate them with each other and his own direct evaluations. The general approach required to render the use of outside specialists practical is discussed in Chapter 5.

Increasing the cooperation between the various suppliers of finance—such as between equipment suppliers and finance companies or between commercial banks and development banks—can also be helpful. Such interaction helps widen the concept of all parties concerning possible financing opportunities and, by joining complementary capabilities, widens the scope of activities they may undertake. Achieving such cooperation again depends upon there being an organization which is motivated and staffed to help

[37] Commercial banks engaged in term lending in the United States also need staff of this type for closely similar reasons. See G. S. Moore, "Term Loans and Interim Financing," in Beckhart, op. cit., p. 224.

bring about a workable division of functions and responsibilities between the cooperating institutions.

Introducing Improved Screening Methods

If measures to stimulate an active approach to screening are successful, the suppliers of funds will themselves seek out better ways of screening applicants. However, direct efforts to improve screening methods are also valuable. Deficiencies in screening methods of particular suppliers of finance as well as possible ways of remedying them have already been discussed in the analysis of the various channels of financing. It may be useful to bring together the essential points on screening stressed there.

The typical situation upon which new methods must improve is one in which a simple adequacy of collateral is the most common screening test. Moreover, requirements tend to be high and the type of collateral acceptable narrowly limited so that many creditworthy applicants are excluded. Further, this procedure provides little guidance concerning whether the financing will have any developmental value.

The collateral test is usually combined with management evaluation of one sort or another. Usually this does not improve the screening process, because lenders have little specific knowledge of the qualities important to success in small enterprises. They may also lack a broad enough knowledge of small industrialists to have an adequate comparative standard for evaluating individual small-industry applicants. Management evaluation often merely means excluding those who are not well known to the lender, which may effectively exclude most small industrialists.

In the exceptional case of special development financing, the allocation method now being used in newly industrializing countries is to an increasing degree project evaluation or detailed technical, economic, and financial analyses of past and future operations. This method has the merit of considering proposed fund uses. In some cases, it has permitted less stringent collateral requirements. It encompasses management evaluation, although frequently in practice much less stress is given to this aspect than to technical, economic, and financial feasibility evaluations. It tends to be an expensive screening method and is dependent upon information and planning abilities which the small entrepreneur in the environment of developing countries may neither possess nor be able to acquire. Even where specialists trained in project preparation have been available to assist entrepreneurs, experience has not been very satisfactory. Projects have not in many cases been accurately prepared and sufficiently explicit about unknown factors to guide implementation. Entrepreneurs have not been sufficiently a part of the planning to know how to apply it to their operations. Moreover, frequently all staff with special knowledge of industrial operations are absorbed by elaborate project screening procedures so that supervision is neglected or entrusted to persons ill equipped to undertake it.

To improve present screening methods, it is not necessary or usually even desirable to eliminate collateral requirements. Rather what is needed is a use of a greater variety of assets and guarantees for this purpose and a lowering of requirements through a greater dependence on other screening approaches and post-allocation measures.[38] Broadening the variety of assets and guarantees acceptable as collateral requires in many cases changes in legislation or new institutional arrangements. In Sweden, for example, it was recently found desirable to establish a separate corporation (although with the same ownership and management as its present Industrial Credit Corporation) which will specialize in lending against second mortgages.[39] The value of various other new institutional measures such as the establishment of field warehouses, industrial estates, or special finance companies equipped to lend against receivables in reducing collateral problems has been discussed elsewhere. Lenders may need to be educated in new techniques and in new concepts concerning the purposes of collateral. Where collateral comes to serve as a supplement to other screening and implementation measures, much lower requirements become possible. Assistance in developing other types of screening capabilities is essential for this purpose. An increased dependence on implementation measures also requires assistance in building up implementation capabilities.

Evaluation of proposed fund uses is important, but less elaborate and more direct procedures than those usually implied by project analysis are favored for most types of financing. It is often not practical in the case of small factories to require detailed and formal reports on past or planned performance or to rely heavily on the information in such reports in evaluating applications. Field investigations by persons with a practical knowledge of industrial operations are essential for accurately appraising the probability of financing being productively used and repaid. If fairly simple written information requirements are combined with a well-rounded field analysis of the enterprise and its competitive position, even though the latter is brief and qualitative, this is often adequate to identify creditworthy small enterprises.

There are of course some legal, psychological, and educational values in requiring applicants to describe in writing their operations and plans. This also simplifies the subsequent field evaluations. However, a relatively brief reply to a simple questionnaire will serve these purposes. While project

[38] See the discussion of implementation in Chap. 11.

[39] Brian Wickremesinghe, *Financing of Small Scale Industrial Enterprises in Sweden,* Företagsekonomiska Institutionen, Uppsala Universitet, 1962, p. 22. In Denmark, officials administering the Ministry of Commerce and Industry loan program reported in discussions with the author in 1965 that they accepted second and even lower-ranking mortgages. This involved some operational disadvantages but had not resulted in a significantly higher level of losses than would have occurred with a first mortgage. See also the experience of Japan's Small Business Finance Corporation in Chap. 13.

analysis as it is commonly carried out may appear to economize on field-work, it is in part an unwise economy and in part a transferring of the responsibility from bank staff to applicants which does not reduce the actual national costs incurred in screening.

There is a need to place greater stress upon oral and visual collection of information, not only because of the undeveloped state of statistical information in many countries, but also because of the nature of the information required. Even in the United States where formal sources of information are very advanced, oral and visual investigation methods are also important for evaluating creditworthiness:

> Additional answers beyond those contained in the agency reports are to be gleaned from direct trade checkings, which are made most effectively by personal interview. Unfavorable comments, if such are circulating, seldom receive currency through the written word. They may be obtained in conversation when prompted by the right questions or they may be implied from an unwillingness to express confidence in the subject. Such matters as general reputation in the trade and even rather personal comments about the principals may come out in the course of the interview. A good investigator will be keen to sense attitudes whether or not explicitly stated and will be alert to pick up leads for further checkings.[40]

This is not the only kind of information that must be gathered in this fashion. Even more important is information relating to the potential of the enterprise:

> Many purposes are served by visiting with the borrower and his organization. Certain questions derived from the analysis of statements may be asked. An opportunity is afforded to meet and to size up other members of the organization, particularly junior men who will be stepping into the responsible positions at a later date. Seeing the plant layout, the production process, the housekeeping practices, the labor force, the kinds of records and controls maintained, the general atmosphere of the organization, and the personal relationships which exist may add not only to the credit analyst's background and understanding of his customer's problems, but in addition to the favorable or unfavorable observations which he is making on the question of credit standing.
>
> . . . in final analysis, the lender must rely on the enterprise and ability of management to cope with unforeseeable as well as predictable happenings. Thus the appraisal of the organization in a broad sense becomes the principal factor in resolving doubts about the credit worthiness of the prospective commercial borrower. This means an appraisal of the competence and depth of executive direction, the strength of competitive position, the efficiency of operations, the reliability of reporting and controls, the soundness of financial planning, the quality of industrial relations, and the resourcefulness in meeting new problems and situations. No doubt, these elements in the appraisal of the organization are more reliable and persistent than uncertain

[40] Roger Murray, "Evaluating Credit Worthiness," in Beckhart, *op. cit.,* p. 87.

expectations regarding the economic climate in which the firm will be operating; these qualities provide the real margin of safety.[41]

As the foregoing commentary by Murray implies, it is only by *observing* an enterprise and its management *in operation* that the dynamic elements so important to the successful use of financing can be evaluated.

In the case of smaller enterprise, the quality of management is of special importance. As has been noted in the United States and applied with even greater force in less-developed countries: "No lender can possibly foresee all the future circumstances that will affect the fortunes of the borrower. But if he has satisfied himself of the superior ability of the management, he can reasonably expect that appropriate adjustments will be made. Appraisal of management is the touchstone of term credit analysis."[42] It is equally fundamental to short-term financing if, beyond the repayment of funds, development results are desired. It is important, therefore, to improve the capacity of those allocating finance to evaluate management accurately and objectively.

Finally, there is a need for less exclusive reliance upon screening to protect the profitability or enlarge the development value of financing, for a greater use of an actuarial approach to risk taking, and for protections such as loss reserves and post-allocation measures to improve implementation. Arrangements for monitoring financing closely enough to detect difficulties in their early stages and to mobilize external assistance to correct such difficulties as they arise are particularly important. Screening, by whatever methods, can never be an exact or automatic process; it will always remain more of an art than a science. Beyond a certain point, post-allocation measures provide a better way of improving results than greater screening efforts do.

Improving screening is not merely a matter of altering techniques. Equally important is assuring an appropriate application of techniques. This may mean channeling funds through types of lenders capable of employing appropriate techniques or of assisting lenders in improving their techniques. Where, for example, modernizing equipment is of basic importance to the future of numerous small enterprises in a country such as Japan, providing such financing by institutional arrangements for discounting installment sales bills of domestic producers of equipment may provide adequate assurance of a reasonable allocation of funds and may at the same time be simpler, more rapid, and more economical than alternative methods. On the other hand, where equipment financing is sought largely for imported equipment by new enterprises in a country with a shortage of foreign

[41] *Ibid.,* p. 91.

[42] N. Jacoby and R. Saulnier, *Term Lending to Business,* National Bureau of Economic Research, New York, 1942, p. 92. The significance of this comment is heightened by the fact that the lenders to whom Saulnier referred had access to, and utilized, elaborate means of analyzing the past and proposed operations of the large enterprises they typically financed.

exchange and idle plant capacity, as was the case recently in Israel, the screening methods suppliers can be expected to employ in these circumstances are likely to be seriously inadequate to what is needed.

A further example of how the appropriateness of a technique may vary with the financing is the contrasting case of short- and longer-term financing: temporary working capital financing may be of development importance, even though it may not be practical to devote great effort to analyzing or influencing the development results of individual allocations. Screening may simply consist of applying standard rules of thumb and easily administered collateral requirements and of trusting applicants as long as past experience, credit reports, and other sources confirm the banking and developmental soundness of doing so. It may be practical and useful to appraise thoroughly on an annual basis the normal financial needs of periodic users to assure that fund approvals the following year will generally conform to the applicant's ability to use them productively. Term financing, on the other hand, may merit more detailed screening, at least where it substantially enlarges a firm's resources. It might involve a preliminary screening on the basis of an interview and/or simple questionnaire; a direct analysis of management, its operations, and its financial affairs; adequate pledging of assets to assure a high repayment incentive; the establishment of provisions for regular financial reporting; occasional field visits to review or counsel operations; and the designing of controls, setting desirable and appropriate limitations on management actions without encumbering normal operations. Term financing to new as compared with established enterprises will require much more detailed investigation of operating plans and of management's abilities to operate the specific enterprise contemplated. More frequent and detailed counseling and supervision may also be required, and the assumption of much more risk must usually be provided for.

These and many other differences in screening situations which suppliers of finance must be capable of dealing with make it important that those allocating funds employ varied and versatile methods. Improving the capacity of a wide range of suppliers of financing in this respect will usually require making readily available to them a responsive service which has close contact with and a practical knowledge of industrial operations and which can supplement the lender's normal capacities with necessary specialized abilities. Improved screening methods depend not only on supplementing the capabilities of those allocating finance, but also on motivating them to adopt more appropriate methods. This requires a convincing demonstration of the general effectiveness and overall practicality of new methods. It may also require assistance in transitional problems such as the training of staff and other inducements. This again requires the assistance of a development-oriented agency closely acquainted and directly concerned with the needs and capabilities of small factories. Methods of achieving appropriate institutional arrangements for this purpose have been discussed in Chapter 5.

Chapter 11
Assuring Implementation

The Need for Post-allocation Measures or Aftercare

A lending institution screens applicants to eliminate types that may fail to keep their commitments conscientiously, that may not be able to repay loans, or that may not apply funds to appropriate uses. Screening, however, cannot be the end of the process of assuring that the financing produces the result intended. Post-allocation supervision, control, counseling, or other aftercare can be equally important.

As the previous chapter has indicated, using screening as a device to assure financing will produce intended results has inherent limitations, since it attempts to determine *future* performance on the basis of *present* plans and conditions and *past* performance. Especially over the period of a medium- or long-term loan, many changes can take place in economic conditions, technology, and management capabilities, motivations, and plans. The future can be estimated, but it cannot be definitely ascertained.

The exclusive reliance on screening to assure financing results has two drawbacks. The assurance screening can provide may be inadequate; or the costs may be unnecessarily high. The possibility of wrong financing decisions arising from unanticipated changes can be reduced by making investigations more extensive or by tightening standards. Investigating everything that might possibly be relevant, however, tends to be costly. Tightening standards so that applicants are rejected whenever there is any possibility of adverse changes or when these possibilities cannot be accurately estimated tends to eliminate many applicants offering sound and important financing opportunities. In newly developing countries where the environment is less stable, information less available, management less experienced, and financing relationships less smoothed by customs and regulations, uncertainty is inevitably higher and, in many cases, not reducible by investigation. If strict standards are relied upon to compensate for this lack of information, many promising borrowers may be eliminated by this means of assuring that all unpromising ones are excluded.

The course of events is not necessarily predetermined, nor need it be left entirely to chance. It can in some degree be shaped, and this is what post-allocation measures are intended to do. Both the need for and possibilities of improving financing results through post-allocation measures are especially great where management is a key factor and where its general level is not very high.

The amount of effort and the methods worth applying to post-allocation measures depend upon what the specific objectives of the measures are. Private banks are primarily interested in aftercare where it helps economize on screening costs or helps detect adverse changes at an early stage so that they can be remedied or losses minimized. Some private banks are also aware that aftercare may even be a profitable policy where it goes beyond this to improving the prosperity of their clients and relations with them. Where a financier's return is tied to the profit of the recipient, this gives rise to a special motive for rendering aftercare which may justify its cost in terms of a higher return.

For the financing institution with development responsibilities, aftercare has an even greater significance. Because a development institution's responsibilities may involve it in more risky types of financing, the contribution that aftercare makes to reducing risks is of particular value. The development institution, moreover, is interested in stimulating the maximum development with a given amount of financing, not merely in improving production sufficiently to assure repayment. While a private vendor may not feel the need for extending much aftercare to a reasonably prosperous client, a development bank, which by reasonable expenditure on aftercare can speed loan repayment or increase productivity of even a prosperous client, has reason to do so.

The need of development institutions to assure that funds are actually applied to development purposes also makes it important for them to provide aftercare. Private lenders also may be concerned with how funds are used, especially term loans, since where they are not used profitably, repayment difficulties may develop. But in many cases, nonproductive uses of funds may not endanger repayment and thus may be of little concern to the private lender. A development bank must be concerned with the use of funds even where repayment is not endangered; it is often nationally important that the funds not be used to facilitate speculation, capital flight, or increased consumption. Because some types of nonproductive activities are often highly profitable in developing countries, because of the exceptional incentives to increase consumption faster than income permits, and because borrowing may be further stimulated by subsidized lending rates, the motivation for applicants in developing countries to divert funds to ineligible purposes is unusually high. Follow-up procedures which will effectively guard against this may differ in many respects from those concerned only with assuring repayment.

Counseling service to borrowers has been much recommended to financial institutions in recent years. A general recognition among both private and public development banks of the desirability of some provision for post-allocation supervision was stimulated by Arthur Lewis's remarks that "lending money to inexperienced small business people without supervision is often equivalent to pouring it down the drain. What these people need is first supervision and advice and only secondarily capital."[1] Lewis's views were also stated in more detail in an earlier report on the Gold Coast, where he advised:

> The writer does not therefore agree that the Industrial Development Corporation should cease to make small loans. He recommends that loans should be continued but the emphasis should be shifted to supervision and advice. When an application is received, the Industrial Development Corporation should examine thoroughly the way in which the business is run, and the proposals now made for its extension. If dissatisfied in important particulars, it should require the applicant to make whatever alterations it thinks fit (layout, keeping of records, staff policy, or whatever is deficient), as a prior condition to granting the loan. The granting of the loan should also be on condition that the owner of the business cannot make certain major changes without the consent of the Industrial Development Corporation—such as to alter the nature of the business, or to sell any of its fixed assets—and that the Industrial Development Corporation will pay regular visits and advice. The Industrial Development Corporation should equip itself with sufficient competent staff to carry out these duties. Its relations with debtors should be those of the family doctor rather than the policeman. All the same, most people dislike being given good advice, even by the family doctor; if the debtor finds the relationship onerous, this may spur him to pay off the debt all the sooner.[2]

The idea of aftercare is thus not new, but few practical arrangements for implementing it are yet in operation. In such programs as exist, little consideration has been given to what types of supervision and counseling are important, to what extent they should be given, or to what administra-

[1] *The Theory of Economic Growth,* George Allen and Unwin, Ltd., London, 1958.

[2] W. A. Lewis, *Report on Industrialization and the Gold Coast,* Gold Coast Government, Accra, 1953, p. 13. An early postwar study in the United States similarly reported: "Those experienced in the affairs of small business stress again and again that improved management is needed far more than new financial aid. In speaking of the experience of the Industrial Corporation of Baltimore, its director stated: 'Thirty years of experience of our corporation, dealing with hundreds of cases has convinced us that small business needs more counsel than cash.' " (Douglas R. Fuller, *Government Financing of Private Enterprise,* Stanford University Press, 1948, p. 178.)

tive arrangements might this service be most economically and effectively provided.

The value of supervision and of the related function of counseling stems from the fact that, particularly in less-developed countries, many more clients might be eligible for financing and the financing extended might be more productively used if industrialists had a broader knowledge of industrial operations and if there were means of assuring that full knowledge was applied to the maximum extent toward purposes within the development financing organization objectives. This approach has a particular appeal in countries where, because of the difficulties in screening and the limited supply of entrepreneurs, it is not possible to rely simply on selecting applicants who are reasonably certain to perform in the way desired and on the setting of loan conditions designed to induce this performance.

Counseling and direct supervision are a promising approach to improving the development possibilities of financing, particularly in the case of small industries. However, like screening, there are limitations on the extent to which it can be applied and the ways in which it can be applied to provide reasonable results at a reasonable cost.

Some of the enthusiasm for counseling, like that for loan allocation on the basis of project analysis, is based on the mistaken premise that business failure can be virtually eliminated by good organization of information. In fact, however, much of the information valuable to successful industrial operations is not available or cannot be known sufficiently in advance to be taken into account in a methodical way. Success, therefore, depends in some degree upon risk or chance and, to a considerable extent, on the flexibility of management to meet new situations by a shrewd assessment of the appropriate course on the basis of very limited information. It depends upon the entrepreneur keeping open several alternative courses and being able to reverse mistaken decisions rapidly. It requires a broad and intimate knowledge of a wide variety of factors bearing upon an enterprise's success and the taking into account of their complex interrelationship. Business decisions, particularly for the small firm in a very unstable environment, are often necessarily "quick and dirty." Specialists, whether bankers, engineers, economists, or others who look at the enterprise from the outside and focus on the particular aspect of the enterprise with which they are familiar may be tempted to think that they could greatly improve the operation of the enterprise. It is easy to improve one particular aspect of an enterprise provided one can safely disregard the implications this may have for many other aspects of the enterprise. The successful entrepreneur, however, cannot be a perfectionist in any one particular aspect until he has fully taken into account the consequences on the rest of the enterprise.

For counseling to be useful to an enterprise, specialized knowledge must be available to the entrepreneur when he needs it. He must know what specialized knowledge is available and enough about it to evaluate its implications for his operations, and he must be motivated to apply such knowledge when it will help improve his operations. Some ways of achieving a framework which will assist and encourage entrepreneurs to do this are analyzed below. It may be well first to look at some of the experiences with counseling and direct supervision of development financing.

Experience Thus Far

Experiments with counseling service for industry have been going on in a number of countries, particularly since the end of World War II. A number of programs which blend industrial counseling with financing exist on paper, but very little practical application has yet been made of this approach.[3]

One of the oldest programs that has sought to blend counseling services with financial assistance is the loan fund of the Danish Ministry of Commerce and Industry, which has been in operation since 1928; its maximum size of loan is less than US$15,000 (100,000 kroner). It has about 1,500 loans outstanding and processes around 300 applications a year. In recent years, increasing funds have been appropriated for this program, with a little over US$2 million being budgeted for loans in 1965.

About one-third of its applications are referred to the Copenhagen Technological Institute for assistance in evaluating the application and in supervising the loan until it is paid. Applications referred to the CTI are usually for amounts over $3,000 going to enterprises employing from 10 to 50, and occasionally as many as 100 or 200, persons. Less than two man-weeks is normally required for evaluating applications, including one-day plant visits by an engineer to evaluate general operations and by a financial specialist to check over accounting procedures and financial matters. Supervision involves primarily an analysis of financial statements which borrowers are required to submit annually, although field visits are made to about one-fifth of the firms showing least success. Several CTI staff members are assigned primarily to assisting the loan program and other specialists are drawn on as required. The CTI is paid a fee by the Ministry of Commerce and Industry for the man-hours devoted to these services.

Loans are extended for relatively long periods (up to 15 years) and secured by a comparatively low ratio of collateral (buildings accepted up

---

[3] For more details on counseling services to small industries than can be provided here, see Joseph E. Stepanek, *Small Industry Advisory Services: An International Study*, the International Development Center of Stanford Research Institute, The Free Press of Glencoe, New York, 1960; Donald Liggett, *Small Industry Development Organization—A World Wide Directory*, the International Development Center of Stanford Research Institute, The Free Press of Glencoe, New York, 1959; International Labor Office, *Services for Small Scale Industry*, Studies and Reports, new series, no. 61, Geneva, 1961; and Eugene Staley and Richard Morse, *Modern Small Industry for Developing Countries*, McGraw-Hill Book Company, 1965.

to 80 percent of their value and equipment up to 50 percent). However, loans are only made to enterprises with at least three years experience and a satisfactory financial record. The loss ratio is estimated to be less than 1 percent.

In general, the program, though small and involving somewhat cumbersome and slow-moving procedures, has had a successful record and is expanding. The experience with loans made with CTI assistance has, on the whole, been more satisfactory than the generally smaller loans made under simpler procedures. Moreover, according to program officials, the provision of a degree of advisory assistance in combination with loans has resulted in marked improvements in the accounting and general productivity of the firms served.[4]

Another of the older programs which in some degree blends financing with consulting assistance is that of the Netherlands Middleclass Bank. This is a largely government-owned commercial-type bank with 178 branches and over $225 million credits outstanding in 1964. Besides its general banking business, it has a variety of special credit and term loans for smaller enterprises. Over $64 million of its credits in 1964 were extended under government guarantee. It is very roughly estimated that one-third of these are term loans to small manufacturers.

When the program was first started, the bank relied heavily on the Netherlands Technical Consulting Services (NTCS) to evaluate loan applications. It also drew upon the assistance of the Government Ministry of Economic Affairs in analyzing the financial aspects of a loan application. These services were provided without charge. As the principal activity of the NTCS was providing largely free advisory services to small firms on technical and managerial problems, and as the Ministry of Economic Affairs was regularly engaged in providing free assistance on accounting problems, contact with applicants at the screening stage often led to assistance being given. In some cases, use of such assistance was made a condition of financing.

The bank has made decreasing use of outside services in recent years. Less than 10 percent of guaranteed loans are estimated to have drawn on NTCS or Ministry assistance. The principal reason for this is that the Bank, as it acquired experience with this type of financing, found it possible to utilize more rapid procedures which are less dependent on a knowledge

---

[4] Based on discussions in 1965 with officials concerned with the loan program in the Danish Ministry of Commerce and Industry and the Copenhagen Technical Institute, and on information previously provided by a former member of the Copenhagen Technological Institute. A similar, but smaller, program is that of the United Kingdom Rural Industries Bureau and Fund. See P. C. Alexander, *Government Assistance to Small Industries in the United Kingdom,* Government of India, Ministry of Commerce and Industry, New Delhi, 1961; and W. M. Williams, *The Country Craftsman,* Routledge and Kegan Paul, London, 1958.

of industrial technology. Evaluations are based on an analysis of financial statements, previous experience with the client as depositor, the client's reputation for meeting his obligations, and the branch manager's ability to assess management capabilities by virtue not of a detailed knowledge of industrial operations but of local residence, close contacts with the business community, and the general impressions that he may obtain from a plant visit. The bank, through its deposit and other relationships with loan applicants can keep well informed on their operations.[5]

Sweden has an unusual program, in that loans and technical assistance are administered through 24 Trade Development Associations (TDAs). These are regional (county) associations of enterprises, but their operations are largely subsidized by the government and their banks include representatives of both the central and regional governments. Each TDA has a staff of from one to five technical officers who provide consulting services to enterprises on such matters as plant layout, accounting, and marketing. Since 1960 the TDAs have also administered loan funds provided mainly by the central government. These are intended to supplement bank credit and thus are often secured by second mortgages or other securities not acceptable to banks. The maximum loan is about US$15,000, with 95 percent of all loans going to firms, principally manufacturers, employing less than 25 workers.

Losses have been significant but tolerable (around 4 percent). The major drawback is that the program is relatively small (loans outstanding in 1961 were around US$10 million). Also TDAs are so thinly staffed that there is considerable delay and very limited advisory service in connection with loans.

Japan is another country which has very advanced financing programs and consulting services for small industry. For the most part, however, there is little integration of the two programs.[6]

In the United States, commercial banks are usually in a position to provide advice on such matters that are closely related to finance and to put a firm in touch with others who can be helpful. They are usually equipped from their knowledge of the balance sheets of other enterprises to provide general advice to a firm on the basis of analysis of balance sheets and project information which he may submit for a loan. They are, of course, also a source of information on credit practices. Many commercial banks maintain field services which keep in regular contact with

[5] Based on discussions in 1965 with officials of the Netherlands Middleclass Bank (Nederlandsche Middenstandsbank, N.V.) and the Netherlands Technical Consulting Service (Rijksnijverheidsdienst) and reports of these organizations. Also of great value were discussions with Dr. G. J. van der Heyden, Director of the Research Institute for Management Science. See his article, "Credit Financing Facilities for Small Industry," International Society for Small Scale Industries, *Bulletin* No. 8, 1965. For a fairly detailed description of the Netherlands' Technical Consulting Services, see also F. J. N. Stades, *Report on Small Industry in India,* Government of India, Ministry of Commerce and Industry, New Delhi, 1960.

[6] See Japan case study in Chap. 13.

their clients so that they are closely familiar with their problems. For the most part, however, they are not prepared to give detailed management advice.[7]

Some of the private finance companies discussed in Chapter 8, particularly some United States SBICs and the ICFC, provide supervision and some counseling, although primarily to medium-scale enterprises. Commercial finance companies in the United States also are reported to have associated management counsel with their financing as early as the 1930s in order to help small concerns with inadequate managerial staff and relatively weak financial standing. They charge fees for their service and maintain relatively high loan charges, which have been important in rendering these services possible.[8]

An interesting United States experiment with combining counseling with credit which has been little analyzed is that of the Smaller War Plants Corporation, which made

> liberal use of engineers and production men in appraising the abilities and improving the operation methods and controls of small manufacturers. The Corporation established a Technical Advisory Service to answer technological questions faced by small enterprises which could not afford to maintain engineering and research staffs of their own. In these activities, the Corporation was handicapped by lack of adequate trained personnel to service its widely scattered borrowers, but its stress upon the need of small businesses for technical advice and managerial assistance, rather than merely financial aid, undoubtedly contributed to a wider recognition by financing institutions of the importance of this aspect.[9]

Unfortunately the Corporation was short lived (1942–1946), and the critical question of the economics of the arrangement seems to have received little attention.

In its successor organizations, first the Reconstruction Finance Corporation and then the Small Business Administration, counseling other than of a very general nature has not been important. In 1964, however, the SBA

[7] Individual banks sometimes go much further in advising individual clients, particularly small ones. Among the rules suggested by a practicing banker for handling the relatively small (average $3,000) business loans to war veterans after some early poor loan experience was one stating: "Be certain that the veteran does not exaggerate the true profit potentialities of his business and study the business periodically to provide him with management counsel." (Earl Parsons, "We're Learning a Lot About G.I. Loans," *Banking*, July, 1946, cited by R. J. Saulnier et al., *Federal Lending and Loan Insurance*, Princeton University Press, Princeton, N.J., 1958, p. 532.) See also E. I. H. Bennett, "Using Your Banker's Advisory Services," *Management Aids for Small Manufacturers* No. 4, Small Business Administration, 1958.

[8] See Neil Jacoby and R. J. Saulnier, *Business Finance and Banking*, National Bureau of Economic Research, 1947, p. 215.

[9] Fuller, *op. cit.*, pp. 154, 155.

launched a new effort to make counseling available to loan recipients in difficulties. It is attempting to mobilize retired executives to staff the counseling service on a voluntary, unpaid basis.[10] Although it received a large response to its initial request for volunteer consultants, it seems doubtful that a counseling service of satisfactory quality and of significant size can be sustained on this basis for long, despite the SBA's hope of doing so.

Among the newly developing countries, both official and private development banks have often been given responsibility for extending counseling services, or separate agencies have been assigned these functions. Such counseling services have differed widely from case to case in staffing, administration, intended services, and results. The Industrial Development Bank of Turkey has in many ways pioneered the combination of technical assistance with financing. Its most notable assistance has been in introducing accounting practices and in assisting in the preparation of projects. It has also carried out some industry and marketing surveys. Much field advisory assistance is precluded by its limited staff, although an annual supervisory visit is made to all but the smallest loan recipients. A 1962 evaluation found the technical assistance aspects of its operation still highly deficient, although improving:

> In the field of technical assistance, the IDB confined its activities to serving its customers filing applications for financing. It preferred to discharge this function with the means at its disposal and without charge. For this reason, the IDB's technical services were confined to a narrow field, caused delays, and cost a great deal of money. Since half of these services were devoted to the rejected projects, the results were hardly satisfactory.
>
> As the technical departments were understaffed, due to the lack of employable skills, and were bogged down in work, the IDB was for a long time unable to determine the productive fields of investment and prepare productive projects. For the past two years, however, it has been possible to conduct such studies and prepare projects. Such projects cannot fail to be of advantage in terms of inducing a number of enterprises to invest their capital in these projects.[11]

The IDB has certainly helped enlarge the knowledge as well as the finances of borrowers by the interchange of ideas which takes place between industrialists and its staff of well-trained and broadly experienced professionals when loan applications are being evaluated or when loan recipients encounter serious problems. Staff limitations and the pressure of a rising volume of applications has kept informational services at a bare minimum. Aftercare services appear occasionally to have fallen below minimum re-

[10] See *Business Week*, Aug. 15, 1964, pp. 94–97.

[11] Columbia University School of Law, Report No. 3, *Public International Development Financing in Turkey*, November, 1962, p. 99. See also *Industrial Development Bank of Turkey 1950–1959*, IDB, Istanbul, 1960.

quirements to assure a satisfactory loan recovery record, although changes in procedures were being adopted in 1965 to assure that this aspect of services would not be neglected. Aside from staff problems, which are unlikely to be overcome without the establishment of an organized training program needed to facilitate major staff additions, the IDB is narrowly restricted by its position as a lender in the kind and extent of advisory services it may directly provide, and there are at present few other organizations which might be drawn upon.[12]

In Israel, the Industrial Development Bank has made a start on aftercare services:

> After the loan is granted there are good follow-up procedures to ensure proper disbursement of funds, by both accounting checks and inspections by the engineering staff as installation progresses. An IDBI engineer tries to visit the project while construction is going on, and occasionally consulting engineers are hired to provide expert opinions. If the borrower cannot produce documentary proof that money has been properly spent, an attempt is made to evaluate the cost of work in progress. Follow-up visits are made to the extent feasible; however, the small engineering staff has only been able to visit about 100 of IDBI's 400-odd borrowers. If difficult technical problems arise, the borrower is referred to an appropriate technical institute or private consultant.[13]

But a page later the source notes:

> Finally, there are practically no facilities to provide advice and technical assistance to borrowers *after* their factories *go into operation,* and while there is some doubt as to whether the enterprise will succeed. The IDBI has personnel that are able to provide such advice, but they are fully occupied with other duties.[14]

The IDBI case is not exceptional. Supervision is often devoted excessively, and sometimes exclusively, to the period during which the loan is spent, neglecting the other stages, but this is not sound practice.

Of Israel's Artisans' Bank, Tenenbaum reports: "If technical advice is considered necessary, it is obtained from the Ministry of Industry. Although the Bank would like to have its own engineer, it does not have a sufficiently large budget to pay for one."[15] Later he adds:

---

[12] Based on the author's brief review of the bank, including discussions with numerous members of its staff in 1965. A joint effort of business groups with Ford Foundation and other international support was being made in 1965 to create an organization which would provide some of the additional informational services needed to accelerate industrial growth.

[13] Edward Tenenbaum, *Israel's Industrial Finances—A Second Look,* Continental-Allied Company, Washington D.C., 1960, p. 159.

[14] *Ibid.,* p. 158 (italics added).

[15] *Ibid.,* p. 176.

Technical assistance for artisans is sadly lacking. Officials of the Ministry of Commerce and Industry do what they can, and recently one engineer has been assigned full-time to this work (for 30,000 artisans!). However, much more needs to be done, both in providing information on manufacturing methods and in developing basic management skills (e.g., rudimentary principles of cost accounting). Israel now has excellent programs for larger enterprises, such as the courses conducted through the Israel Management Association, but these are not accessible to artisans.[16]

The counseling services of the Industrial Development Corporation of the Union of South Africa have been highly praised:

> Once again, the experience of South Africa's IDC may be cited as an example of the range of help that a development bank with adequate resources may provide. A borrower from IDC may without charge make use of IDC's production or marketing specialists and technical experts in various fields. As a part of its normal procedure prior to backing an entrepreneur, IDC performs extensive services in the form of laboratory and market tests as well as cost and capital requirement estimates. Independent investigations, research and experimental work builds up a backlog of information about the economy from which the new investor may draw. In short, a full range of facilities is offered.[17]

Another report describes the IDC program further:

> Its "aftercare program" is closely linked to the initial project investigation. IDC has three investigation sections: production; financial; and commercial and economic. A group comprised of one staff member from each section is responsible for evaluating the proposal and recommending IDC action. . . . The same group is automatically responsible for subsequent supervision. . . . The group tries to visit each enterprise as a rule once a year, more often if difficulties arise, less frequently if the enterprise is successful.[18]

Later the same report notes: "The Industrial Development Corporation of South Africa provides technical assistance, apart from that incident to loan supervision, only to the smaller of its clients; it encourages the larger enterprises, which can afford it, to purchase such services elsewhere."[19]

The features of the IDC services described above are good, but there are limitations which should not be overlooked. An important element in the

---

[16] *Ibid.*, p. 177.

[17] J. D. Nyhart, "Factors Affecting the Operation of Development Banks in Very Underdeveloped Countries of Africa," unpublished paper, Harvard Law School, 1958, p. 27.

[18] Shirley Boskey, *Problems and Practices of Development Banks,* International Bank for Reconstruction and Development, Washington, 1959, pp. 98, 99.

[19] *Ibid.*, p. 100.

success of the IDC in extending such assistance to its small-industry borrowers is its ability to support its operations from its larger loans. Over 90 percent of its financing has gone to enterprises requiring several hundred thousand dollars or more, even though these make up less than a fourth of its clients. Smaller borrowers in terms of numbers are relatively few; only 10 to 20 small enterprises are financed per year.[20] Despite the undoubled merits of the program, it has not progressed to the stage where it is able to serve large numbers of enterprises on an economical basis.

The program in Puerto Rico of the Industrial Development Company (PRIDCO) for providing financial and technical assistance to local enterprises, although small, is gradually being enlarged and improved.[21] In Nicaragua, the development bank has on its staff a few persons who directly advise clients both on management and technical matters. Although assistance is fairly limited, it appears to have been very helpful.[22] A few other development banks in Latin America can claim a similar degree of aftercare for loan recipients. The lending procedures of many Latin American development banks, however, tend to be like that of the Industrial Bank of Argentina prior to its recent reorganization. Elaborate screening procedures were followed by rather legalistic post-allocation checking on the client's adherence to the loan contract. These appear to have added greatly to red tape without contributing much to the assurance that funds are used in a productive way. The Bank of Northeast Brazil similarly invested a great deal of time and a highly trained staff in screening but gave little attention to aftercare except of a perfunctory sort. A rather elaborate "Supervised Industrial Credit Program" was announced in Bolivia in 1958 but, despite some foreign advisory assistance and several reformulations, did not achieve a satisfactory operational basis and was replaced in 1963 by a private development finance corporation.[23]

In India, as in Japan, despite the variety of institutions and services, an effectively coordinated relationship between financing and counseling is for the most part lacking. The Small Industries Service Institutes do carry out surveys intended to be of assistance to lending institutions and on occasions have evaluated the technical competence of applicants for bank loans. In Pakistan, which has similar types of programs, recent efforts to link technical and financial assistance have been absorbed by staff

[20] Industrial Development Corporation of South Africa, Ltd., *Annual Reports and Accounts.*

[21] See case study of Puerto Rico, Chap. 3.

[22] Based on experience of the author in working with INFONAC in 1960 and subsequent brief studies of the organization in 1961 and 1964.

[23] For a description of the supervised credit effort up to 1961, see USOM, *Supervised Industrial Credit,* 1960, La Paz, and Murray Bryce and John P. Powelson, *Report on Supervised Industrial Credit Program in Bolivia,* USOM, La Paz, 1961.

and administrative inadequacies.[24] Progress along these lines is reported in Ceylon.[25]

The Medium Industry Bank of Korea has begun industry and sample plant surveys and the dissemination of general information through literature, courses, and demonstrations. In 1962 it opened a Small Industry Consultation Office in each of 37 branches to provide specific and specialized advisory services free of charge. So far, however, these seem to have largely served to advise and assist on loan arrangements.[26]

The need for counseling in the newly emerging African countries has long been stressed by program advisers. Ghana, known prior to independence as the Gold Coast, was one of the earliest to receive such advice, as previously indicated. Professor Lewis's advice in 1953 on coupling supervision and counseling with finance was gradually implemented; by 1961 the Industrial Development Corporation had a staff of over 100, including 19 in its small loan department.[27] The IDC reported during the mid-1950s that this approach was helping to reduce delinquencies and other problems.[28] Yet by 1961, the IDC was in serious difficulties. Although its small-industry loan program involved less than one-fifth of its staff and even a smaller portion of its funds, its problems contributed at least proportionally to the IDC's total difficulties.

Although a complete account of the small loan program's difficulties is not available, they were obviously serious. The IDC has indicated that delinquencies continued to be a problem and that staff shortages and other problems resulted in a slow processing of applications. The seriousness of the problems is suggested by the drastic changes in the program the IDC itself suggested.[29]

One source of the IDC's small-industry program's difficulties was that the minimum staffing requirements to undertake this activity were much

[24] Harwood, Duncan, and others, *Encouraging the Growth of Small Industry in Pakistan,* Stanford Research Institute, 1963.

[25] See Francis Godwin, "The Research Institute as a Key Industrial Development Instrument," *U.S. Papers Prepared for the U.N. Conference on the Application of Science and Technology,* vol. IV, pp. 96–102, and Frank Mayer Engineering Company, *Final Progress Report to Agency for International Development to Ceylon Institute of Scientific and Industrial Research,* Los Angeles, 1962.

[26] See The Medium Industry Bank publications: *The Profile of The Medium Industry Bank,* 1962; *The Small Enterprise in Korea,* 1963; *Annual Report,* 1962; *Quarterly Statistical Review,* January and May, 1963.

[27] Porter International Company, *The National Investment Bank of Ghana,* 1962, p. 19.

[28] IDC, *Reports and Accounts,* 1956–1957.

[29] IDC, "Small Industry Development in Ghana," 1960. (Mimeographed.) Different but equally drastic changes were suggested by the Porter International Company which, without being specific, emphasized the need to guard against a repetition of its small business loan experience (*The National Investment Bank of Ghana,* Porter International Company, Washington, 1962, p. 20).

larger than the IDC could afford on the basis of its volume of financing and its requirement to operate on a self-supporting basis while keeping lending rates low. The limited management capabilities of loan recipients and average loan size of about $3,600 made the task more difficult. It was further complicated by the fact that projects were widely and thinly scattered over all parts of the country. The IDC could not afford sufficient staff to provide a resident adviser in all the areas where loan recipients operated, but it found that resident advisers who could be in regular and intimate contact with borrowers were needed to provide the quality of counseling and supervision required. Its staff was also too limited to provide specific and practical advice to such a diversity of lines of enterprise in which its borrowers operated.[30]

Finally, the absence of reliable accounting in the enterprises financed—a situation which the program was not equipped to remedy—greatly enlarged the supervising and counseling problem.

In Nigeria, a World Bank Mission in 1955 noted:

> Use of the loan proceeds is often unsupervised; sometimes the proceeds are used for purposes entirely unrelated to the project for which the loan was granted. The Mission was informed that the Western Board has begun to supervise loan funds and pays over loan proceeds only upon proof of payment for the goods financed by the loan. This kind of supervision is essential, but it is not enough. Even after completion of the project, the boards should keep themselves informed of the manner in which the borrower conducts his business and should advise him where necessary.[31]

Despite these recommendations, however, the situation does not seem to have improved much since.[32]

In Kenya, employees of the Department of Trade and Supply frequently travel through provinces and advise individual businessmen as well as local loan boards seeking to bring the promising small traders and industrialists together with the sources of finance and advising individuals how to get started in business or how to improve operations.[33] Although the Kenya

[30] In 1960, besides a loan officer and his assistants, the small loan program had seven very low-salaried debt collectors, a bookkeeper, and five clerical workers. As this is four fewer than reported in 1961, the account may not be complete. Also, the small loan program appears to have utilized in addition staff from other departments to a limited degree (IDC, "Small Industry Development in Ghana," 1960 [mimeographed]).

[31] IBRD, *The Economic Development of Nigeria*, The Johns Hopkins Press, Baltimore, 1955, p. 93.

[32] A recent paper notes that less than half of the borrowers of the Federal Loans Board may be considered successful, despite general good loan administration and substantial advisory assistance, and concludes that the problem is a shortage of viable enterprises. (Sayre P. Schatz, "Government Lending to Nigerian Private Enterprise; The Federal Loans Board," unpublished paper, 1963.)

[33] See Martin S. Klein, *African Trade in Kenya*, United Research, Inc., Cambridge, Mass., 1961.

financing and advisory services appear to be of value, they suffer from the same problems noted about a similar program in Uganda:

> The experience of all these funds in helping small business has been similar and rather disappointing . . . . The time and trouble spent in administering the funds is out of all proportion to the loans made. The assessment of applications, seeking out of possible enterprises of merit, guidance of the principals, and supervision of commitments have demanded more experienced staff than have been available.[34]

The study recommended rationalizing the various efforts within a unified program. In brief, the services, though useful, need to be improved in quality and put on a more economic basis. One way of achieving this, according to Klein, would be to set a loan minimum of £100. This would reduce the number of loan applications to manageable proportions permitting an adequate job of screening and supervision to be done with the limited staff available for at least the more important loans.[35] As with the effort to blend counseling with financing in Ghana and a great many other countries, a good part of the reason for difficulties appears to be underestimating the minimum requirements for doing this successfully.[36]

The Relevance of Supervised Agricultural Credit Experience to Small-factory Financing

Experiments with combining counseling with financial assistance have been carried on in agriculture longer than in industry. There are, moreover, some similarities between the problems in extending development financing to small industrialists and small farmers. In both cases, there is the economic problem of serving small units. The units served in both cases typically employ a relatively inefficient technology, in part because of their size, but also because of the limited knowledge and resources of the owners. This in turn, in combination with other factors, results in the units having a relatively low or unstable income, which diminishes the possibilities of internal financing and increases the risks of external financing. Finance remains, nevertheless, one of the essentials for improving the productivity of these units.

These similarities in problems, together with the more advanced experience in supervised agricultural credit, have suggested to some observers the possibility of drawing on agricultural credit experience in designing programs for extending development financing to small industry. Tenenbaum, impressed by the supervised agricultural credit program in Taiwan, was stimulated to suggest:

[34] IBRD, *Economic Development of Uganda,* pp. 286, 287.
[35] Klein, *op. cit.,* p. 6.
[36] For these see Chap. 5.

By far the most important contribution industrial credit might obtain from the agricultural credit program is the possibility of learning something from the techniques of "supervised agricultural credit." It is not necessary for Taiwan's industrial credit experts to travel abroad to learn how to look for neglected smaller customers, how to develop sound production plans, how to make follow-up visits, how to lend on economic feasibility rather than on collateral security. They can learn all this by studying—and adapting—the methods of JCRR's "supervised agricultural credit program" (perhaps together with the "extension agents" available from the China Productivity and Trade Center).[37]

The possibilities are there, but the analogy must not be pushed too far. In particular, it should not be assumed that *supervised* agricultural *credit* has had the long experience and the same success in developing practical operating techniques as agricultural *extension programs*. While the experience of the latter has been of considerable value to industrial extension programs, the experience of agricultural credit programs has so far been not only more limited, but also less applicable to industry than has agricultural extension experience.

There are a number of fairly obvious differences between supervised agricultural credit and small-industry development financing which make necessary different techniques. The geographical scatter of units is very different, a significant factor since location greatly influences the cost of direct contact with units. The types of information required by small units tend to be more standardized, more readily available, and more easily disseminated in agriculture than in industry. On the other hand, it may be as difficult to get farmers to apply counseling as small industrialists, or even more so. The average amount of financing required by small factories is much larger than that usually required by farmers, which greatly influences the economics of financing services. The forms and types of financing required and the risks involved are largely different.

There is also a fundamental difference between the needs which supervised agricultural credit is intended to meet and those which small-industry development financing must usually serve, a difference which has an important bearing on lending policies and procedures. Supervised agricultural credit is concerned with farm productivity because of its direct effect on farm incomes and the standard of living of farm families. Small-industry development financing is ordinarily concerned only with the small unit as a producer—with the contribution which improving its productivity will make to the economy as a whole. Increasing the income of small units

[37] Tenenbaum, *Taiwan's Turning Point,* Continental-Allied Company, Washington, n.d., 1961?, p. 55. In Bolivia, also, the possibility of learning from agricultural experience led to the establishment of a "supervised industrial credit program" initially in an agricultural bank with the assistance of a consultant from the International Development Services, a consulting group experienced in agricultural credit programs.

in this case is not a basic goal of the program—as it is in supervised agricultural credit—but only a means to the goal of enlarging productivity and productive capacity. Social objectives must usually be a basic part of supervised agricultural credit, whereas in small-industry development financing, concentrating on economic objectives is what is most important and all that is really necessary. Since in mixing objectives one or the other is apt to be neglected, an exclusively economic focus is often absolutely essential to effective small-industry development financing programs.

The difference being stressed is a matter of goals. The latter are, of course, a matter of choice. The logic of the two situations, however, usually dictates different choices. If we were discussing the nonfactory type of small-industry unit, such as cottage enterprises, individual craftsmen, and small workshops, the differences from agriculture would be fewer. However, the small industrialists to which we refer are not usually a major segment of society, as small farmers often are, nor are they at the bottom of the scale in terms of income or of knowledge of business and technology. They may lack funds for operating their enterprises in the most efficient way, but their incomes are close to or above the national average. To the extent that small industrialists have a personal income problem, the assistance they require need not be separated from social programs for other urban residents. Their income problem does not require distinctive treatment to the extent that it may in the case of small farmers with their distinctive way of life.

The small industrialists may lack formal education, special skills important to their enterprises, and complete up-to-date information on matters relevant to their operations, but they tend, nevertheless, to be intellectually more advanced and more economically motivated than the average of the society. The small industrialist, unlike the small farmer, is not personally deprived. His plight is less one of income or personal needs than of having a productive potentiality that is not being as fully utilized as it might be. He need not be served by a paternalistic program and is unlikely to be receptive to one.

The difference in objectives between small-industry and agricultural financing has one further very important operational aspect. Small-industry development financing, being concerned with maximizing production results, must be extended on a highly selective basis, aiming at the exceptional enterprise rather than being equally available to most small units. This will provide the greatest increase in output, since there tend to be major differences in the potentiality of individual enterprises for expanding productivity with given amounts of the types of assistance that can be extended. Whether or not this may increase the inequalities of income among small-industry units is of no economic and little social importance. Supervised agricultural credit, on the other hand, if it is to justify its cost, must in the long run influence the activities of the mass of small units and in one way or another raise the productivity and income of the mass of present small farmers.[38]

Because of the basic differences between supervised agricultural credit and small-industry development financing programs and because supervised agricultural credit is popularly conceived of as a paternalistic, socially oriented government program, psychologically it is probably not a good tactic to use the term "supervised credit" in relation to programs for small factories.[39] This, however, is not to deny that there are some parallels. Some degree of direct supervision and counseling must be combined with financing in both cases to give a satisfactory level of results, and in both cases techniques must be found for doing this effectively and at a cost compatible with the achievements attainable. The specific techniques suitable to each, on the other hand, may not have much in common.

Fostering Implementation with a Minimum of Aftercare

Some aftercare measures such as direct supervision and counseling tend to be expensive or, for other reasons, difficult for lenders to provide. Lenders, therefore, must usually keep these activities to a minimum compatible with the results they are seeking. There are several ways by which they can be achieved.

The problems of aftercare may be reduced by taking them into account in the process of screening. Although screening cannot always correctly identify the future course of events, it may identify types of applicants who are unlikely to encounter problems with which they are not equipped to deal or who have the resourcefulness and drive to overcome unexpected adversity, who will be frank in discussing adverse developments with the lender and cooperative in joint efforts to overcome them, and who will be motivated to assume the primary burden of such adversity.

The establishment of collateral requirements is, as we have previously indicated, a means of reducing the need for supervision and assistance to borrowers. It does not assure that they will use funds productively or profitably, but it tends to increase motivation to repay finance and to co-

---

[38] Supervised agricultural credit may, of course, also follow the technique of serving first the units with the greatest potential in the expectation that the results will either radiate out to other farmers or, by increasing competition, cause other farmers to change their occupation to a more remunerative one.

[39] The popular image of supervised agricultural credit is not necessarily a correct one. Some authorities on agricultural supervised credit stress that financing in the case of agriculture also should be selectively extended; should not be made generally available; should be extended as credits, not grants; and should not have a generally paternalistic approach. In any case, however, all seem to agree that supervised agricultural credit must be concerned with improving family living as well as production (see, for example, Horace Belshaw, *Agricultural Credit in Economically Underdeveloped Countries,* Food and Agricultural Organization of the United Nations, Rome, 1959).

operate with the lender in working out repayment difficulties, should these occur. Collateral also provides an alternative source from which at least part of funds lent can be recovered. A similar provision is the requirement that a certain share of the capital be provided by equity. This is intended to assure that owner-managers will continue to be motivated to overcome temporary operating problems even after a period of losses. Where their equity is large, they may absorb substantial losses and still have a sufficient stake in the enterprise to strive to save it from bankruptcy.

Usually, the shorter the loan period, the less the need for aftercare. Even though further loans may be made to most clients when loans are made for a short period, this arrangement has the advantage from the lender's point of view of making necessary a frequent review of financing allocations and makes it relatively simple to cease financing where experience or trends are adverse. The reluctance of many commercial bankers to enter into term financing reflects in part an appreciation of this fact. The need for aftercare not only increases with a shifting from periods of a few months to those over a year, but also rises rapidly as loans are lengthened from one, two, or three years to five, ten, or more. More thorough screening often facilitates the transition from commercial financing to medium-term financing; screening is much less valuable for reducing the risks as loan periods approach five or more years, particularly in less developed countries.[40]

Providing for loan repayment at frequent and regular intervals is another valuable means of minimizing supervision requirements. This helps keep the lender roughly informed of the financial condition of the borrower. Even more importantly, it compels the borrower to reexamine his financial position at regular close intervals and to set aside a small amount for loan repayment. Lack of planning, rather than any real shortage of funds, is often the cause for delinquencies when payments are relatively large and fall due only once or twice a year. In the opinion of some of the staff of the Industrial Development Bank of Turkey this has been a major cause of delinquencies. Similar problems have been observed in Latin American countries. Quarterly or monthly repayments are commonly required by the more successful lending institutions serving small manufacturers in the industrially advanced countries. This practice needs to be more widely adopted in less developed countries, despite the additional administrative work involved.

[40] Beckhart stresses the need for increased protection for financing of longer periods in the United States: "Bankers will probably learn by hard experience that greater margins of safety are a credit necessity in term lending. At best, it is difficult to estimate economic conditions even twelve months ahead, much less then ten years! . . . And so, depending upon the amounts and time involved, the lender must allow for geometrically increasing margins of safety in term lending, increasing with the length of the payment period." (*Business Loans of American Commercial Banks,* The Ronald Press Company, New York, 1959, p. 224.)

Specific requirements and prohibitions incorporated in loan agreements are a further means of reducing the extent of aftercare needed by recipients of finance. The agreement may contain provisions limiting the payment of dividends or salaries to management, the extension of loans or advances by the creditors to others or further borrowing by the creditor, the making of capital expenditures and other major commitments without prior consultation with the lender. In order to assure that adequate working capital is maintained, a minimum ratio of current assets to current liabilities may be established, as well as an overall debt limit and provisions against pledging assets to others.

Agreements usually provide penalties for any breach of contract, such as an immediate termination of the loan. These give the bank effective authority in case a borrower is unable or unwilling to maintain the agreement to bring about changes in the enterprise when violations are uncovered.[41]

The terms of loan agreements—and particularly repayment schedules—cannot, however, be regarded as a fixed pattern from which no deviation can be permitted. It is never possible, particularly in a less developed country, to forecast capacity to repay accurately. Flexibility is essential but must not deteriorate into slack loan recovery policies. It is important for loan officers to be well informed on borrowers' financial conditions and to be firm in enforcing their judgment concerning the extent to which the original terms may be modified. Decisions of this nature should also be closely and intelligently reviewed by a higher authority. Institutions in less developed countries do have difficulty in obtaining the information and staff competence required for good loan supervision. Essentially, however, the same policies need to be pursued as are customary in industrially advanced countries:

> The lender must have procedures established to follow compliance with the terms of the loan agreement. More importantly, he must have a program and procedures established to follow the extent to which actual operations vary from the estimates on which the loan was based, or by which construction costs exceed or fall short of budget estimated. The borrower may need help in many ways. The term lender must live with the term borrower for the entire life of the loan if a successful and mutually agreeable result is to be expected from the lender-borrower relationship. There are few term loans which do not need readjustment during their life. If close contact is main-

[41] For a description of some of the typical contractual terms used for medium-term loans in the United States, see William G. F. Price, "Medium-Term Credits in the United States of America," in Nederlandse Bankiersvereniging, *Trends in Bank Credit and Finance*, Martinus Nijhoff, The Hague, 1961, pp. 111ff.; Jacoby and Saulnier, *op. cit.*, p. 141; *Robert Morris Associates Bulletin*, September, 1954, pp. 16, 17; and the suggested contract provisions for term lending in Ghana, *The National Investment Bank of Ghana*, pp. 68ff., and appendix.

tained, the readjustments are readily and understandably made, and problems are often met in time for their solution.[42]

The need for close and direct contact with the borrower is particularly great in less developed countries. Communications are slow. Accounts are often nonexistent or of uncertain meaning or reliability. The possibility of problems which the borrower is unable to solve is far greater. Without visits to the borrower's operations, there are few dependable means of knowing how he is progressing. To be informative, visits must be made by persons who have knowledge of the fundamentals of the operations in question and some comparative knowledge of similar types of enterprises. If problems are to be detected in their early stages when they are easiest to remedy, visits must be reasonably frequent. If supervision is carried to this point, the step to some types of counseling is a short one. What types is a critical question discussed below.

Practical Approaches to Direct Supervision and Counseling

The results thus far of programs which have attempted to combine direct supervision and counseling with financing for small industry have tended to suffer from one or both of two defects: (1) programs have not been able to extend a very significant volume of financing; or (2) they have not achieved the quality of counseling and supervision required. In some cases, these deficiencies have been simply a matter of inadequate staffing either in number or, more seriously, in the high skill requirements of the counseling and supervision function. Sometimes this difficulty has been enlarged by an attempt to provide unnecessarily elaborate and diverse services, with the results that costs have been higher and individual functions more thinly staffed than they would have been if efforts had been concentrated on the bare essentials. High costs and low effectiveness are also in part the result of the smallness of programs, which has often not permitted sufficient specialization of staff. The general solutions to these deficiencies, though fairly obvious, are not easily achievable because of the absolute shortage of the quality of skills required. Some of the more specific steps important to establishing adequate programs for combining direct supervision and counseling with financing are considered below.

Supervision or counseling must rest on a thorough knowledge of the economics of the enterprise, its major strengths and deficiencies, and the kinds of problems it is likely to encounter. For most small enterprises, a fairly brief informal analysis by several industrial specialists in production equipment, plant organization, business management, markets, competition, and other internal and external aspects of operations is usually sufficient. Indeed, one really well-rounded and experienced industrial consultant may be more useful, as well as more economical, than several more narrowly

[42] Beckhart, op. cit., p. 226.

specialized analysts, but skill of the former type is often not available in less developed countries.[43] The analysis of the firm required for supervision is needed in any case for sound loan decisions, so this requirement presents no additional problem. A problem may arise, however, if screening and supervision are conducted by separate staff, unless the staffs are closely linked. Many of the basic insights into the enterprise provided by brief analyses of this type are unlikely to be fully and explicitly recorded.

This rounded view of the enterprise must be kept up to date and, in some cases, refined. Where an adequate accounting system does not exist to provide a good measure of the enterprise's present condition and progress, this must usually be instituted both to minimize supervision and counseling costs and to increase the effectiveness of such efforts. If regular plant visits are not required for this purpose, they will in any case be required to supplement the rather limited supervision which can be exercised through a review of such accounting reports and other information which small industrialists can be expected to submit.

Plant visits for supervisory purposes must be of a type which will inspire the full cooperation of the client and which will update the initial board analysis. In general, this requires that it be conducted by a staff member with a practical knowledge of the fundamentals of industrial management, an understanding of the entrepreneur's point of view, an ability to discuss industrial operations in colloquial business terminology, and a personal acquaintance with a good part of the local business community. Although there is no general rule concerning how frequently visits should be made, annual visits would be an improvement over present practices in some cases, and quarterly or at least semiannual visits seem nearer to what the minimum limit should be for small enterprises in most developing countries. How frequent and how lengthy visits need to be depends a good deal on the extent to which entrepreneurs know their problems or are willing to discuss them, as well as on how frequent and serious their problems are likely to be.

Supervisory visits are more likely to be successful in obtaining information as well as in serving the broad purposes of financing if they bring some services to the entrepreneur which he values. Counseling services of a liaison type often will serve this purpose without significant additions to supervisory

[43] In Japan, the diagnosis of enterprises to suggest improvements in productivity usually involves three specialists for a given period of from a few days up to one week. In Denmark, loan evaluations of small manufacturers normally require plant visits of one day each by a financial and an engineering specialist, plus several man-days of office analysis and other investigation. The practice in the Netherlands is similar. A proposed program of the Bank of Northeast Brazil, which was to follow the Netherlands experience adapted to local conditions, suggested the analysis might require two men for 10 days (BNB, Departamento Industrial e de Investimentos, "Diretrizes para o Financiamento a Pequena Industria," unpublished memorandum, 1961).

costs. More elaborate counseling, moreover, may be difficult because the field officer cannot by himself have specialized knowledge in all lines and aspects of industrial operations with which he must usually deal.

Supervisory visits also are more likely to be successful where an officer resides in the general community of the clients he serves. Such residence contributes to the building up of local knowledge and relationships important to acquiring the confidence of local industrialists and obtaining a complete insight into the nature of the problems and operations.[44] Small programs, however, may have to substitute frequent and extended field visits for local residence or reduce the geographical limits of the service.

For some types of enterprises, more detailed advisory services than the minimum suggested above are likely to be required. In countries where industrial experience is very limited, small-industry financing, if at all possible, seems likely to require more detailed counseling. Even India with its substantial industrial experience may have a large group of small enterprises which cannot be usefully financed unless they are also extended advisory assistance capable of improving their marketing arrangements. A good many units, as one writer notes, tend to be at the mercy of one or two buyers. "The close relationship between finance and marketing makes it impossible for policies of financial assistance or of marketing assistance to small-scale industries to have an appreciable effect unless they are conceived as parts of an integrated program."[45]

Where substantial advisory assistance must be extended, it is usually no longer possible to incorporate this as a part of the lending institution's direct responsibilities, and yet close coordination is essential. (See Chapter 5.) At this point, well-designed arrangements become particularly important to assure economy and effectiveness. Lending institutions should not, in any case, overlook the possibility of enlarging the counseling services to clients and potential clients by stimulating and assisting other organizations which are in a position to provide much greater informational services than they are presently extending. Such organizations include (1) those having interbusiness relationships with the financed firm; (2) service organizations such as consultants, accounting firms, research institutes, and testing laboratories; (3) industrial and trade associations; and (4) local and regional organizations.

There is a danger of too much counseling as well as of too little, or at least a danger of counselors seeking to direct rather than advise. Coun-

---

[44] This is emphasized in the approach of the Netherlands Technical Service to counseling. Considerable effort is devoted to building close relationships with the enterprises to be advised, and great care is taken to avoid anything that might diminish business confidence in the Service (see Stades, *op. cit.,* pp. 35–37, 45).

[45] K. S. Krishnaswamy, "Some Aspects of Finance for Small Industry," *Productivity Journal of NPC,* August, 1962, p. 908. Japan has been, and to some extent still is, confronted with a similar problem, particularly for very small enterprises. See **Chap. 13.**

selors, however competent or however frequent their visits, remain outsiders to the enterprise, both in motivation and in familiarity with details. Over-intervention may diminish the initiative of the entrepreneur or his general receptivity to counseling. It tends to split the management function so that no one assumes the full initiative and integrating responsibility. What has been said of research-based enterprises of medium size in New England is true in large degree for owner-operated enterprises everywhere: "With this high degree of involvement and the high stakes in the success and reputation of his venture, the technical-entrepreneur is difficult to advise and usually impossible to direct."[46] Moreover, in many countries entrepreneurs exhibit a great desire to keep their business affairs secret and a general mistrust of the motivations of others. In brief, counseling involves a delicate relationship which may be easily destroyed by overzealous efforts.

The Uganda Development Corporation Limited in its contrasting situation of financing small enterprise under African conditions, reports the same problems:

> The stipulation that an essential feature for any investment must be the need for technical knowledge and guidance is, in practice, extremely difficult to maintain. Although it can hardly be said that most of the applicants are experienced men in their field, they nevertheless appear primarily for a loan and often accept only the broadest advice as to the best use of the money. Indeed, to control the spending of the money really effectively would be a major administrative effort requiring a quite disproportionate number of UDC staff, in effect, doing the job for them.[47]

The report goes on to acknowledge that some advice could be given but notes that "success almost inevitably rests with the enthusiasm, intelligence and integrity of the borrower."[48]

One of the attractions of combining counseling with financing is the inducement as well as the means which financing provides for implementing counseling. This leverage, however, is best applied in a circumspect manner. How extensively and forcefully it may be possible to extend advice to recipients of financing depends a great deal on the quality of the counseling system and of its staff and on the general receptivity of entrepreneurs to advisory assistance.[49] In general, the limits to counseling need to be approached

---

[46] Albert Rubenstein, *Problems of Financing and Managing New Research-based Enterprises in New England,* Federal Reserve Bank of Boston, 1958, p. 51.

[47] *Development of Small Industries,* Uganda Development Corporation, Ltd., Kampala, 1959, p. 3. (Mimeographed.)

[48] *Ibid.*

[49] Development banks in many countries are frequently criticized for overintervening in the affairs of financed companies, discouraging desirable types of applicants, and sometimes reducing the efficiency of the enterprise. Such criticism is generally directed against excessive supervision by organizations lacking real counseling capabilities (e.g., the Orissa State Financial Corporation in 1959) but not always. See,

with caution through experimentation with assistance to those more easily assisted. An overestimation of the counseling possibilities is not only expensive in a variety of ways, but also may create a general climate of opinion about counseling damaging to reasonable programs.

Long before the kinds of limits on counseling we have so far been discussing have been reached, a restriction on the extent of counseling arises in many countries by a simple inadequacy of staff or the cost of the service. In such cases, selectivity concerning what enterprises are to be extended counseling, in what degree, and of what type becomes particularly important. It is especially important to select for financing only entrepreneurs with a strong interest in and aptitude for improving their management capabilities. Selectivity may also be applied in other ways to obtain better results from limited aftercare abilities. Only the minimum of attention need be given to some enterprises because of the character and ability of management and other assurance of productive use and repayment of funds. Other enterprises may require much more advisory assistance. Financing arrangements should be flexible enough to permit counseling and supervision to be applied where it is the most useful. Suggestions on organizational arrangements intended to provide the greatest amount of service with limited staff have been considered in Chapter 5.

---

for example, the comments on El Salvador's Institute for the Promotion of Production in Robert R. Nathan Associates, Inc., *Investment and Industrial Development in El Salvador,* 1961, pp. 166, 167 and on Ghana's Industrial Development Corporation in *The National Investment Bank of Ghana,* p. 19.

Part Five
Additional Case Studies

Chapter 12
Colombia[1]

COLOMBIA HAS ONE of the more favorable political and economic settings in Latin America for successfully implementing a development financing program. The special environmental problems with which small factories and special programs for financing their development must cope in Colombia are nevertheless broadly those which tend to prevail in newly industrializing countries. Examining Colombia's experience and requirements in concrete detail may help to illustrate the kinds of small-industry development financing needs, the problems involved in meeting them, and possible solutions in such countries. The first half of this chapter presents a capsulized picture of basic conditions, institutions, and financial needs in Colombia in 1962; the second half describes how an effective development financing program might be most usefully established in this setting.

Political and Administrative Conditions

Colombia's political stability depends upon the durability of a 1957 agreement between the two major political parties to rotate the Presidency and to share the seats in Congress. Bitter civil strife between the Liberal and

[1] This chapter has been based on the author's experience as a member of a Stanford Research Institute team which assisted the Banco Popular in carrying out a study on this subject in 1962 the results of which were reported in *Small and Medium Industry in Colombia's Development*, Banco Popular, Bogotá, 1962. The author is indebted to the Banco Popular and to his colleagues, Eugene Staley and Richard Morse, for permission to draw upon this work. The chapter is concerned with the situation in 1962, which is adequate for the purpose here of illustrating the financial needs of small manufacturers and means of meeting them in a developing country. There have, however, been a number of interesting developments in Colombia since 1962 not reported on here, such as the establishment of a "Private Investment Fund," the expansion of the operations of private financieras, and a gradual implementation of some of the program suggestions. Changes since 1962 have in general not been covered, although some are indicated in footnotes.

Conservative parties, which flared up in 1948 and marked much of Colombian history in the nineteenth century, has, it is hoped, been permanently resolved. The agreement met the test of elections in 1962 with the peaceful succession of the Liberal party President by a Conservative party President. However, the succeeding government has much less unified support than the preceding one, and there remains a disturbing, if diminishing, heritage of banditry in some parts of the country as a result of the earlier civil war.

The capacity of government for daily administration is indicated by the nature of local criticism. This focuses on questions of efficiency and effectiveness, or occasionally partiality, rather than on complaints of corruption. Government staffs in Colombia, relative to other countries in the region, have a fairly high proportion of well-trained personnel. They are nevertheless still inadequate in relation to their responsibilities and the inertial mechanism through which they must often operate.

Economic Foundations

Colombia occupies 440,000 square miles; its population in 1960 was 14 million. A rapidly growing population and large unsettled areas contribute to its development potential. Improvement in transportation is bringing into healthy competition several well-established economic centers once isolated by mountains. Its primary economic problem is a dependence on the export of coffee and the declining coffee prices in recent years. The rapid economic expansion of the early 1950s almost stopped in the mid-1950s; recently, an annual growth rate of 3 to 4 percent in gross national product has been achieved; however, this implies a very small per capita increase, since population is expanding by over 2 percent a year.[2] Average per capita income in 1960 was around $180, but there are wide disparities in income distribution.

Characteristics of Industry

Industry accounts for nearly 17 percent of gross national product. It expanded by an average annual rate of 5.4 percent from 1950 to 1959.

There are over 3,600 small factories engaging between 10 and 99 persons with a total employment of over 93,000 persons. They account for 27 percent of value added and 38 percent of the persons employed in manufacturing. There are 6,500 additional enterprises employing less than 10 workers; these account for 12 percent of manufacturing employment. The remaining 50 percent of manufacturing employment is accounted for by the 400 enterprises employing 100 persons or more.

[2] The 1964 census revealed a growth rate of more than 3 percent and a total population of 17 million.

Seven departments,[3] and primarily nine or ten industrial centers within them, contain 90 percent of Colombia's small factories. A little over a third are concentrated in the department of Cundinamarca, primarily in Bogotá and surrounding towns. Another third is almost evenly divided between the departments of Antioquia and Valle del Cauca, again primarily in their major cities, Medellín and Cali, and in their industrial suburbs. Other important centers are the cities of Barranquilla, Bucaramanga, Cartagena, Manizales, Pereira, and Armenia.

The most important product lines in which small factories are concentrated are: (1) food products, accounting for nearly one-fifth of the total plants, primarily bakeries and other grain-processing enterprises, but also including a small number of milk products, confectionery, and food preservation enterprises; (2) clothing, 13 percent; (3) nonmetallic minerals, largely cement products and other building materials, 9 percent; (4) metal products, 7 percent; and (5) chemicals, 6 percent (over half of which are pharmaceuticals and one-fourth are soap and related products). Other significant lines, each accounting for over 3 percent of the total small factories are printing, vehicle repair, shoes, and furniture. The remaining 27 percent are distributed over a wide variety of lines.

Small factories increased in both number and employment by over 4 percent per year from 1953 to 1959; the increase in production was probably higher. Their growth was, nevertheless, less rapid than the 7 percent increase in employment in larger enterprises. On the other hand, it contrasts with the substantial decline recorded for enterprises employing less than 10 persons.

Some of the highest rates of increase were registered in metal products, machinery, and vehicle repair. Nonmetallic minerals, printing, furniture, clothing, and many minor lines also showed higher-than-average rates of increase. In a few minor lines, such as tobacco, beverages, and textiles, expansion by larger establishments was partly at the expense of small ones.

General Monetary and Banking Conditions

A degree of inflation has accompanied Colombian growth. The average price rise from 1950 to 1956 was about 4 percent per year; it was 17 percent in 1957 and 13 percent in the year following. Fiscal and monetary measures reduced the average price increases in the period 1959–1962 to about 6 percent per year.[4]

The most important initial counterinflationary measures applied were: (1) higher income and import taxes, which discouraged imports and strengthened government revenues, thereby producing budget surpluses; and (2) the imposition of advance deposit requirements on imports, which

[3] A *department* is a major political subdivision, equivalent to a state or province.
[4] The annual average price increase rose to over 20 percent for the period 1963–1965.

also discouraged imports and generally tightened monetary conditions. Central bank measures to tighten credit were applied early, but effective measures were not achieved until 1961.

Central Banking

A modern central bank structure has long existed, and, as recent measures have indicated, the Central Bank is capable of effective action.[5] The Central Bank until recently has had only two main tools of monetary management—rediscount policy and legal reserve requirements. The former was weakened by the practice of setting liberal rediscount quotas for each bank, but recent measures have sharply reduced these quotas. Selective credit controls to allocate a greater share of credit to important development activities are also now being applied, although with uncertain results. Measures are being taken to improve the operation of selective credit controls, such as the training of a qualified inspection staff and the replacement of excessively complicated regulations with more operational ones.[6]

Institutions Financing Industry

Colombia has an exceptional range of institutions which contribute to the financing of industry. Its extensive commercial banking system is supplemented by many specialized institutions. It includes many private ones and others which are owned partly or wholly by the central or local governments. The diversity of Colombian institutions makes it difficult to categorize them, but five broad groups discussed below may be distinguished for the purposes here.

Commerical Banks

There are 18 commercial banks in Colombia with approximately 475 offices and over 4.7 billion Colombian pesos (Col$) assets.[7] Two of these, the Banco de Bogotá and the Banco de Colombia, account for over 45 percent of the assets and nearly 60 percent of the offices. Three others account for roughly another third of both assets and offices. The remainder

---

[5] Colombia's central bank system and banking legislation are patterned after that of the United States. The Banco de la República is owned by member banks, although three of its nine board members are appointed by the central government. An independent government agency under the Superintendent of Banks is responsible for bank examination.

[6] Since the study, control over monetary policies was transferred to a Ministerial Monetary Council, of which the Central Bank is one of five members. It has been able to impose extremely tight controls over credit, but these have not prevented rising inflation due to major increases in government deficits and other pressures.

[7] The free exchange rate varied from 8.7 to 9.0 pesos to a United States dollar during the period of this study. Subsequent inflation has reduced the value of the pesos to an exchange rate of 18 to 1 United States dollar.

include branches of five foreign banks and eight small domestic banks, some of the latter being quasi-public or specifically oriented toward local requirements.

Colombia's commercial banks have a tradition of effective operations and have been adjusting their credit programs to new industrial needs. They have been authorized since 1950 to extend credit for up to five years and, since 1955, to purchase guaranteed industrial mortgage bonds extending up to 10 years. Selective credit measures recently have increased the incentives to make medium-term development loans. Although very little medium-term credit appears so far to have been extended to small enterprises, banks are extending an increasing amount to larger enterprises.[8] Because of the relatively low interest rate set on medium-term development credit, this credit is highly sought after by borrowers. On the other hand, banks tend to limit the volume of such lending to the minimum permitted under bank regulations, since they regard the margin of return on this type of lending as low and the required loan procedures as unfamiliar and complicated.[9] Inevitably, such loans as are made go to the largest or most favored clients.

At least one or two of the larger banks are giving some attention to adapting short-term credit arrangements to the needs of small factories. For example, installment loans up to one year have been made to quite small enterprises and, at least in a few cases, on liberal collateral arrangements. A number of banks have established *popular credit* departments under the provisions of a 1960 decree (No. 1790) intended in part to improve the availability of credit to small industry. However, the actual volume of credit extended by commercial banks under these provisions has been extremely small.[10]

[8] Industrial development loans made by commercial banks under provisions of decree No. 384 of 1950 rose to over 800 loans for more than Col$140 million in 1961, nearly doubling in value from the preceding year; they accounted at the end of 1961 for roughly one-fifth of the value of all commercial bank loans outstanding to industry. While bank statistics on these loans may be entirely reliable, since there were strong incentives for banks to classify loans as decree No. 384 development loans, they are probably indicative of the general level and trend of medium-term lending to industry. No data are available on the average term of these loans, but interviews with bankers and industrialists suggest that most are for periods of around three years, with a few for as long as five years. The authorized period has been increased since this study was made to 10 years, and by 1965 the average was reported to be about five years.

[9] In 1961, loans under decree No. 384 bore a maximum interest rate of 8 percent and were rediscountable at 3 percent. Most other bank loans were made at 10 to 12 percent, and the effective rate including fees was higher. By 1965, the official rates were about two percentage points higher, and the margin on loans under decree No. 384 was reduced to two percentage points.

[10] The general tightening of credit since 1962 is reported to have greatly reduced even the limited commercial bank services to small manufacturers that existed in 1962.

One aspect of bank services to small factories on which there has been some debate is whether or not small factories are better served by banks in the largest industrial centers than by banks in the smaller cities. Most of the banking facilities as well as the experience in industrial lending is concentrated in the three largest cities. Industrial loans also appear to be more concentrated in these cities than is industry itself. On the other hand, small enterprises tend to be much more overshadowed by large ones when they seek finance in the main centers. Also, a few enterprises surveyed reported choosing smaller cities for their plant location, specifically because of the possibility of establishing better banking connections. The practice of banks of managing branches through *local* boards of directors contributes greatly to the ability of industrialists in smaller cities to obtain a sympathetic and informed hearing of their needs.

Special Institutions with Commercial Bank Functions

Colombia has four special institutions which conduct an important share of normal commercial bank business: the Caja de Crédito Agrario, Industrial y Minero (popularly known as Caja Agraria), the Banco Cafetero, the Banco Ganadero, and the Banco Popular. Together they have over Col$3.5 billion assets and about 550 offices; thus they are roughly comparable in size to the total of commercial banks.

The Caja Agraria is by far the largest of the four; it possesses about half the assets and nearly three-fourths the offices of the combined total of special institutions. It was founded in 1931 as an autonomous institution. Its shares are primarily government-owned, although around one-fourth are owned by the Federación Nacional de Cafeteros (National Coffee Growers Federation). It has several types of long-term resources. It issues agricultural bonds to which, by law, banks must subscribe in proportion to their assets. These bonds provide 12 percent of the Caja Agraria's total resources. Another 20 percent were derived in 1961 from rediscounts with the Banco de la República. Since 1935, the Caja Agraria has administered the largest savings bank in Colombia, the Caja Colombiana de Ahorro, and formally absorbed it in 1955. Savings deposits now account for over 20 percent of the Caja Agraia's total resources.

The Caja Agraria's main activity is financing agriculture, but it also engages in such activities as credit insurance, loan supervision for other lenders, agricultural extension services, and the distribution of agricultural supplies and equipment. It was originally given responsiblity for financing industrial as well as agricultural development, but unsatisfactory industrial loan experience in its early years resulted in this type of financing being sharply curtailed.

Under decree No. 1156 of 1940, its industrial loans were restricted exclusively to small industry. At present, loans may be made to industrial enterprises with assets of Col$300,000 or less and in amounts not in excess of Col$25,000 where the enterprises are related to agriculture; where they are not, the limit on assets is Col$120,000 and on the amount of loans in Col$5,000. Loans may be made for working capital purposes for periods up to one year and for fixed capital purposes, up to three years. Normal collateral requirements are high, although the Caja Agraria has been permitted to make loans against personal guarantee since 1958. Lower-than-normal collateral requirements apply to loans of less than Col$10,000 made under the popular credit provisions of the 1960 decree (No. 1790). The interest rate including an insurance fee is reasonably low—7 percent on short term and 9 percent on medium term.

The industrial lending operations of the Caja Agraria have been extremely limited, amounting to one-third of 1 percent of its total portfolio in June, 1961, or a little over Col$3 million. Loans have been primarily short term and for petty amounts; new industrial loans in the last half of 1961 averaged less than Col$3,000. Field interviews suggest they have been used primarily by very small enterprises in very small towns. Even these enterprises tended to regard the Caja Agraria loans as of minor importance because of the conservative collateral and related loan requirements and the limitations on maximum loan size.

The Banco Cafetero is the second largest of the special institutions. In assets, it is about half the size of the Caja Agraria or about the same size as the largest commercial bank; in terms of banking offices, however, it is much smaller than either, having only 56 offices in 1960.

The Banco Cafetero was established in 1954 by the National Coffee Growers Federation, a quasi-official organization. It is authorized to undertake all normal commercial bank operations and is subject to the usual regulations applying to private commercial banks. It is nevertheless classified as a development bank (banco de fomento) and has special responsibilities with regard to coffee, members of the National Coffee Growers Federation, and coffee-growing regions. It undertakes, for example, the financing of the resettlement of small farmers. It has participated in the formation of investment banking corporations, being the major shareholder in Corporación Financiera de Caldas and Financiera-Valle. It also administers a program for the National Coffee Growers Federation under which short- and medium-term finance is extended to purchasers of imports made in connection with bilateral payments or barter agreements designed to stimulate coffee exports.

The last-mentioned program is of particular interest, since it provides for some medium-term finance. Under this program, industrialists may receive finance for 9 to 18 months on imported materials and 18 to 36 months on imported equipment. The interest rate is 6 percent, but if other costs are taken into account, the effective rate is substantially higher. Loan guarantees which are normally required may increase the effective cost to 9 percent. The required foreign exchange usually must be purchased at premium rates. Advanced deposits generally required for imports also apply in these cases, and somewhat greater delays may be involved. The importer must take delivery at the production point abroad and make all shipping arrangements, which adds to the expense and difficulty of this type of transaction, particularly for the small industrialist. Countries from which such imports can be made may not be able to provide the desired item at competitive standards of quality and price. Despite limitations such as the foregoing, the program has been helpful to industrialists, including some of medium size and a few small ones. No special attention, however, has been given in the program to smaller factories or to adapting procedures to their particular needs.

The other two special institutions with important commercial bank functions need only be briefly mentioned. The larger and more important for our purposes, the Banco Popular, will be separately treated after other institutions have been briefly summarized, since it is the primary institution with developmental responsibilities toward small and medium industry. It also carries on regular commercial banking and is roughly comparable in size to the fourth largest commercial bank. The other special institution, the Banco Ganadero, was established by the Caja Agraria and the Colombian Confederation of Cattle Raisers in 1956 to serve the cattle industry in the same way as the Banco Cafetero serves the coffee industry. It is still relatively small; at the end of 1961 it had less than Col$200 million assets and 14 offices. Its concern with industry is intended to be limited to enterprises directly related to cattle raising. Like the other special institutions, it also engages in commercial banking. It may also develop special regional interests as the Banco Cafetero has done.

Mortgage and Savings Institutions

There are only a few mortgage and savings institutions which have potential significance in small-factory financing. Savings amount to over Col$700 million and are collected primarily through departments of commercial or special banks rather than by separate institutions; over half the total is accounted for by the savings department of the Caja Agraria. A portion of the savings deposits become indirectly available to industry through their investment in the bonds and notes of the Banco Central Hipotecario.

The combined resources of 70 insurance companies and five capitalization (lottery-type savings) associations are a somewhat larger source of funds than savings departments. An important share of these is invested in industrial bonds and shares, in bonds of the Banco Central Hipotecario, and in mortgage or policy loans to industrialists. Although these go primarily to large industry, medium-size enterprises have obtained policy loans and loan guarantees in at least a few cases.

The Banco Central Hipotecario was established in 1932 by the Banco de la República, which owns 85 percent of its shares, and by the commercial and special banks which own the remainder. It had total assets at the end of 1961 in excess of Col$1 billion and 28 offices. Most of its assets are derived from the sale of bonds and notes, including some made attractive by lottery features. Its issues are sold (1) to a voluntary market, (2) to institutions which are required to hold a portion of their assets in these issues, and (3) to the Banco de la República. Its funds have been devoted largely to housing, although it has been extending some finance to industry in recent years. Most of this has gone to large enterprises. At the end of 1960, it had 241 loans for Col$103 million outstanding to industry, of which 28 loans totaling Col$8 million went to enterprises with 100 or fewer workers.

The Banco Central Hipotecario can issue loans up to 10 years (and in some cases, up to 20), although field interviews suggest that loans to smaller enterprises do not generally exceed five years. It does not lend funds, but rather issues bonds which the borrower sells to an insurance company or other buyer who usually has agreed in advance to make the purchase. Loans are also repaid in bonds which the borrower repurchases in the market. The Banco Central has recently increased its lending rate to 12 percent; if the losses the borrower normally incurs on the bond transactions involved in its loan procedures are taken into account, the effective rate to the borrower is between 13 and 14 percent. Borrowers must sometimes also incur other costs, such as purchasing an insurance policy from the prospective bond buyer to assure the availability of a market. The Banco Central cannot lend in excess of 60 percent of the value of collateral and sometimes lends on a more conservative basis in the case of smaller enterprises.

The conservative and fairly costly basis on which Banco Central loans are made are not, however, the most important limit on their use by smaller enterprises. Its loans are still much cheaper than loans from private sources. More important is the simple unavailability of funds even for many enterprises which could meet cost and collateral requirements. Also important is the lengthy period—reported by some loan recipients to range from four to eight months—required for action on loan applications.

The Instituto de Crédito Territorial is another organization which merits brief mention, though it has been concerned so far with financing only low-cost housing. It is a government organization (with business and employee representation on its board of directors) and has been in operation since 1939. It derives funds from budget allotments, bonds, and, recently, from substantial funds provided under the United States AID program. The Institute has carried on research and acquired direct experience in urban development problems and, with its increasing resources, might provide valuable assistance to programs concerned with improving the availability of industrial buildings for smaller enterprises.

Private Investment Institutions

Among the promising new institutions for financing industry are four private finance corporations. Before considering them, two other private institutions (the Crescinco Fund and Promotora de Empresas Privadas, S.A.), which are of more limited interest, merit brief mention.

Mutual fund organizations made a start in Colombia with the opening in 1959 of the Crescinco Fund by the International Basic Economy Corporation. Although there appears little immediate possibility that mutual funds will purchase shares in small- or medium-scale enterprises in Colombia, financial organizations basically of the mutual fund type have in some parts of the world broadened their functions and services to a point where they have been able to provide equity finance to medium-scale enterprise.

Promotora de Empresas Privadas, S.A., is a corporation worth noting as an illustration of the basic problems involved in seeking to develop small factories through private financial institutions. Promotora was formed about 1959 with a capital of Col$671,000 to provide equity finance and other assistance to promising small enterprises. It had 31 shareholders, largely Colombian, but the initiator and major shareholder was a United States industrialist concerned with demonstrating the value of private enterprise in newly developing countries. The underlying concept appeared to be that the financed enterprises through their resulting growth would provide a demonstration to entrepreneurs, government officials, and the country as a whole of the potentialities of small private enterprises. At the same time, the financial success of Promotora would demonstrate to the financial community the economic soundness of extending such finance.

Promotora operated for about two years, extending finance to nine enterprises before the shareholders decided to liquidate its operations. It was not a failure in all respects. A few of the enterprises financed are successful and growing enterprises and attribute a substantial part of their success to the financial assistance from Promotora.

The major difficulties of Promotora appear to have stemmed from: (1) underestimating the cost of financing small enterprises; (2) focusing on enterprises of such a small scale that there was relatively slender possibility of finding enterprises with substantial and readily developable potential; and (3) expecting the successful industrialists among the shareholders to have the time, incentive, and ability to provide sufficiently informed evaluation of finance applications and also to extend subsequent supervision and advisory assistance to enterprises financed.

Among the lessons to be drawn from the experience of Promotora is that the evalution of loan applications and the extension of advisory assistance requires a highly informed and organized approach. The fact that some of the firms financed were successful suggests that advisory services are not always essential, provided that selection procedures are adequate to identify sufficiently promising firms. Small-industry finance services, however, need to be priced realistically if substantial private finance is to be attracted to such undertakings.

Private finance corporations were authorized by legislation in 1957. In each of the four succeeding years, one of the finance corporations existing at the time of this study (1962) was established. They are: Corporación Financiera Colombiana de Desarrollo Industrial (CFC-Bogotá); Corporación Financiera Nacional (CFN-Medellín); Corporación Financiera de Fomento Industrial y Agropecuario (Financiera-Valle); and Corporación Financiera de Caldas (CFC-Manizales).[11] These institutions are intended to provide most of the usual services of private investment banks, serving as a source of equity and medium- and long-term loan funds for industrial, agricultural, and extractive enterprises of all sizes. They have, however, some special interest in small manufacturing enterprises.

The share capital of the corporations is drawn primarily from domestic financial institutions, business concerns, and individuals. However, a small but significant portion of shares has been sold to financial institutions abroad. The other major resources of the corporations are derived from rediscounts with the Banco de la República and domestic and international bank loans. The Corporations may obtain further funds by issuing bonds or accepting trust funds or deposits of 90 days or more. Rediscount privileges apply only in the case of loans made for fixed capital purposes and otherwise qualifying under the provisions of decree No. 384 of 1950. The amount of rediscount was set initially at 100 percent of capital and reserves, but rediscount privileges are to be gradually reduced and eliminated at the end of six years.

Although the operations of all four corporations are fundamentally the same, there are some important differences in the nature of shareholders and their approaches to term lending. The CFC-Bogotá was officially constituted at the end of 1958 with an authorized capital of Col$20 million. It is located in Colombia's capital and largest industrial center. In 1962, it opened a branch office in Bucaramanga although initially with only the function of receiving applications. The two largest commercial banks and several smaller ones as well as insurance and industrial companies are among the shareholders of the CFC-Bogotá. A major addition to its funds was US$2 million long-term loan secured by convertible notes from the International Finance Corporation in 1961.

Of more importance from the point of view of financing small enterprises was another loan in 1961 from the Inter-American Development Bank of Col$4 million together with US$500,000. The Inter-American Development Bank funds are to be relent to enterprises with net assets of not over Col$1 million. Individual loans are not to exceed Col$600,000, and at least 50 percent of the loans must be for amounts less than Col$300,000.

[11] A fifth, the Corporación Financiera del Norte, has since been formed.

Loans are to be made for fixed asset purposes only, for periods of three to 10 years and at an interest rate not over $9\frac{1}{2}$ percent plus $\frac{1}{2}$ percent fee where technical assistance is provided.

The CFC-Bogotá has found it difficult in practice to lend the dollar portion of the loan, since few borrowers are prepared to bear the required exchange risk. There is ample demand for peso funds. Peso loans to small factories, however, are not expected to be financially profitable in view of high lending costs, despite a margin of roughly 4 percent between borrowing and relending rates. Such loans were undertaken by the CFC-Bogotá as a part of its general development or public service functions. It feels able to do so since these are a small part of its total financial transactions, and other loans, particularly those extended for raw materials, provide a much higher return.

The CFN-Medellín was established in July, 1959, with an authorized capital of Col$25 million. Like the CFC-Bogotá, its shareholders include commercial banks, insurance and industrial companies, and individuals. One of the banks among its shareholders is Colombia's third largest commercial bank. Also like the CFC-Bogotá, it received a US$2 million loan from the International Finance Corporation in 1961. Its financing activity is similar to the CFC-Bogotá's, differing primarily in the geographic center of its operations. It makes a significant number of loans to small and medium enterprises but depends for profits primarily on its financial services to large concerns.

The Financiera-Valle was established in April, 1960, with an authorized capital of Col$25 million. Its shareholders include the Banco Cafetero, the Banco del Comercio, the Corporación Autónoma Regional del Valle del Cauca, sugar mills, and other industrial concerns. In view of the quasi-public character of major shareholders and the special social problems of its area of operations (the Valle del Cauca), its policy is to give primary attention to financing new enterprises which will add significantly to employment. It has demonstrated greater interest than other finance corporations in making loans to agriculture for fixed installations. It has found it generally difficult in its region to make industrial loans on a formal project basis, particularly to smaller enterprises. It has therefore generally regarded Col$100,000 as a minimum limit on loan size.

The CFC-Manizales was established in May, 1961, with an authorized capital of Col$15 million. Its major shareholders are the Banco Cafetero, the Federación Nacional de Cafeteros, and Empresa Colombiana de Petroleos (Ecopetrol), the latter a government petroleum company. Insurance and industrial companies also own a small part of the shares.[12] In its first year of operation, it issued Col$8.6 million in loans including a number to small and medium enterprises, although few loans were less than Col$100,000. It has concentrated its activities in the department of Caldas;

[12] Since this study, the International Finance Corporation has also become a shareholder.

three-fourths of the amount of its loans in the first year were in the city of Manizales.

The potential contribution of finance corporations to the growth of small manufacturing enterprises is indicated by some assistance which they have already provided. At the same time, a number of obstacles are evident which could prevent their financing of small factories from reaching a significant volume. They have found few opportunities of interest to them for extending equity finance. They generally base their medium-term loans on evaluations of projects submitted by applicants, but they find few small enterprises that can prepare projects in sufficiently organized and detailed form to permit quick and low-cost evaluation.

The various solutions being experimented with so far by the different corporations include: (1) the building up of a technical staff which can convert information obtained from applicants into projects that can be tested; (2) adding heavy collateral requirements to loan terms so that less attention need be given to testing the projects submitted; and (3) relying less on project testing than on a quick field evaluation of the borrower and his enterprise by a loan officer.

Although each of these approaches has some merit, each has dangers if incorrectly applied. Building up a technical staff within a financial institution may prove costly. Bank personnel, because of their position of responsibility, may give excessive attention to individual projects; this will increase the costs on an inevitably expensive service and may result in bank staff becoming too directly involved in matters better left to the responsibility of the enterprise. The second approach, that of requiring collateral, has the merit of stimulating borrowers to greater concern for repayment; however, if collateral becomes the primary criterion, then some of the most promising enterprises may be eliminated from consideration. The third approach has the merit of speed and economy, which is important, particularly in the case of smaller enterprises. But it can result in serious losses from unwise loans unless it is carried out by staff having a high level of training and experience in industrial loan evaluation and easy access to data on environmental factors such as competition, markets, and economic trends. A limitation of all these approaches is that none makes adequate provision for remedying the situation where initially sound loans fall into difficulty because of a change in conditions—a not uncommon circumstance.

Each of the finance corporations may in its own way develop practical methods of financing smaller enterprises. Their ability to move in this direction will be greatly strengthened if supporting programs (described later) are established.

Government Development Organizations

A number of government development organizations exist which could contribute to the financing of small factories. The Instituto de Fomento Industrial is the most important of these. It was established in 1940 to assist the establishment of important types of enterprise not immediately attractive to private investment. Its activities are related primarily to large enterprise, but some are of significance at least to medium enterprise.

In its early years, it helped establish numerous companies ranging from steel and basic chemical plants to fiber bag and meat-packing enterprises. Many of these have since been disposed of, so that it now owns shares in only 10 industrial companies. These, however, account for about half of its Col$47 million assets, and much of the remainder is in mining and other long-term investments.

A shortage of investment resources, and differences within the government concerning what financial activities it should undertake, have resulted in the Instituto's giving greater emphasis in recent years to conducting studies of investment opportunities and their feasibility. A staff of about 25 economists, statisticians, and engineers in two departments are engaged primarily in such studies. The development of exports is another field to which it has given special attention in recent years. At the same time it has been seeking an international loan to enable it to undertake development lending to medium-scale enterprises. It is also a participant in other organizations which have industrial development responsibilities; one of these engaging in small-industry financing is the Development Fund of Santander, described below.

The Development Fund of Santander was formed in 1960 out of the reorganization of an earlier agency and the selling of the latter's shares in several industrial enterprises. About two-thirds of the Fund's capital of Col$900,000 is owned by the department of Santander and most of the remainder by the Instituto de Fomento; a very small amount has derived from private shareholders. It operates with part-time management and the assistance of the local community. It is authorized to finance enterprises within the department in amounts not exceeding Col$200,000 per loan. By March, 1962, it had disbursed most of its funds in seven loans to enterprises of various sizes, primarily of small and medium scale. The normal loan period is two to three years and the rate of interest 10 percent.

Other development organizations of some relevance are regional and local development corporations. These have not so far been directly concerned with financing industry. They have, nevertheless, an interest in industrial development and industrial zoning. In some cases, they also have substantial development resources. Their autonomous nonpolitical character, together with the preceding characteristics, qualify them as potentially valuable participants in industrial estate and related programs intended to alleviate industry's need for building finance.

The Banco Popular

The Banco Popular, a largely government-owned institution, was established in 1950 primarily to provide pawn loans to individuals at a regulated rate of interest. Its operations were broadened in 1951 to include commercial bank functions, with special attention to small industry. In the following year, it was authorized to make medium-term mortgage loans. This mixture of social purpose, commercial, and development financing has handicapped the bank in evolving clear objectives and priorities in its operations.

In 1955, a United Nations consultant was brought in to evaluate small-industry needs and make program suggestions, including those required for improving the bank's lending program. Despite this effort, by 1957 the bank had fallen into serious financial difficulties because of political interference and mismanagement.

Following the change in government in 1958, the new administration refinanced the bank and set in process a reorganization of its operations and a reformulation of its objectives. Law No. 49 of 1959 permitted the bank to write off its past losses and provided it with Col$30 million additional capital and special government deposits. A firm collection policy was applied toward delinquent and defaulting creditors to discourage the recurrence of unsound loans as well as to recover a portion of past bad debts. The bank's statutes were modified in order to direct a large part of the bank's functions to the development of small industry. A reevaluation of its branch and staff requirements was begun, resulting in gradual alterations in both. Several of the government institutions lending to small borrowers, including the bank's subsidiary, the Banco Hipotecario Popular, were put into liquidation. In February, 1962, the Banco Popular initiated a study of the requirements for a coordinated and efficient development program for small factories. The Banco Popular and other appropriate authorities are now in the process of implementing the program suggestions of this study.

At the end of 1961, the Banco Popular had total assets of about Col$500 million. This represented 14 percent of the total assets of special banks of 6½ percent of the combined total for special and commercial banks. It had paid up capital of Col$43 million; capital and reserves were nearly Col$57 million. Seventy-five percent of its total shares since its recapitalization in 1959 have been owned by the central government, 10 percent by municipalities, 9 percent by departments, and 6 percent by numerous small private shareholders.

Despite government ownership, the bank's present resources are not well suited to development financing. Over half are current deposits which reportedly are subject to exceptional fluctuations because of the inclusion of a high proportion of government accounts. Savings and term deposits account for 13 percent of resources, and rediscounts with the Banco de la República, another 4½ percent. The remaining resources include little besides capital, reserves, and a small amount derived from the sale of bonds that are suitable for medium-term lending.

The bank has a substantial network of branches covering all major cities and a number of minor ones. At the end of 1961 it maintained 78 offices in 53 cities or towns. About a fifth of the offices were in Bogotá. The number of its branches has gradually increased during the last few years, despite the closing of some, including all those abroad.

The bank's present portfolio consists primarily of short-term loans. Total loans outstanding at the end of 1961 were Col$273 million, of which 84 percent were short-term (less than one year), 14 percent medium-term (one to six years), and 2 percent long-term (over six years).

Loans to industry amounted to Col$58 million, or about 21 percent of total loans. Extractive, construction, and service enterprises such as hotels and transportation accounted for another 14 percent of loans; commerce for 32 percent; agriculture and cattle raising, 15 percent; loans to public entities, or for housing rehabilitation and other social purposes, 8 percent; and small consumer loans, 10 percent. Consumer loans are much more important than their share of value may suggest, particularly in their effect on bank operating costs. They constituted nearly two-thirds of the total number of loans and averaged only a little over Col$600 each.

The average loan size was small, reflecting the effect of the aforementioned consumer loans as well as legal restrictions on the size of loans the Banco Popular may make. Popular credit institutions (or departments of banks devoted to popular credit) are required to make at least 55 percent of their loans in amounts of not more than Col$50,000 per borrower; in both of these cases, the net assets of a borrower may not exceed Col$300,000. The remaining 15 percent of loans must be lent to borrowers with net assets not over Col$500,000, although exemptions to this limit can be made with special approval. The average size of short-term loans at the end of 1961 was Col$3,500; of medium term, Col$13,200; and of long term, Col$6,100. If loans to industry only are considered, but without regard to loan period, the average size was a little over Col$24,000.

The Banco Popular makes industrial loans under the same general regulations as are applicable to commercial banks. These regulations include decree No. 384 of 1950, which authorizes rediscountable medium-term industrial loans for fixed capital purposes, and decree 1790 of 1960, authorizing rediscountable short and medium multipurpose loans to small industry. The bank has accounted for a relatively small share of total loans under decree No. 384—less than 1½ percent in 1961, although as much as 6 percent in 1960. On the other hand, it has accounted for most of the decree No. 1790 loans, its share being around 90 percent, even though the inducements to make such loans are equally available to other banks.

In terms of the bank's total loans to industrial enterprises, loans under both of these development-oriented provisions have been relatively small, although decree No. 1790 loans have been by far the more important. Together they constituted only a little over one-fourth of the bank's outstanding industrial loans at the end of 1961. If the roughly equal volume of decree No. 1790 credit extended in 1961 under temporary provisions to nonindustrial types of enterprises (primarily taxicabs) were included under industry, the proportion would be much higher; on the other hand, total No. 1790 credit to all sectors as a percent of total Banco Popular loans was only about 10 percent. Thus, although the bank has made a substantial start toward providing development finance to small and medium industry, this activity is so far still a small part of its total operations.

Ancillary Services for Institutions Financing Industry

Colombia has a wide variety of institutions which have made a start on performing services essential to effective development financing. Of particular importance are those which assist in the collection, analysis, and dissemination of information helpful to production or financing decisions, to their implementation, or to direct improvement in the production abilities of potential and actual recipients of financing.

The Instituto de Investigaciones Tecnológicas (IIT) is Colombia's leading institution serving needs of this type. Its professional staff comprises about 100 persons of whom over one-third hold advanced degrees. It operates on an annual budget of about Col$6 million. The IIT was established in 1955 by the Caja Agraria, primarily to carry on technological research related to agriculture. Its sponsorship and functions have since been widened. Four additional organizations, the Banco de la República, Federación Nacional de Cafeteros, Ecopetrol, and the Instituto de Fomento Industrial are now represented on its board and contribute to its basic finance.

The IIT undertakes contract research for both private enterprises and public entities, particularly with regard to agriculture and agricultural processing and chemical industries. It carries out physical testing and studies of industrial processes. It has also undertaken a number of economic feasibility studies or project evaluations of particular enterprises for development and financial organizations.

A new program which it added in 1962 with the assistance of the United Nations is technical assistance to small industry. As a first step, it has begun surveying the technical assistance requirements of selected industries, including foundries, bakeries, soap manufacturers, and food preservation enterprises. It has started a technical assistance program for a small group of foundries in Bogotá. On the basis of this experience, it plans to undertake similar programs for other industries and possibly other areas.

The Universidad Industrial de Santander in Bucaramanga is another institution of rapidly increasing potential for rendering service in this field. Its primary activity is training engineers. It expects to increase its annual graduates from 108 in 1960 to around 280 in 1967 as the result of financial assistance from the United Nations. It is also creating facilities for direct service to industry by an institute of chemical research and testing, a standards institute, and an institute of industrial consultants. Although the institutes are just being formed and will require time to accumulate experience, staff, and equipment, they reflect energetic and imaginative planning and will gradually increase important services to industry.

Universities and technical schools in such cities as Medellín, Bogotá, Cali, Barranquilla, and Pereira are also making important contributions to the training of industrial technicians and are providing a small amount of testing or consulting services.

The Instituto Colombiano de Administración (INCOLDA) has already begun providing management training through seminars and performing some management assistance. INCOLDA was started in 1958 by Colombia's major industrial association, the Asociación Nacional de Industriales (ANDI), with the assistance of the United States AID program. Its major source of current income is fees which it charges for participation in its seminars. It now has a staff of one to three persons in each of five cities. It also engages local and foreign consultants as required to lead management seminars which it holds on such topics as: "Executive Accounting," "The Role of the Supervisor," "Sales Management," and "Industrial Economics." Although its programs have been criticized for being overly general and expensive, it has probably been as successful as most other programs of this type have been in their early stages. It has been exploring the idea of providing extension service where more direct and concrete business advisory assistance might be given. It is already conducting an experimental program of direct advisory assistance to a cooperative of small foundries.

The Escuela de Administración y Finanzas in Medellín is another institution for management training recently founded under ANDI auspices, with the assistance of the United States AID program. It plans to train students from about the high school graduate level over a period of five and one-half years, alternating business course work with in-service training in business enterprises.

Business administration programs are being started in a number of universities. Business training courses and advisory services are also provided on a fee basis by 15 to 20 private individuals or concerns. Although much of the business community tends to be critical of the cost and quality of the work of local private consultants, their survival is some testimony to their usefulness.

The Servicio Nacional de Aprendizaje (SENA) initiated a program in 1959 with the assistance of the International Labour Organization and the United Nations for training workers and employees, from the foreman level downward. It is primarily financed by a 1 percent payroll tax paid by enterprises above a specified size. It is carrying out surveys of skill requirements, is establishing training centers in various parts of the country, and has begun training in some of them. It expects to train some 32,000 persons over a five-year period.

Economic surveys are another service important to effective development financing which Colombian institutions have already begun to provide. A leading example is the Centro de Estudios sobre Desarrollo Económico in the Universidad de los Andes. It was started in 1958 with the assistance of the Rockefeller Foundation and Michigan State University and now has a staff of over 20. It has carried out a wide range of surveys and economic studies. One or two other universities are now starting similar economic investigation centers. Economic and technoeconomic analysis of industrial opportunities are part of the work of government organizations such as the Instituto de Fomento Industrial and the Office of Industrial Economics in the Ministry of Development. The related activities of the IIT have already been referred to.

Business associations are a final type of organization in Colombia actively seeking to provide some of the services important to effective development financing. Shortly after the founding of the Banco Popular, its manager initiated the founding of the Asociación Colombiana Popular de Pequeños Industriales (ACOPI). This association was intended to provide an organizational framework within which small industrialists might provide for themselves many of the required services. However, according to the United Nations consultant brought in to reevaluate the small-industry program in 1955, ACOPI had not by that date acquired the organizational unity and financial strength to perform effectively and had lost many of its members when it became apparent that membership did not assure Banco Popular financing. The enthusiasm of a few members has enabled ACOPI to survive, although without acquiring much strength or adequate membership to be representative of small industry. Despite continued difficulties, it has been active on behalf of its membership; it has started an industrial estate and has strongly campaigned for improved financing for small industry, going so far as to seek permission and funds to found a new institution of its own for this purpose.

Among other industrial associations of importance to small and medium industry is the Federación Popular Colombiana (FEPOCOL), which once was affiliated with ACOPI. It has been active primarily in the Valle del Cauca area.

Colombia's major industrial association, ANDI, includes some smaller enterprises as well as most larger ones. A number of its important and varied activities have already been referred to.

There are in addition organizations in individual lines of industry. A few of these, such as Federación Metalúrgica Colombiana (FEDEMETAL) for metalworking enterprises, have undertaken activities such as surveying production capabilities and technologies of its membership and providing members with up-to-date information on equipment, production techniques, and market prospects for products.

One further type of association which has potential importance in Colombia for facilitating development financing of small factories is that of banking institutions. The Asociación Bancaria meets annually to consider joint activities which will improve banking. It agreed at its 1961 meeting, for example, to study the possibility of a service through a Technical-Economic Department to collect types of information essential to evaluating development credit requirements of enterprises. Another important measure it is considering is a centralized credit rating service. The ability of the Asociación Bancaria to unify both private and public financial institutions on group action of these types is an important asset that can be utilized in improving the financing of small factories.

Financial and Related Needs of Small Factories

In 1962, 120 small-scale factories representative of significant industries and regions in Colombia were studied to assess their growth capacity and to identify the major factors limiting their expansion and modernization. Both financial and other needs which might be met in part by external agencies were evaluated in order to determine what programs and priorities were appropriate for stimulating small-factory development.

Since the needs of enterprises with real capacity for significant growth normally deserve priority in development programs, this summary of the survey findings concentrates first on the 70 enterprises rated in the Banco Popular survey as capable of significant expansion. Then the relative importance and needs of firms are reviewed for each of several size subgroups.

Needs of Firms with Significant Growth Potential

The highest priority requirement for significant expansion among the 70 growth-potential firms was medium-term finance for equipment purchase or working capital expansion. Such medium-term credit was essential for output expansion or reduction of production costs of 50 of these firms, about 70 percent of the growth-potential group.[13]

About half the group, 34 firms, required equipment finance; of these, 28 firms would simultaneously need expanded working capital on one- to two-year terms in order to reach and maintain a higher operating level; 15 of the firms would require long-term credit for factory construction, together with both equipment and working capital finance.

Medium-term working capital expansion, together with long-term building finance, was required by nine other firms, while seven additional firms required medium-term working capital expansion in order to utilize their present equipment and buildings to fullest capacity. Thus a total of 44

---

[13] Given the size of the sample, the percentages reported here represent orders of magnitude only and are intended principally to illuminate the major differences between groups of firms in capacity and needs. The financial needs of small enterprises have undoubtedly increased greatly since this study was made, because of greater restrictions on credit availability and an increase in the rate of inflation.

firms required medium-term working capital, although in most cases it was required as a supplement to equipment and/or building finance.

The total number of growth-potential firms requiring long-term building finance was 28, about 40 percent of the group. Most of these, as indicated above, required some equipment and/or working capital funds also, although four required only long-term building finance, to permit better layout and utilization of the present equipment.

Over 30 percent of the growth-potential firms required increased short-term working capital in order to expand output or to cut costs. Most of these required it both for financing materials and finished stock, and 10 required financing also for accounts receivable.

In interpreting these financial needs, it is of prime importance that more than 60 percent of the growth-potential firms were judged to be able to expand significantly with financial assistance only. This finding emphasizes the potentially great contribution which an effective credit program can make to the development of small and medium Colombian industry. Three important qualifications must be noted, however:

1. The 70 firms analyzed were those with significant growth potential which typically were managed by better-than-average entrepreneurs. Only half of the total 120 firms interviewed were judged to have significant growth prospects if aided by loans alone.
2. Direct counsel in the enterprise's *financial* planning was essential or important for two-thirds of those outstanding firms that could expand significantly with financial assistance alone. Such counsel was needed, for example, in planning the firm's balance between fixed and working capital expansion, or in preparing and analyzing cash-flow budgets to determine the appropriate amount and timing of loans.
3. The effectiveness of financial assistance to the most promising firms would be multiplied substantially by simultaneous provision of other elements of management counsel. In the case of the 40 percent of the growth-potential firms which were judged *unlikely* to expand significantly through provision of finance alone, complementary developmental counsel was essential or highly important.

The types of simultaneous or supplementary development counsel most essential may be briefly summarized. Production management counsel was essential or important to the expansion of nearly 60 percent of the growth-potential firms. More plants were judged to require guidance on such industrial engineering problems as work standardization and simplification, plant layout and work flow, or production scheduling and inventory control than on specific technical problems limited to their own type of production process. Nevertheless, over one-third of the growth-potential firms required advice or information on technical production problems and methods for their present product line. A much larger number would require specific technical guidance in order to undertake new products which they had the general competence and capacity to manufacture.

Nearly 60 percent of the growth-potential firms required new or improved market information or distribution methods on either their existing or new products in order to achieve and maintain significantly increased sales. This was true even though the greatest difference between the growth-potential firms and the others visited was that over 90 percent of the growth-potential firms enjoyed a favorable sales outlook for their present products, whereas only 25 percent of the others had good sales prospects. It could be said that the major single evidence of superior capacity of the most promising entrepreneurs was their greater knowledge of market opportunities and their success in selecting products of the right design, price, and quality to command increasing sales. Nevertheless, in order for their present products to achieve and maintain the sales volume they deserve, it was judged that nearly 40 percent of the growth-potential firms needed better information on market trends. In order successfully to introduce new products, supplementing present lines, about half the promising firms required product-focused market studies. Those firms judged to have only moderate or low growth potential were obviously less well informed on market trends, on the average, and had even greater need for product-focused market studies.

About half of the growth-potential firms required assistance in the design and installation of improved accounting systems geared to the special needs and administrative limitations of small firms.

To summarize, each small firm with great or substantial growth capacity had its individual complex of strong features and problems. Although developmental finance coupled with financial counsel could take many of these firms ahead significantly, the maximum realization of expanded output and employment in the small-medium sector can only be achieved when such firms have simultaneous and direct access to sources of management and technical counsel. The counseling agency must possess the judgment and information necessary to make a total appraisal of the firm's scope and needs in the context of the immediate economic environment and must also be flexible enough to respond to each firm's unique needs or to obtain specialized assistance from cooperating agencies for such specialized needs.

Needs of Firms of Different Sizes

Firms by Employment Size

In plants engaging fewer than 10 persons, only 1 out of 15 owner-managers was judged to have great or substantial capacity for expanding his manufacturing operations, as against 11 with moderate capacity and 3 of doubtful capacity. Five out of the fifteen displayed a positive response to the idea of technical and management advice. The low proportion of owner-managers found to have promising growth capacity in this size category confirms the advisability of focusing early development efforts on firms having 10 or more persons. But program boundaries should be sufficiently flexible to seek out the exceptional firm even below the 10-person level, especially in significantly mechanized activities in which the sales turnover and capital commanded are above average for plants of this work force.

Of the visited firms engaging 10 to 24 persons, 19 out of 34 firms were judged to possess great or substantial growth capacity, as against 12 with moderate capacity and 3 with doubtful capacity. The receptivity of entrepreneurs in this group to technical, marketing, and management counsel equaled their evident capacity for growth.

In larger plants, an even greater proportion was judged to have substantial growth potential: 25 out of 28 firms engaging 25 to 49 persons; 17 out of 19 firms engaging 50 to 99 persons; and 8 out of 10 firms engaging 100 or more persons. The motivation of entrepreneurs for improvement and receptivity to outside counsel showed a positive response as follows: 20 out of 28 firms engaging 25 to 49 persons; 15 of 19 firms with 50 to 99 persons; and 4 out of 10 firms engaging over 100 persons. The need for selectivity in allocating development assistance obviously must include as a criterion the attitude of the firm's management toward overall improvement. Those who give evidence of both capacity and willingness to modernize techniques should receive preference. Their example may eventually stimulate improvement on the part of those competing firms whose owners are presently indifferent to the quality of their production and management operations.

Firms by Asset Size

The asset characteristics of firms are of greater relevance in a financing program than the number of persons employed, although these tend to be related. Of firms visited which possessed Col$200,000 to Col$499,000, 60 percent were judged to have great or substantial growth potential. (These included firms in both the 10- to 24-person and 25- to 49-person categories). Of those having gross assets from Col $500,000 to Col$999,000, 80 percent were growth-potential firms. (Most of these engaged between 25 and 49 persons, although some employed as many as 70 persons.) Among the firms visited having gross assets of Col$1 million and over, some 90 percent were judged to have significant growth capacity.

Manufacturing enterprises selected as capable of growth in the asset class Col$200,000 to Col$499,000 appeared to merit the highest priority for developmental finance assistance. Nearly 75 percent evidenced the capacity to grow with only financial counsel and financial assistance. At the same time, they had a high need for finance. Over 70 percent needed medium-term working capital for expansion. Some 60 percent required equipment finance. Over half required long-term capital for factory construction. Nearly half also required increased short-term working capital—principally for materials for inventories—in order to expand output in the short run.

Despite the ability of a large proportion of growth-potential firms in the Col$200,000 to Col$499,000 asset class to benefit substantially from financial assistance by itself, varied managerial and technical counsel was important to their future success. Although financial counsel and assistance can start promising firms of this asset strength on a path of expansion, the existing problems of these firms and the increasing complexity of management will quickly set limits on their growth unless supporting technical and business management counsel are provided, particularly in accounting, production planning, and control and marketing.

Next priority for financial assistance was found to lie with the promising firms in each of two asset groups: the group from Col$500,000 to Col$999,000 and the group below Col$200,000. The two groups will be considered separately.

Two-thirds of the growth-potential firms visited which had assets between Col$500,000 and Col$999,000 showed promise of significant growth with improved credit and financial counsel. Many firms in this asset class had grown to the point where they needed long-term building finance for plant expansion or new factory construction: expanded plant facilities were essential for nearly 60 percent of these firms. An equal number required medium-term working capital to reach a higher output level. Over 30 percent required medium-term equipment finance. Short-term working capital was required by over 20 percent. On the average, firms of this scale had less need than smaller firms for strictly technical assistance, since they more frequently employed qualified engineers, some of whom kept abreast of technical developments through engineering and industrial journals. However, a majority could benefit from counsel on such matters as plant layout and production planning and control.

Firms with assets less than Col$200,000 having great or substantial growth capacity had the highest average need of any asset group for financial assistance but also showed the highest average need for technical and management counsel in order to utilize improved credit to full advantage. Nearly 90 percent of the growth-potential firms evaluated in this group were in critical need of medium-term credit to expand output, usually to exploit immediate sales potential. Equipment finance was needed by 70 percent of these firms. Enterprises of this size received the least-effective credit from suppliers of materials and machinery; credit from suppliers was either not feasible or needed great improvement for all the growth-potential firms visited in this category. Over 60 percent of such firms were seriously handicapped by shortage of short-term credit for materials, stocks, or receivables financing, even to utilize their present plant to capacity. Around 40 percent required building finance for the degree of expansion that would be possible in the near future if the above elements of financial need were fulfilled.

Nevertheless, only about half of the promising small firms having assets below Col$200,000 were judged capable of expansion through financial counsel and improved credit alone. On the average, this group had the highest need for in-plant technical guidance on production problems: at least 60 percent of these firms had important problems in such operations as materials selection, cupola design and operation, machine utilization and maintenance, use of jigs or molds, and control of quality. Problems of layout, work simplification and scheduling, and similar problems of production management appeared equally important. Over two-thirds of these enterprises could make important improvements in their accounting systems if they were effectively assisted. Their need for market analysis on existing products was less than that of firms in the Col$200,000 to Col$499,000 asset category, but over 65 percent of the smallest growth-potential firms required guidance in correct selection of new products in order to expand to the apparent limit of their overall capacity.

Lowest priority for developmental assistance in this program was attached to the group of enterprises which possessed gross assets of over Col$1 million; this was because of the lower incidence of needs in these firms. Even though more promising firms were in this asset category than in any other single category, less than half of these firms showed both a significant need for added credit and the ability to use it effectively without other assistance. Most of the remainder had established channels of credit that were adequate for the degree of expansion which they contemplated.

Measures for Improving Small-factory Development Financing

It will be useful to turn, now that the financial needs and services in Colombia have been sketched, to the measures suggested in 1962 for transforming existing services into those more useful to stimulating small-factory development. These provide fairly comprehensive and concrete illustrations of how the principles discussed in Chapters 4 through 11 may be applied in a specific situation. The main elements of the program suggested for Colombia are reviewed below.[14]

[14] By 1965, some implementation of the basic suggestions had been achieved and efforts were continuing. Implementation, however, suffered a heavy setback soon after the program was drawn up by an announcement of the newly elected government of a plan to transform the Banco Popular into a "Workers' Bank" (Banco Obrero). Although this plan was not put into effect, it prevented the bank from obtaining assistance for which it was negotiating from the United States AID program and suspended for some time progress in instituting changes in the bank which were essential to improving its capacity for extending development financing to small manufacturers.

Need for an Integrated Program

A variety of things which aid in small-industry development are being done now by public, quasi-public, and private agencies. But in nearly all these fields the existing services are not as widely available as they need to be for effective nationwide development of small-industry, or they are in practice more oriented toward large firms, or the small industrialists do not know about them and have no adequate means of learning how to make use of them. Also, there are certain kinds of economic and technical guidance and certain kinds of financial services needed by small industrialists which are almost totally lacking. Furthermore, the assistance which is available (at least potentially) comes from scattered sources and in uncoordinated form, with the result that each type of help is less effective because of the absence of other supplementary kinds.

What is needed is a more comprehensive approach to small-industry development which emphasizes certain key elements and fills certain gaps. The lack of one or two elements can impair the effectiveness of otherwise good developmental work. For example, excellent technical advice may be wasted if the small industrialist cannot get capital to install a required machine. Or a loan may be useless or even harmful if the recipient is producing the wrong product because of lack of sound economic advice, is not marketing properly, or is failing to maintain quality because of some technological weakness.

The requisites for accomplishing these needs are chiefly:

1. An agreed program of action, reflecting a clear sense of direction and of the policies and methods required for moving in the desired direction;
2. An effective development-oriented organization for maintaining close contact with small industrialists and for integrating the aids available from other cooperating and supporting organizations;
3. Specially trained and devoted staff in this organization and in the cooperating and supporting organizations;
4. Funds to pay the costs of attracting thoroughly competent staff personnel and training them in the new methods of work.

Chart 1 shows the seven elements in the recommended program. The key elements are a Development-counseling Service and a Development-financing Program; supporting elements include industrial research, industrial training, interfirm assistance, regional development, and government policies.

Development-counseling Service

The creation of this type of service is an important first step for stimulating the expansion of small enterprises. It would be the chief instrument for bringing to a focus all the types of aid potentially available from various

CHART I

INTEGRATED PROGRAM FOR SMALL-INDUSTRY DEVELOPMENT

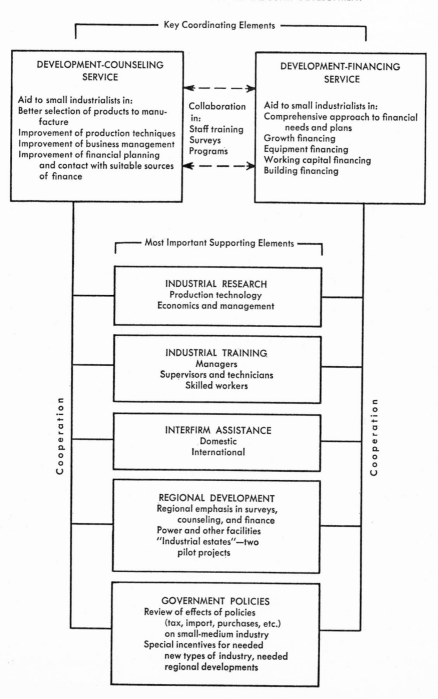

Key Coordinating Elements

DEVELOPMENT-COUNSELING SERVICE

Aid to small industrialists in:
Better selection of products to manufacture
Improvement of production techniques
Improvement of business management
Improvement of financial planning and contact with suitable sources of finance

Collaboration in:
Staff training
Surveys
Programs

DEVELOPMENT-FINANCING SERVICE

Aid to small industrialists in:
Comprehensive approach to financial needs and plans
Growth financing
Equipment financing
Working capital financing
Building financing

Most Important Supporting Elements

INDUSTRIAL RESEARCH
Production technology
Economics and management

INDUSTRIAL TRAINING
Managers
Supervisors and technicians
Skilled workers

INTERFIRM ASSISTANCE
Domestic
International

REGIONAL DEVELOPMENT
Regional emphasis in surveys, counseling, and finance
Power and other facilities
"Industrial estates"—two pilot projects

GOVERNMENT POLICIES
Review of effects of policies (tax, import, purchases, etc.) on small-medium industry
Special incentives for needed new types of industry, needed regional developments

Cooperation

Cooperation

sources to promote modernization and growth in this sector. In close co-operation with the new Development-financing Program, and drawing upon supporting services from other organizations, a well-managed service could significantly improve the environment for industrial progress.

At the end of a build-up period of several years, the Development-counseling Service should be operating service centers in some 6 to 10 locations throughout Colombia. It should everywhere cooperate closely with existing regional and local institutions, even in some cases contracting with such institutions for the actual running of the service centers, in order to avoid duplication, encourage local initiative, and develop local institutions.

Each service center would have a number of industrial counselors on its staff. Their task would be to become well acquainted with the small industrialists (existing and potential) in their district and to aid them in every feasible way—directly, and indirectly by putting them in touch with more specialized sources of aid when needed. The counselors would in this manner promote: (1) better selection of products for manufacture; (2) improvement of production techniques and production management (e.g., choice of processes and equipment, plant layout, maintenance, quality control) ; (3) improvement of commercial and business management (e.g., marketing, purchasing, accounting, personnel relations) ; and (4) improvement of financial planning and establishment of working relations with suitable sources of capital and credit (in close cooperation with the Development-financing Program).

The counselors would be men with good professional training and experience either in industrial engineering and production management or in some combination of economics, business management, and finance. They would receive supplementary training in methods of analyzing the technical, management, and financial problems of small industrial enterprises; in the planning and execution of industrial economic surveys; in the purposes and policies of the development program and the sources of aid available under it; and in the best methods of establishing relations of confidence with small and medium industrialists in order to help them adopt modern practices.

The Development-counseling Service, in collaboration with the Development-financing Program (and particularly with the proposed new program of the Banco Popular), would operate a Training and Survey Division. This would in fact, be the first part of the service to be established, before any of the centers. This division, aided in the first years by external consultants, would combine the training of staff with the carrying out of technoeconomic surveys. The first surveys would be focused on particular industries or branches of industries, with the object of analyzing their development possibilities and problems. After a fair amount of specific industrial knowledge had been assembled in this way, regional surveys would be undertaken, in order to discover the most promising opportunities for small industry in each region. Participation in several of these surveys under expert guidance, together with a certain amount of seminar work, is recommended as the best method of training counselors. Each new staff member of the Development-counseling Service, the key staff member of the Development-financing Program, and perhaps some key staff members of cooperating and supporting organizations should receive this training.

Development-financing Program

Those seeking to accelerate industrial growth by the extension of finance are confronted with three types of problems:

1. The borrower, on receiving the loan, may so rearrange the total resources available to the enterprise that the loan in effect constitutes little or no net addition to the productive capital employed;
2. The funds may constitute a net addition but without having the desired effect because (*a*) they are inadequate for minimum expansion needs, (*b*) some essential complementary element is lacking, or (*c*) the expansion opportunity envisaged is illusory or too short lived;
3. The borrower may prove unable or unwilling to repay, whether or not he expands his production.

To prevent frustration of development objectives, the screening of loans and supervision measures must be adequate to cope in a significant degree with all three types of problems. Although it would be economically impractical, if not impossible, to devise methods that would be entirely successful in preventing losses or diversion of funds, much can be done to improve conventional practices, as suggested in the following program.

The essence of the suggested financing program is that one institution devote its primary effort to meeting the major needs through a type of program which, by its comprehensive approach, will be more certain of assuring a developmental effect than do normal lending procedures. The Banco Popular might appropriately assume this responsibility.

Suggested Program for the Banco Popular

A first essential step is to equip the Banco Popular to undertake development financing of small industry. The bank would, of course, have to undergo some transformation if it is to serve this purpose. The transformation relates essentially to its basic policies, the types of applicants to be served, types of financing to be undertaken, resources, and organizational and staffing arrangements.

The bank's policies and functions would need to be clearly development-oriented, with appropriate staff and resources for this purpose. It is therefore important that the bank adopt as its primary function the financing of development of small industry and that it transfer to more appropriate institutions functions not closely related to, or which are administratively incompatible with, this objective.

The appropriate scale of enterprises to which the bank will need to give its primary attention will vary over the years, depending upon changing industrial needs, activities that other institutions are undertaking, and the resulting major gaps in the financial structure. It is recommended that the limit on the size of loan the bank should make and the size of enterprises it should serve be established along the following lines: During the initial two years, while its new program is being established, roughly 20 percent of its loans in terms of value might go to enterprises with gross assets of less than Col$200,000. Another 50 percent might go to enterprises with gross assets between Col$200,000 and Col$500,000, and the remaining 30 percent to enterprises with gross assets between Col$500,000 and Col$2 million. Primary consideration should be given, in the case of the last category, to enterprises with gross assets of less than Col$1 million, although no rigid limitations should be set in this regard.

By the end of two years, when the bank's staff and resources should have substantially improved, it should be possible to increase the share of loans going to enterprises with less than Col$200,000 to 25 or 30 percent. The share going to enterprises with assets over Col$500,000 could be decreased by an offsetting amount, since by that time the finance corporations and alternative sources of finance should be in a much better position to serve the needs of enterprises in this scale.

Even if the bank were to continue to serve enterprises of the same average size as at present, the present limits on the size of loans granted should still be raised. The developmental type of financing recommended for the bank, particularly where medium- and long-term loans are involved, will necessarily constitute a larger share of the total resources of an enterprise than has been common heretofore. Moreover, its operations become costly if many very small loans are made. The size of loan may be expected to vary according to the type of loan. The maximum loan size should in no case exceed Col$500,000 and would ordinarily, even in the case of medium-term loans, be much smaller.

The bank should serve primarily owner-managed enterprises, where the majority owners are devoting most of their time and finances to this enterprise. Enterprises controlled by larger companies or wealthy owners do not ordinarily have the special need for financing that the bank's new program is intended to serve. A limitation might therefore be set that to be eligible the majority owners should not have gross assets outside the enterprise in excess of Col$500,000.

This program will require sufficient and suitable resources. There are many reasons why the Banco Popular should not continue to place great reliance on current deposits as a source of finance for its development program. The instability of its current deposits poses special problems even for short-term lending in the case of the proposed new program. Moreover, it is important that its officers be freed from the concern with generating deposits, usual in commercial banks. Its development financing program needs to be independent of this influence if its loans are to go to enterprises now inadequately served by commercial banks. The handling of current deposits is, of course, a useful supplementary function to servicing and supervising eligible borrowers, as well as a source of short-term funds. It would be desirable, nevertheless, that this function occupy only a secondary position so that it does not exercise influence on basic bank policy.

Medium-term loans—and ultimately long-term loans—which should gradually become a major element in the Banco Popular's lending activity, will require special resources. Funds will be needed on a sufficiently stable basis so that no problem of uncertainty of resource availability for commitments can arise. Moreover, resources need to be made available in increasing volume in accordance with the need for expanding loan programs.

The Banco Popular's new program will require some alterations in its present organization and staffing. Initially, there should be set up a special training and operational unit to undertake the special growth-financing program described below. This unit is intended to be dissolved into regular divisions devoted to industrial loan analysis and supervision at the end of two years. It will also be desirable to build up gradually an advisory service on financial planning and accounting. The function of this service would be primarily to help clients set up their financial planning and accounts on a sound basis, facilitating both the growth of the enterprise and bank supervision of its finances. The bank will also need to gradually build up an economic analysis division, which will be devoted largely to keeping industrial loan officers and top management informed on industrial, monetary, and other economic trends of policy importance, particularly in respect to medium- and long-term loans.

It is essential to build up a staff with the special competence required for the new services proposed. Approximately 10 to 15 specially trained industrial loan officers will be required by the end of five years. The accounting and financial advisory service should, at its maximum, require only a few key persons—three to five—each with broad regional responsibilities. They should normally draw on private contract services where detailed services to clients are required. The economic analysis division should also consist only of a few high-level persons—three at most—who would draw on contract sources for special studies beyond their capacity.

The bank's interim growth-financing program should be designed to fill some of the more urgent gaps in financing development, in providing technical assistance to industry, and in training program staff. The program will focus on a few carefully selected firms, meeting their total needs for external finance. A consultant long experienced in this type of program will be essential to the success of the program.

While this and other immediate programs are going on, longer-term, more comprehensive, and more economical programs can be installed. These will supplement and gradually take over some of the functions assigned initially to bank staff in the growth-financing program. This will enable the bank staff to shift its concentration to analyzing the evaluations provided by other institutions, supplementing these with its own studies of the quality of management and of its finances. The bank should continue to provide financial counseling and general loan supervision, although drawing increasingly on the assistance of collaborating organizations.

It is recommended that the growth-financing program be started immediately on a pilot basis. It would be preferable to start in one of the smaller but rapidly industrializing cities such as Pereira or Bucaramanga, where the industrial, financial, and commercial communities are of a size that permits easy and close acquaintance and where, at the same time, many promising applicants for such a program exist.

Initially, it should be staffed by a consultant and four staff associates. The consultant will participate in the selection of four staff members to work with him in an operational program in which the selected staff will acquire on-the-job training in the specific techniques required for this program. The selected staff members should be seasoned, well-trained officers who, with brief guidance in these specific techniques, may graduate to senior positions in charge of industrial loan programs in major branches of the Banco Popular. Two should be graduate industrial engineers, and two should be graduates, preferably economists, with substantial specialized work in accounting and finance. Each of these persons should also have had several years of experience in industry, industrial research, or industrial finance.

At the end of three to six months of work on the first pilot center, a second similar center should be selected and the staff divided. This process of in-service training with periodic subdivision of those trained and the splicing in of new staff might continue for about two years. At the end of the second year, other programs should be sufficiently developed to undertake many of the loan evaluation and supervision functions, permitting the bank staff to assume positions as directors of Industrial Development Departments in branches or in the head office of the Banco Popular. The merging of the growth-financing program into the bank's maturing regular industrial loan operations should not result in contraction in services but in a broadening of the same service through slightly different procedures.

Under the growth-financing program, the analysis of an application by a fully trained staff should not normally require over one to two man-weeks, although initially more may be required. The objectives of the analysis are threefold: (1) to arrive at a first approximation of the abilities of management and the potentialities of the enterprise by a thorough understanding of their present situation and recent evolution; (2) to determine the major strengths and weaknesses of the enterprise and ways in which the weaknesses can be most effectively remedied and the strengths built upon in the course of an expansion program; and (3) to assist management, if otherwise eligible for financing, in formulating a program for expansion.

It will not be possible in these brief analyses, considering the limited industrial and commercial data available, to analyze markets or other aspects of the environment of the enterprise in much detail. Therefore, until industrial and other survey information becomes available from other programs, loans under this program should be limited to enterprises where markets or other external conditions are not likely to be a major uncertainty.

Also, consideration should be given in the beginning only to that fairly substantial group of enterprises found during the survey to show a strong possibility of successfully making a major expansion solely on the basis of financial assistance. Loan recipients should at the same time be industrialists who are eager to improve, even in minor ways, their plant efficiency and managerial abilities and who have the capacity for using external guidance to achieve this. They should give evidence of a potentiality, if so assisted, of being able to assume the management of an enterprise several times the size of their present one within the course of the next 5 or 10 years. A further important requirement is a willingness to reinvest profits other than a minimum provision for salary and dividends in the enterprise during the period of the loan.

The bank's counseling service, once a project has been approved, should adopt the approach of being the right hand of management, meeting "felt needs" wherever it has the competence. At the same time, it should seek to make management aware of important unrecognized needs which it has the competence to serve. Counseling must nevertheless be limited, focused on improvements easily achieved. Probably not more than an average of two additional man-weeks a year of direct counseling can be provided to each firm, and part of this will be more in the nature of ascertaining that the firm is proceeding soundly along agreed lines. As other institutional arrangements for various types of technical assistance to enterprises come into effective operation, the counselors will be able to draw on these arrangements to speed the development of the management in enterprises they are serving.

Supervision should be discreet and largely incidental to visits intended to assist management with its problems. Visits should be made no less than once quarterly to update the general appraisal of the enterprise, its progress, and its problems, and to seek out areas in which the counselor may be of assistance. These visits should also provide visual verification of information derived from analysis of accounts and other regular reports submitted by the firm.

Financing should be based on the total external requirements of the firm over a period of three years. It is to be expected, in view of the selection criteria, that additional finance, possibly in larger amounts and on longer terms, will be required for further expansion by the firm at the end of three years. Terms need to be tailored to individual firm requirements and capacity, at the same time keeping in mind(1) the need of the entrepreneur to have sufficient stake in the enterprise to be personally committed to its success and (2) the need to limit expansion to a rate at which the entrepreneur is able to adapt to the changing requirements.

Suggested Programs for Other Institutions

A bank devoting special attention to development financing of small industry, however substantial, well focused, well managed, and truly effective it may be, is not likely by itself to meet all the requirements of small enterprises. It is fortunate that in Colombia's case there are many long-established institutions with a variety of characteristics and special merits which can lend their strength to broadening the sources of financial assistance for the development of small industry.

It is not merely the extent and variety of these enterprises and their needs which make it difficult for a single institutional arrangement to serve them fully; even more, it is the dynamic and diversely changing nature of the needs of small enterprises that complicates the task. A variety of approaches supplementing each other and even overlapping in some areas gives better assurance that all types of needs will be met. The use of a variety of approaches provides the degree of competition between different institutions needed to stimulate the maintenace by each of a high standard of service. It builds into the system a readiness to meet new contingencies or previously small requirements which have since grown large. It greatly simplifies the task of the institution with the primary responsibility by permitting it to focus its efforts more narrowly in the beginning and thus enhancing the probability of its success. This approach of drawing on many institutions is the more necessary because of the volatile conditions of developing countries. It will give the Banco Popular at least a brief time to expand its experience and to experiment in a modest way with bolder programs holding promise of breaking through the difficult institutional barriers inhibiting adequate financing for the development of small and medium enterprises.

A few of the possibilities for strengthening other important institutions are explored below. These and other possibilities need to be examined and elaborated through the joint effort of the Banco Popular, the Development-counseling Service, relevant government bodies, and, of course, the institutions in question.

Private Finance Corporations

The four finance corporations each give some attention to small or medium enterprise. It seems likely that there will be some overlap between the enterprises eligible for finance under the new program of the Banco Popular and under those of the finance corporations. This is as it should be. There are a number of factors which will limit the ability of the finance corporations to serve those enterprises eligible under the Banco Popular program. In the case of smaller firms, travel costs and related problems (in analyzing or supervising firms) will tend to restrict the distance from their offices at which it will be practical to service applicants. Secondly, although each of the finance corporations is adopting a somewhat different course, the present tendency is to concentrate largely on enterprises that can provide substantial guarantees and submit detailed projects. The smaller enterprises which the corporations are able to serve thus tend to be those owned by persons with substantial personal resources or exceptional financial connections. Many, especially the rapidly growing small enterprises, will not be able to meet either the guarantee or project requirements.

Another limiting factor on the scope of operations of the corporations among small enterprises is the need of many of the latter for detailed assistance in programming their expansion and for at least occasional guidance in its implementation. Although the corporations are building up technical staffs for project analysis, the counseling which they will be able to extend to applicants or loan recipients will probably never be very large. The problem is essentially one of cost and the fact that the finance corporations, particularly the two in Bogotá and Medellín, are expected by their shareholders to more or less maximize profits. Although they have already undertaken some loans to smaller enterprises and indicate an intention to continue to give some attention to such enterprises, in the long run the natural concern of shareholders to maximize dividends might be expected to limit such operations to types and amounts that do not cut heavily into the profit potentials.

The activity of the corporations in serving small industry should be given every possible encouragement. Making available to them funds that are restricted to loans to enterprises of a specified maximum size, along the lines of the present Inter-American Development Bank loans to the Corporación Financiera Colombiana, is undoubtedly a useful approach which might be more widely applied. The establishment of an exchange insurance fund along the lines suggested below for the proposed Banco Cafetero equipment financing program might enable greater international funds to be channeled through these corporations. The authority to make medium-term working capital loans to growing concerns with expanded working capital needs could be helpful. As firms with such needs often also need better financial planning and as the supervision of the use of such funds is fairly difficult, the corporations would need at the same time to arrange with other institutions for the necessary counseling and supervision.

Caja de Crédito Agraria, Industrial y Minero

The Caja Agraria has branches in probably every town where even a small nucleus of industry has begun. Although it finances primarily agriculture, it has given some attention to very small industrial enterprises. It might be appropriate, therefore, for the Caja Agraria to initiate a program along lines similar to those of the Banco Popular but keyed more to enterprises located in towns smaller than the ones in which the Banco Popular can afford to maintain branches. It might also similarly service all enterprises that fall below or in the lower ranges of the scale that the Banco Popular's program is designed to assist. The Caja Agraria's experience in financing agriculture as well as its past program for very small industry should give it some preparation for the task of financing workshops and very small factories. Its maximum loan size will need to be considerably increased, and its lending procedures will need to undergo major changes along the lines suggested for the Banco Popular.

The Banco Cafetero

The present program for financing equipment imports on a medium-term basis administered by the Banco Cafetero for the Federación de Cafeteros provides an excellent foundation for a much broader program. Already a number of small enterprises have acquired imported equipment on generally satisfactory financial terms through the Banco Cafetero's assistance. Moreover, the Banco Cafetero has acquired experience and competence in administering this type of program.

To expand the impact of the program, special attention might be given to channeling financing of imported equipment to small and medium industry. The need of this sector for special equipment finance, particularly in the case of foreign equipment, is undoubtedly much greater than among larger enterprises. A substantial proportion of such finance and of staff time might be set aside for applicants for small industry. Special assistance in preparing applications, selection of equipment, arranging for transport and import will in many cases be necessary, particularly in the case of very small enterprises. This will be a logical function for the Development-counseling Service once it is established. In the interim it might be the most expedient solution if the Banco Cafetero assigned special personnel in each of its branches to carry out this function. Such staff also might serve a public relations function of making better known among small and medium industrialists the existence of the program, the nature and conditions of the service available, and the countries from which equipment could be obtained.

The program administered by the Banco Cafetero might also be broadened in another respect. If the number of countries from which equipment could be obtained were increased, the program would be of substantially greater value for some types of equipment. Partly, this expansion may be obtained along present lines under barter or compensation agreements. However, in countries where such arrangements are not likely to be made, alternative arrangements for securing the import of equipment without exchange risk to the buyer and on medium-term credit might be considered.

Possibly the Banco Cafetero could establish a similar program with countries such as the United States, Germany, and the United Kingdom under which equipment would be financed, on medium term, by a semiofficial institution in the exporting country (e.g., the Export-Import Bank in the United States). The exchange risk might be eliminated by sharing it between three parties:

1. An insurance fund financed by the addition of two or three points to the interest rate on the loan. This would also serve to discourage the importation of equipment if domestic sources were available.
2. The exporting country, through a special government fund (e.g., one established by AID in the United States) might bear half of any risk not covered by the insurance fund. This would be justifiable in the exporting country (a) as a general aid measure to developing countries, (b) in recognition of the partial responsibility of industrialized countries for the pattern of exchange rates in developing countries, and (c) in the interest of encouraging its own exports.
3. The final half of any risk not covered by the insurance fund should be covered by a Colombian government agency. This would be justifiable in Colombia in view of the national responsibility for the determination of future exchange rates and in the interest of stimulating general development.

For small industry, a higher but certain cost is a minor problem compared with the burden imposed by uncertainty arising from loans in foreign exchange.[15]

Instituto de Fomento Industrial (IFI)

The Instituto de Fomento Industrial in the past concentrated primarily on large industry. However, its studies in identifying investment prospects and preparing projects have been in some cases relevant to medium-scale enterprises. It is also a participant in the Fondo de Santander, which has financed small- as well as medium-scale enterprises. The IFI is in the process of assessing its programs and possible resources with a view to recharting its objectives and programs in the years ahead. There are two areas in which the IFI appears uniquely equipped to fill important gaps in the program for assisting small and medium industry.

One such area is the fostering of export industries. This is already among the basic functions which IFI has adopted, although as yet it has little exercised this function. The IFI is also already organized and staffed in some degree to provide the comprehensive type of assistance required. The assistance of the Colombian Federation of Exporters, which is largely

---

[15] This problem has been greatly underlined since this study by the decline in the value of the peso from 9 to 18 pesos to 1 United States dollar between 1962 and 1965. The cost of the insurance arrangements to the two governments, however, would have been much higher than anticipated at the time the recommendation was made, in view of the rapid change in exchange rates.

financed by the IFI, would also probably be readily available to supplement the IFI's activity. Over the long run, the growth and even survival of many of Colombia's small and medium enterprises may depend on their ability to export. The recent formation of the Latin American Free Trade Area enhances this possibility. The potentiality of small industries to make major contributions to exports is illustrated by Japan's experience, which also illustrates the extensive and varied types of assistance that enterprises, especially the smaller ones, require to become successfully established in export operations.

A program of assistance to export industries would require the collaboration of various other government agencies which the IFI might be in suitable position to obtain, i.e., the assistance of Colombian consulates in the collection of market information abroad, the assistance of custom authorities in expediting the return of duties paid on imported requirements for producing export goods, and the assistance of appropriate authorities in negotiating tariff exemptions with other countries for potential export industries. Assistance to enterprises in arranging marketing connections abroad, in export financing, and in both attaining requisite standards of quality and in establishing a system for assuring foreign buyers of this standard are other important types of service which would be important. The high initial cost per enterprise of this assistance could be minimized by concentrating this function in one agency such as the IFI, which could build on each experience in extending similar assistance to other enterprises. The program would nevertheless need to be regarded as a long-run investment basic to the country's future growth and thus appropriately financed out of government revenues.

Another activity which the IFI might be in an advantageous position to undertake, especially because of the activity's relation to export assistance, is assisting enterprises to locate and to arrange licensing and partnership agreements with enterprises abroad. The type of activity required is not only similar to the foregoing, but many of the firms requiring the assistance may be the same ones requiring assistance to engage in export operations. Few owners of small enterprises have the opportunity of the wide international contact needed even to become aware of the often large possibilities that exist. The value of such arrangements in improving production technology is illustrated in the clothing and many other industries in Colombia; the need for guidance on the limitations and alternatives of such arrangements is also illustrated by a number of ill-advised arrangements. It will thus be important to identify the sources and possibilities of such assistance abroad, to interest the enterprises abroad in concluding desirable types of arrangements, and to advise and assist local enterprises in concluding advantageous agreements.

In both export and licensing assistance, the IFI contributions might be strengthened by collaboration with the finance corporations and commercial banks, particularly with the foreign banks; the close connections of these institutions with private enterprises and institutions abroad could provide a valuable addition to the IFI's own special resources.

The Banco Central Hipotecario

Under present arrangements, some savings or long-term investment funds, such as insurance funds, are channeled to the financing of industrial buildings through the Banco Central Hipotecario. Very little of these funds benefits small industry. This is partly because the procedure is time-consuming and difficult for small firms to comply with. It is also partly because insurance companies have less interest in supplying funds for loans to small firms, since these firms are not normally important policy holders or potential borrowers of large sums. This source of funds, however, could be made to be of service to small industry.

To do so, it would probably be necessary to open a special division in Banco Central Hipotecario which would handle only loans for small industry. Alternatively, the Banco Popular could be authorized to carry out the same type of operation for small industry now performed by the Banco Central Hipotecario for industry generally. Under the present system, the selection of borrowers, in practice, appears to be made in two stages: first, approval must be obtained from the insurance company; second, approval must be obtained from the Banco Central Hipotecario. There seems to be little merit in the first screening, and some harm in the case of small industry, since insurance companies may favor important policy holders or oversell insurance coverage. As the insurance company assumes no risk, there is little need for its intervention in the selection process. The administering banking institution might therefore assume the responsibility for seeking out funds for all clients as lending opportunities arise. As soon as the Development-counseling Service comes into full operation it might be requested to assist in processing loan applications by providing, on a contract basis, preliminary appraisals of small concerns as to their collateral, technical ability, economic outlook, and developmental importance. This will greatly expedite loan application processing and will assure that applications of all eligible concerns possible receive due consideration.

Commercial Banks

Commercial banks are a basic source of external finance for small industry. With the proper incentives, their contribution might be much larger than it is. Aside from the many important services that the Development-counseling Service can render to commercial banks as well as to other financial institutions, several additional approaches might induce and facilitate a greater participation by commercial banks in financing small industry.

Credit insurance programs have been found useful in many countries for inducing banks to lend to small enterprises. Such programs require some government assistance but should not provide for a transference of all risks to government or an effective elimination of the responsibility for loan application screening on the part of the lender.

An adequate system of credit information interchange between financial institutions is basic to enabling banks to broaden their lending activities to include entrepreneurs who are unable to provide a high ratio of property guarantees for loans and who, at the same time, are not personally well known to bank management. It is recommended that the Asociación Bancaria and the Banco de la República take such measures as are necessary to bring about the establishment of a fully adequate system for the exchange of credit information.

Central banking and monetary policies have not been studied in detail, but partial information acquired in the survey suggests that general banking practices might be improved if a number of policies were revised:

1. Interest rates. The whole rate structure needs to be reexamined to determine if the incentives intended by rate differences are having the desired effect. For example, banks appear to have nearly ceased discounting bills receivable, because more favorable rates can be earned on lending against notes of six months or more, guaranteed by bills. Because the discounting of bills is normally a simple and economical procedure, it can usually be a valuable credit form for meeting very short term needs on an economical basis.

   Another case that appears worth investigating is the 8 percent rate set on loans under decree No. 384 of 1950. This relatively low rate probably plays no role in stimulating companies to expand, since the uncertainties of new investments far outweigh a few percentage points in the cost of finance. It is enough, however, to induce companies, particularly large ones, to seek to utilize this source for expected needs rather than more expensive sources. It thus may provide incentives for ineligible borrowers to misrepresent their qualifications without being of special stimulus to expand production. A rate comparable to or higher than the current short-term rate might serve the objective better.

   One further example of interest policy worth reexamining is the wide margin that banks are able to earn on loans out of current deposits, since the latter bear no interest and may be lent on simple procedures for undefined purposes so long as repayment is certain. The return made on loans for special development purposes appears to be much less. If this is true, banks can be expected to prefer the former, a part of which may go to inflationary or nondevelopmental purposes.

2. The incentives and controls under decrees No. 384 of 1950 and No. 1790 of 1960 do not appear to be as effective as they might be. The net expansions of loans for the objectives intended may, on careful study, prove to be quite limited. Present regulations seem to be a cause for delay in issuing such loans as are being made.[16]

[16] A well-informed private commercial banker in Colombia has suggested that tighter credit conditions since 1962 have further reduced commercial bank interest in serving

3. In-plant financing is discouraged by present regulations. The policies encouraging warehouse loans may also contribute to the scarcity of in-plant financing. As this is normally one of the more economical and convenient forms of credit for some types of enterprises, it may be helpful to reexamine these policies and regulations.

Industrial Research Services

Beyond counseling and finance, the next most urgent area where special services are important to small-industry development is industrial research, both technological and economics-management research. A Development-counseling Service must have research support, and a Development-financing Program will be much sounder if allied with good industrial research.

The Development-counseling Service and the Development-financing Program therefore need to maintain close working relationships with the several organizations in Colombia that are doing valuable work in various aspects of industrial research. It is highly desirable to strengthen their facilities and to help them make their services more widely available, especially to small industrialists who cannot usually afford to undertake research within their own firms. Contracts could be entered into with these research organizations, in appropriate cases, for research services required to guide and assist the small-industry development effort.

It is also important for the Development-counseling Service to recruit and train its own staff to make technoeconomic surveys, to analyze the problems of small firms, and to carry on continuous analyses, national and regional, designed to discover very specific new industrial opportunities for small industry and to orient each region toward its most promising lines of industrial development.

Industrial Training Services

One of the most important factors in industrial advancement is development of personnel—competent, well trained, well motivated, and able and eager to apply the best modern methods. Such personnel are needed for overall management, for supervisory and technical positions, and as skilled workers in plants and offices. They are needed by small industry as well as large industry, but small firms are less able than large firms to provide for the training of their own personnel by in-service training courses, by sending selected employees abroad, and similar means. Therefore, it is particularly important for the modernization and growth of small industry that appropriate training be widely available through agencies that serve the whole community. The Development-counseling Service can be of great

---

small manufacturing to such an extent that unless regulations provide for earmarking a specific share of bank funds for loans to small industrialists, the latter are unlikely to receive adequate financing. This may well be true, although in 1962 the author believed that less drastic and less controversial measures should be attempted first.

assistance to these programs in identifying entrepreneurs and subject matter deserving priority and in following up with further assistance after the foundations of basic training have been laid.

Interfirm Assistance

ANDI, ACOPI, FEDEMETAL, FEPOCOL, and other industrial and trade associations, in cooperation with the Development-counseling Service and the Development-financing Program (or even in advance of the establishment of these) might usefully launch an organized campaign to promote closer working relations between large-scale and small and medium manufacturing firms. Specific information should be assembled on the kinds of items which large firms need to purchase from outside suppliers and on the manufacturing capabilities (existing and potential) of the small firms. This information should be exchanged, and the large firms should be persuaded to take a positive interest in seeking out capable smaller firms with which to place "educational" orders for parts or supplies. They should combine with these orders such technical and even financial help as might be required to develop high-quality and low-cost sources of regular supply, thus benefiting themselves, the smaller producers, and the industrial growth of the country.

The Development-counseling Service and the Development-financing Program could establish, in cooperation with the Instituto de Fomento Industrial and other organizations interested in international assistance and connections for Colombian industry, a special liaison service by which small industrialists can be brought into contact with reliable firms abroad and can be aided to work out mutually advantageous arrangements for provision of technical know-how and, if desired, for capital investment on a joint-venture basis. Large firms are able to locate such opportunities and make arrangements on their own; small and medium firms could in many cases benefit by similar arrangements but need help and advice.

Regional Development

It is important that the activities of the Development-counseling Service and the Development-financing Program be regionalized and localized. They cannot be effective unless they respond sensitively to local needs and opportunities. There should also be strong regional emphasis on the industrial surveys which will guide the counseling and financing programs, and special surveys should be undertaken to discover the most promising opportunities for industrial development in particular regions.

In some localities the field inquiries showed that lack of electric energy is a real handicap to further industrial development. Until additional power facilities are installed, adequate to serve existing industry and some new undertakings, it would be a waste of effort to mount an intensive campaign to foster further industrial expansion. High priority should be given to remedying already known lacks of electric power facilities (or transport, water, and other needed industrial facilities) in those localities where this would open the way to promising industrial development. The Development-counseling Service and the Development-financing Program should also concern themselves with carrying out, either on their own initiative or more probably through other appropriate agencies, realistic studies of the probable future needs for power and other industrial facilities in all of the most promising industrial centers—to be followed by timely action.

Pilot experiments need to be undertaken in the use of a potentially valuable tool of small-industry development and of community planning: the *industrial estate*.

Government Policies

An appropriate agency of the government should undertake a careful review of the effects of government policies, regulations, and procedures which impinge in one way or another on small industry, particularly from the point of view of the way they affect the modernization and growth of existing enterprises and the establishment of new enterprises. The Development-counseling Service and the Development-financing Program, after they have been functioning for some time, will be able to contribute useful information to such a review. But it is not advisable to delay the review until that time; rather, such a review should be repeated from time to time.

Particular attention should be given to: (1) various ways in which import and export policies, regulations, and formalities impinge on the operations of small industrial firms and the possibilities of simplifying procedures that unduly discourage small (but potentially growing) transactions, especially on the export side; (2) the extent to which government purchasing procedures offer convenient opportunities for small industrial firms to enter bids and the extent to which payments for government purchases might be made more promptly, in order to ease the strain on the working capital of the supplying firms and thus remove one obstacle to the expansion of their operations; (3) the effects of tax policies and procedures on small and medium enterprises, and especially on their ability to grow by plowing back earnings.

The national government and also departmental and local governments should explore various incentives which might be offered to encourage desired kinds of industrial growth, especially: (1) the starting of new types of industrial production which studies show to hold definite promise but which have not yet been undertaken in Colombia and (2) the introduction of promising types of industrial enterprise into particular areas where, for good policy reasons, it is desired to make special development effort. In any such incentive program it is important to be highly selective. Lists of desired new industries, based on careful studies, might be prepared and kept up to date.

However, it is important to think carefully about the kinds of incentives offered. Some types will have more positive developmental effects than others. Incentives that take the form of shielding a firm from competition, or granting it a money subsidy, or exempting it from taxes paid by other firms help the particular firm at the expense of other firms or of the general community. They may encourage the speculator, who is looking for a quick profit, rather than the long-range builder of an industry which will be self-sustaining and permanent. They involve rather arbitrary decisions which grant special favors and, therefore, are difficult to administer equitably and may even be a temptation to corruption. Exemption from taxes lessens the public revenues available for public facilities needed by all industry and by the general community. On the other hand, alert national, regional, and local authorities can devise other types of incentives which will be much more positively developmental—that is, they aid the particular firm by helping it to become more productive. This increases the national product at the same time that it increases the firm's profits. Among such incentives are market surveys and technical research services made available free or at nominal cost, suitable factory premises (perhaps in industrial estates) for lease at reasonable rates, aid in finding needed financing, and aid in finding and training a suitable work force.

Chapter 13
Japan[1]

JAPAN IS, IN many respects, one of the more highly industrialized countries in the world today. In 1962, for example, Japan derived 30 percent of its national production from manufacturing as compared with 29 percent in the United States and 35 percent in the United Kingdom. Its world leadership in the manufacture of some new and technically complex products is widely recognized.

It is nevertheless also true that Japan has not yet achieved the income levels of the most industrially advanced nations, although its per capita

[1] This study was largely carried out in 1961 and 1962, but some updating has been possible as the result of a brief trip to Japan in 1965. In preparing this chapter, the author was assisted by investigations carried out under his direction by the Osaka Prefectural Government Institute of Economic Research (IER) during the last half of 1961. The IER conducted interviews with 128 small manufacturers in six lines of industry (lighting fixtures, screws, plastic molding, men's socks, brocade, and ceramics) in the prefectures of Osaka, Fukuoka, Kyoto, and Aichi. Lending institutions and government agencies were also surveyed, primarily in Tokyo and Osaka and in the prefectures of Fukuoka, Toyama, Gumma, Shuzuoka, and Yamaguchi.

The author is indebted to Mr. Ichiro Oshikawa, secretary-general of the Asian Productivity Organization, for facilitating arrangements with the IER, and to Mr. Tsutomu Nakamura and his associates at IER and collaborating organizations who conducted these investigations. Mr. Nakamura, now a professor of economics at Nanzen University in Nagoya, has also been kind enough to review this draft and to offer suggestions on interpretations and qualitative judgments.

The author is also very much indebted to Mr. Yoh Kikukawa, now chief of the Loan Department of the Small Business Finance Corporation's Osaka Branch, who assisted in planning the study in 1961 while an international fellow at Stanford Research Institute, and provided invaluable assistance to the author in fieldwork and revisions carried out in 1965. Similar assistance was generously provided by Mikio Abe and other members of the Nomura Research Institute, both while at SRI for advanced training and during fieldwork in Japan. The author is, of course, solely responsible for any errors or omissions in the findings presented here.

income has been rising rapidly and was equivalent to US$450 in 1962. Its accumulated capital in industrial plant and equipment is only about one-fifth of that of the United States on a per capita basis.[2] About 45 percent of its manufacturing output in 1961 was produced by firms having less than 300 employees. A great many of these small firms employ relatively little equipment and outdated methods as compared with the producers of similar products in the older industrial nations.

Financing the growth and modernization of small factories has been a matter of special concern to the Japanese since the 1930s, but most especially since World War II. Japan's already highly advanced banking system was further modernized in the postwar period and given an enlarged role in the economy. A small part of United States reconstruction funds were earmarked for smaller enterprises, giving further impetus and capability for reviving and improving programs for financing small-factory development. Japan's extensive testing of diverse program measures for stimulating small-factory development during the past 10 to 15 years and the similarity of some of its small-factory financing problems to those of newly industrializing countries makes Japan's experience of particular interest.

The Postwar Japanese Economy

Japan is a densely populated island economy of 95 million persons (1962) which must trade to support its present population. Having lost its colonies as well as nearly half of its industrial plants and equipment during the war, it had an urgent postwar need to develop new means of production and new trade relationships. A concerted development effort supported by a high and rising rate of investment—18 percent of gross national product went into gross domestic fixed capital formation in 1955 and 34 percent in 1962—has increased real national output by an average of over 10 percent per annum in the decade 1951 to 1961. Exports have also been expanded by an average of over 10 percent per annum, and in 1962 they represented 13 percent of gross national product. Trade relationships have been developed with a wide variety of countries, the most important partner being the United States, which took 28 percent of Japan's exports and supplied 32 percent of its imports in 1962. Approximately 90 percent of exports are manufactured goods ranging from traditional exports such as textiles (12 percent of exports in 1962) to newer types of exports such as machinery and transport equipment (25 percent).

The major restraint on postwar growth has been periodic balance-of-payments crises, which since 1952 have been overcome primarily through mone-

---

[2] Equipment investment per worker in Japanese manufacturing enterprises employing over 30 workers averaged $636 in 1960 (*Industrial Statistics,* Ministry of International Trade and Industry, 1961). Equipment investment per worker in manufacturing enterprises in the United States in 1960 was $2,934 (*Statistical Abstract of the United States,* 1962).

tary measures. The effectiveness of monetary measures has been strengthened by postwar policies which have facilitated and in some degree compelled greater dependence by industry on bank credit.[3] Interest rates have been set at high (although gradually declining) levels. The tightening of credit to cope with periodic balance-of-payments problems has manifested itself primarily in a reduced availability of credit, particularly for smaller enterprises.

Because of the foregoing conditions, Japan's efforts to improve the credit facilities for small enterprises have had two principal objectives: (1) to mitigate the effect of periodic restrictive monetary measures on the output of small enterprises; and (2) to assist and stimulate them through better credit facilities to modernize and enlarge their production capabilities. Measures have been taken to improve the credit facilities for small enterprises generally—commercial and service as well as industrial enterprises, artisan as well as factory enterprises. Small factories, however, are a sector on which many measures have concentrated, and it is with these that we will be primarily concerned here.

Characteristics of Japan's Small Factories

There are nearly 129,000 manufacturing enterprises in Japan employing between 10 and 299 workers. About 72 percent of these employ less than 30 workers, and most of the rest, less than 100 workers. In terms of employ-

[3] Sixty-two percent of Japanese corporate investments in the period 1954–1957 were estimated to be financed from external sources, primarily banks, as compared with 26 percent for American corporations in the same period. Banks in Japan accounted for between 48 and 57 percent of the external sources of industrial funds in this period as compared with less than 10 percent from 1934 to 1936. See Hugh Talbot Patrick, *The Bank of Japan: A Case Study in the Effectiveness of Central Bank Techniques of Monetary Control*, doctoral dissertation, University of Michigan, 1960, pp. 105–107.

Table 3. Small Manufacturing Enterprises in Japan, 1961

Size of enterprise by number of workers	Manufacturing enterprises		Employment		Value added	
	Number	Percent	Number (in thousands)	Percent	Amount (in millions of US dollars)*	Percent
10 to 29	92,773	72.1	1,677	35.2	2,047	26.6
30 to 99	29,312	22.8	1,743	36.6	2,806	36.5
100 to 299	6,534	5.1	1,343	28.2	2,831	36.9
Total	128,619	100.0	4,763	100.0	7,684	100.0

* All data in this report which have been converted from yen to dollars are converted at 360 yen per one United States dollar.

SOURCE: Ministry of International Trade and Industry (MITI), *Statistics of Manufacturing Industries.*

ment and output, enterprises in the three subcategories—10 to 29, 30 to 99, and 100 to 299 employees—are each of roughly equal importance. Although all three categories have been growing, the relative importance of the smallest has been declining.

Taken together, enterprises employing from 10 to 299 workers account for 54 percent of the total manufacturing employment and 42 percent of the value added in manufacturing in 1961. Another 14 percent of manufacturing employment and 3 percent of value added are accounted for by enterprises employing less than 10 workers. The remaining 32 percent of employment and 55 percent of value added are accounted for by enterprises employing 300 workers or more. Manufacturing is one of the most rapidly expanding sectors of the Japanese economy and accounted in 1963 for 30 percent of net national output.

Small manufacturing enterprises are of special importance in Japan as a major source of exports and exchange earnings, the expansion of which is critical to Japan's growth. They are estimated to have accounted for slightly less than half of Japan's total exports in the prewar period; their share was increased to somewhat over half during the 1950s but declined toward 50 percent in recent years.[4] This is exclusive of the many small-industry products which are incorporated as components in other exported goods.

The postwar task of reviving and expanding the exports of small manufacturing enterprises was made more difficult by Japan's loss of its special position in the previously important Chinese market and by the rising competition in textiles and other traditional exports. It thus became important to help small enterprises to modernize and diversify as well as to expand. New products and higher quality standards were required to sell to the United States and other markets where Japan's postwar export opportunities were the greatest.

In the early postwar period, Japan's small manufacturing firms relied primarily on labor-intensive methods and were able to employ labor at much lower wages than those paid by larger enterprises. During most of the 1950s, the average monthly wages paid by manufacturers employing between 30 and 99 workers was only 55 to 60 percent as high as those employing over 500 workers. Average wages in firms employing less than 30 employees were even lower, and those in firms employing 100 to 299

---

[4] The share of exports of manufactured goods accounted for by enterprises employing less than 200 persons was estimated at around 48 percent in the prewar period. In 1952, their share was 45 percent but rose steadily in subsequent years to a peak of 56 percent in 1956; the share has gradually fallen since then to 51 percent for 1963. Enterprises employing between 200 and 300 workers may have accounted for another 10 percent of manufactured goods exports. The recent decline in the share is principally explained by the more rapid growth of exports in lines in which large enterprises predominate. (Data provided by the Smaller Enterprise Agency, Ministry of International Trade and Industry, Government of Japan.)

workers were between 60 and 70 percent of the average in firms employing over 500.[5]

Productivity, however, was also low because of reliance on labor-intensive methods.[6] Major changes were needed to enable these firms to meet Japan's postwar production needs, particularly in exports. One of the first requirements, mechanization, involved (1) large investments, which the owners often could not afford and which banks could not extend on the basis of past profit records; (2) the adoption of production and marketing methods new to management; and (3) the training of some workers and the displacement of others. The rapid postwar growth of the general economy and special government measures facilitated these changes.

By 1960, a change in the labor situation intensified the need for more efficient and capital-intensive production methods—the labor market had become so tight that wages in Japan's small enterprises were rapidly catching up with those in larger firms. Wages in manufacturing enterprises employing 10 to 99 workers rose by 9.1 percent in 1960 as compared with 3.4 percent in firms employing 1,000 or more workers.[7] The ratio of wages in firms employing 30 to 99 workers to those in firms employing over 500 climbed from 56 percent in 1959 to 69 percent in 1963.[8]

Other major characteristics of Japan's small factories which have an important bearing on their financing are the special nature of interbusiness relationships in Japan and the major changes taking place in these relationships during the postwar period. It may be sufficient to mention these here as they will be further discussed in the section on interbusiness financing.

Government Policy on Small Industry

The Japanese government in close cooperation with the business community has for many years been engaged in a concerted effort to speed up the industrialization and general modernization of the Japanese economy. Special policies for smaller enterprises became important only in the 1930s.[9] The Central Bank for Commercial and Industrial Cooperatives was formed in 1936, the Tokyo Credit Guarantee Association in 1937,

[5] JPC, *Small Business in Japan,* p. 17, and Small Business Finance Corporation, *Present State of Small Business Financing in Japan,* 1960 edition, p. 4.

[6] "Capital Structure by Firm Size," *Economic Bulletin* No. 6, Government of Japan, Economic Research Institute, 1961.

[7] SBFC, *op. cit.,* p. 5.

[8] The Japan Development Bank, *Facts and Figures on the Japanese Economy,* Tokyo, 1964, p. 122.

[9] For a brief resumé in English of the financial problems of small enterprises in Japan which led up to earlier assistance measures, see T. Yamanaka, "Historical Sketch of Japanese Small-Medium Industries," *Symposium on Small Business Development,* vol. III, Asian Productivity Organization, Tokyo, 1964. For a more detailed account, see Hisashi Matsuzaki, *Study of the Financing of Small Industries in Japan,* 1928 (in Japanese).

and an official bank to make petty loans in 1937. The main concern initially was with artisans and small businesses suffering from their decreasing ability to compete with larger and better-equipped enterprises employing modern techniques.

In the postwar period, the need to restore production by the most rapid means possible and to implement a policy of reducing the dominance of business by a few large companies led to increasing stress being placed on assisting both small- and medium-size enterprises. Policy has been directed toward assisting a broad group of enterprises usually defined to include: commercial and service enterprises employing up to 30 workers, manufacturing enterprises employing up to 300 workers, and mining enterprises employing up to 1,000 workers. In the case of lending programs, small business is defined to include enterprises with a share capital of less than 10 million yen (¥) (about US$28,000) or since August, 1963, of less than ¥50 million (about US$139,000).[10] Programs continue to have responsibility for artisans, retail shops, and other very small types of business enterprises. Increasing emphasis, however, has been given in the postwar period to serving modern types of enterprises with growth potential, particularly in manufacturing, and measures and institutions designed to serve the particular needs characteristic of these types of enterprises have been introduced.

One of the earliest postwar measures was the Antitrust Law of 1947 which restricted the formation of trusts and cartels but exempted from these provisions cooperatives and associations formed by smaller enterprises. In the same year the prefectural governments began extending counseling services primarily to small and medium enterprises. Some special provisions for financing smaller enterprises were also made by the Reconstruction Finance Bank, which operated from 1947 to 1952. Special funds for loans to small enterprises were also made available to other banks by the Bank of Japan from 1948 to 1955. The actual amounts of assistance extended through these measures were small, but they helped to some extent to offset the decreased availability to small enterprises of internal and interbusiness sources of finance brought about by fiscal and monetary measures taken during this period to curb inflation.

The establishment of the Smaller Enterprise Agency under the Ministry of International Trade and Industry in 1948 provided an organizational base for a more concerted effort to assist small enterprises.[11] It was given specific responsibilities for gathering and analyzing information and formu-

[10] Enterprises are eligible for financing if they can qualify on the basis of either employment or capital. The share capital of a small Japanese firm is usually less than one-third or one-fourth of its total resources.

[11] This organization is most commonly designated in English as the Smaller Enterprise Agency, although various designations, including the Small Business Administration, are sometimes used. A literal translation would be the Medium-Small Enterprise Agency.

lating and implementing policies and measures for stimulating the development of small enterprises.

The SEA has a staff of 167 persons (1965) about equally divided between three main functions: research, planning, and industrial promotion and assistance. It operates principally at the research planning and policy formulation level. Although it has engaged in direct implementation of policies and measures in some degree, for the most part it has relied upon assisting other existing organizations or upon creating new organizations to carry out and administer the operational aspects of special assistance measures. Thus it has aided and guided the formation of cooperatives and has helped formulate and enforce cooperative legislation. It has provided grants and informational assistance to prefectural, municipal, and other local government and business associations to enable them to carry out management consulting and special financing programs. It has helped bring into existence special lending institutions and to induce and enable existing ones to improve their financial services to small enterprises. The budget of the Smaller Enterprise Agency in fiscal 1965 amounted to ¥22 billion—about US$60 million and nearly double the budget for 1963. Most of these funds were reallocated to other agencies for special loan programs.[12]

The adoption and rapid implementation by the Japanese government of a complex of interacting measures in the postwar period and the continuous improvement of measures in the light of experience have been greatly facilitated by the broad and continuing analytical work of the Smaller Enterprise Agency and by its having the staff, funds, and some authority to bring about the implementation of new policies and measures its investigations have found are needed. The Smaller Enterprise Agency has also achieved a greater degree of coordination than would otherwise have prevailed among the various organizations responsible for extending financial and other assistance to small enterprises. The coordination, however, has been primarily at the upper levels on broad policy matters. At the operating level, the financial counseling and other services extended by different organizations are not as yet closely coordinated or integrated.

Government policies on assisting the development of small enterprises have been expressed primarily through measures intended to strengthen them (1) organizationally, (2) technologically, or (3) financially. Even the first two types of measures have some bearing on finance, particularly in their effect on the availability of internal funds and interbusiness financing and will be further referred to in these discussions. Measures adding to or improving the sources of finance are, of course, of direct and primary interest here and will be elaborated further in the discussion of the various sources of finance.

[12] Information provided by the SEA. Of the funds allocated to other agencies in 1963, approximately ¥6.7 billion was to finance industrial parks and ¥5.3 billion was to be lent to small enterprises for financing equipment.

Internal Funds

Very few small factories in Japan depend exclusively on internal funds; only about 5 percent of the total small factories did so according to a 1961 survey, and these were primarily very small units.[13] Large as well as small factories in Japan typically raise a much smaller proportion of their funds internally than do factories in other countries.[14]

Within the small-factory category, the dependency on internal funds tends to decline as the size of the factory increases. A sample survey in 1961 found that 39 percent of the funds of factories employing between 10 to 29 workers were raised internally as compared with 37 percent for those employing 30 to 99 workers and 31 percent for those employing 100 to 299 workers.[15] This may be explained by a much greater problem in Japan of obtaining access to institutional finance as the size of enterprise falls below 100 workers.

Although the data are known to understate the reliance of small manufac-

[13] Survey for this study by the Osaka Prefectural Government Institute of Economic Research (IER). A nationwide survey in 1957 by the Smaller Enterprise Agency of the Ministry of International Trade and Industry found that between 6 and 7 percent of small factories relied exclusively on internal funds, (*Report on Coordinative and Fundamental Survey of Small Enterprises,* Tokyo, 1958). Data cited refer to factories employing between 10 and 299 workers; in the case of manufacturing enterprises employing less than 10 workers, the 1957 survey showed that 44 percent relied exclusively on internal sources of funds.

[14] Official statistics for 1960 show that the net assets of Japanese manufacturers employing between 50 and 299 workers were 24 percent of their combined liabilities and net assets, and in the case of those employing 300 workers or more, the proportion was 31 percent (Bank of Japan, *Economic Statistics of Japan,* 1961). Roughly comparable data for the United States in 1958 shows the proportion for manufacturing corporations with assets of less than $250,000 was 52 percent, and for manufacturing corporations of all sizes, 67 percent. (United States Federal Trade Commission—Securities and Exchange Commission, *Quarterly Financial Report for Manufacturing Corporations,* fourth quarter, 1958. See also the discussion of internal finance in Chap. 6). The comparison is much less valid for the smaller category, since the data on these in Japan is heavily biased by the practice of owners of small enterprises of providing a major part of their own funds in the nominal form of a loan to the enterprise and understating the owner's assets on company records. An examination of the accounts of a few small manufacturers suggests that their share of equity, though much higher than official data indicate, is still lower than is usual for comparably sized manufacturers in the United States or other countries.

[15] Survey by IER. Data are for 85 enterprises, 26 employing 10 to 29 workers, 42 employing 30 to 99 workers, and 17 employing 100 to 299 workers. The proportions given are subject to the same general downward biases indicated for Bank of Japan data on firms employing 50 to 299 workers. Dependency on internal funds is calculated somewhat differently than in the case of the Bank of Japan data cited in the previous footnote. If dependency on internal funds is calculated from Bank of Japan data in the same way used for the IER data, the Bank of Japan would show 27 percent reliance on internal funds for manufacturers employing 50 to 299 workers and 37 percent for those employing 300 or more.

turers on internal funds, the real proportions are believed to be quite low, because of such factors as the well-developed state of institutional and interbusiness credit sources, the large and long-continued postwar impetus to expand and modernize, the relatively low level of small-factory profits and other internal sources of funds, the high level of postwar taxation, and the traditional operation practice in Japan of paying out a large portion of profits as they are earned.

A low degree of dependence on internal financing has not always been the case for Japanese small enterprises. In the immediate postwar period, internal financing was a major source of financing as the result of the high level of profits available in a goods-short economy and the general shortage of bank and interbusiness credit. However, the counterinflation measures introduced in 1949 sharply reduced the profit opportunities for small enterprises and imposed heavy tax burdens upon them.

The initial efforts to ease the resulting serious financing problems for small enterprises were primarily directed toward enlarging the availability of institutional financing.

Measures to increase the availability of internal financing have also been introduced in recent years. Special depreciation allowances were granted on new equipment, initially in a form primarily useful to large enterprises, but since 1957 with special provisions for equipment used by smaller enterprises. Limitations on the types of equipment eligible and the general unfamiliarity of many small enterprises have resulted in only about 30 percent of corporations having assets of less than ¥5 million (about US$14,000) taking advantage of special depreciation allowances.[16] A variety of new tax benefits for small enterprises were authorized in 1963.[17]

The government has indirectly contributed to enlarging the internal funds available to small factories by facilitating the adoption by them of more efficient production methods—and thus tending to increase the availability of profits for reinvestment. One way it has done this, which will be discussed later, is by making possible the purchase of more efficient equipment through loan programs.

A second way in which the government has indirectly helped to make more profits available for investment is through making industrialists acquainted with more efficient production methods. Research and counseling services have long been provided in Japan by various central and local government agencies. The Department of Industrial Science and Technol-

---

[16] *Small Business Development Program in Japan,* Japan Productivity Center, 1960, p. 28.

[17] An interesting and important one, designed to encourage the amalgamation of small firms into larger ones, permits firms with assets recorded on their books at much less than their true value to revalue them at their true value when they amalgamate without incurring a tax liability. For tax reasons, the accounts of small firms often show assets at much below their true value.

ogy of the Ministry of Trade and Industry and over 170 independent local laboratories and institutes throughout the country have engaged in technical research and provided information services. Prefectural services are illustrated by Osaka, where an Industrial Research Institute with a staff of around 200 provides research and laboratory testing services at subsidized rates. Osaka prefecture has also had an Institute of Industrial Management since 1925. The latter was expanded in the postwar period and now has a staff of about 50 persons. It carries out analyses of the operations for industrial firms (involving about 10 man-days each) and whole industries, provides management seminars, and also evaluates loan applications for the prefectural government's loan program. No charge is made for these services.

The Smaller Enterprise Agency, since its establishment in 1948, has helped to enlarge the abilities of local government institutes, chambers of commerce and industry, and private consultants in extending counseling services to small enterprises. It has provided training programs and grant funds to facilitate such activities. Its budget for fiscal 1965 included ¥267 million for grants to prefectures for consulting and related services to small enterprises and ¥376 million for the Japan Small Business Advisory Work Center, which provided training in management consulting—a total of about US$1.8 million, and an increase of about 80 percent over 1963. The various local government agencies performing operations analysis or advisory services assisted 2,630 factories in 1961, of which 82 percent employed between 11 and 300 workers, 15 percent employed 10 or fewer workers, and 3 percent more than 300 workers.[18] No charge is made for these services.

Though government and quasi-public research and advisory services are large and varied compared with those available in many countries, they are still small in relation to the number of small enterprises in Japan. According to Professor T. Nakamura, as well as a number of other well-informed Japanese observers of the program, achievements have been more significant for the consciousness they have aroused of the need for utilizing research and improving efficiency and for the stimulation they have given to other sources of these services than for services directly extended. A great many consultants have been trained for private firms and business associations.[19] Large companies have been made aware of the value of

[18] This includes only one of the many services extended by these agencies and does not include the large volume of services extended to enterprises other than factories. (Information provided by the Smaller Enterprise Agency.)

[19] Besides thousands of private consulting firms which have sprung up in Japan in the postwar period, the Chambers of Commerce and Industry were reported to be operating some 432 small business consulting offices in 1959. (*Small Business Development Programs in Japan,* p. 18.) The Japan Productivity Center also has had a small business department since 1957 and has undertaken programs for training consultants, providing technical information, developing cost accounting for small

assisting and compelling small subcontractors to adopt better production methods. Small firms have themselves been stimulated to take the initiative in procuring better equipment and modernizing their operations.

A third way in which government has contributed to enlarging the internal funds available to small enterprises has been the provision of subsidies or subsidized services. This has largely been confined to free advisory services, described above, and interest-free equipment loans extended by prefectures and discussed below in the section on official sources of finance.

A final way in which government has contributed to enlarging the internal funds available to small enterprises is through measures to strengthen their bargaining position in interbusiness relationships. These measures will be discussed in the following section.

Interbusiness Financing

Interbusiness credit in Japan is the most important external source of funds for small manufacturers. It accounted for 57 percent of the liabilities or 36 percent of the combined liabilities and net worth of manufacturers employing 50 to 299 workers in 1960. Enterprises employing 300 workers or more, in contrast, obtained only 36 percent of their liabilities or 17 percent of their combined liabilities and net worth from interbusiness credit.[20]

Small manufacturers not only receive credit from other firms, but also extend credit to their customers. They engage in extension, moreover, to a much greater degree than do large firms. In 1960, enterprises employing between 50 and 299 workers had 23 percent of their assets in credit due from customers as compared with 16 percent in the case of enterprises employing 300 or more workers.[21]

Enterprises employing between 50 and 299 workers were nevertheless heavy net recipients of interbusiness financing, according to the above Bank of Japan data. This, however, is subject to qualification. The IER survey in 1961 confirms that enterprises employing from 100 to 299 workers were substantial net recipients, with 85 percent of their purchases being on credit but only 70 percent of their sales. For enterprises in the next two categories, 30 to 99 and 10 to 29 workers, however, the reverse was true, with only 75 percent of their purchases in both cases being on credit but with 83 and 81 percent of their sales on credit. The net position of firms employing less than 10 workers was far more unfavorable.[22] Although there were marked differences between different types of manufactures, only the ceramics industry of the seven industries surveyed showed a higher percentage of credit pur-

---

enterprises, and rendering similar services. The Asian Productivity Organization in Japan also operates a training program for management consultants.

[20] Bank of Japan, *Economic Statistics of Japan,* 1961.
[21] Bank of Japan, *Business Analysis of Small Industries,* 1960.
[22] Survey by Osaka Institute of Economic Research.

chases than of credit sales. The ceramics industry's favorable situation is due to the large proportion of sales going to exports, where sales are usually for cash.

The unfavorable net position of smaller firms is shown to be worse when the terms of interbusiness credit are considered. Interbusiness credit is extended or received principally in the form of bills receivable. The length of the bills on credit extended averaged 97 days as compared with 87 days on credit received. Small manufacturers did not receive interest when they extended credit against bills. However, depending on trade and credit conditions, they sometimes paid from 11 to 18 percent interest on credit received and also lost cash discounts.[23]

Postwar Japanese policies with regard to interbusiness credit can be best understood in the context of the general nature of interbusiness relationships in Japan. In the prewar period most small manufacturers, particularly those producing for export, obtained their financing and raw materials from a large mercantile firm which was also the principal buyer of their output. These economic relationships were combined in many cases with traditional hierarchic local and personal relationships which together kept the small manufacturer in a dependent position. Small manufacturers having subcontracting relationships with larger manufacturers were also becoming an important group in the prewar period, but in these cases, also, the small firm was typically closely tied to a particular large concern.

In the postwar period, the general dependency of small manufacturers on larger firms for credit has decreased. The role of mercantile firms, being based largely on relationships to artisan-type enterprises, was reduced by the war and by postwar emphasis on industrialization and on mechanized factory production methods.[24] Small manufacturers have been assisted in shifting to alternative sources of financing by improved profit opportunities and greater access to lending institutions. Their ties to large firms, nevertheless, are still substantial, although now more commonly with large manufacturers and less with wholesalers. It is estimated that between 40 and 60 percent of the manufacturing firms employing less than 300 workers work primarily on a subcontract basis.[25]

This general pattern of relationships between large and small firms has been subject to much criticism in Japan. Large enterprises are said to take advantage of their dominant position, keeping the profits of smaller enterprises low and shifting to them the burden of any adjustments received by changing economic conditions, such as contracting markets or tightening

[23] Survey by Osaka Institute of Economic Research.

[24] The transformation is illustrated by the decline in the share of enterprises employing less than 30 workers in Osaka prefecture from 89 percent in 1933 to 67 percent in 1957 and of those employing less than 5 workers from 74 percent to 14 percent. *Statistical Yearbook of Osaka Prefecture.*

[25] Estimate by Japan's Smaller Enterprise Agency.

credit supplies. From the point of view of the total economy, it may be argued that the use of dependent small firms by larger enterprises as a buffer against adverse changes is economical. It may be less wasteful if some of the small firms are required to shut down when materials, finance, or markets are temporarily inadequate than if the production of the less flexible larger enterprise is cut back. Whether or not the system permits the smaller enterprise to attain a level of profits to make bearing the costs of these risks equitable is, of course, a separate question.

Apart from doubts as to its equity, some Japanese officials have also felt that the system has not always worked well from a development point of view. Particularly in the case where a small enterprise has dealt with a merchant, who in turn is separated from the market by other intermediaries, the pressure for reduced prices has, in some cases, been so great as to force down wages and the quality of production and to prevent investments in more efficient production facilities. As an American observer noted:

> Most trading companies carry 200 or more very diverse commodities and perform a great number of services. Under such circumstances they can become merely order takers. They have neither the time, the research organizations, nor the desire to undertake market research, market promotion, or extensive analysis of any kind. They are neither innovators nor enterprisers in the full meaning of these words. Their whole organization inhibits technological development and initiative on the part of individual producers.[26]

There have been cases, on the other hand, where larger enterprises, usually manufacturers, have recognized the long-run advantage to be gained from modernization of dependent firms. Particularly under the conditions of recent years, favoring rapid expansion, large manufacturers have found it to be in their own interest to utilize their controlling position and their superior financial, technical, and other resources to bring about improvements in the technical standards of the smaller subcontractor.

Various government measures have been taken to strengthen the general bargaining position of small firms in their interbusiness relationships with larger ones. For example, the Law Pertaining to the Prohibition of Private Monopoly and the Maintenance of Fair Trade, passed in 1947, was intended to reduce the dominance of business by a few large enterprises. Various measures to facilitate joint action by small enterprises have also been enacted, such as the Small Business Cooperative Association Law (1949),

[26] Charles Hatton, "The Position of Small Industry in Japan," United States Operations Mission in Japan, Nov. 8, 1956. (Mimeographed.) The adverse influence of wholesalers' usual policies and relationships with small manufacturers on the efforts of the latter to grow or modernize are also described at length in W. S. Lander, "Survey of Japanese Industrial Productivity," United States Operations Mission to Japan, Jan. 1, 1956. (Mimeographed.)

the Law on Formation of Small Business Associations (1958), and the Law on Formation of Society of Commerce and Industry (1960).

The Smaller Enterprise Agency has also made some effort to encourage large firms to utilize their relationships with dependent concerns to assist the latter in improving their operations. It has, for example, provided consulting assistance to the subcontractors of large firms where the latter are also ready to contribute to improving the efficiency of their subcontractors.[27]

The only measure so far taken in Japan which is directed specifically toward the financial aspects of interbusiness relations is the Law on Prevention of Delayed Payments to Subcontractors (1956). This was intended to discourage the practice whereby some large enterprises held up payments for long periods, particularly during times of financial stringency. By doing this they were, in effect, requiring small subcontractors to finance them. There have been difficulties in enforcing the provisions of the law, because small enterprises are generally reluctant to lodge complaints, fearing they will not receve orders in the future if they do. The law may be contributing to discouraging payment delays by placing them under public disapproval, but it has not been adequate.

Institutional Sources of Financing

Japan has a highly developed credit system with a wide variety of private, public, and quasi-public institutions. Japan's lending institutions had loans outstanding to manufacturing in October, 1963, of ¥8,883 billion (about US$25 billion) of which ¥1,953 billion (about US$5 billion)—or 22 percent—went to enterprises capitalized at no more than ¥10 million (about US$28,000).[28] Although the volume of institutional credit to small manufacturing enterprises in Japan is large and rising, it is nevertheless probably less than proportional to the contribution which these enterprises make to Japan's manufacturing output.[29]

The four main groups of institutions providing credit to small manufac-

[27] The subcontractors of 25 firms were assisted in 1964, and about double the number were expected to be served in 1965. Some of these firms have as many as 100 or 200 subcontractors. (Information provided by officials of the Smaller Enterprise Agency.)

[28] The Small Business Finance Corporation, *Financial Statistics Monthly*, January, 1964. SBFC data on small manufacturers up through August, 1963, cover enterprises capitalized at more than ¥10 million (about US$28,000). Since that date, SBFC data have covered enterprises capitalized at not more than ¥50 million (about US$139,000). Loans to small manufacturers under the new definition in June, 1964, amounted to ¥3,868 billion (about US$10.7 billion) or 39 percent of the institutional loans to manufacturing. *Ibid.*, September, 1964.

[29] Current data are not available to verify this, but disparity between small factories' contribution to output and their share of institutional funds indicated by data for 1957 does not appear from general trends to have been eliminated, although it probably has been somewhat reduced. See Table 4.

turing enterprises are: (1) commercial banks; (2) mutual savings and loans banks and credit associations; (3) other private institutions (long-term credit banks, investment trusts and investment banks), and (4) official and quasi-official institutions.

Commercial banks are by far the most important, accounting for over half of the total institutional credit to small manufacturing enterprises. Most of their credit is short-term, but they are also a significant source of medium-term equipment financing. The relative share of their manufacturing loans going to small enterprises, however, has always been modest and has steadily declined over the past decade. The proportion of *manufacturing* loans of "all banks" going to enterprises with a capital of not over ¥10 million (about US$28,000) was 32 percent in December, 1953, 26 percent in December, 1958, 24 percent in December, 1960, and 20 percent in August, 1963.[30] The proportion not only has had a declining trend, but also has tended to contract markedly during periods of tight credit and to recover in part as the credit situation eases. The share of small manufacturers in *total* "all banks" loans in August, 1963, was slightly less than 10 percent and has also declined over the past decade.

Mutual savings and loan banks and credit associations together account for nearly 30 percent of the total institutional credit to small manufacturers. Like commercial banks, most of their loans are short-term, but the 14 percent of their credit to small manufacturers in medium-term loans makes them the second most important source for the latter type of financing.

Official institutions account for about 14 percent of the institutional credit to small manufacturing enterprises. They are the most important source of equipment financing and extend credit primarily on a medium-term basis. Official institutions also contribute to strengthening the flow of private institutional financing to small enterprises through guarantee arrangements.

The remaining institutions, the long-term credit banks, the trust banks, and the investment banks, account for less than 2 percent of the institutional financing outstanding to small manufacturers, although the long-term credit banks are of somewhat greater relative importance in the case of plant and equipment financing.

The preceding four categories are obviously very broad. Each includes subtypes of institutions having important differences from one another, particularly in the extent to which they serve small manufacturing enterprises. (See Table 4.) The characteristics of the major types of institutions in each category are examined in more detail in the following sections.

[30] "All banks" in Japanese banking terminology are defined as the commercial and long-term credit banks, but the latter are of comparatively minor importance in the overall totals. Data are from Bank of Japan, *Economic Statistics of Japan,* 1961, and SBFC, *Financial Statistics Monthly.*

Table 4. *Percentage Distribution of Outstanding Loans to Manufacturing Enterprises by Size of Enterprise for Various Sources of Financing, 1957*

	Enterprises employing							Grand total†
	1–10	10–49	50–299	Subtotal	300–999	1,000 or more	Subtotal	
Commercial banks:								
City banks	*	5	12	17	15	69	84	100
Local banks	5	20	25	50	14	36	50	10
Mutual banks and credit associations:								
Mutual banks	17	44	23	84	4	11	15	100
Credit associations	23	49	21	93	1	6	7	100
Credit cooperatives	32	46	19	97	3	*	3	100
Official institutions:								
Central Bank for Cooperatives	7	34	44	85	9	7	16	100
SBFC	6	42	49	97	3	*	3	100
PFC	34	46	6	86	1	12	13	100
Japan Development Bank	*	1	5	6	10	84	94	100
Long-term banks and trusts	*	1	4	5	8	86	94	100
Other:								
Customers	11	19	38	68	17	16	33	100
Money lending	31	42	14	87	13	—	13	100
Relatives and acquaintances	34	52	13	99	1	1	2	100
Other	3	8	14	25	15	59	74	100
Total	3	11	15	29	13	58	71	100
Share of Value Added (1957)	7	17	19	43	12	46	58	100

* Less than 0.5 percent
† Totals may not add because of rounding.
Source: Smaller Enterprise Agency, *Comprehensive and Basic Survey of Small Manufacturing Industries*, Chuso Kiggo Sōgōkihon Chosa, 1958.

Table 5. Offices and Loans to Small Manufacturers by Type of Lending Institution, December, 1960

Loans to small manufacturing enterprises[a]

	Number of banks	Number of offices	Total loans Amount (in billions of yen)	Percent	Plant and equipment loans Amount (in billions of yen)	Percent	Operation loans Amount (in billions of yen)	Percent
Commercial banks:								
City banks	13	1,791	464	26	13	5	451	30
Local banks	64	3,822	510	29	18	7	492	32
Total	77	5,613	989[e]	55[e]	37[e]	14[e]	952[e]	63[e]
Mutual banks and credit associations:								
Mutual banks[c]	72	2,485	281	16	49	20	232	15
Credit associations[c]	538	2,698	238[b]	13[b]	24	9[b]	214	14[b]
Credit cooperatives[c]	461	1,082	[b]	[b]	[b]	[b]	[b]	[b]
Total	1,071	6,265	519[b]	29[b]	73[b]	29[b]	446[b]	29[b]
Official institutions:								
Central Bank for Cooperatives[c]	1	56	102	6	23	9	79	5
Small Business Financing Corporation	1	14	97	6	84	33	13	1
People's Finance Corporation	1	87	29	2	13	5	16	1
Japan Development Bank	1	8	2	[g]	2	[g]	[d]	[d]
Export-Import Bank of Japan	1	1	[d]	[d]	[d]	[d]	[d]	[d]
Total	5	166	230[d]	14	122[d]	47	108	7
Long-term credit banks and trusts:								
Long-term credit banks	3	22	24	1	20	8	4	[g]
Trust banks	7	166	13	1	1	[g]	12	1
Total	10	188	37	2	21	8	16	1
Grand Total[f]	1,163	12,232	1,775	100	253	100	1,522	100

[a] Refers to manufacturing enterprises with a capital of less than 10 million yen, except where otherwise noted. Because this definition has no minimum size limit, data includes loans to artisans and workshops as well as to factory-type enterprises.
[b] Data are not available for credit cooperatives, but the amount of loans to manufacturing enterprises is believed to be small.
[c] Refers to all manufacturing enterprises financed, although most are believed to have a capital of less than 10 million yen.
[d] Data are not available for the Export-Import Bank, but the amount to small manufacturing enterprises is believed to be small.
[e] Include loans from commercial and trust accounts not separately shown.
[f] Table may not add because of rounding.
[g] Less than 1 percent.
Source: The Bank of Japan, Economic Statistics of Japan, and SBFC, Annual Report on Financial Statistics.

349

Table 6. Loans to Small Manufacturing Enterprises by Japanese Lending
Institutions, June, 1964
(in billions of yen)

	Total loans		Operating loans		Plant and equipment loans	
	Amount	Percent	Amount	Percent	Amount	Percent
All banks †	2,093.4	54	1,930.8	59	162.6	27
Trusts	29.8	1	11.2	‡	18.6	3
Mutual banks §	714.6	19	602.0	18	112.6	19
Credit associations §	636.8	17	554.7	17	82.1	14
Central Bank for Cooperatives §	201.5	5	154.2	5	47.3	8
Development Bank	10.1	‡	0.1	‡	10.0	2
Export-Import Bank	0.9	‡	0.9	‡		
Small Business Finance Corporation	181.2	5	17.1	1	164.1	28
Total ¶	3,868.2	100	3,271.0	100	597.2	100

* Small manufacturing enterprises are defined here by the new definition of having capital of less than 50 million yen, unless otherwise noted.
† "All" banks refers to the city and local commercial banks and the three private long-term credit banks.
‡ Less than 1 percent.
§ See note C, Table 5.
¶ Totals may not add because of rounding.
SOURCE: SBFC, *Financial Statistics Monthly*, September, 1964.

Commercial Banks

Japan's commercial bank system includes 13 city banks with 1,791 offices and 64 local banks with 3,882 offices.[31]

The *city banks* are distinguished from local banks primarily by being generally larger and by their dominant role in the banking business of the major cities and in the financing of larger enterprises. They tend to have very close relationships with prime customers with whom there may be interlocking ownership. Most of their loans go to large enterprises, employing 1,000 workers or more.[32] A little over one-fifth of city bank loans to manufacturing at the end of 1960 went to enterprises with a capital of less than ¥10 million (about US$28,000), and this accounted for somewhat over one-fourth of the institutional financing outstanding to small manufacturers.[33]

Not only are city banks important sources of small-industry financing, but, moreover, 12 of the 13 have established customer service centers to extend informational assistance primarily to small industry. Most of these

[31] See Table 5.
[32] See Table 4. For a discussion of postwar relationships between banks and industry, see Hugh Talbot Patrick, *op. cit.,* pp. 70ff.
[33] See Table 5.

were set up in 1950 in response to government suggestions.[34] In the case of the Fuji Bank, which is fairly representative, it presently has two centers, one in Tokyo and another in Osaka, although none at branches elsewhere. Each center employs about a dozen persons who extend advisory services on management, industrial relations, accounting, financing foreign trade, and laws and regulations. Services are free. About 200 enterprises a month are served by each center, of which over two-thirds have a capital of less than ¥10 million.[35]

The city bank attention to small manufacturers, despite a large enterprise orientation, stems, in part, from the way many small enterprises are linked to major enterprises in Japan. Banks are prevailed upon by large enterprises to serve closely associated smaller enterprises. City bank interest in small enterprises also stems from a desire to generate deposits and, in addition, to find an outlet for surplus funds when the general money market is slack. Public opinion and government emphasis on the need to provide better financing for small enterprises has been a further influence on city bank policies.

The city banks have been highly selective in the small industries which they serve. They employ regular staff to actively seek out the best small enterprises in the most promising lines of industry, and there is keen competition between banks for such clients. Chance customers on the initiative of clients are rare except where they are introduced by parent enterprises or other large clients of the bank with whom they have connections.

New clients, before they receive financing, must generally undergo a trial period of at least two or three months—and more usually six months—during which they maintain an account with the bank and allow the bank an opportunity to become closely acquainted with the turnover of deposits, the operation of the enterprise, the character of management, and related matters.

Banks, before they accept a client, also examine the general trend of the industry of which the enterprise is a part and its relative performance from balance sheets and profit and loss statements, make limited checks on the reliability of financial data, and make inquiries of other banks and the enterprise's suppliers and customers.

Loan decisions tend to be made by the head offices, although branch managers are sometimes given authority in making smaller loans. The investigation tends to be more detailed when financing is in the form of notes than in the form of discounting of commercial bills. In the latter case, beyond examination of the quality of the bills offered, general credit investigations are repeated once or twice a year.

[34] See Small Business Financing Specialists Study Team, *Small Business Finance in Japan,* Japan Productivity Center, 1958, p. 17.

[35] Description of the policies and procedures of banks is based on information collected through interviews with banks by IER, except where otherwise indicated.

New customers are normally financed initially on the basis of discounting bills for periods ranging from 30 to 120 days. A part of established customers eventually qualify for short-term loans of three to six months on a note basis. In 1960, 38 percent of city bank financing was in the form of discounted bills, 60 percent on single name notes, and the remainder on overdrafts or deeds. Specific data are not available for the proportions in the case of small manufacturers, but it is estimated that in their case discounted bills are 60 percent, and single name notes, 40 percent. City banks rarely make loans to small enterprise except on a short-term basis. Less than 3 percent of their loans to small manufacturers in 1960 were for plant and equipment loans, and these constituted only about 5 percent of the institutional plant and equipment loans outstanding to small manufacturers. Equipment loans, according to bankers contacted, normally are installment loans of three years duration but may vary between one and seven years.

Loans are normally secured in the case of small industries. Even where financing is extended in the form of discounting commercial bills, additional security besides the bill itself, up to 20 to 30 percent of the value of the funds extended, is often, but not always, required of small enterprises. Deposits are the most common type of security. Real estate is the second most important. Other forms are rare. Personal guarantees are normally required, and liens may be taken on machinery and personal property to reinforce other collateral. The amount of compulsory deposits required against financing varies greatly from case to case. The average deposit requirement is variously estimated from as low as 10 percent to as high as 30 to 50 percent. The higher figures are more in accord with the information obtained in our survey of firms.

Deposits serve as a means not merely of guaranteeing repayment, but also of raising the effective interest rate. The formal interest rate of city banks ranges from as low as 7.7 percent in the case of good bills to as high as 9.1 percent. However, the effective cost of loans to small enterprise is substantially raised by *compulsory deposits,* which are discussed briefly above, and also by so-called *deduction deposits.* The latter, which may amount to 1 to 1½ percent up to a maximum of 5 percent, are in effect additional interest charges deducted in advance. As large enterprises normally are not subject to deduction deposits and are subject to lower compulsory deposits, the spread in interest rates between different sizes of enterprises is much greater than the spread in formal rates of 1 to 1½ percentage points.

Local banks are subject to the same banking regulations as city banks but are regionally rather than nationally oriented. They were drastically reduced in number during the late 1920s and 1930s. Demand for more banks to serve small enterprise in the postwar period resulted in 12 new local banks being licensed up to 1954, but additional local banks have not been authorized since. The 64 existing local banks vary greatly in size with 10 having deposits of ¥9 billion (about US$25 million) or less and 5 having deposits of ¥100 billion (about US$278 million) or more. The larger ones have numerous branches, but most are concentrated within the limits of one or two prefectures.

The operating procedures of local banks are very much like those of city banks, although local banks tend to be more lenient in their standards, generally accepting—particularly in the larger cities—clients who cannot gain access to the more prestigious city banks. A little over 45 percent of local bank loans to manufacturing went to enterprises with less than ¥10 million (about US$28,000) capital in 1960, and these made up 29 percent of the institutional loans outstanding to small manufacturing enterprises.[36] Some local banks adopt procedures more closely suited to local client needs than city banks, particularly in smaller towns where local banks know their clients well, although others are much less progressive. There is a greater tendency for local banks to maintain business relations with clients despite changing business conditions out of a sense of obligation. Their security requirements are generally similar to those of city banks. However, they make more use than city banks of guarantees through credit guarantee associations to enable applicants to qualify for financing. Interest rates tend to be slightly higher than those of city banks, generally ranging between 8½ and 9½ percent. Loan periods are similar to those of city banks.

Less than 4 percent of local bank loans to small manufacturers in 1960 were for plant and equipment. These constituted 7 percent of the institutional plant and equipment loans outstanding to small manufacturing enterprises.

The Mutual Savings and Loans Banks and Credit Associations

This group includes three distinct but related types of institutions: mutual savings and loans banks, credit associations, and credit cooperative associations. In the aggregate, they are second only to commercial banks as a source of institutional finance for small manufacturers. As is shown in Table 4, between two-thirds and three-fourths of their loans to manufacturing enterprises go to those employing less than 50 workers, and most of the rest go to enterprises employing between 50 and 300 workers. Because of their special importance to small enterprises, the government has sought to strengthen them in various other ways, including making available to them special government deposits.

There were 72 mutual savings and loans banks with 2,485 offices in Japan in 1960. They provided 16 percent of the total institutional loans outstanding to small manufacturing enterprises in 1960 and 20 percent

[36] See Table 5. Their share of loans going to different employment sizes of enterprises in 1957 is shown in Table 4.

in the case of plant and equipment loans.[37] The mutual savings and loans banks developed out of a traditional type of mutual financing companies. Since they have been brought under the Mutual Loans and Savings Bank Law of 1951, their operations have resembled that of commercial banks except that they are more restricted as to area of operations, size of loans, and financing activities. They accept deposits, discount bills, and extend loans as well as enter into mutual savings and loans contracts. Normal bank-type loans and discounts are of increasing importance in their operations and accounted for 78 percent of their financing in 1960. Except in the case of savings and loans contracts where savers automatically become borrowers, loan procedures, deposits, and collateral requirements are generally similar to those of commercial banks. Interest rates nominally range from 9 to 10½ percent, but effective rates are much higher. Loans for equipment are more frequently made than in the case of commercial banks—18 percent of their loans to small manufacturing enterprises being for equipment. The loan period for plant and equipment averages around 20 months and does not usually exceed 40 months.

There were 538 *credit associations* with 2,698 offices and 461 *credit cooperative associations* with 1,082 offices in 1960. Credit associations of various types have a long history in Japan. The primary difference between credit associations and credit cooperative associations under regulations established in 1951 is that credit associations can accept deposits and installment savings from the public at large, while the cooperatives can accept deposits only from members, their relatives, and public institutions. Credit cooperatives tend to serve much smaller enterprises, primarily those in commerce rather than in manufacturing. Further discussion focuses on the credit associations, which are more often used by small manufacturers than cooperatives are.

Credit associations are nonprofit organizations owned by small business enterprises and individuals who are also the borrowers these organizations are intended to serve. Credit associations have on the average about 3,300 members each. Only about 3 percent of their resources are derived from member subscriptions, which averaged a little over ¥13,000 (about US$36) per member in 1961.[38] Deposits make up 94 percent of their resources, and the remainder is derived from loans. Some credit associations also do an important volume of agency business for other lending institutions, such as the Central Bank for Industrial and Commercial Cooperatives, the Small Business Finance Corporation, and the People's Finance Corporation.

Nearly one-third of their loans in 1960 went to manufacturing, primarily

[37] See Tables 5 and 6.
[38] SBFC, *Present State of Small Business Financing in Japan,* Tokyo, 1961, pp. 19, 20.

to enterprises with a capital of ¥3 to 5 million (about US$8,000 to 14,000).[39] Credit associations provided 13 percent of the institutional financing of small manufacturing enterprises in 1960.

Credit associations discount bills and also lend on a note basis. Loans are primarily to meet short-term working capital needs, with less than 10 percent of their loans going to financing plant and equipment in 1960. Plant and equipment loans are usually for periods of one to three years. Working capital loans are made for periods up to one year. They also provide emergency funds for periods as short as three days.

New members, before admission to the association, are thoroughly investigated as to character and credit status by officers of the association. Loans are secured both by deposits of 35 to 50 percent of the loan value and by real estate or other collateral. Interest rates range between 10 and 11 percent.[40]

Other Private Institutions

Other private institutions serving small enterprises include Japan's seven trust banks, three long-term banks, and three recently formed small business investment companies. The *trust banks* engage principally in trust business, although they also carry on ordinary commercial banking. About 5 percent of their loans in 1960 went to small manufacturers, almost wholly for working capital purposes. These accounted for less than 1 percent of small manufacturers loans from institutional sources.

The *long-term banks* also accounted for less than 1 percent of total borrowings of small manufacturers. In the case of plant and equipment financing, however, their share was 8 percent. Loans to small manufacturers accounted for somewhat less than 5 percent of the long-term banks' loans to manufacturers or less than 3 percent of their total loans.

The long-term credit banks extended loans primarily for plant and equipment, but also for working capital on a term basis of three to five years, repayable in installments. Loans are secured by mortgages and bear an interest rate of 9½ or 10½ percent. The resources of long-term banks are largely derived from the issuance of medium-term bonds which are purchased by commercial banks, the general public, and to some extent by the government Trust Fund Bureau. Long-term banks may receive deposits only from borrowers and government agencies, and in 1960 deposits were equivalent to about 6 percent of loans outstanding.

The oldest of the long-term banks is the Industrial Bank of Japan, first established as a quasi-government organization in 1902, although presently

---

[39] Data on their loans by employment size of enterprises is shown in Table 4.
[40] Interest rates of credit cooperatives associations are higher, ranging from 12 to 14 percent.

operating under the provisions of the Long-term Credit Bank Law of 1952 as a private long-term lending institution. It has had a separate small business department since 1923. It played a leading role in small-industry lending programs in the prewar period and was instrumental in bringing into operation the Central Bank for Commercial and Industrial Coopera- tives in 1937. It facilitated the establishment of the Small Business Finance Corporation (SBFC) by lending experienced staff for key positions, some of whom are still serving the SBFC. In its small-industry financing it has emphasized selecting well-established enterprises demonstrating long-term growth potential. Thus, it began financing such now large and well-known enterprises as Canon Camera Company, Inc., and Honda Motor Company, Ltd. around 1950, when both were quite small. Since the establishment of the SBFC in 1953, the Industrial Bank has tended to concentrate its small-enterprise financing on firms in the upper ranges of the size category and on subcontractors of large companies.

The newest of the long-term credit banks is the Hypothec Bank of Japan, established in 1957 to make loans to small enterprises on the security of real estate. Although a private bank, over 40 percent of its initial capital was derived from the government. The share of its financing going to small enterprises is somewhat larger than the other two long-term banks, although even the Hypothec Bank focuses primarily on medium-scale enter- prises with a capital of ¥100 million to ¥500 million (about US$278,000 to 1.4 million).

The *small business investment companies* (SBICs) were authorized by legislation in 1963 which provided special government assistance for com- panies extending equity financing to small enterprises under its regulations.[41] Three SBICs, differing in ownership and regional specialization, had been formed up to 1965, one each in Tokyo, Osaka, and Nagoya. The Tokyo SBIC is the largest, with a capital of ¥2.5 billion (about US$7 million) and a staff of 37; the Nagoya SBIC is the smallest, with a capital of ¥1 billion (about US$2.8 million) and a staff of 20.

The government, through the Small Business Finance Corporation, may provide up to one-third of the capital of such companies in the form of 6.5 percent 15-year redeemable nonvoting preference shares, although its subscription of such shares has amounted to only 10 to 12 percent of the capital of the three existing companies. The respective local governments have provided an additional 17 to 20 percent of capital in common shares. Private financial institutions own the majority of shares in all three SBICs,

---

[41] The description of the SBICs draws on discussions with officers of the Tokyo and Osaka SBICs in 1965. A brief description of the SBICs is provided in "Outline of Government-affiliated Institutions for Small Business Financing in Japan—1964," reproduced in *Symposium on Small Business Development,* Vol. I, Asian Productivity Organization, Tokyo, 1964, and also published separately as a pamphlet by the Government-affiliated Institutions, Tokyo, 1964.

and the remainder of the shares are held by securities dealers associations and industrial companies.

The somewhat different orientation of the three companies is suggested by the institutions from which the managing directors have been drawn. The Tokyo SBIC's managing directors come from the Bank of Japan, the Small Business Finance Corporation, and the Tokyo city government; in Osaka they come from the chamber of commerce and the two largest city banks; and the senior managing director of the Nagoya SBIC is from a large local bank with head offices in Nagoya.

SBICs may finance only enterprises with a capital—before SBIC financing—of less than ¥50 million (about US$139,000), purchasing not less than 15 percent of more than 50 percent of shares issued. Only enterprises in 23 designated industries (principally various types of manufacturing and mining, construction, transportation, and warehousing) may be financed. To be eligible, firms must also have paid dividends of at least 10 percent per annum over the past 18 months, show promise of growth, and be unable to raise capital from other sources.

Initially, SBICs were only authorized to provide financing by the purchase of newly issued shares, but regulations were amended in 1965 to permit them to purchase debentures bearing maximum interest of 10 to 11 percent, convertible to equity within four years. The SBICs are not expected to seek representation on the boards of directors of companies they finance or otherwise gain control of; at the same time they are expected to provide consulting services. Each of the SBICs has a consulting department which, in the case of the Osaka SBIC, consists of an engineer and a specialist from a stockbrokerage firm. The Osaka SBIC requires detailed monthly reports from financed firms and meets quarterly with their top management to review operations. It also plans to bring the officers of client companies together periodically to review common operating problems.

As of September, 1965, the three SBICs had together made a total of about 75 investments in a wide variety of enterprises. Investment policy is directed toward selecting the most promising firms in a diversity of types of industry. The shareholders of SBICs, particularly the SBFC and private banks, have assisted the SBICs in identifying promising clients.

Official and Quasi-official Institutions

Japan has five official or quasi-official institutions which extend financing in some degree to small manufacturers. These institutions are intended to supplement private lending institutions and particularly to soften the effects of monetary restrictions on enterprises with important financial needs. Two, the Central Bank for Commercial and Industrial Cooperatives and the Small Business Finance Corporation extend the largest part of their financing to small manufacturing enterprises. Two others serve primarily larger enterprises, and the fifth serves primarily artisans, merchants, and very small factories. There are in addition to official lending institutions, government-insured agencies which provide guarantees to other institutions lending to small enterprises. Finally, there are prefectural programs which, for the most part, provide funds to financial institutions enabling them to undertake special financing programs for small enterprises.

The Central Bank for Commercial and Industrial Cooperatives (CBCIC) is the oldest of the official or quasi-official institutions focusing on small enterprises. It was established in 1936 with capital in part provided by the government and in part by cooperative organizations. Its capital in 1962 amounted to ¥12 billion (about US$33 million) of which ¥7.7 billion was owned by government and ¥4.3 billion by more than 13,000 cooperative organizations. Its local resources amounted to ¥277 billion (about US$778 million), of which 65 percent were derived from debentures, 30 percent from deposits, 4 percent from share capital, and 1 percent from loans. Its debentures, about one-third of which are subscribed by the government, bear interest of 6 to 7 percent. It pays between $2\frac{1}{2}$ and $3\frac{1}{2}$ percent for its current deposits and between 6 and 8 percent for one-year time deposits. Deposits are derived primarily from members of cooperatives, although about 10 percent are derived from local governments.

As of June, 1964, 59 percent of CBCIC loans outstanding went to small manufacturing enterprises with less than 300 employees. Such borrowers typically employed around 40 workers and, in the case of term loans, borrowed on the average about ¥3 million (about US$8,000). CBCIC lending has been rapidly expanding in recent years. Its loans outstanding to small manufacturers in June, 1964, amounted to ¥201 billion (about US$558 million), or practically double the volume in December, 1960. However, it still accounts for only 5 to 6 percent of the total institutional financing of small manufacturers, and its relative importance has not increased in recent years.[42]

The CBCIC was originally intended to deal only with the cooperative organizations themselves. However, because of the weakness of some cooperatives, it was authorized in 1952 to finance the membership of cooperatives directly. By the end of 1960, 29 percent of its total loans—and practically all of its term loans—were extended directly to members applying at one of the CBCIC's 64 offices, and 71 percent were extended to cooperative members through the 178 credit cooperative organizations serving as CBCIC agencies.

The CBCIC extends loans principally for working capital purposes, these accounting for 78 percent of its loans outstanding to small manufacturers

[42] See Tables 5 and 6. The relative shares of institutions in the two tables are not quite comparable as a result of somewhat different definitions of small manufacturers and the omission of the financing by credit cooperative associations from Table 6.

in 1960. Of the 78 percent, 35 percent are accounted for by loans on short-term notes of 4 to 12 months, 24 percent by the discount of 90- to 150-day bills, and 19 percent by term loans for working capital, usually for periods of about three years, but extending in some cases up to five years. Plant and equipment loans for periods of two to five years account for 22 percent of its loans. Term loans for working capital and plant and equipment purposes taken together thus account for 41 percent of its financing. In 1961, the CBCIC also began to take an active part in the financing of industrial estates.

Interest rates have been gradually reduced since 1955 from a level of 13 percent to 8.8 percent for short-term loans and 9.2 percent for loans of two years in 1964. These rates refer to loans through associations; direct loans are one-tenth of a percentage point higher. In the case of bill discounting, a 1 percent deduction deposit is usually required. Compulsory deposits average about 15 percent of the value of the loan. Thus, taking into account its relatively low deposit requirements, its present effective lending rates may not be much higher than those of city banks.

In addition to deposit requirements, collateral is usually required except in the case of high-quality bills presented for discounting or in the case of loans guaranteed by a credit guarantee association. Real estate is preferred but may be combined with equipment or other assets. The manager of the enterprise must also give his personal guarantee and, in the case of loans through cooperative association, the additional guarantees of the officers of the association.

Its loan application screening procedures in the case of direct lending require applicants to provide financial records and other data indicating in some detail the enterprise's record during the past two or three years, its planned use of funds, and estimated future profits. In the case of loans through associations, procedures are somewhat simpler, resting in part on the record of the association. Bill discounting is primarily carried out through associations on the relatively simple basis of quotas set by annual investigations.

The CBCIC has been a relatively successful channel for financing small enterprises. Its losses from bad debts have been negligible. Considering the high cost of its funds, its lending rates are reasonable. It is uncertain how satisfactory its screening procedures are from a development point of view, but they have not been subject to any marked criticism and have enabled the Bank to reach a large number of small manufacturing enterprises.

The Small Business Finance Corporation (SBFC) is a second institution of special importance here because it focuses its operations primarily on small-factory enterprises. Manufacturing firms, to be eligible for its financing, must employ not more than 300 persons or have a capital of not more than ¥50 million (about US$139,000).[43] Mining enterprises employing not more than 1,000 workers and a wide variety of service enterprises employing not more than 50 workers are also eligible for SBFC financing, although manufacturers have accounted for around 70 percent of SBFC loans in recent years. The average SBFC borrower in 1964 had 48 employees and a capital of ¥5.1 million (about US$14,000) and received a loan of ¥5 million (about US$13,900).[44]

The SBFC was established as a wholly government-owned corporation in 1953. It took over the special small-business financing activities initiated in the early postwar period by the Reconstruction Finance Corporation, subsequently transferred to the Japan Development Bank and ultimately to the SBFC. The SBFC has grown rapidly since its establishment. Its total resources in 1964 amounted to ¥257 billion (about US$714 million) of which 10 percent consisted of share capital and the remainder primarily of loans from the Government Trust Fund Bureau.[45] Its operations by March, 1964, were conducted by a staff of 1,487—of which somewhat over half were male university graduates. It operates through 36 offices, supplemented by 782 lending institutions with around 7,000 offices which serve as agents of the SBFC.

It issues directly or through agents around 25,000 to 30,000 loans a year. Loans outstanding at the end of 1960 amounted to ¥147 billion (US$408 million), of which ¥97 billion (about US$269 million) went to small manufacturing enterprises. By July, 1965, loans outstanding had risen to ¥307 billion (about US$853 million), of which ¥214 billion (about US$600 million) went to small manufacturing enterprises. Its share of the total institutional loans to small manufacturers, however, remains small—5 to 6 percent—and has not increased in recent years.[46] Its role in plant and equipment financing, however, is much larger—the SBFC accounted for 27 percent of the institutional loans to small manufacturers for plant and equipment in 1964.[47]

The SBFC extends only term loans for periods usually between one and five years, although in exceptional cases up to 10 years. The average loan period in 1964 was three years and eight months. Loans are usually repaid

[43] The capital limit was raised from ¥10 million (about $28,000) in September, 1963.

[44] This average relates to all borrowers; separate data are not available for manufacturing enterprises. The total resources of small manufacturers in Japan are often three to four times as large as paid-in-capital, and the ratio may be much higher in the case of these firms, since a number are commercial and service enterprises.

[45] The Trust Fund Bureau obtains its resources primarily from post office savings deposits and post office life insurance funds.

[46] See Tables 5 and 6. Its share of total institutional loans to small manufacturers in June, 1964, under the new definition (enterprises with capital of less than ¥50 million or about US$139,000) was 4.7 percent.

[47] Its share in 1960 under a narrower definition of manufacturers was 33 percent. See Table 5.

in monthly installments. Nearly 90 percent of its loans go for the purpose of financing plant and equipment. Working capital loans have been authorized in recent years where term loans for this purpose are essential.

One of the main purposes of establishing the SBFC was to provide small enterprises with a less expensive source of term financing. Its initial lending rate was set at 10 percent but has since been reduced to 9 percent; it has been directed by parliament to seek to lower its rate ultimately to 7½ percent. As the SBFC does not require either compulsory or deduction deposits, the 9 percent rate is attractive in terms of the alternatives of most small factories and only 1 to 1½ percent higher than the effective rate paid by the most favored large borrowers of city banks.

SBFC loans are fully secured by mortgages, although second mortgages may be accepted. Mortgaged assets consist principally of real estate but may also include personal property, machinery, and assets being acquired with the loan. In addition, the loan must be guaranteed by two officers of the company, or by a business association of which it is a member, or by other responsible individuals. The use of second mortgages is reported to involve some administrative inconvenience, although no significant losses have occurred because of the acceptance of second mortgages.

The SBFC initially allocated and administered all its loans through the agency of other lending institutions and still relies on this method for more than half of its lending, particularly for smaller loans. It experimented during its early years with a procedure under which it retained final authority over such loan decisions and also bore most of the risks. This procedure proved administratively unsatisfactory and was abandoned in 1956. The present method is to allocate quotas to agents quarterly, which they may lend subject to basic terms set by the SBFC on such matters as: (1) scale and type of enterprise, (2) maximum loan size, (3) use of funds, (4) rate of interest, (5) period of loan, and (6) security and guarantees. The agent agrees to bear 80 percent of any losses. However, there is very little risk problem, since where collateral does not provide adequate protection, credit guarantees may be used, the fee for these being borne by the borrower. The agent receives a commission for his risk and administrative responsibilities of 29 percent of the interest in the case of loans of less than ¥3 million (about US$8,300) and 25 percent in the case of loans over ¥3 million. The maximum size loan normally made through agents at present is ¥10 million (about US$28,000).

The SBFC exercises control over agents' lending operations through the selection of agents, contractual arrangements, guidance, and supervision. Lenders must forward information to the SBFC on loans as well as installment payments as they are made. Repayment records are reported to be followed and inquiries made where delinquencies occur. Whether this serves a useful purpose is uncertain, since losses have rarely occurred in agency loans. The SBFC's most important means of controlling agents is its staff of 18 experienced inspectors. A team of two normally devote a week annually to reviewing operations of each major agency and inspect smaller ones every two or three years. Inspectors audit transactions, review applications and other records, and, where necessary, visit borrowers. Agents are rated according to their performance, and these ratings are taken into account in fixing future loan quotas. About 2 percent of those inspected in 1964 were denied new quotas the following year, and quotas of others were revised upwards or downwards. As financial institutions until recently were fully lent and operations were profitable, they have been anxious to obtain quotas.

The SBFC has had some problems with its use of agents, particularly in early years when it was less well equipped to supervise agency operations. Loans were not always allocated in the most developmentally useful way. Favored bank customers tended to be given preference over applicants having greater development needs for financing. Screening methods relied on assuring conservative collateral protection. Interest rate controls were sometimes evaded by deposit requirements or other practices difficult to check. This, in particular, still continues to be a matter of concern to the SBFC.

Inadequacies in the agency system led the SBFC to begin its own direct lending operations in 1955, which have since expanded as rapidly as the necessary staff and branch facilities could be acquired. Direct loans rose to about 20 percent of total financing in 1960, and to over 38 percent by August, 1964.[48]

Direct loan operations are intended to supplement agency loans rather than compete directly with them. Direct lending gives special attention to export enterprises and those seeking to modernize their production methods and facilities. It also tends to concentrate on the larger eligible enterprises and is not extended to retailers or other merchants. Enterprises financed through direct loans in 1964 received an average of nearly ¥16 million (about US$44,000) each and employed on the average 117 persons each.

In the case of direct loans, the SBFC makes a thorough evaluation of the management and outlook of the enterprise. Since it does not engage in deposit banking, it may not have had any previous business relations with the applicant or knowledge of his particular operations. A loan officer makes a preliminary evaluation of an application for a loan on the basis of an interview with the applicant, a review of financial statements and sales records for the preceding two years, and information on the history of the enterprise, experience of the principal officers, collateral available, and the proposed program. If these findings are satisfactory, the applicant is asked to submit a detailed written application, together with appropriate documents. These, together with previous submissions, are turned over to

[48] SBFC, *Financial Statistics Monthly*, March, 1961, and September, 1964.

a credit analyst who will spend about two man-weeks making a detailed evaluation. The analyst, sometimes accompanied by an engineer, will make a plant visit to evaluate operations and assets directly. Customers and suppliers of the applicant are also contacted. The bank's extensive files on client firms and its periodic surveys of clients are drawn on in evaluating the competitive abilities and prospects of an applicant firm. The evaluation stresses: (1) market conditions in the applicant's line of industry; (2) profitability; (3) long-run prospects and competitive capacity; (4) financial conditions and prospects; and (5) management. Management is regarded as the most important of these. The findings and recommendations of the credit analyst are reviewed by a loan officer, who compares these with his preliminary impressions and arrives at a loan decision. Loans over ¥5 million (about US$14,000) must be approved by a director, and those involving sums over ¥30 million (about US$83,000) by the board of directors.

After a loan is made, it is supervised by the authorizing loan officer, who makes a plant visit when the investment program has been completed and again a year later. No further supervisory visits are made if no problems develop. Greater supervision is regarded as desirable but impractical in view of staff limitations and present responsibility of each officer for about 70 loans.

The main shortcomings in the SBFC's direct lending operations from the point of view of borrowers are the extensive information requirements and the several months taken to reach loan decisions.[49] Although the SBFC has from the beginning had staff well experienced in this type of lending— by virtue of staff lent by other institutions, particularly the Industrial Bank of Japan—it has had inadequate staff to manage the volume of loan applications as expeditiously as it might otherwise have done.

The SBFC has been quite successful from the point of view of loan repayment record, its written-off losses being negligible. It has extended a large and rapidly rising volume of term financing. Its services appear to be reaching a large proportion of small manufacturers employing 30 workers or more and a substantial number of much smaller enterprises. Through its agency system it has been able to provide funds to enterprises throughout the country and to serve quite small enterprises on a fairly economical basis. It has been able to administer the large-agency program and to conduct a direct loan with an average loan size of about US$44,000

[49] Of 286 enterprises replying to a mail questionnaire, 55 percent considered the SBFC's screening procedure too complicated, and 60 percent objected to the period required to obtain a loan decision. Objections on these accounts were voiced by a much smaller share of enterprises in the case of all other lending institutions except the Japan Development Bank, where the proportions were 67 and 60 percent respectively. Discussions with enterprises during field interviews indicated many enterprises which had received SBFC loans regarded the delay and procedural problems as serious. (Surveys by IER in 1961.)

with an operating cost (exclusive of interest costs and agency fees) in 1964 equal to about 1½ percent of its direct loans outstanding.

Other official institutions serving small manufacturing firms include the People's Finance Corporation, the Development Bank, and the Export-Import Bank of Japan. In none of these is small-factory financing more than a minor part of total activities.

The People's Finance Corporation (PFC) is a wholly government-owned corporation established in 1949, succeeding two earlier institutions. Its total resources in 1964 amounted to ¥108 billion (about US$500 million) of which 11 percent is derived from government share subscriptions and the remainder largely loans from the government Trust Fund Bureau.

The PFC is intended to serve individuals and very small enterprises which cannot obtain financing elsewhere. Its primary clients are small merchants, and its normal maximum loan is ¥500,000 (about US$1,400). Its loans outstanding to manufacturing enterprises in 1964 amounted to ¥48 billion (about US$133 million) or about 30 percent of its total loans. Data for 1960 indicate its loans accounted for less than 2 percent of the institutional loans to small manufacturing enterprises. Moreover, 55 percent of its manufacturing loans by value went to enterprises employing a maximum of 10 workers and 90 percent to enterprises employing a maximum of 30 workers. Thus the manufacturing enterprises among its clients are mostly artisans and workshops and the very smallest of factory-type enterprises.

The PFC extends term loans repayable on an installment basis for periods up to 5 years; 91 percent of loans by value are for periods from 19 to 36 months. Loans are usually secured by the guarantee of a Credit Guarantee Association or other cosigner. Loans may also be secured by collateral, although only 3 percent of PFC loans (or 6 percent of the amount) are so secured. The interest charge is 9 percent.

The PFC screening policies take into account social as well as economic considerations in extending loans. The procedure is simple, involving the submission of business records, an interview, and a brief plant visit by a credit officer. Loan decisions are reached within about 20 days, which is considered relatively prompt in Japan. Most loans are made directly through one of the PFC's 84 offices, although around one-fourth are made through its 735 agents. Agents assume one-half of any losses on loans they make.

The PFC's operations have resulted in only modest repayment problems for this type of financing. Bad debts amount to about 2 percent of the number and 0.9 percent of the value of loans; delinquencies amount to 3 percent of the number and 1.6 percent of the value of loans. The desire of its clients for continued access to the PFC seems to be an important factor in keeping repayment problems low.

The PFC's operations are conducted with reasonable efficiency considering that a large part of its borrowers are new. In June, 1961, it had a ratio of 196 direct loans outstanding to every staff member. The PFC does not have the staff or funds to serve many applicants eligible for its financing. This stems in part from the relatively attractive terms on which it extends financing and in part from the very large number of enterprises in the smaller size categories.

Both the Japan Development Bank and the Export-Import Bank of Japan extended only a small fraction of 1 percent of their total financing to small enterprises, the total loans outstanding to small manufacturing enterprises in June, 1964, for the Development Bank being a little over ¥10 billion (about US$28 million) and of the Export-Import Bank being less than ¥1 billion. The Development Bank transferred the limited small-industry financing activities it inherited from its predecessor, the Reconstruction Finance Bank, to the SBFC when the latter was formed in 1953. It again became involved in a financing program serving primarily small factories as the administrator of ¥11 billion (about US$31 million) made available by the government in 1956 for loans under the Temporary Act on the Development of Machine Industries. With the extension and revision of this program in 1961, the SBFC was designated as a second channel for these funds, diminishing the Development Bank's future responsibilities for small enterprises. Loans under this program were initially lent at 6½ percent, which was raised to 8½ percent in 1961.

Other Special Financing Programs

The Credit Guarantee Program

The Credit Guarantee Program dates from the mid-1930s, when credit guarantee societies were established in Tokyo, Kyoto and Osaka. The system became widespread in the postwar period and was put on a more organized basis with the passage of the Credit Guarantee Association Law in 1953. There are at present 52 associations, of which 46 were sponsored and financed primarily by prefectural governments and 6 by municipal governments.

The function of a credit guarantee association is to evaluate loan applications and, on the basis of this evaluation, to guarantee lenders against loss on those approved. Associations are expected by virtue of their staff and specialized function to be able to approve loans in cases where collateral or financial reports which applicants can provide are inadequate by bank standards. They assess the prospects of enterprises by visiting the plant, checking basic records, and examining actual assets and operations. Applicants must usually provide the association with collateral, although as the result of the association staff's better knowledge of the true value of the collateral, requirements need not be as high as those of banks. The guarantee association, through its extensive credit records and personal contacts with small entrepreneurs and their business connections, is also able to assess the character, personality, and credit reputation of such applicants.

Processing a guarantee application of the above type usually requires about two weeks and involves about one day of actual investigation work in the case of the Osaka Prefecture Small and Medium Enterprise Credit Association. It also issues some guarantees almost immediately, without investigation, where suitable bills are offered as collateral.[50]

An apparent deficiency of the system is that the guarantee association, after issuing a guarantee, has no contact with the client unless and until default occurs. Collection and supervision are the responsibility of the lender. Once default has occurred and the association has compensated the lender for funds due, collection becomes the responsibility of the association.

Guarantees are issued by associations to lending institutions on loans up to a maximum size of ¥10 million (about US$28,000) per industrialist or up to ¥30 million (about US$83,000) per cooperative association. Any private or official bank, mutual savings and loan, credit association, or related financial institution having a contract with the guarantee association may request a guarantee on eligible loans which it has authorized. Very small enterprises having a capital of less than ¥1 million (about US$2,800) and employing less than 20 workers and cooperatives meeting certain requirements may also approach the guarantee association directly and request a loan guarantee and assistance in obtaining a loan from a financial institution.

Guarantees are generally issued for periods of less than one year in the case of working capital loans (typically for three months), and for periods of less than three years (typically one year) in the case of plant and equipment loans. Guarantee charges vary but average close to 2 percent per annum. In Tokyo, for example, rates—depending on the security offered—range from 1.7 percent to 2.5 percent per year for loans over ¥500,000 (about US$1,400), and from 0.9 percent to 1.4 percent for smaller loans. In Osaka prefecture, the rate is 1.8 percent per annum on loans over ¥500,000 and 1.3 percent on smaller loans. Guarantee charges are borne by the borrower and are additional to annual interest charges.

The 52 associations together had nearly 429,000 guarantees outstanding for a total of ¥301 billion (about US$836 million) in June, 1964. This represents a 66 percent increase in the number and a 159 percent increase in the value over June, 1961. Although the program has shown a fairly rapid rate of expansion over the past 10 years, it started from a relatively small basis; the total value of the guarantees outstanding in June, 1964,

[50] Discussions with officers of the Osaka Prefecture Small and Medium Enterprise Credit Guarantee Association. A description (in English) of another major guarantee association is provided in *The Tokyo Credit Guarantee Association*, Tokyo, 1959.

was still only 3.2 percent of the value of the total institutional loans to small enterprises.[51]

The 52 associations experienced defaults on 1.7 percent of the guarantees accepted up to September, 1960; as about half of the funds on defaulted loans are ultimately recovered, net losses are less than 1 percent.[52] The default rate in recent years has been about 1 percent.[53]

A Small Business Credit Insurance Corporation (SBCIC) was established in 1958 in order to strengthen the guarantee societies. The SBCIC succeeded an earlier insurance program which had operated since 1950. The SBCIC's capital was wholly provided by the national government and amounted to ¥22 billion (about US$61 million) in 1964. The main functions of the SBCIC are to insure the guarantees extended by the guarantee societies and to extend loans to the latter. The value of the SBCIC's insurance contracts amounted to ¥93 billion (about US$258 million) in 1960 and rose to ¥259 billion (about US$719 million) by June, 1964. Total loans outstanding as of March, 1964, amounted to ¥14.3 billion (about US$40 million).[54]

Guarantees are generally issued for periods of less than one year in the case of working capital loans (typically for three months) and for periods of one year for loans from ¥500,000 to ¥7 million (about US$19,000). In the early years of the program, insurance was also provided to guarantee societies on a basis which allowed the latter to select the guarantees to be insured. A similar insurance was also offered to financial institutions on loans. However, despite somewhat higher rates, these types of insurance proved uneconomic for the SBCIC and were dropped from SBCIC's services in 1961.

The insurance program in its early years incurred substantial losses—losses up to March, 1960, exceeded ¥1 billion (about US$3 million) or equal to about one-third of the gross receipts to that date.[55] The simplification of its services in 1961 has since resulted in a major improvement in its operating record.

The insurance program by June, 1964, provided coverage on over 85 percent of the guarantees issued on small business loans. It thus provides reasonable assurance that the guarantee societies will be able to meet their obligations.

The insurance cost makes up a relatively large part of the guarantee

---

[51] SBFC, *Financial Statistics Monthly,* September, 1964. The data refers to all types of small business; separate data are not available for guarantees on loans to small manufacturing enterprises.

[52] Unpublished speech by Mr. Tsutomu Nomiyama, director of the Small Business Credit Insurance Corporation, 1961.

[53] SBFC, *Financial Statistics Monthly.*

[54] For a fairly detailed description of these operations, see *Outline of Small Business Credit Insurance Corporation, SBCIC,* Tokyo, 1964.

[55] T. Nomiyama, *op. cit.*

charges. The guarantee rates may, in turn, tend to retard the expansion of the program, although the rate of expansion in recent years may well be as high as can be soundly managed.

Prefectural Loan Programs

The prefectural governments not only contribute to the funding of guarantee societies, but also provide various loan programs for small enterprises. For example, a loan program for modernizing industry was begun in 1954. Funds are provided jointly by the central and prefectural governments; the latter must contribute at least one-half of the funds, and in practice have provided nearly two-thirds. Loans are extended for periods up to five years on an interest-free basis. Loans outstanding under this program amounted to ¥3.4 billion (about US$9 million) in 1960, and to ¥7 billion (about US$19 million) in 1961. Of the loans outstanding in 1960, 20 percent went to enterprises employing less than 20 workers, 77 percent to those employing 20 to 199 workers, and 3 percent to larger enterprises. About half the total went to 1,777 machinery and metalworking enterprises.[56]

There has been considerable criticism of the way in which these have been allocated and administered. Since 1960, loans have been restricted to lines of industry annually designated as meriting priority by the Smaller Enterprise Agency of the central government. An effort has been made in recent years also to restrict loans to enterprises unable to obtain financing from other sources but at the same time showing reasonable economic prospects. In some prefectures, such as Osaka, the assistance of industrial specialists in government-sponsored industrial management institutes is drawn on in evaluating applications. Since 1963, the demand for equipment financing has slackened, reducing allocation problems but also reducing the need for a program of this type.

Another important loan program of prefectural governments is designed to meet the needs of small industry during the two main seasons in Japan when the demand for funds is highest. Other programs are designed to meet other special needs. Frequently, the administration of such lending programs is delegated to the Central Bank for Commercial and Industrial Cooperatives or other financial institutions, although in some cases prefectures administer them directly.

Industrial Estates[57]

Industrial estates have been increasingly employed in recent years, not only as a means of channeling financial and other assistance to small and medium enterprises, but also as a means of decentralizing industrial growth away from the main metropolitan areas of Tokyo and Osaka. Efforts to

[56] Data provided by the Smaller Enterprise Agency.

[57] This section has drawn principally on the detailed report of Tokeo Matsunaga, *Industrial Estates in Japan,* Japan Productivity Center, Tokyo, 1963.

encourage estates were strengthened in 1959 by an extensive study of the most desirable locations for industrial plants from a national development point of view and by setting up arrangements for regulating and giving advisory assistance on plant locations. This was followed in 1961 by the Promotion Law for the Development of Industries in the Underdeveloped Areas, specifying areas to be developed as centers for small and medium enterprises and providing incentives for establishing estates.

Industrial estates are being established by: (1) local governments, (2) groups of small and medium enterprises wishing to locate in an estate, (3) the Housing Corporation, and (4) private groups such as real estate companies, financial organizations, and railways. The first two are of the greatest importance. Local governments up to 1962 had invested ¥544 billion (about US$1.5 billion) in estate projects with an area totaling 343 million square meters. The main focus of this program is on attracting and assisting industry in locations designated as meriting priority for industrial expansion.

Small and medium enterprises are the other major sponsors of industrial estates and are of particular interest here. An important objective of these estates is to increase the productivity and general growth of small and medium enterprises. Special incentives are granted to encourage the formation of such estates. Prefectural governments extend interest-free loans for the acquisition and development of land, construction of buildings, and establishment of common facilities. Loans for the acquisition of land are for two years and for most other purposes for five years. The Central government meets a part of the cost of providing interest-free loans. Funds budgeted for this rose from ¥300 million in 1961 to ¥6.7 billion (about US$185 million) in 1965.[58] Financing for equipment and for housing may also be obtained from the prefectural governments. Other assistance includes long-term loans from the Central Bank for Commercial and Industrial Cooperatives and the Small Business Finance Corporation, special tax benefits, survey assistance, and any required improvements or connections of roads, water, power, telephone, or other public utilities.

Estates to be eligible for these incentives must be sponsored by a group of over 20 small and medium enterprises. All of the latter must be members of an association for business cooperation and must normally be in the same or related lines of industry. The estate must be located in an area designated for industrial development and must meet building and layout standards and certain other requirements.

The growth of these estates has been impeded by organizational and administrative problems. However, 10 estates were established in 1961, 20 in 1962, 25 in 1963, 26 in 1964, and 31 were expected to be established in 1965. The estates range in size from the minimum accommodations for 21 enterprises up to several times that size. Most serve enterprises in

[58] Data provided by the Smaller Enterprise Agency.

one general line of industry, such as woodworking, machinery, or clothing, although one of the larger estates includes enterprises from the machinery, synthetic fiber, lumber, and food industries.

An example of these estates is the Toyama Machine Industry Center which was established by 39 enterprises previously operating in and around Toyama city. Most produce machinery for the Fujikoshi Steel Company, Ltd. The estate includes, in addition to factory buildings, a restaurant and joint facilities for product testing and for educating employees.

A second illustration of a small-industry estate is the Okayama Iron Industries Center. In 1962 it included buildings for 22 factories, and plans were under way for constructing 10 more. It also planned to provide housing for workers and joint facilities for types of equipment which estate tenants could not afford to own individually. The total investment up to 1962 was ¥191 million (about US$531,000) of which 19 million was provided by members, 25 million from welfare annuity funds (used for housing), 92 million by a loan from the Central Bank for Commercial and Industrial Cooperatives, 51 million by a loan from the prefecture, and 5 million unspecified.

The Adequacy of Financial Services

A measure of the adequacy of the finances available to small manufacturers in Japan is their ability to expand their output and increase in number. The smallest category (employing 10 to 29) showed a 20 percent increase in number of enterprises and 119 percent increase in net output from 1956 to 1961. Those employing 30 to 99 increased by 31 percent in number and 149 percent in net output. Those employing 100 to 299 increased 50 percent in number and 151 percent in net output. Together, their net output increased by an average of 17 percent per year as compared with 18 percent for all manufacturing enterprises.

Another way of evaluating the adequacy of finance is to examine the operation of particular types of financial services and the forms of finance available. This reveals a number of deficiencies. In interpreting these, however, it is important to keep in mind that rapid growth has nevertheless taken place and that financial services in Japan have tended to respond to changing needs as well as to improve generally.

Small firms have made heavy use of external sources of short-term financing, either from interbusiness associates or financial institutions. All but a very small percent of small firms employing over 10 workers do obtain external financing, and the average dependence on external funds is heavy, far exceeding the internal funds used. Only in the case of enterprises employing less than 30 workers is there substantial borrowing from moneylenders, friends, or relatives. Even for these, only one-fifth of external funds came from these sources, and not all of this, perhaps very little, was short-term financing.

The main problems with the short-term financing available are that over half of it is normally derived from interbusiness financing and that the financing available is at best moderately expensive. Dependence on interbusiness finance tends to reduce the bargaining position of small firms and to add to their borrowing costs and uncertainties, particularly during periods of tight credit. Where manufacturers were quite small and dealt principally with wholesalers, such as in the case of sock and brocade manufacturers, interbusiness credit terms were often quite unfavorable. There may also be a credit access problem for new firms as the result of the practice by most institutions to extend credit only on a secured basis and after a period of deposit relationships and detailed investigations.

Term financing for equipment has permitted a rapid increase in the mechanization of small units as well as an expansion in output. Equipment financing tends to be more readily available to firms with a profit record. However, firms needing to modernize or expand despite an unsatisfactory profit record were frequently able to obtain funds. In some cases, such as in the machinery industry, interbusiness connections with large firms facilitated access to funds. However, even the brocade industry, which sells largely to wholesalers, was found in the survey to be rapidly shifting from hand to power looms capable of producing finer products, despite a generally depressed condition in the brocade market. Similarly, many cotton-socks manufacturers faced with competition from nylon socks were adding machinery capable of producing more competitive products, although firms in this industry were having more difficulty in obtaining finance than firms in more profitable lines. Firms with less than 29 workers had much more difficulty than somewhat larger enterprises in obtaining equipment financing. Only 45 percent of the firms having 10 to 29 workers were found in a sample survey to have equipment loans, as compared with 71 percent for those employing 30 to 99 workers and 79 percent for those employing 100 to 299 workers.[59]

The principal deficiency of the equipment financing available was that the period of financing was quite short, usually one to three years. It was available principally through official institutions or banks acting as the agents of official institutions. A high proportion of sample enterprises surveyed regarded delays and the complicated nature of screening procedures as important drawbacks. Nevertheless, there was a high appreciation of the usefulness of these services.[60]

Other limitations on term financing in Japan are that it is usually secured and usually restricted to equipment needs. Nevertheless, second mortgages and other less-desirable types of guarantees are sometimes accepted. Also, term financing is in some cases extended for working capital and other purposes.

[59] IER survey in 1961.
[60] IER survey in 1961.

Long-term financing to meet building needs is not yet widely available. The industrial estates program, to which increasing emphasis is being given, may help to fill this gap, although the program has encountered many as yet unresolved administrative problems.

A solution to the need of small enterprises for greater amounts of equity financing has not yet been found, but there has been considerable experimentation. Efforts are being made to strengthen and thus enlarge internal resources through extending free or low-cost technical assistance, facilitating cooperation between small enterprises, reducing the bargaining strength of larger enterprises in their relations with smaller enterprises, establishing tax concessions, and in other ways. New institutional arrangements for extending equity financing are also being tried. Although some of these measures or experiments are costly in terms of government expenditures or revenues foregone, progress is being made. This aspect of financing is, moreover, receiving increased attention, which strengthens the possibilities that better approaches will be developed.

The Continued Evolution of Program Measures

The Japanese program has been concerned on one hand with increasing the contribution of the whole range of private sources of financing to the development of small factories. It has, on the other hand, also created specialized semiofficial or official institutions where these have seemed to be required. It has simultaneously given great emphasis to the analysis of small-factory operations and to the provision of informational assistance. It has established a strong agency to study small-enterprise needs and the operation of various assistance measures and to recommend revisions in policies and measures in the light of accumulating experience. Japan's program thus shows no sign of becoming rigid or stagnant despite the substantial achievements of present measures. New departures in policies are, for example, indicated in the most recent legislation, the Basic Law for Smaller Enterprises and the Small Business Modernization Promotion Law, both enacted in July, 1963.

What are perhaps most needed in Japan's program efforts now are a greater coordination and a sharper focus of the various assistance efforts, particularly between financial and information assistance. The breadth of the program responsibilities and the diversity of sources and types of assistance being drawn on make this of particular importance. Progress, however, is being made in these respects. The mechanism for achieving the degree of coordination and focus required exists in the resources and responsibilities of the Smaller Enterprise Agency. The outlook thus is good for a continued evolution of Japan's program measures with experience and changing needs.

Index

Accardo, Francesco, 184
Accounting, 152, 156
  in Argentina, 88
  in Colombia, 310
  in India, 50
  introduction by Fondo, 174
  prices, 236
  problems of small manufacturers, 14
  role of income tax in fostering, 87
  tool for enterprise appraisal, 232–233
  (*See also* Counseling)
Adams, P., 103
Advanced countries, relevance of their experience to less developed countries, 104
Africa, 147, 154, 218, 220, 244
Aftercare (*see* Implementation)
Agency for International Development, 188
Agricultural credit, 276–279
Alexander, P. C., 22–23, 38, 39, 40, 41, 42, 267
American Bankers Association, 121, 147
American Economic Review, 91
American Machine and Foundry Company, 124
Argentina, 70, 152, 169, 172, 191–192
  finance companies in, 164–165
  Industrial Bank of, 70, 191–192, 203, 208, 210, 273
Asian Productivity Organization, 343
Asian Productivity, 7
Australia, commercial finance companies in, 165
  Commonwealth Development Bank, 195–196
Austria, 124, 135

Banerji, Sabita, 20, 24
Barron's, 178
Barton, H. C., Jr., 53, 57
Basu, S. K., 26
Bates, James, 126

Beckhart, B. H., 23, 137, 143, 152, 173, 239, 251, 256, 259, 269, 280, 282
Beckwith, A. R., 164, 169, 172
Beers, John de, 55
Belgium, 124
  cooperative banks in, 148
Belshaw, Horace, 279
Bennett, E. I. H., 269
Berna, James J., 4–5, 20, 22, 24, 45
Bhatt, R. S., 22
Block, L. de, 205–206
Bolivia, 277
  Industrial Bank of, 196
  supervised industrial credit program of, 273
Boskey, Shirley, 186, 236, 244, 272
Bottomley, A., 112
Brandenburg, Frank, 143
Brazil, 77, 131, 134, 135
  Bank of Northeast, 13, 81, 198, 220, 222, 244, 273, 283
  cooperative banks in, 148
  Development Bank of, 196
  interest rates on supplier credit, 127
  program objective deficiencies in, 70
  supplier credit in, 119
  tax exemption in, 106
Brooks, James R., 218
Bryce, Murray, 273
Bulletin d'Information de la Caisse Nationale des Marchés de l'Etat, 184
Burma, 132
Burn, Duncan, 114
Burroughs Clearing House, 204, 222, 252
Business Week, 86, 123, 124, 129, 144, 153, 168, 169, 180, 231, 233, 270

Cambodia, 6
Capital deposit ratios of banks, 135
Canada, 79
  guarantee arrangements in, 154–155
  Industrial Development Bank of, 96, 195, 201, 216, 222, 223, 255

Central America, development finance companies in, 16
   industrial park development program for, 103
Ceylon, 274
   Agricultural and Industrial Credit Corporation of, 196
   Development Finance Corporation of, 186, 244
Channels of finance, complementarity of, 103, 109, 322
Chase, Samuel B., Jr., 156
Checchi and Company, 208, 218
Chevrolet, 124
Chewning, David L., 64, 65
Chile, 106, 236
   commercial banks in, 148
   Economic Development Corporation of, 195
Chopur (see McCrory, James T.)
Chrysler, 123
Collateral (see under Security)
Colombia, 5, 70, 72, 74, 77, 107–108, 118, 127, 133, 134, 148, 152, 160, 218, 289–332
   Banco Cafetero, 294–296, 324–325
   Banco Central Hipotecario, 296–297, 327
   Banco Ganadero, 294, 296
   Banco Popular, 5, 72, 222, 294, 296, 302–305, 317–322
   Caja Agraria, 294–295
   Central Bank, rediscount rate on small business loans, 149
   Central Mortgage Bank of, 238
   commercial banks in, 134
   credit information in, 152
   Crescinco Fund, 298
   Finance Corporation of Caldas (CFC-Manizales), 186, 299–300, 322–323
   Industrial Development Finance Corporation (CFC-Bogotá), 185, 192–193, 299–300, 322–323
   Instituto de Credito Territorial, 297
   Instituto de Fomento Industrial, 301–302, 307, 325–327
Colombia, Instituto de Investigaciones Tecnológicas (IIT), 305
   surveys, 81
   insurance companies, loans by, 160
   National Finance Corporation of (CFN-Medellín), 185, 299–304, 322–323
   Popular Association of Small Industrialists (ACOPI), 307
   program objectives, deficiencies in, 70
   Promotora de Empresas Privadas, S. A., 298
   reinvestment propensities of small entrepreneurs, 107–108
   survey for program design, 74
Columbia University School of Law, 270
Combinations and interactions, principle of, 11
Commercial banks, 134–158, 164–165, 248–249
   basic characteristics of, 135
   branch operations of, 22, 254–255
   evaluation of term loans in, 246
   in India, 21, 24–26, 48–51
   in Japan, 347–353
   limitations of, 140–147
   merits of, 137–140
   in Puerto Rico, 55–56
   reducing lending risks of, 151
   relation, to finance companies, 163, 169
      to official financial institutions, 215
   role in U.S. SBICs, 177
   suggested measures to improve, 147–158
   tradition of aloofness in, 253–254
   (See also Chapters 12 and 13)
Commercial and Financial Chronicle, 178
Community Development Corporation, 103
Complementarity of channels of finance, 103, 109, 322
Confidential business information, protection of, 89
Continental-Allied Company (see Tenenbaum, E. A.)

Cooperative credit institutions, 103, 148, 198
  in India, 26, 29–30, 51
  in Japan, 347–350
  (*See also* Colombia, Banco Popular)
Costs (*see* Interest rates, and lending costs)
Counseling, 84–86, 106
  on accounting, 87–89, 93, 96, 267
    (*See also* Accounting)
  assistance, by banks, 138–139
    in Ghana, 7
    in Japan, 341–342, 350–351
    in U.S., 268–269
  by finance companies, 166–167
  financial, 86, 94, 113–114, 133
  importance for small manufacturers, 14
  by Japanese SBICs, 357
  on management and production technology, 89–90, 95
  need for in Colombia, 309–310
  by official institutions, 210–211
  as offset to adequate evaluation, 229
  on partnership formation, 114, 116
  receptivity of borrowers to, 264, 278, 285
  role in financing, 264–279
  suggested program for Colombia, 314–317, 321
  by suppliers and customers, 124, 129, 132–133, 326, 330
  by U.S. SBICs, 179–180
  value of surveys in determining need for, 82, 305
Cowan, Edward, 169
Credit, cards, 245–246
  extension by small firms in India, 22
  guarantees, 48–51, 154–156, 365–368
  information, 131, 151–152, 183, 250–251
  insurance, 131
  lines of, 136
  regulations and qualitative controls, 157
  supplier or interbusiness (*see* Interbusiness financing)
  (*See also* Interbusiness financing)

Crosse, Howard D., 156, 253–255
Crum, M. C., 168
Coutsoumaris, George, 6

Dahmén, Erik, 105
Davenport, R. W., 70, 75, 77, 103, 106, 118, 119, 127, 134, 158, 166, 170, 186, 187, 203, 204, 219, 242, 244
Debentures, 176
Debt equity ratios in finance companies, 163, 172, 176
Deere and Company, 121
Definition of small manufacturer, 8–10, 19
Denmark, 6, 79, 258, 283
  accounting in, 87
  Copenhagen Technological Institute, 266–267
  Finansieringsinstituttet for Industri og Handvaerk A/S, 185
  lending costs in, 15
  Manufacturing and Manual Industries' Finance Corporation, 184–185
  Ministry of Commerce and Industry loan program, 266–267
Deutsches Handwerksblatt, 156
Development criteria, use of, by commercial banks, 136
Development finance companies (*see* Finance companies, special)
Development fund, use of, to activate other institutions, 158
Development orientation in financing, 10–12, 157, 235–236, 250, 263–264
  active approach to, 253–257
  basic problems in achieving, 317
  special costs involved in, 14–15
Dhar, P. N., 20, 36
Diamond, William, 186
Dominant-dependent relationships (*see* Interbusiness financing)
Drake, Milton J., 230, 234
Duke, K., 103
Duncan, Peter D., 158, 166, 170, 187, 204, 274

East Africa, 200
  (*See also* Kenya; Tanzania; Uganda)
Economist, 168, 240
Ecuador, National Development Banking
  System in, 208
Edokpayi, S. I., 117
El Salvador, 145
  Development and Investment Finance
    Corporation of, 186
  Institute for the Promotion of Produc-
    tion, 286
  Salvadorean Finance Company for
    Small Industry, 197
Ellis, Howard S., 144
Engle, Nathaniel, 149, 186, 190, 191
Enlarging profitability of small factory
  financing, 149–151
Enterprise appraisal, 83–84, 229,
  232–238, 282–283
  (*See also* Evaluation)
Enterprise, 184
Equipment financing, 167–168, 213,
  243
Equipment leasing (*see* Leasing of
  equipment)
Equity and other risk-bearing financing,
  111–112, 120, 190, 197
  in India, 26, 29–30
  in Japan, 356–357
  merits of internal funds in, 105
  by moneylenders, 110
  by special finance companies, 170–171,
    176
  (*See also* Interbusiness finance;
    Internal finance)
Ethiopia, Development Bank of, 195
European Productivity Agency, 184
  (*See also* Organisation for European
    Economic Co-operation)
Evaluation, assistance to commercial
  banks, 157
  collateral or recourse, 238–245,
    257–258
  (*See also under* Security)
  by commercial banks, 136, 146,
    151–153
  factors affecting cost of, 115

Evaluation, by Fondo, 174
  improvement of methods for, 257–
    260
  of loan applications, 12–13, 227–261
  by banks in India, 50
  by Credit Guarantee Association,
    365–366
  by Government Development Bank,
    Puerto Rico, 60
  by Industriekredit Bank, 183
  by Japanese banks, 351
  by Japan's SBFC, 362–363
  by National Small Industries Cor-
    poration, India, 35, 37
  by PFC, 364
  State-Aid-to-Industries Acts, 27–28
  by State Banks in India, 46
  by State Finance Corporations,
    India, 33–34
  of management, 228–232, 239, 257,
    259–260, 265, 279, 286
  by official institutions, 202–206, 209,
    214
  of performance, 245–247
  procedures, of Copenhagen Tech-
    nological Institute, 266
  of Industrial Bank of Argentina,
    273
  of Middleclass Bank, 267–268
  role of accounting in, 87
  by savings institutions, 159
  by SBICs, 179–182
  by special finance companies in Colom-
    bia, 301
  suggested procedures for Banco Popu-
    lar, 320–321
  by suppliers, 122–123
  value of surveys in, 82, 93
  (*See also* Enterprise appraisal)
Exchange in international loans, 324–325

Factoring, 166
Far Eastern Economic Review, 109, 111
Fassnacht, B., 156
Favoritism by lending institutions,
  202–205, 232

Finance companies, 162–193
  commercial and related, 165–170
  general characteristics of, 162–165
  special, 170–193, 248
  (*See also* specific country)
Financiers, private, and moneylenders,
    23–24, 104, 109–118, 163
Financing, evaluation of, need for, 69,
    72–73
  improved, need for, 1–8, 20–23, 72–73,
    308–313, 370–372
Finland, 131
  Industrialization Finance Corporation,
    196
Flink, S. J., 86, 115, 178, 179, 181, 182
Ford Foundation, 271
Foreign advisers, 89
Foreign banks, role of, 144–145
Foreign exchange, 324–325
France, 135, 157, 184
  commercial finance companies, 165
  cooperative banks, 148
  Regional Development Companies, 184
  TEFICA, 184
Francis, Amadeo I. D., 53, 55, 59
Frank Mayer Engineering Company, 274
Friedmann, Wolfgang C., 236
Fuller, Douglas R., 207, 264

Germany, 79, 124, 156
  cooperative banks in, 148
  Industriekreditbank, 79, 183–184
  Kreditanstalt für Wiederaufbau, 189
Ghana, 6, 77, 92, 281
  financial need in, 7
  guarantee arrangements in, 154
  Industrial Development Corporation
    of, 7, 70, 264, 274, 275, 286
Godwin, Francis, 274
Gold Coast (*see* Ghana)
Gordon, the Honourable Walter L., 216
Greece, 104–105
  Center of Economic Research, 105
  commercial banks in, 144, 148
  financial need, 5–6
  internal finance, 105

Guarantee arrangements, 154, 242
  in Japan, 353, 359, 365–368
  in the Netherlands, 267
Guarantees, of lending programs by sav-
    ings banks, 159
  Reserve Bank of India, 48–51
Guatemala, 148

Halcrow, A. G., 14
Harbridge House, Inc., 64
Harwood, Wilson F., 274
Hatton, Charles, 345
Hayes, Samuel, 178, 180, 181
Heyden, G. J. van der, 268
Hire-purchase, 26, 34–37, 103, 125–126,
    239–240
  (*See also* Term financing, of
    equipment)
Hodgman, Donald R., 141
Hogan, Warren P., 164
Honduras, 132, 141–142, 143
  Honduran Finance Company, 186
Hungate, Robert T., 120, 123, 125, 128,
    148
Hunt, Pearson, 122, 156, 168

Implementation, 262–286
  by commercial banks, 153, 156
  problems with internal funds, 105
  relation to evaluation procedures, 249
  role, of accounting in, 87, 275, 283
  of collateral in, 243–244
  in performance testing, 247
  value of surveys to, 93
India, 3–5, 19–52, 77, 83, 93, 107, 109,
    118, 126, 135, 152, 206
  All India Manufacturers' Association,
    48
  commercial banks in, 24–26, 51,
    134–135, 148
  cooperatives in, 26, 29–30
  counseling services in, 83, 96
  credit information in, 152
  equity financing in, 26, 29–30
  Estimates Committee, 36

India, financial need in, 3–5, 20–23
  Government of, Central Small Indus-
    tries Organisation, 20–21, 25, 27,
    31, 34
    Handloom Board, 19
    International Perspective Planning
      Team, 19, 36–42, 52
    International Planning Team
      (1953), 34
    Khadi and Village Industries Com-
      mission, 19
    Small Industries Service Institutes,
      28, 29, 44–45, 50–51, 81, 273
  Hyderabad Seminar on Financing
    Small-Scale Industries, 48
  ICICI, 185, 186
    lending procedures, 191
    staffing, 190
  Imperial Bank of, 43
  indigenous bankers in, 23–24
  Industrial Commission (1916), 26
  Industrial Development Bank of, 31,
    51
  internal financing in, 21–22, 104, 107
  Japanese Delegation on Small-Scale
    Industries, 30, 32, 33, 35–36
  Life Insurance Corporation of, 41
  managing agency firms in, 163
  measures to improve small industry
    financing in, 26–27
  metalworking firms in, 3–5, 22
  moneylenders in, 23–24, 109
  National Small Industries Corporation,
    26, 34–37, 47, 195, 197
  partnerships in, 117
  program objective deficiencies in, 70
  relationship between financing and
    counseling programs, 273
  Reserve Bank of, 26, 27, 31, 32, 33,
    34, 43
    credit guarantee programs of, 48–51,
      154
    other programs of, 51
  Second Five Year Plan, 27
  Society for Social and Economic
    Studies, 20, 22, 32
  State-Aid-to-Industries Acts, 26–29, 31

India, State Bank of, 21, 32, 49, 50
  small industry financing programs
    of, 43–48
  training programs of, 47
  State Finance Corporations, 30–34, 45,
    49
    Kerala, 13, 33
    Madras, 30–31
    Orissa, 197, 285
  Working Group on Small-Scale Indus-
    tries (1959), 48
Indonesia, 132
Industrial and Commercial Finance Cor-
  poration (U.K.), 185, 230–231
Industrial Corporation of Baltimore, 264
Industrial Credit Company, Ltd. (Ireland), 252–253
Industrial estates, 103
  financing of saving banks, 160
  in India, 26, 38–42
  in Japan, 368–370
  in Puerto Rico, 58–59, 65
Inflation, 17
Installment repayments, 280–282
Institut de Droit Comparé, Université
  de Paris, 156
Insurance companies, 160, 248, 299, 327
Insurance of deposits, 156
Interaction of finance and supporting
  services, 285
  in Colombia, 314–315
  in India, 38, 42, 44–45, 77, 90
  in Puerto Rico, 63–65
Interaction of financial and other problems in India, 23
Inter-American Development Bank, 187,
  192, 299
  (See also Davenport, R. W.)
Interbusiness financing, 104, 109,
  118–133
  evaluation of, 248
  factors encouraging the growth of,
    120–124
  general characteristics of, 118–120
  limitations of, 126–129
  merits of, 124–126
  need for counseling services in, 86

Interbusiness financing, in newly indus-
    trializing countries, 17
  in India, 20–21, 24
  in Israel, 121
  in Japan, 343–346
  open-book credit, 118
  payment delays in, 22, 132–133
  role of finance companies in, 169
  suggested measures to improve,129–133
Interest rates, on deposits, 112
  and lending costs, 87, 111–115, 122,
    125–127, 131, 139–140, 149–151,
    159, 167, 170, 172–174, 185,
    188–189, 205, 212, 233
  in Colombia, 293, 297, 328
  effect, of geographic dispersion of
    clients on, 221, 277
  of specialization on, 217
  in India, 23–24, 25, 27, 32, 35–36,
    46
  influence of loan procedures on,
    236, 245–246, 262
  in Japan, 352–353, 354, 359, 361,
    363–364, 366
  as obstacle to financing small manu-
    facturers, 14–16
  in Puerto Rico, 56, 60
  U.S. SBICs, 176, 181
  regulation of, 113, 135
Internal finance, 86, 104–109
  in India, 21
  in Japan, 340–343
International Bank for Reconstruction
    and Development, 159, 186, 188,
    241, 242, 275, 276
International Development Association,
    188
International Finance Corporation, 32
International Financial News Survey, 114
International Labour Office, 128, 266
Iran, 73
  IMDBI, 185, 190
  Iran-American Industrial Guarantee
    Fund, 149
Iraq, 195
Ireland, Industrial Credit Company of,
    196

Israel, 73, 113, 114, 121, 130, 132, 145,
    152
  Artisans' Bank of, 215–216, 219,
    271–272
  Industrial Development Bank of, 244,
    271
Italy, 124, 184
  Centro Banca, 184, 195
  Ente Finanziamenti Italiani, 184
  Medio Banca, 184
Ivory Coast, 220

Jacoby, N. H., 14, 119, 125, 136, 154,
    167, 168, 260, 269
Jain, L. C., 23
Jamaica, Industrial Development Cor-
    poration of, 195
Japan, 6, 48, 72, 79, 83, 95, 105, 109,
    112, 118, 129, 130, 135, 155, 246,
    283, 333–372
  accounting in, 87
  "all banks," 347, 350
  Bank of, 343
  Central Bank for Commercial and
    Industrial Cooperatives, 356–359,
    368–370
  commercial banks in, 135, 148, 347–353
  credit associations in, 72, 347–350,
    353–355, 365–368
  guarantee arrangements in, 154–155
  long-term banks in, 349–350, 355–356
  mutual savings and loan banks in,
    347–350, 353–355
  People's Finance Corporation, 364–365
  Productivity Center, 88, 337, 341, 342
  Small Business Credit Insurance Cor-
    poration, 367–368
  Small Business Finance Corporation,
    79, 138, 148, 195, 197, 220, 222,
    337, 346, 356–357, 359–365, 367
  Small Business Investment Companies,
    356–357
  Smaller Enterprise Agency, 6, 338–340,
    342–344, 346, 368–369
Jenkins, H. L., 252

Jones, O., 164, 169, 172
Jordan, 155
  commercial banks in, 148
  Development Bank of, 196
*Journal Officiel de la République
  Française*, 184

Kaplan, A. D. H., 229
Katona, George, 139
Kelley, Richard E., 178
Kenya, 6, 200, 244, 275
  Industrial Development Corporation
    of, 195, 196
Kilby, Peter, 89, 240
Kirkpatrick, H., 132, 142, 220
Klein, Martin S., 128, 244, 275, 276
Knier, Lawrence T., 251
Korea, 6, 87, 109, 111, 114, 134,
    143–144, 148, 150
  interest rates in, 111
  moneylenders in, 109
  Small and Medium Industry Bank,
    114, 196–198, 221, 274
Krishnaswamy, K. S., 284

Ladd, William C., 218
Lander, W. S., 345
Landriscina, Giovanni, 184
Laud, G. M., 30
Law, Warren A., 168
Leasing of equipment, by banks, 137
  by finance companies, 166, 168
Lending costs (*see* Interest rates, and
  lending costs)
Lending procedures, 28, 33, 61, 181–182,
    206–209, 213–214, 238
  (*See also* Evaluation; Imple-
    mentation)
Lending programs (*see* Objectives and
  priorities in lending programs)
Lewis, W. A., 264, 274
Liaison service as form of counseling,
    84–85, 131, 283–284
Liberia, 218
  Development Bank of, 196
  guarantee arrangements in, 154

Liggett, Donald, 266
Little, Arthur D., Inc., 70, 88, 108, 175,
    191–192, 203, 208, 220
Loan evaluation (*see* Evaluation)
Lydall, H. F., 20, 36

McCrory, James T., 3–4, 20, 21, 22, 24,
    28, 74, 107, 117, 126, 206, 212
McGuire, Joseph W., 229
Madan, Bal Krishna, 23
Malawi, Industrial Development and
    Loan Board, 195
Malaysia, 6
  Industrial Development Finance, Ltd.,
    of, 231
  Rural and Industrial Development
    Authority, 195, 204, 241
Management of small factories, 12–13
  in Argentina, 88
  in Nigeria, 89
  in newly industrializing countries, 17
Management evaluation (*see* Evaluation,
  of management)
Manning, Eric, 132, 208
Markel, Howard, 207
Marks, Leonard, 246
Marks and Spencer, Ltd. (U.K.),
    128–129
Marquez, Javier, 198
Mason, Lester, 168
Matsunaga, Tokeo, 369
Matsuzaki, Hisashi, 337
Merwin, Charles L., 129
Mexico, 6, 123, 143, 158
  Asociación de Banqueros de, 174
  Centro Industrial de Productividad,
    175
  equipment leasing in, 168
  finance companies (*Financieras*) in,
    162, 165, 171–175
  Fondo de Garantia y Fomento a la
    Industria Mediana y Pequeña,
    148, 171, 173–175
  Nacional Financiera, 160
  Sears, Roebuck in, 123
Mittra, K. C., 31, 49, 50
Moneylenders, 23–24, 104, 109–118, 163

Monitoring, of commercial banks, 157,
    362
  of measures to improve internal financ-
      ing, 106–107
  of official institutions, 213
  of programs, 78, 82, 94
  suggested role in Peru, 158
Moore, G. S., 256
Moore, O. Ernest, 172
Morocco, National Bank for Economic
    Development, 196
Morse, Richard, 8–9, 11, 77, 81, 85, 266
Mosk, Sanford A., 143, 173
Murray, Roger, 259–260
Myers, Margaret G., 143, 166, 173

Nanjundan, S., 81
Nathan, Robert R., Associates, Inc., 61,
    64, 65, 119, 127, 133, 242, 286
Nebolsine, George, 186
Ness, Gayle, 204
Netherlands, 6, 79, 93, 205–206
  accounting in, 87
  equity financing in, 197
  guarantee arrangements in, 154
  lending costs in, 15
  Middleclass Bank, 154–155, 197, 220,
      267–268
  Research Institute for Management
      Science, 268
  Technical Consulting Services, 92–93,
      267–268, 284
New England, research-based enterprises
    in, 113, 285
New York Times, 178
New Zealand Finance Corporation, 186
Newly industrializing countries, special
    financing problems of, 16–18
Nicaragua, 135
  Instituto de Fomento Nacional
      (INFONAC), 187, 195, 198, 221,
      230, 273
  Nicaraguan Investment Corporation,
      187
Nigeria, 6–7, 89–90, 96, 117, 119, 127,
    133, 147, 154, 240–241, 242

Nigeria, Federal Loans Board, 185, 275
  Finance Corporation of Western Re-
      gion, 238
  Nigerian Industrial Development
      Bank, 186
Nomiyama, Tsutomu, 367
Noninstitutional sources of finance, 104
  (See also Financiers)
Norway, 124
  Bank for Industry, 196
  District Development Fund, 195
Nyasaland (see Malawi)
Nyhart, J. D., 6–7, 117, 272

Objectives and priorities in lending pro-
    grams, agricultural versus industrial,
    277–279
  need for defining, 69–74
Obstacles to small-factory financing,
    11–16
  (See also Interest rates, and lending
      costs; Risks, and losses in lending)
Odle, Harry B., 252
Official and quasi-official financing insti-
    tutions, 170–171, 194–224
  in Colombia, 301–305
  in East Africa, 200
  in India, 19–52
  in Japan, 347–350, 357–365
  limitations of, 201–211
  merits of, 198–201
  in Puerto Rico, 53–66
  specialization in, 217–224
  suggested measures to improve,
      213–224
  shareholding, 214–216, 220
Ogren, Arne, 105
Open-book credit, 118
O'Regan, Dermot, 231
Organisation for Economic Co-operation
    and Development (OECD), 105
Organisation for European Economic
    Co-operation (OEEC), 124, 137,
    159, 166
Organizational measures in official insti-
    tutions, 214–224

Osaka Prefectural Government Institute
of Economic Research, 340, 343,
344, 371
Overdrafts, 25

Paauw, Douglas, 208
Pakistan, 6, 72, 96, 273–274
Industrial Credit and Insurance Cor-
poration (PICIC), 186, 190–193,
244
Panama, 255
cattle development loan program,
255
Industrial Development Corporation
of, 186
Parsons, Earl, 269
Partnerships, 64, 86, 116–117
Pawley, Francis R., 165
Pension fund, 160–161
People's banks (see Cooperative credit
institutions)
Pereira, H. Felix de C., 239
Peru, 108, 158, 165–166, 170
Peruinvest, 187
Rehabilitation and Development
Council of Arequipa, 204
Phelps, Clyde W., 131
Philippines, 135, 148, 154
Development Bank of, 186–187, 203
Industrial Development Center, 88,
148, 166
Private development banks, 186–187
Private Development Corporation,
185–186
Pico, Rafael, 53, 61
Popular banks (see Cooperative credit
institutions)
Porter International Company, 7, 70, 274
Post-allocation measures (see Imple-
mentation)
Powelson, John P., 273
Price, William G. F., 199, 281
Program evaluation, 71–72
Project analysis, 232, 235–238, 257–259
Psilos, Diomedes, 105
Puerto Rico, 6, 53–76, 81, 134

Puerto Rico, Caribe Nitrogen Company,
61
commercial banks in, 55–56, 139
Economic Development Administration, 57–58, 59, 63–65
Government Development Bank,
56–57, 59–62, 195, 240
Industrial Development Program, 56–57
industrial estates in, 65
joint ventures, 64
PRIDCO, 58–59, 61, 65–66, 195, 273
supporting services in, 62–64

Quandt, Richard, 220

Ramakrishna, K. T., 33
Rao, Madav V., 46
Reader's Digest, 255
Receivable financing by finance companies, 165, 190
Regional and local development, 103,
184, 196, 302, 330–331
(See also India and Japan)
Regulation, of banks, 135, 139–140,
144–145, 199
of finance companies, 163, 164–165,
169, 170–173, 186, 188, 196
of savings banks, 159
(See also Organizational measures in
official institutions)
Reinvestment propensities of small entrepreneurs, 107–108
Relationships, of financial institutions and
clients, 95, 145, 153, 211, 253–255
of counseling staff and clients, 284, 321
Relatives and friends as source of
finance, 109–110
Resources (see Sources of funds)
Risk-bearing finance (see Equity and
other risk-bearing financing)
Risk-reduction through insurance, 160
Risks, and loss reserves, 212
and losses in lending, 12–13, 49, 61,
151–157, 175, 181–182, 359,
363–364, 367
effect on costs, 115

Risks, and losses in lending, by finance companies, 169
in inter-business finance, 127
Risks, and losses in lending, in inter-business finance, 127
methods of reducing, 153
in official banks, 201
by pension funds, 161
in savings banks, 159
by suppliers, 122
Risk-sharing (*see* Guarantees)
Risk-taking in evaluation, 250, 260
Robert Morris Associates, 251, 252, 281
Robinson, H. J., 164, 169, 172
Robison, H. E., 81
Roll-over of short-term loans, 136
Rosen, George, 23
Rubinstein, Albert, 113, 285
Russell, Allen H., 186

Sales financing by finance companies, 166
Saulnier, R. J., 14, 119, 125, 131, 136, 154, 167, 168, 200, 260, 269
Savings institutions, 158–161, 165
in Colombia, 294, 296–298
in Japan, 347–350, 353–355
Sayers, R. S., 157
SBA (Small Business Administration) definition of small business, 177
SBICs (small business investment companies), size problems in, 179
Schatz, Sayre P., 6, 117, 127, 275
Schisgal, Oscar, 255
Screening of loan applications (*see* Evaluation, of loan applications)
Security, as tool for implementation, 279–280
value in reducing risks, 153
Security problems of small manufacturers, 14
Security requirements, 13, 25, 32, 34, 45, 50, 55, 60–61, 65, 136, 159, 226–227, 250, 352, 355, 361, 364, 365–366
Seiden, Martin H., 12, 120, 122
Shah, C. K., 20
Singapore Development Board, 148

Singh, Baljit, 128
Small business investment companies (*see* SBICs)
Social and political conditions in developing countries, 17–18
Small Business Administration (*see* SBA)
Société d'Etudes et de Documentation Economiques, Industrielles y Sociales, 184
Society for Social and Economic Studies (India), 20, 22, 32
Sources of funds, 30–31, 61, 184–187, 303, 318–319, 358
of commercial banks, 140–141, 148
of finance companies, 164, 166, 172
in Colombia, 299–300
insurance companies as source for other lenders, 160
of interbusiness credit, 121, 130, 131
of investment trust, mutual, and pension funds, 161
of private development finance companies, 188–189, 191
of private financiers, 113, 163
of savings institutions, 159
of SBICs, 176
South Africa, Union of, Industrial Development Corporation, 195, 272–273
Spain, 148, 159, 241
Special financing problems of developing countries, 16–18
Specialization by financial institutions, 217–224
Stades, F. J. N., 93, 268
Staffing, 17, 27–28, 32, 47, 57–58, 65, 96, 98–99, 185, 189–190, 206, 210, 216, 238, 255–256, 268–270, 272–276, 282–283, 286, 298, 301, 316, 319–320, 339, 360, 363
of commercial banks, 146, 149, 153–154
for development financing, 78–79
for evaluation, 83–84
of finance companies, 165
of savings banks, 159
of SBICs, 179, 182–183
Staley, Eugene, 8–9, 11, 77, 81, 85, 266
Stanford Research Institute, 96, 164, 266

Stead, William H., 57
Stepanek, J. E., 73, 85, 131, 266
Supervised agricultural credit, 276–279
Supervision (*see* Implementation; Monitoring)
Supplier credit, 118–119
    (*See also* Interbusiness financing)
Supporting services, 51, 62, 77–78, 84–85, 90–99, 182, 222, 256, 284, 305–308, 329
    (*See also* individual service, e.g., Counseling, Training, etc.)
Surveys, 69–76, 80–83, 93, 108, 153, 202, 234–235, 252, 255, 305, 307
Sweden, 104, 105, 155, 156, 157, 159
    Industrial Credit Corporation, 207–208, 258
    Trade Development Associations, 268
    (*See also* Wickremesinghe, Brian)

Taiwan, 83, 87, 109, 111, 115, 130, 148, 150, 151, 196, 204, 239, 243, 276–277
Tanzania, 200
Taylor, James, 132, 142, 220
Tenenbaum, E. A., 73, 83, 87, 109, 111, 112, 113, 114, 115, 121, 130, 132, 142, 143, 145, 151, 152, 201, 204, 219, 220, 239, 243, 244, 271, 277
Term financing, 30–34, 72, 79, 136–137, 146–150, 159, 170–171, 183, 185, 190, 200, 209, 218–221, 230, 261, 280–282
    in Colombia, 293, 295–297, 301–305, 318–319, 321–322, 324
    in Denmark, 266–267
    of equipment, 167–168, 213, 243
    in India, 47–48
    in Japan, 349–350, 352–356, 359–360, 364
    by Mexican *financieras*, 173
    in Puerto Rico, 55–56, 60
    by SBICs, 170
Tew, Brian, 231
Thailand, 7

Thailand, Industrial Finance Corporation of, 185, 229–230
Thompson, Louis, 201
Thunholm, Lars-Erik, 157
Tinbergen, Jan, 236
Tobi, E. J., 154
Trade bills and acceptances, 118, 130, 136, 241, 243
    in Japan, 344, 352, 359, 366
Training, 16, 47, 50, 52, 78–80, 82–83, 93, 192, 255
    in Colombia, 306–307, 316–317, 319–320, 329
    in Japan, 245
    in Puerto Rico, 64–65
Tudor Engineering Company, 208
Turkey, 79
    Industrial Credit and Investment Bank of, 186
    Industrial Development Bank of, 81, 87–88, 186, 189–190, 216, 270–271, 280
Turnkey plants, 124

Uganda, 159, 200, 242, 276
    Development Corporation Ltd., 285
Union of South Africa, Industrial Development Corporation, 195, 272–273
United Kingdom, 129, 165, 168
    Commonwealth Development Corporation, 188–189
    Development Area Treasury Committee Fund, 195
    Industrial and Commercial Finance Corporation, 185, 230–231
United Nations, 7, 132, 141, 218, 219, 236, 305, 306
United States, 6, 48, 72, 79, 80–81, 83, 86–87, 90, 104–105, 114, 119, 120, 122, 125, 126, 127, 131, 135–137, 139, 144, 147, 149–150, 154, 155, 160, 162, 165, 166, 168–170, 234, 246, 251–254, 259–260, 268–269, 281
    Agency for International Development, 188–189

United States, Agency for International
    Development, programs in various
    countries, 148
Bank of America, 153
Ex-Im (Export-Import) Bank, 148
Federal Land Banks, 215
Federal Reserve System, 105, 119, 121,
    123, 126, 131
Federal Trade Commission-Securities
    & Exchange Commission, 105,
    120, 135, 137, 340
Foundation for Commercial Banks, 231
National Bureau of Economic Re-
    search, 14
Reconstruction Finance Corporation,
    13, 200, 207, 269
Small Business Administration, 79, 80,
    84–85, 168, 175–177, 182, 195,
    211, 220, 222, 269–270
    in Puerto Rico, 62, 65
Small Business Investment Companies,
    116, 175–182, 209, 269
Smaller War Plants Corporation, 207,
    269

Venezuela, Development Finance Com-
    pany, 196
Venkatappiah, B., 49
Venture capital organizations, 162–163
Viet-Nam, Industrial Development Fi-
    nance Corporation of, 196

Wall Street Journal, 179
Wattles, M. S., 87
Weissner, G., 156
Wheeler, Oliver P., 230
Wickremesinghe, Brian, 155, 156, 159,
    207–208, 258
Williams, Bruce R., 105
Williams, M. W., 267
Wilson, J. S. G., 157
Wolf, Charles, Jr., 90–91
Woods, Donald, 178, 180, 181

Yamanaka, T., 337